Aristotle

Aristotle's History of Animals

In Ten Books

Aristotle

Aristotle's History of Animals
In Ten Books

ISBN/EAN: 9783337002510

Printed in Europe, USA, Canada, Australia, Japan

Cover: Foto ©Thomas Meinert / pixelio.de

More available books at **www.hansebooks.com**

ARISTOTLE'S

HISTORY OF ANIMALS.

IN TEN BOOKS.

TRANSLATED BY

RICHARD CRESSWELL, M.A.,

ST. JOHN'S COLLEGE, OXFORD.

LONDON: GEORGE BELL & SONS, YORK STREET,
COVENT GARDEN.
1878.

PREFACE.

THE following Translation of Aristotle's History of Animals has been made from the text of Schneider. In a work of considerable difficulty it is hardly possible entirely to avoid errors; but it is hoped that those which have escaped are neither numerous nor important. The notes of Schneider have been consulted throughout; and in places of difficulty the English translation by Taylor, the French of Camus, and the German of Strack, have been severally referred to.

The work itself is the most ancient and celebrated contribution to science which has come down to us; and it is hardly possible, when we consider the means of observation which were accessible at the time, to imagine a work of more accurate observation. From the numerous quotations in which our author avails himself of the experience of his predecessors in the same field, as well as corrects their errors, there can be no doubt that Aristotle had the advantage of many works which have perished in the lapse of ages. In the Appendix to the present Translation will be found the Essay of Schneider on the sources whence Aristotle derived his knowledge of the animals he describes; and these sources, together with his own accurate observations, are probably sufficient to account for the correct knowledge of the history of animals displayed throughout the work.

It is right, perhaps, to observe in this place, that Dr. Smith, in his Dictionary of Biography, speaks of the 'History of Animals' as partly the result of the royal liberality of Alexander; and doubtless Aristotle would gladly have introduced into his work any fresh materials which might have been made available to him either during his residence at the Macedonian court, or by the subsequent victories of Alexander in the East, if the information so obtained had reached Athens in sufficient time to be incorporated. But in the first instance he would naturally use the materials ready to his hand in the works of his predecessors, and these were not few. The animals also which he describes are principally those of Greece and of the countries with which the enterprising Greeks had frequent and commercial intercourse. He says little of the animals of the interior of Asia and of India, and speaks very cautiously of such as he does mention; and one who quotes his authorities so freely would hardly have failed to notice the sources of his information.

The study, or at least the knowledge of the classification of animals appears to have been carefully pursued in the earliest period of man's history. The oldest records that we possess contain abundant notices of the peculiarities of animals. The Mosaic law abounds in them, in its distinctions between the clean and the unclean, a distinction not then first established, but of the most remote antiquity. Indeed it could hardly be otherwise than that men engaged in the pursuits of agriculture and the chase should study the habits of the animals that were valuable to them, as well as those which were injurious. A study thus commenced by necessity, would eventually be pursued for its own sake; and not a few would be found who would investigate, and, as far as they could, record the various phenomena they observed. The paintings of Egypt and the sculptures of Assyria are our witnesses of the skill with which animals and plants were drawn, and of the minute perception of their external forms; and the knowledge thus gained in the ancient centres of civilization would be sure to circulate and increase when the intercourse with foreign nations spread the knowledge and philosophy so acquired.

In the writings of Homer we find that the knowledge of the anatomy of the human body had already made considerable progress; and the inspection of the animals offered in sacrifice cannot fail to have added much to the general knowledge of their history. A century later, we have the poems of Hesiod, devoted to the encouragement of agriculture and rural pursuits. Pythagoras, in the seventh century B.C., may perhaps have left no writings, but we know that he was an eminent student and exponent of natural phenomena. His contemporary, Alcmæon of Crotona, is especially mentioned by Aristotle; and he is eminent among natural philosophers as the first who is said to have recommended to his followers the practice of dissection. Empedocles of Agrigentum left a work on the phenomena of nature, of which a few fragments still remain, and there were also others who, if they did not enter into the details of what we now call natural history, treated generally of the nature of things, and opened the field to those who would study the subject in its particular parts. The empire of Persia was still the dominant power, and was carrying the civilization of the East to every part of the known world when Ctesias wrote his great works, of which, unhappily, only a few fragments remain. He described not only the history of his own time, but also the natural history of Persia and of India, and that probably with more accuracy than has been usually attributed to him. India he had not visited personally, so that he could only describe it from the information of others; but this implies that he was not alone in the studies which he devoted to natural objects. With such predecessors and aided by his own acute observations, we need not wonder that Aristotle produced a work which has ever been admired by naturalists, and must continue to rise in their estimation the longer it is in their hands.

The Index to the present volume has been formed on the basis of that of Schneider, and considerable pains have been taken to add as many names as possible from other sources, especially the Index of Strack, and Külb's recent translation of the History of Animals, both of which contain identifications of a great many animals. A few identifications have also been added from Liddell and Scott's Lexicon, as well as from Professor Bell's Catalogue of Animals in Captain Spratt's work on Lycia; and the cephalopods are named from Professor Owen's article on that class, in the Cyclopædia of Anatomy. It is hoped, therefore, that the Index will be found to contain a greater number of suggestions for the identification of the animals mentioned by Aristotle than have been hitherto published collectively. It is also right to add, that it has been compiled after the translation was completed; and, therefore, in any differences which may be found between the identifications at the foot of the page and those given in the Index, the reader will rather prefer the latter, as the result of later research in works which were not accessible when the translation was made.

April 30, 1862. R. C.

Analytical Table of Contents.

Book I.—The work commences with a general review of the animal kingdom, and several suggestions for a natural arrangement of animals in groups, according to their external form or their mode of life, a comparison of animals among themselves, and a description of some of their habits. Aristotle then introduces the human form, the best known to man, as the standard of comparison to which he refers the rest of the animal kingdom. The concluding chapters of this book are occupied with a description of the several parts of the human body, both internal and external.

Book II.—In the second book the different parts of animals are described. The animals are arranged in various groups, viviparous and oviparous quadrupeds, fish, serpents, birds. The only animals described are those with red blood: the description of the rest being reserved for the fourth book. Their internal organs are also described; and in the course of the book a few animals, as the ape, elephant, and chameleon, are especially noticed.

Book III.—The third book commences with a description of the internal organs, beginning with the generative system. A considerable portion of the book is devoted to the course of the veins; and Aristotle quotes from other writers, as well as states the result of his own observations. He then describes the nature of other constituent parts of the body, sinews, fibres, bone, marrow, cartilage, nails, hoofs, claws, horns, and beaks of birds, hair, scales, membranes, flesh, fat, blood, marrow, milk, and the spermatic fluid.

Book IV.—Animals without blood, and first, the cephalopods, are described; then the crustaceans, testacea, echinidæ, ascidians, actiniæ, hermit crabs, insects. In the eighth chapter the organs of sense are considered, and afterwards, the voice, sleep, age, and differences of the sexes in animals are described.

BOOK V.—In the former books animals are for the most part described with reference to their several parts. In the fifth book they are treated as entire, and especially with regard to their mode of reproduction. First of all, our author treats of spontaneous reproduction, and then of those animals which spring from a union of the sexes; and from this he proceeds to some detail with respect to different groups of animals, testacea, crustacea, insects. The book concludes with a long description of bees and their habits.

BOOK VI.—In this book the same subject is continued through the several classes of birds, fish, and quadrupeds. This account of the reproduction of animals includes also the consideration of the seasons, climates, and ages of animals, and how far these influence their reproduction.

BOOK VII.—The seventh book is almost entirely devoted to the consideration of the reproduction of man, and an account of man from his birth to his death. This book ends abruptly, and is probably imperfect.

BOOK VIII.—In the eighth book Aristotle passes on to the most interesting part of his work, the character and habits of the whole animal world, as it was known to him. The amount of detail which he has collected and arranged on this subject is most interesting. He treats, first of all, of the food of animals, of their migrations, their health and diseases, and the influence of climate upon them.

BOOK IX.—The subject of the eighth book is continued, with an account of the relations in which animals stand to each other, and especially the friendship and hostility of different species; and these are for the most part referred to the nature of their food, and their mode of procuring it. The notices of fish are not so numerous as those of other groups: this would necessarily arise from the difficulty of observation. At the conclusion of the book, an essay on bees and their congeners is given at considerable length.

Book X.—This book, in all probability erroneously ascribed to Aristotle, is occupied with a treatise on the causes of barrenness in the human species. It appears to be rather a continuation of the seventh book, which ends abruptly; but it is well placed at the end, as no genuine work of our author.

THE HISTORY OF ANIMALS.

BOOK THE FIRST.

Chapter I.

1. Some parts of animals are simple, and these can be divided into like parts, as flesh into pieces of flesh; others are compound, and cannot be divided into like parts, as the hand cannot be divided into hands, nor the face into faces. Of these some are not only called parts, but members, such as those which, though entire in themselves, are made up of other parts, as the head and the leg, the hand and the entire arm, or the trunk; for these parts are both entire in themselves, and made up of other parts.

2. All the compound parts also are made up of simple parts, the hand, for example, of flesh, and sinew, and bone. Some animals have all these parts the same, in others they are different from each other. Some of the parts are the same in form, as the nose and eye of one man is the same as the nose and eye of another man, and flesh is the same with flesh, and bone with bone. In like manner we may compare the parts of the horse, and of other animals, those parts, that is, which are the same in species, for the whole bears the same relation to the whole as the parts do to each other. And in animals belonging to the same class, the parts are the same, only they differ in excess or defect. By class, I mean such as bird or fish, for all these differ if either compared with their own class or with another, and there are many forms of birds and fishes.

3. Nearly all their parts differ in them according to the opposition of their external qualities, such as colour or shape, in that some are more, others are less affected, or

sometimes in number more or less, or in size greater and smaller, or in any quality which can be included in excess or defect. For some animals have a soft skin, in others the skin is shelly; some have a long bill, as cranes, others a short one; some have many feathers, others very few; some also have parts which are wanting in others, for some species have spurs, others have none; some have a crest, others have not. But, so to say, their principal parts and those which form the bulk of their body, are either the same, or vary only in their opposites, and in excess and defect.

4. By excess and defect I mean the greater and the less. But some animals agree with each other in their parts neither in form, nor in excess and defect, but have only an analogous likeness, such as a bone bears to a spine, a nail to a hoof, a hand to a crab's claw, the scale of a fish to the feather of a bird, for that which is a feather in the birds is a scale in the fish. With regard then to the parts which each class of animal possesses, they agree and differ in this manner, and also in the position of the parts. For many animals have the same parts, but not in the same position, as the mammæ which are either pectoral or abdominal. But of the simple parts some are soft and moist, others hard and dry.

5. The soft parts are either entirely so, or so long as they are in a natural condition, as blood, serum, fat, tallow, marrow, semen, gall, milk (in those animals which give milk), flesh, and other analogous parts of the body. In another manner also the excretions of the body belong to this class, as phlegm, and the excrements of the abdomen and bladder; the hard and dry parts are sinew, skin, vein, hair, bone, cartilage, nail, horn, for that part bears the same name, and on the whole is called horn, and the other parts of the body which are analogous to these.

6. Animals also differ in their manner of life, in their actions and dispositions, and in their parts. We will first of all speak generally of these differences, and afterwards consider each species separately. The following are the points in which they vary in manner of life, in their actions and dispositions. Some animals are aquatic, others live on the land; and the aquatic may again be divided into two classes, for some entirely exist and procure their food in the water, and take in and give out water, and cannot live without it;

this is the nature of most fishes. But there are others which, though they live and feed in the water, do not take in water but air, and produce their young out of the water. Many of these animals are furnished with feet, as the otter and the latax[1] and the crocodile, or with wings, as the seagull and diver, and others are without feet, as the water-serpent. Some procure their food from the water, and cannot live out of the water, but neither inhale air nor water, as the acalephe[2] and the oyster.

7. Different aquatic animals are found in the sea, in rivers, in lakes, and in marshes, as the frog and newt, and of marine animals some are pelagic, some littoral, and some saxatile. Some land animals take in and give out air, and this is called inhaling and exhaling; such are man, and all other land animals which are furnished with lungs; some, however, which procure their food from the earth, do not inhale air, as the wasp, the bee, and all other insects.[3] By insects I mean those animals which have divisions in their bodies, whether in the lower part only, or both in the upper and lower. Many land animals, as I have already observed, procure their food from the water, but there are no aquatic or marine animals which find their food on land. There are some animals which at first inhabit the water, but afterwards change into a different form, and live out of the water; this happens to the gnat in the rivers, and .. .. ..[4] which afterwards becomes an œstrum.[5]

8. Again, there are some creatures which are stationary, while others are locomotive; the fixed animals are aquatic, but this is not the case with any of the inhabitants of the land. Many aquatic animals also grow upon each other; this is the case with several genera of shell-fish: the sponge also exhibits some signs of sensation, for they say that it is drawn up with some difficulty, unless the attempt to remove it is made stealthily. Other animals also there are which are alternately fixed together or free, this is the case with a certain kind of acalephe; some of these become separated during the night, and emigrate. Many animals are separate from each other, but incapable of voluntary movement, as

---

[1] Beaver, Castor fiber.   [2] Medusa, or perhaps Actinia, or both.
[3] Under the class ἔντομα are probably included all annulose animals.
[4] Some words appear to be lost in this place.   [5] Tabanus, gad-fly.

oysters, and the animal called holothuria.[1] Some aquatic animals are swimmers, as fish, and the mollusca,[2] and the malacostraca, as the crabs. Others creep on the bottom, as the crab, for this, though an aquatic animal, naturally creeps.

9. Of land animals some are furnished with wings, as birds and bees, and these differ in other respects from each other; others have feet, and of this class some species walk, others crawl, and others creep in the mud. There is no animal which has only wings as fish have only fins, for those animals whose wings are formed by an expansion of the skin can walk, and the bat has feet, the seal has imperfect feet. Among birds there are some with very imperfect feet, which are therefore called apodes; they are, however, provided with very strong wings, and almost all birds that are similar to this one have strong wings and imperfect feet, as the swallow and drepanis;[3] for all this class of birds is alike both in habits and in the structure of their wings, and their whole appearance is very similar. The apos[4] is seen at all times of the year, but the drepanis can only be taken in rainy weather during the summer, and on the whole is a rare bird.

10. Many animals, however, can both walk and swim. The following are the differences exhibited by animals in their habits and their actions. Some of them are gregarious, and others solitary, both in the classes which are furnished with feet, and those which have wings, or fins. Some partake of both characters, and of those that are gregarious, as well as those that are solitary, some unite in societies and some are scattered. Gregarious birds are such as the pigeon, stork, swan, but no bird with hooked claws is gregarious. Among swimming animals some fish are gregarious, as the dromas,[5] tunny, pelamis,[6] amia.[7]

11. But man partakes of both qualities. Those which have a common employment are called social, but that is not the case with all gregarious animals. Man, and the bee, the wasp, and the ant, and the stork belong to this class. Some of these obey a leader, others are anarchical; the stork and the bee are of the former class, the ant and many others belong to the latter. Some animals, both in

[1] Perhaps some species of Zoophyte. [2] Cephalopods.
[3] Perhaps Sand martin.   [4] Swift.   [5] Some migratory fish.
[6] A kind of tunny, still called palamyde at Marseilles.
[7] A kind of tunny, Les Bonitons (Camus.)

the gregarious and solitary class, are limited to one locality, others are migratory. There are also carnivorous animals, herbivorous, omnivorous, and others which eat peculiar food, as the bee and the spider; the former eats only honey and a few other sweet things, while spiders prey upon flies and there are other animals which feed entirely on fish. Some animals hunt for their food, and some make a store, which others do not. There are also animals which make habitations for themselves, and others which do not. The mole, the mouse, the ant, and the bee, make habitations, but many kinds both of insects and quadrupeds make no dwelling.

12. With regard to situation, some are troglodite, as lizards and serpents, others, as the horse and dog, live upon the surface of the earth. Some kinds of animals burrow in the ground, others do not; some animals are nocturnal, as the owl and the bat, others use the hours of daylight. There are tame animals and wild animals. Man and the mule are always tame, the leopard and the wolf are invariably wild, and others, as the elephant, are easily tamed. We may, however, view them in another way, for all the genera that have been tamed are found wild also, as horses, oxen, swine, sheep, goats, and dogs.

13. Some animals utter a loud cry, some are silent, and others have a voice, which in some cases may be expressed by a word, in others it cannot. There are also noisy animals and silent animals, musical and unmusical kinds, but they are mostly noisy about the breeding season. Some, as the dove, frequent fields, others, as the hoopoe, live on the mountains; some attach themselves to man, as the pigeon. Some are lascivious, as the partridge and domestic fowl, and others are chaste, as the raven, which rarely cohabits.

14. Again, there are classes of animals furnished with weapons of offence, others with weapons of defence; in the former I include those which are capable of inflicting an injury, or of defending themselves when they are attacked; in the latter those which are provided with some natural protection against injury.

15. Animals also exhibit many differences of disposition. Some are gentle, peaceful, and not violent, as the ox. Some are violent, passionate, and intractable, as the wild boar. Some

are prudent and fearful, as the stag and the hare. Serpents are illiberal and crafty. Others, as the lion, are liberal, noble, and generous. Others are brave, wild, and crafty, like the wolf. For there is this difference between the generous and the brave—the former means that which comes of a noble race, the latter that which does not easily depart from its own nature.

16. Some animals are cunning and evil-disposed, as the fox; others, as the dog, are fierce, friendly, and fawning. Some are gentle and easily tamed, as the elephant; some are susceptible of shame, and watchful, as the goose. Some are jealous, and fond of ornament, as the peacock. But man is the only animal capable of reasoning, though many others possess the faculty of memory and instruction in common with him. No other animal but man has the power of recollection. In another place we will treat more accurately of the disposition and manner of life in each class.

Chapter II.

1. All animals possess in common those parts by which they take in food, and into which they receive it. But these parts agree or differ in the same way as all the other parts of bodies, that is, either in shape or size, or proportion or position; and besides these, almost all animals possess many other parts in common, such as those by which they reject their excrements, (and the part by which they take their food,)[1] though this does not exist in all. The part by which the food is taken in is called the mouth, that which receives the food from the mouth is called the stomach. The part by which they reject the excrement has many names.

2. The excrement being of two kinds, the animals which possess receptacles for the fluid excrement have also receptacles for the dry; but those which have the latter are not always furnished with the former. Wherefore all animals which have a bladder have a belly also, but not all that have a belly have a bladder; for the part appropriated to the reception of the liquid excrement is called the bladder, and that for the reception of the dry is called the belly.

3. Many animals possess both these parts, and that also by which the semen is emitted. Among animals that have the power of generation, some emit the semen into them-

[1] The words in brackets should probably be excluded from the text.

selves, and some inject it into others. The former are called female, the latter male. In some animals there is neither male nor female, and there is a diversity in the form of the parts appropriated to this office. For some animals have a uterus, others have only something analogous to the uterus. These are the most essential organs; some of which exist in all animals, others in the majority only.

Chapter III.

1. There is only one sense, that of touch, which is common to all animals; so that no exact name can be given to the part in which this sense resides, for in some animals it is the same, in others only analogous.

2. Every living creature is furnished with moisture, and must die, if deprived of this moisture either in the course of nature or by force. But in what part of the body this moisture resides is another question. In some animals it is found in the blood and veins, in others the situation is only analogous, but these are imperfect, as fibres and serum.[1] The sense of touch resides in the simple parts, as in the flesh and in similar places, and generally in those parts which contain blood, at least in those animals which have blood; in others it resides in the analogous parts, but in all animals in the simple parts.

3. The capacity of action resides in the compound parts, as the preparation of food in the mouth, and the power of locomotion in the feet or wings, or the analogous parts. Again, some animals are sanguineous, as man, the horse, and all perfect animals, whether apodous, bipeds, or quadrupeds; and some animals are without blood, as the bee and the wasp, and such marine animals as the sepia and the carabus,[2] and all animals with more than four legs.

Chapter IV.

1. There are also viviparous, oviparous, and vermiparous animals. The viviparous, are such as man, and the horse, the seal, and others which have hair, and among marine animals the cetacea, as the dolphin and those which are called selache.[3]

---

[1] Fibres and serum, as compared with veins and blood, refer to the circulation in animals without red blood.

[2] Palinurus, Spiny Lobster.   [3] Cartilaginous fishes.

Some of these are furnished with a blow-hole, but have no gills, as the dolphin and the whale. The dolphin has its blow-hole on the back, the whale in its forehead; others have open gills, as the selache, the galeus,[1] and the batus.[2] That is called the egg of the perfect fœtus, from which the future animal is produced, from a part at first, while the remainder serves for its food. The worm is that from the whole of which the future animal is produced, and the fœtus afterwards acquires parts and increases in size.

2. Some viviparous animals are internally oviparous, as the selache; others are internally viviparous, as mankind and the horse. In different animals the fœtus assumes a different form, when first brought into the world, and is either a living creature, an egg, or a worm. The eggs of some animals, as birds, are hard-shelled, and are of two colours. Those of the selache and some other animals are soft-skinned, and have only one colour. Some species of the vermiform fœtus are capable of motion, others are not. But in another place, when we treat of generation, we will dwell more accurately on these subjects.

Chapter V.

1. Some animals have feet, others have none; of the former some have two feet, as mankind and birds only; others have four, as the lizard and the dog; others, as the scolopendra and bee, have many feet; but all have their feet in pairs.

2. And among apodous swimming animals some have fins, as fish; and of these some have two fins in the upper and two in the lower part of their bodies, as the chrysophys[3] and labrax;[4] others, which are very long and smooth, have only two fins, as the eel and conger; others have none at all, as the lamprey and others, which live in the sea as serpents do on land, and in like manner swim in moist places; and some of the genus selache, as those which are flat and have tails, as the batos and trygon, have no fins; these fish swim by means of their flat surfaces; but the batrachus[5] has fins, and so have all those fish which are not very thin in proportion to their width.

3. But the animals which have apparent feet, as the cepha-

---

[1] Squalus galeus.　　　[2] Raia batos.　　　[3] Sparus auratus.
[4] Perca labrax.　　　[5] Lophius piscatorius and also L. barbatus.

lopods, swim both with their feet and fins, and move quickly upon the hollow parts of their bodies, as the sepia, teuthis, and polypus: but none of them can walk except the polypus. Those animals which have hard skins, as the carabus, swim with their hinder parts, and move very quickly upon their tail, with the fins which are upon it, and the newt both with its feet and tail, and (to compare small things with great) it has a tail like the glanis.[1]

4. Some winged animals, as the eagle and the hawk, are feathered; others, as the cockchafer and the bee, membranaceous wings; and others, as the alopex[2] and the bat, have wings formed of skin. Both the feathered and leather-winged tribes have blood; but the insects, which have naked wings, have no blood. Again, the feathered and leather-winged animals are all either bipeds or apodous, for they say that there are winged serpents in Ethiopia.[3]

5. The feathered tribe of animals is called birds; the other two tribes have no exact names. Among winged creatures without blood some are coleopterous, for they have elytra over their wings, as the cockchafer and the beetles, and others are without elytra. The animals of this class have either two or four wings. Those with four wings are distinguished by their greater size or a caudal sting. The diptera are either such as are small, or have a sting in their head. The coleoptera have no sting at all; the diptera have a sting in their head, as the fly, horse-fly, gad-fly, and gnat.

6. All bloodless animals, except a few marine species of the cephalopoda, are smaller than those which have blood. These animals are the largest in warm waters, and more so in the sea than on the land, and in fresh water. All creatures that are capable of motion are moved by four or more limbs. Those with blood have four limbs only, as man has two hands and two feet. Birds have two wings and two feet; quadrupeds and fishes have four feet or four fins. But those animals which have two wings or none at all, as the serpent, are nevertheless moved by four limbs; for the bendings of their body are four in number, or two when they have two wings.

[1] Silurus glanis, L. (Strack). [2] Probably some kind of flying squirrel. [3] Herodotus, ii. 76: "the form of this serpent is similar to that of the water-snake; its wings are not feathered, but like those of bats:" the *draco volans* may have given rise to this story.

7. Those bloodless animals which have more than four feet, whether furnished with feet or wings, always have more than four organs of locomotion, as the ephemera, which has four feet and four wings; and in this it not only agrees with its peculiar manner of life, from which also it derives its name, but also that it is winged and four-footed; and all creatures, whether they have four feet or many feet, move in the same direction, for they all move in the long way of their bodies. All other animals have two leading feet, the crab alone has four.

Chapter VI.

1. The following are the principal classes which include other animals—birds, fishes, cetacea. All these have red blood. There is another class of animals covered with a shell, and called shell fish, and an anonymous class of soft-shelled animals (malacostraca), which includes carabi, carcini, and astaci; and another of mollusca, such as teuthis, teuthos, and sepia; and another class of annulose animals. All these are without blood, and the species with feet have many feet. There are no large classes of other animals; for there are many forms which are not included under a single form, but either stand alone, having no specific difference, as man, or have specific differences, but the classes are anonymous.

2. All animals with four feet and no wings have blood. Some of these are viviparous, others oviparous. The viviparous are not all covered with hair, but the oviparous have scales. The scale of a reptile is similar in situation to the scale of a fish. The class of serpents, sanguineous land animals, is naturally without feet. Though some have feet, this class is also covered with scales. All serpents, except the viper, are oviparous. The viper alone is viviparous, so that not all viviparous animals have hair; for some fishes also are viviparous. All animals, however, that have hair are viviparous; for we may consider the prickles of the hedgehog and porcupine as analogous to the hair of animals; for they answer the purpose of hair, and not, as in marine animals that are so covered, of feet.[1]

3. There are also many classes of viviparous quadrupeds,

[1] The Echinidæ.

but they have never received names. Each kind must, therefore, be taken separately, as man, as we speak of lion, stag, horse, dog, and of others in like manner. There is, however, one class of those that have a mane called lophuri,[1] as the horse, ass, mule, ginnus,[2] hinnus, and those which in Syria are called mules,[3] from their resemblance, though not quite of the same form. They copulate and produce young from each other, so that it is necessary to consider well the nature of each of them separately.

4. We have now treated of these things in an outline, for the sake of giving a taste of what we are afterwards to consider, and of how many. Hereafter we will speak of them more accurately, in order that we may first of all examine into their points of difference and agreement; and afterwards we will endeavour to inquire into the causes of these things, but it will be a more natural arrangement to do so when we treat of the history of each. For it is evident from these things what they are, and what we have to demonstrate.

5. Our first subject of consideration must be the parts of which animals are made up, for these constitute the chief and the whole difference among them; either because they have them or are without them, or these parts vary in position or arrangement, or in any of the differences mentioned before, in form, size, proportion, and difference of accidents. First of all, then, we will consider the parts of the human body; for, as every one can best understand the standard of money with which he is most familiar, so it is in other things. And of necessity, man must be the best known to us of all animals. The parts of the body are, indeed, plain enough to every one's common sense; but, that we may not forsake our arrangement, and may have reason as well as perception, we will speak, first of all, of the organic, and afterwards of the simple, parts.

Chapter VII.

1. These are the principal parts into which the whole body is divided. The head, neck, trunk, two arms, and two legs,

---

[1] Animals with long hair on their tails.
[2] Ginnus is the offspring of a mule and mare. Book vi. 24, 1.
[3] Hemionus, perhaps the foal of a horse and wild ass, and so distinct from oreus, the foal of the he-ass and mare.

The whole cavity, from the neck to the pudenda, is called the trunk. That part of the head which is covered with hair is called the cranium, the fore part of this is called the sinciput. This is the last formed, being the last bone in the body which becomes hard; the hinder part is the occiput, and between the occiput and sinciput is the crown of the head. The brain is placed beneath the sinciput, and the occiput is empty;[1] the cranium is a thin spherical bone covered with a skin without flesh. The skull has sutures: in women there is but one placed in a circle; men have generally three joined in one, and a man's skull has been seen without any sutures at all. The middle and smooth part of the hair is called the crown of the head; in some persons this is double, for there are some people double-crowned, not from any formation of the bone, but only from the division of the hair.

Chapter VIII.

1. The part immediately beneath the cranium is called the face in mankind alone, for we do not speak of the face of a fish or of an ox; the part immediately beneath the sinciput and between the eyes is called the forehead. Those in whom this feature is large are tardy; those who have a small forehead are easily excited; a broad forehead belongs to those who are liable to be carried away by their feelings; a round forehead is a sign of a passionate disposition.

2. Under the forehead are two eyebrows; if they are straight, it is a mark of a gentle disposition; the eyebrows bent down to the nose are an evidence of an austere temper; if they incline towards the temples, of a mocker and scoffer; if they are drawn down, it is a sign of an envious person. Beneath these are the eyes, which by nature are two in number: the parts of each eye are, first, the upper and under eyelid, the edges of which are furnished with hair. Within the eye, the moist part with which we see is called the pupil; round this is the iris, and this is surrounded by the white. Two corners of the eye are formed at the junction of the eyelids, one in the direction of the nose, the other towards the temple. If these corners are large, they are a sign of an evil disposition; if those near the nose are fleshy, and have a swollen appearance, they are an evidence of wickedness.

---

[1] This mistake is again repeated in Ch. xiii.

3. All other classes of animals have eyes, except shell-fish, and some other imperfect creatures, and all viviparous animals except moles have eyes. A person might, however, conclude from the following observation, that it has eyes, though it is quite without them, for it certainly does not see at all, nor has it any external eyes; but, when the skin is taken off, there is a place for the eyes, and the iris of the eye is in the place which it would naturally occupy on the outside, as if they had been wounded in their birth, and the skin had grown over the place.

4. The white of the eye is generally the same in all animals, but the iris is very different. In some it is black, in others decidedly grey, in others dark grey, and in some it is the colour of the goat's eye, and this is a sign of the best disposition, and is most to be prized for acuteness of vision. Man is almost the only animal which exhibits a variety of colouring in the eye; there are, however, some horses with grey eyes.

5. The eyes of some persons are large, others small, and others of a moderate size—the last-mentioned are the best. And some eyes are projecting, some deep-set, and some moderate, and those which are deep-set have the most acute vision in all animals; the middle position is a sign of the best disposition. Some people have an eye which is perpetually opening and closing, others have an eye always intent, and others a moderately-intent eye: this last is the best disposed; of the others, the one is impudent, and the other a sign of infirmity.

Chapter IX.

1. The part of the head by which we hear, but do not breathe, is the ear; for Alcmæon is mistaken when he says that goats breathe through their ears. One part of the ear has not received any name, the other part is called the lobe. The whole ear is made up of cartilage and flesh. Internally, the ear has the nature of a shell, and the last bone is similar to the ear itself. The sound reaches this part last, as it were in a chamber. There is no passage from the ear into the brain, but there is to the roof of the mouth; and a vein extends from the brain to each ear.[1] The eyes also are connected with the brain, and each eye is placed upon a vein.

[1] Eustachian tube.

2. Man is the only animal with ears that cannot move them. Among animals which have the faculty of hearing; some have ears, and others, as winged and scaly creatures, have no ear, but an open orifice in the head; all viviparous animals, except the seal, and the dolphin, and other cetacea, have ears; the selache also are viviparous. The seal has open orifices by which it hears; the dolphin can hear, though it has no ears; all other animals can move their ears, but man alone does not move them.

3. The ears (of man) lie in the same circle with his eyes, and not above them, as in some quadrupeds. The ears are either smooth, hairy, or moderate. These last are the best for hearing, but they do not in any way indicate the disposition. They are large, or small or middling, or they are erect, or not at all, or only moderately erect. The moderately erect are a sign of the best disposition; large and erect ears are an evidence of foolish talking and loquacity. The part of the head between the eye and the ear is called the temple.

4. In the middle of the face is the nose, the passage for the breath, for through this animals inhale and exhale, and through it also they sneeze; this is the expulsion of a concentrated breath, and is the only kind of breathing which is esteemed ominous or sacred: moreover, inhaling and exhaling is into the chest, and without the nostrils it is impossible to inhale or exhale, for inhaling and exhaling is from the breast by the windpipe, and not from any part of the head. But it is possible to live without this respiration through the nostrils. The smell also resides in this part; this is the sense of odour. The nostril is very moveable, and not naturally immoveable like the ear.

5. One part of the nose, namely, the division between the nostrils, is cartilaginous, but the passage is empty, for the nose is formed of two divisions. In the elephant, the nostril is very large and strong, and it answers to the purpose of a hand, for the animal can extend it, and with it take its food, and convey it to its mouth, whether the food is moist or dry. This is the only animal that can do so.

6. There are also two jaws, the upper and the under. All animals move the lower jaw, except the river-crocodile, and this moves the upper jaw only. Below the nose are two lips, the flesh of which is very moveable. The mouth is the

centre of the jaws and the lips. The upper part is called the roof of the mouth, the lower, the pharynx. The tongue is the organ of taste. This sense resides in the tip, and, if food is placed on the broad part of the tongue, the taste is less acute. The tongue partakes of all the other sensations, as harshness, heat, and cold, as well as that of taste, in common with the rest of the flesh.

7. The flat part of the tongue is either narrow or moderate in size, the moderate is the best, and most apt for clear elocution. The tongue may be either too loose, or tied down, as in stammerers and inarticulate speakers. The flesh of the tongue is porous and spongy. The epiglottis is a portion of the tongue, the double part of the mouth is the tonsils; that in many divisions the gums, they are fleshy, and in them are fixed the bony teeth. Within the mouth there is another part, the uvula, a pillar filled with blood. If this part is swelled with relaxation, it is called a grape, and chokes.

CHAPTER X.

1. THE neck is the part between the head and the trunk; the front part is called the larynx, behind this is the œsophagus. The voice and the breath pass through the front part, the trachea, which is cartilaginous, but the œsophagus is fleshy, and placed farther in, near the vertebra of the neck. The back of the neck is called the epomis. These are the parts as far as the thorax. The parts of the thorax are some before and some behind. First of all, below the neck is the breast with two mammæ; on these are two nipples, through which the milk of the female passes. The mamma is porous. There is also milk in the breasts of men. The flesh of the mamma in men is thick, in women it is spongy and full of pores.

2. The part below the thorax, in front, is the belly, and of this the navel is the centre. Beneath this centre, the part on each side is called the iliac region; the part in the centre, beneath the navel, is called the hypogastric region; the lowest part of this is called pubes; above the navel is the epigastric region; the lumbar region is situated between the epigastric and iliac regions.

3. Of the hinder parts the loin forms the division of the body, whence also its name is derived (ὀσφύς quasi ἰσοφύς). The part of the central region which is like a seat is the but-

tock; that on which the thigh turns, the cotyledon. The peculiar part of women is the uterus; of men the penis, it is external, at the extremity of the trunk in two parts; the upper part is fleshy and smooth, and is called glans; this is covered with an anonymous skin, which, if it is cut asunder, does not unite again, neither does the cheek nor the eyelid.

4. Common to this and the glans is the prepuce, the remaining part is cartilaginous, readily increases in size, and it is drawn in and out, contrary to that of the class of animals called lophuri. Beneath the penis are two testicles, surrounded by a skin called the scrotum; the testicles are not of the same nature as flesh, nor are they made of flesh. In another place we shall treat of the nature of all these parts more accurately.

5. The pudendum muliebre is contrary to that of the male, for it is hollow under the pubes, not projecting like that of the male, and the urethra is outside the womb, for the passage of the semen of the male, and for the fluid excrement of both. The part of the body which joins the neck and the breast is called the jugulum; that which unites the side, the arm, and the shoulder is the arm-pit. The region between the thigh and the hypogastric region is called the groin; the part common to the thigh and the buttock on the inside is the perineum, that of the thigh and buttock on the outside is called hypoglutis.

6. We have previously treated of the trunk. The hinder part of the breast is called the back: the parts of the back are two shoulder blades and the back-bone; below the thorax, and opposite the stomach, are the loins; the ribs belong both to the back and the front of the trunk, and are eight on each side, for we have never heard anything worthy of credit concerning the Ligyes, who are said to have seven ribs.

Chapter XI.

1. Man has upper and lower side, the front and the back, and right and left side. The right and the left are nearly alike in their parts and in every particular, except that the left side is the weaker; but the back parts are not like the front; nor the lower parts to the upper, except in this particular, that the parts below the hypogastric region are full-fleshed or lean in proportion to the face, and the arms also answer

to the proportion of the legs. Those persons who have a short humerus have also generally a short thigh: those who have small feet have also small hands.

2. One of the double parts of the body is the arm. The parts of the arm are the shoulder, humerus, elbow, cubitus, and the hand; the parts of the hand are the palm and five fingers; the jointed part of the finger is the condyle, the unjointed part the phalanx. The thumb has but one joint, all the rest have two. The bending of the arm and finger is always inwards. The arm is also bent at the elbow: the inner part of the hand is called the palm; it is fleshy, and divided by strong lines. Long-lived persons have one or two lines which extend through the whole hand; short-lived persons have two lines not extending through the whole hand. The joint of the hand and arm is the wrist. The outside of the hand is sinewy, and has not received any name.

3. The other double part of the body is the leg. The double-headed part of the leg is called the thigh, the moveable part is called the patella, that which has two bones the tibia; the front of this part is the shin, the hind part the calf of the leg. The flesh is full of sinews and veins; in those persons who have large hips, the flesh is drawn upwards towards the hollow part under the knee, in those who have not it is drawn down. The lowest part of the shin is the ankle, and this is double in each leg. The part of the leg with many bones is called the foot, the hind part of which is the heel. The front part is divided into five toes; the under part, which is fleshy, is called the sole of the foot; the upper part, (the instep,) is sinewy, and has not received any name. One part of the toe is the nail, the other is the joint; the nail is on the extremity of the toe, and the toes are bent inwards. Those who have the sole of the foot thick, and not hollow, but walk upon the whole of the foot, are knavish. The common joint of the thigh and the leg is the knee.

Chapter XII.

1. These parts are possessed in common by the male and female; the position of the external parts, whether above or below, before or behind, on the right side or the left, will appear on mere inspection. It is necessary, however, to enumerate

them, for the reasons which I have mentioned before, that its proper place being assigned to each part, any difference in their arrangement in man and other animals may be less likely to escape our notice.

2. In man, the parts of the body are more naturally divided into upper and lower than in any other animal, for all the upper and lower parts of his body are arranged according to the order of nature above and below; in the same way, also, the fore and hind parts, and those on the right and left, are placed naturally. But in other animals some of these parts are either not at all so placed, or they are much more confused than in man. The head is placed above the body in all animals, but in man alone, as we have said, is this part corresponding to the order of all things.

3. Next to the head is the neck, then the breast and the back, the one before and the other behind; and each of them in the following order:—the stomach, loins, pudenda, haunch, then the thigh and leg, and, last of all, the foot. The legs have the joint bent forwards, in which direction also is their manner of walking, and the more moveable part of the legs as well as the joint is bent forward: the heel is behind. Each of the ankles is like an ear. From the right and left side come arms, having the joint bent inwards, so that the flexures both of the legs and arms are towards each other, especially in man.

4. The senses and the organs of sense, the eyes, nostril, and tongue are in the same position, and in the anterior part of the body; but the hearing, and its organ, and the ears are at the side, and upon the same circumference as the eyes. Man has the eyes closer together, in proportion to his size, than other animals. The sense of touch is the most accurate of the human senses, and next to this the taste. In the rest of his senses he is far surpassed by other animals.

Chapter XIII.

1. The external parts of the body are arranged in this manner; and, as I have said, are for the most part named and known from habit. But the internal parts are not so well known, and those of the human body are the least known. So that in order to explain them we must compare them with the same parts of those animals which are most nearly allied.

2. First of all, the brain is placed in the fore-part of the head, and it occupies the same position in all animals that have this part, which belongs to all sanguineous and cephalopodous animals. In proportion to his size, man has the largest brain of all animals, and the moistest. Two membranes enclose the brain: that outside the skull is the strongest; the inner membrane is slighter than the outer one. In all animals the brain is in two portions. The cerebellum is placed upon the brain at its lowest extremity. It is different from the brain both to the touch and in appearance.

3. The back of the head is empty and hollow in all animals in proportion to their size, for some have a large head, but the part lying under the face is less in those animals which have round faces; others have a small head and large jaws, as the whole tribe of Lophuri. In all animals the brain is without blood, nor does it contain any veins, and it is naturally cold to the touch. The greater number of animals have a small cavity in the centre of the brain. And round this a membrane filled with veins: this membrane is like skin, and encloses the brain. Above the brain is the smoothest and weakest bone in the head—it is called sinciput.

4. Three passages lead from the eye to the brain; the largest and the middle-sized to the cerebellum, the least to the brain itself. The least is that which is nearest the nostril; the greater are parallel, and do not meet; but the middle-sized passages meet: this is most evident in fishes, and these passages are nearer to the brain than the larger, but the least separate from each other, and do not meet.

5. Within the neck is the œsophagus, which also derives its additional name, the isthmus, from its length and narrowness, and the trachea. The trachea lies in front of the œsophagus in all animals which possess this part, that is, all animals which breathe from the lungs. The trachea is cartilaginous in its nature, and contains but little blood: it is surrounded with many smooth rings of cartilage, and it lies upon the upper part towards the mouth, opposite the passage from the nostril to the mouth, wherefore, also, if any liquid is drawn into it in drinking, it passes out of the mouth through the nostrils.

6. Between the passages is the epiglottis, which can be folded over the passage which extends from the trachea to the

mouth; by the epiglottis the passage of the tongue is closed, at the other extremity the trachea reaches to the middle of the lungs, and afterwards divides to each side of the lungs. For the lung is double in all animals which possess this part, though the division is not so marked in viviparous animals, and least of all in man. The human lungs are anomalous, neither being divided into many lobes, as in other animals, nor being smooth.

7. In oviparous animals, such as birds and the oviparous quadrupeds, the parts are very widely separated, so that they appear to have two lungs; they are, however, only two divisions of the trachea extending to each side of the lungs; the trachea is also united with the great vein and with the part called the aorta. When the trachea is filled with air, it distributes the breath into the cavities of the lungs, which have cartilaginous interstices ending in a point; the passages of these interstices go through the whole lungs, always dividing from greater into less.

8. The heart is connected with the trachea by fatty and cartilaginous muscular bands. There is a cavity near the junction, and in some animals, when the trachea is filled with breath, this cavity is not always distinguishable, but in larger animals it is evident that the breath enters it. This then is the form of the trachea, which only inhales and exhales breath, and nothing else either dry or moist, or it suffers pain till that which has passed down is coughed up.

9. The œsophagus is joined to the mouth from above, near the trachea, being united both to the spine and the trachea by membranaceous ligaments. It passes through the diaphragm into the cavity of the stomach, is fleshy in its nature, and is extensible both in length and breadth. The human stomach is like that of a dog, not a great deal larger than the entrail, but like a wide bowel; after this there is an entrail simply rolled together, then an entrail of moderate width. The lower part of the abdomen is like that of a hog, for it is wide, and from this to the seat it is short and thick.

10. The omentum is united to the abdomen in the middle, and is in its nature a fatty membrane, as in other animals with a single stomach and teeth in both jaws. The mesenterium is over the bowels; it is membranaceous, broad, and fat; it is united to the great vein and the aorta: through it extend

many numerous veins at its junction with the intestines, reaching from above downwards. This is the nature of the œsophagus, trachea, and the parts of the abdominal cavity.

Chapter XIV.

1. The heart has three cavities: it lies above the lungs, near the division of the trachea. It has a fat and thick membrane, by which it is united to the great vein and the aorta, and it lies upon the aorta near the apex; and the apex is placed in the same situation in all animals which have a chest; and in all animals, whether they have or have not a chest, the apex of the heart is forwards, though it often escapes notice by the change of position in the parts when dissected. The gibbous portion of the heart is upwards; its apex is generally fleshy and thick, and there is a sinew in the cavities.

2. In all other animals which have a chest the heart is placed in the centre; in man it is rather on the left side, inclining a little from the division of the mammæ towards the left breast in the upper part of the chest; it is not large; its whole form is not long, but rather round, except that the extremity ends in a point It has three cavities, as I have said. The greatest is that on the right, the least on the left, the middle one is of intermediate size. They are all perforated towards the lungs. It has both the two smaller, and all of them perforated towards the lungs, and this is evident in one of the cavities downwards from its point of attachment.

3. Near the principal cavity it is attached to the great vein to which also the mesenterium is united, and in the middle it is attached to the aorta. Passages lead from the lungs to the heart, and they are divided in the same way as the trachea, following the passages from the trachea throughout the whole lungs, and the passages leading from the heart are on the upper part. There is no passage which is common to them both, but by their union they receive the breath and transmit it through the heart; for one of the passages leads to the right cavity, and the other to the left. We will hereafter speak of the great vein and the aorta in the portion of our work which treats of these parts.

4. In all animals which have lungs and are viviparous, either internally or externally, the lung has more blood than all the

other parts; for the whole lung is spongy, and through each perforation branches of the great vein proceed. Those persons are deceived who say that the lungs are empty, drawing their conclusion from dissected animals, from which all the blood has escaped. Of all the viscera the heart alone contains blood, and in the lungs the blood is not in the lungs themselves, but in the veins by which they are perforated. But in the heart itself the blood is in each of the cavities, but the thinnest blood is in the middle cavity.

5. Beneath the lungs is that division of the trunk which is called the diaphragm. It is united to the ribs, the hypochondriac region, and the spine. In the centre is a smooth membranous part, and there are veins extending through it. The human veins are thick in proportion to the size of the body. Under the diaphragm, on the right side is the liver, on the left the spleen, alike in all animals which are furnished with these parts in their natural form and without monstrosity, for already there has been observed an altered order in some quadrupeds. They are joined to the abdomen near the omentum.

6. The appearance of the human spleen is narrow and long, like that of the hog. Generally speaking, and in most animals, the liver is not furnished with a gall, though this is found in some animals. The human liver is round, like that of the ox. This is the case also in animals offered for sacrifice, as in the district of Chalcis, in Eubœa, where the sheep have no gall, and in Naxos it is so large in nearly all the animals, that strangers who come to sacrifice are surprised, and think that it is ominous, and not at all natural. The liver is united with the great vein, but has no part in common with the aorta. For a vein branches off from the great vein through the liver, at the place where the gates of the liver, as they are called, are situated. The spleen also is only connected with the great vein, for a vein extends from this to the spleen.

7. Next to these are the kidneys, which lie close to the spine. In their nature they are like the kidneys of oxen. In all animals that have kidneys the right kidney lies higher than the left, and is covered with less fat, and is more dry than the left. This is the same in all animals. Passages lead from them to the great vein and to the aorta, but not to the cavity; for all animals, except the seal, have

a cavity in their kidneys, though it is greater in some than in others. The human kidneys, though similar to those of oxen, are more solid than in other animals, and the passages that lead to them end in the body of the kidney; and this is a proof that they do not pass through them, that they contain no blood in the living animal, nor is it coagulated in them when dead; but they have a small cavity, as I said before. From the cavity of the kidneys two strong passages lead to the bladder, and two others, strong and continuous, lead to the aorta.

8. A hollow, sinewy vein is attached to the middle of each kidney, which extends from the spine through small branches, and disappears towards the hip, though it afterwards appears again upon the hip. The branches of these veins reach to the bladder; for the bladder is placed lowest of all, being united to the passages which proceed from the kidneys by the neck which reaches to the urethra; and nearly all round its circumference it is united by smooth and muscular membranes, very similar in form to those upon the diaphragm of the chest.

9. The human bladder is moderately large in size, and the pudendum is united to the neck of the bladder, having a strong passage above and a small one below. One of these passages leads to the testicles; the other, which is sinewy and cartilaginous, to the bladder. From this are appended the testicles of the male, concerning which we will treat in the part devoted to their consideration. These parts are the same in the female, who differs in none of the internal parts except the womb, the appearance of which may be learned from the drawings in the books on anatomy. Its position is upon the entrails. The bladder is above the uterus. In a future book we will speak of the nature of the uterus generally; for it is not alike, nor has it the same nature in them all.

These are the internal and external parts of the human body, and this is their nature and their manner.

BOOK THE SECOND.

Chapter I.

1. Of the parts of other animals some are common to them all, as I have said before, and some belong to particular classes, and they agree and differ in the manner often before mentioned. For almost all animals which differ in kind, have also their parts different in form, and there are some which have only a proportionate resemblance, but differ in kind, and others agree in kind, but not in form, and many parts belong to some which others have not. Viviparous quadrupeds have a head and neck, and all the parts of the head, but they differ from each other in their forms. The lion has one bone in the neck, but has no vertebræ, and when laid open its internal parts are like those of a dog.

2. Viviparous quadrupeds have fore-legs instead of arms, and in all quadrupeds, especially those which have the fore-feet much divided, they are analogous to hands, for they use them as hands, and the left legs are less at liberty than in men, except in the elephant, and this animal has the toes less perfectly jointed, and its fore-legs much larger than the hind ones; it has five toes, and short ankles to its hind legs. It has a trunk of such a nature and length as to be able to use it for a hand, and it drinks and eats by stretching this into its mouth; this also it lifts up to its driver, and pulls up trees with it; with this organ it breathes as it walks through the water. The extremity of the proboscis is curved, but without joints, for it is cartilaginous.

3. Man is the only ambidextrous animal. All animals have their chest analogous to man, but not similar to his, for he has a wide chest, and theirs is narrow: no animal but man has pectoral mammæ; the elephant has two mammæ, but not on the breast, though they are in that direction.

4. All animals, excepting the elephant, bend both their fore and hind legs in contrary directions; and also contrary to the way in which a man's limbs are bent. For in viviparous quadrupeds, except the elephant, the joints of the

fore-legs are bent forwards, and those of the hind-legs backwards, and they have the hollow part of their circumference opposite to each other: the elephant is not constructed as some have said, but is able to sit down, and bend his legs, but, from his great weight, is unable to bend them on both sides at once, but leans either to the right side or the left, and sleeps in this position, but its hind legs are bent like a man's.

5. In oviparous quadrupeds, as the crocodile, lizard, and such like, both the fore and hind legs are bent forwards, inclining a little to the side, and likewise also in other animals with more than four feet, except that the middle joint of their last pair of legs is always doubtful, and is rather bent towards the side. And man also has both the flexures of his limbs in the same direction, and those of his arms and legs contrary to each other, for he bends the arm backwards, except that the external part of the arm is a little inclined inwards, towards the side; the legs bend forwards.

6. No animal bends the joints both of its fore and hind legs backwards. The flexure of the cubitus and fore-leg is in a contrary direction to the flexure of the shoulder in all animals, and the flexure of the knee is contrary to that of the hip; so that since man bends his joints in the contrary direction to many animals, those which have such joints as man's also bend them in a contrary direction to many animals. Birds bend their limbs in a direction similar to that of quadrupeds, for being bipeds, they bend their legs backwards, and have wings instead of arms, or fore-legs, and these bend forwards.

7. The seal is like a maimed quadruped, for immediately beneath the scapula it has feet like hands, as are also those of the bear, for they are five-fingered, and each of the fingers has three joints, and a small claw: the hind feet are five-fingered, and each of the fingers has joints and claws like those upon the fore-feet; in shape they are very like the tail of a fish.

8. The movements of animals, whether they have four feet or more, are in the direction of the longer diameter of their bodies, and thus also they stand, the commencement of motion is always on the right side of their bodies. The lion and the camel, both the Arabian and Bactrian, walk with the hind-foot following the fore-foot on the same side, and this means that the right foot is not put before the left, but follows it.

Chapter II.

1. Whatever parts a man has before, a quadruped has beneath: those that are behind in man, form the quadruped's back; most animals have a tail, the seal has a small one, like that of a stag; hereafter we shall speak of apelike animals. All viviparous quadrupeds are, so to say, rough, with hair, and not like man, who, except on his head, has not much hair on his body, and what there is, is very fine; but his head is more massy than that of other animals.

2. And all creatures that have their upper part rough with hair, are quite smooth, or only slightly rough beneath; but man is contrary to this: and again, each eyelid in man is furnished with lashes, and he has hair on the cheek, and pubes; other animals are not so furnished, having no hair on the lower eyelid, or only a few hairs under the eyelid.

3. But some hairy quadrupeds are rough all over, as the hog, the bear, and the dog; the neck of others is the roughest part, as in those which have a mane, like the lion; in others which have a mane, the back of the neck from the head to the point of the shoulder is hairy, as the horse and the mule, and among wild animals with horns, the bonassus. The hipellaphus,[1] as it is called, has a mane upon the point of its shoulder, and so has the pardium,[2] though both these have a thin mane from the head to the shoulder, and the hipellaphus has a beard upon its larynx.

4. Both of these are horned, and have a cloven hoof: the female hipellaphus has no horns, it is about the size of a stag; there are hipellaphi in the country of the Arachotæ, where also are buffaloes. The wild differ as much from domesticated oxen, as wild hogs from tame ones; for they are black, and of great strength; their nose is curved like an eagle's beak, and their horns lie backwards; the horns of the hipellaphus are very like those of the dorcas:[3] the elephant is the least hairy of all quadrupeds. The tails of animals are like their bodies in roughness, and smoothness, in as many as have tails in proportion to their size, for some have very small tails.

---

[1] Perhaps Nylghau (Liddel and Scott's Lexicon), or some large kind of Stag.   [2] Cameleopard. (Schneider.)
[3] Gazelle or antelope, so named from the brightness of its eyes.

5. Camels have a part peculiar to themselves, called the hump upon the back; the Bactrian camel differs from the Arabian; the one has two humps, the other but one; and they have another hump below, like the one on their back, upon which the rest of their body is supported, when they go down upon their knees. The camel has four mammæ, like the cow, and a tail like an ass, and the pudendum is behind; it has but one knee in each leg, and not many joints, as some persons say; this appearance arises from the position of the abdomen. It has a a talus like that of an ox, misshapen, and small in proportion to its size.

6. The hoof is cloven; it has not teeth in both jaws. The cloven hoof is formed in this manner; the lower part is somewhat cloven, as far as the second joint of the toes, but the upper part is four-cleft as far as the first joint of the toes; there is a membrane uniting the cloven parts as in geese, the foot is fleshy underneath like that of a bear, wherefore, when camels are used in war, and become footsore, their drivers put them on leather shoes. All quadrupeds have their legs bony and sinewy and without flesh, that is all animals with feet are so formed, excepting man, and they are without hips; this is particularly the case with birds. But on the contrary, the hips, thighs, and legs of man are more fleshy than almost any other part of his body, for even the calf of his leg is fleshy.

7. Some sanguineous and viviparous quadrupeds have many divisions in the foot, like the hands and feet of man; for some, as the lion, the dog, and the panther, have many divisions of the foot; others are cloven-footed, and instead of nails have hoofs, as the sheep, the goat, the stag, and the river-horse. Some are without divisions in the foot, as the solidunguli, the horse, and the mule. The genus of swine belongs to both classes; for in Illyria, Pæonia, and other places, there are swine with a solid hoof. Those with a two-cleft hoof have two divisions, before and behind; in those with a solid hoof this is continuous.

8. Some animals have horns, others have none; most of those with horns have also cloven feet, as the ox, the stag, and the goat. We have never seen an animal with a solid hoof with two horns, and there are only a few that have a solid hoof and one horn, as the Indian ass, and the oryx.[1]

[1] Antelope Oryx.

Of all animals with a solid hoof, the Indian ass alone has a talus. Swine, as I said before, belong to both classes, so that they have not a well-formed astragulus.

9. Many animals with cloven hoofs have a talus; no animals with their feet in many divisions have a talus, nor has man. The lynx has as it were half a talus, and so has the lion, but it is more intricate, as some pretend. The talus is always in the hind leg, and it is placed upright upon the gamb, with the lower part outwards, and the upper part inwards; the parts called Coa[1] turned inwards towards each other, and the Chia turned outwards, and the projecting portions upwards. This is the position of the talus, in all animals which are furnished with this part. Some animals have a cloven hoof, and a mane, and two horns turned towards each other, as the bonassus, an animal which inhabits the country between Pæonia and Media.

10. All animals with horns are four-footed, unless there is any animal which metaphorically, and for the sake of a word, is said to have horns, as they say that the serpents in the neighbourhood of Thebes in Egypt have, though it is nothing more than an appendage, that is called a horn. The stag is the only animal that has solid horns, the horns of all other animals are hollow for a part of their length, and solid at the extremity; the hollow part is principally formed of skin, and round this is arranged the solid part, as in the horns of oxen. The stag is the only animal which casts its horns; they are reproduced; this takes place every year after the animal has attained the age of two years; other animals never lose their horns unless destroyed by violence.

Chapter III.

1. The parts of the mammæ also, and the organs of generation, are different in man and in other animals For some have the mammæ forward on or near the breast, and two mammæ with two nipples, as man and the elephant, as I said before, for the elephant has two mammæ near the armpits; in the female they are small, and do not bear any proportion to the size of the animal, so that they are scarcely visible in a side view; the males also have mammæ as well as the females, but they are exceedingly small.

[1] Coa, the highest throw with the Astragalus with the convex side uppermost, opposed to Chia, the lowest throw, sixes and aces.

2. The bear has four, other animals have two mammæ upon the thighs, and two nipples like sheep; others have four nipples, as the cow; some animals have not their nipples on the breast and thighs, but on the abdomen, as the dog and the hog, they have many nipples, but not all of the same size; other animals also have more than two, as the panther, which has four on the abdomen; the lioness has two on the abdomen, the camel has two mammæ and four nipples, like the cow.

3. Among animals with a solid hoof the males have no mammæ, except some horses which bear a resemblance to their dams. Some males have the penis external, as man, and the horse, and many others; some internal, as the dolphin. Of those animals in which it is external, some have it in front, as those which I have named; and some of these have both the penis and testicles loose, as in man; others have them close to the abdomen; some have them more, others less loose, for this part is not equally free in the boar and the horse.

4. The elephant has a penis like a horse, but small and less in proportion to the size of its body; its testicles are not external but internal, and near the kidneys, wherefore also the work of copulation is quickly performed. The female has the pudendum in the same position as the udder of the sheep, and when excited with desire, it is lifted up outwards, so as to be ready for copulation with the male; and the orifice of the pudendum is very wide. Most animals have the penis in the same direction, but some are retromingent, as the lynx, lion, camel, and hare. In some males, as I have said, the direction of the penis is different, but all females are retromingent, for even in the female elephant the pudendum is placed under the thighs, as in other animals.

5. The penis is very different in different animals, for in some it is cartilaginous and fleshy, as in man; the fleshy part does not swell, but the cartilaginous portion is erected; in others it is sinewy, as the camel and the stag; in others it is bony, as the fox and the wolf, the weasel and the martin, for the martin also has a bony penis.

6. Again, man being a perfect animal, has the upper part of his body less than the lower part; the contrary is the case with other sanguineous animals: by the upper portion of his body we mean the portion of his body from the head to

the anus; and by the lower, the parts from hence downwards. In those animals which have feet the hind leg is the lower part of the body in point of size; and in those without legs, the same relation is observed in their various kinds of tails. Such is the nature of perfected animals, but they differ in the development of their parts. Man in the young state has the upper part of his body greater than the lower; but as he grows the proportion of his parts changes, wherefore also he is the only animal which does not move in the same way when young and when grown up, for at first a child crawls like a four-footed animal.

7. Some animals grow in the same proportion throughout, as the dog—others when they are first born have their upper part proportionally less than the lower, but as they approach maturity, the upper parts increase in size, as in the lophuri, for in these animals the part from the hoof to the haunch never grows after their birth.

8. There is a great difference in the teeth of animals, both among themselves and from the human type; all viviparous and sanguineous quadrupeds have teeth; some have teeth in both jaws, which others have not; this is the first distinction. Those which have horns do not possess teeth in both jaws, for they have no front teeth in the upper jaw. There are others, as the camel, which, though it has no horns, has not teeth in the upper jaw.

9. Some animals have tusks like the boar, others have not; some have pointed teeth, as the lion, panther, and dog; the teeth of others have an even surface, as the ox and the horse. Animals with pointed teeth have their teeth fitting into each other; no animal has both tusks and horns, neither those with pointed teeth nor any others. Most animals have their front teeth sharp, and their hind teeth flat; all the teeth of the seal are sharp pointed, showing an approximation to the race of fishes, for all fishes have pointed teeth.

10. None of these genera have a double row of teeth. But, if we may believe Ctesias, there are some which have this peculiarity, for he mentions an Indian animal called martichora, which had three rows of teeth in each jaw; it is as large and as rough as a lion, and has similar feet, but its ears and face are like those of a man; its eye is grey, and its body red; it has a tail like a land scorpion, in which there

is a sting; it darts forth the spines with which it is covered instead of hair, and it utters a noise resembling the united sound of a pipe and a trumpet; it is not less swift of foot than a stag, and is wild, and devours men.

11. Man sheds his teeth, and so do other animals, as the horse, the mule, and the ass; man sheds his front teeth, but no animal sheds the molar teeth; swine do not shed any of their teeth. About dogs, there is some doubt; some persons think they do not shed their teeth at all, others that they shed only the canine teeth; but it has been observed that they do shed their teeth like men: perhaps it has escaped notice, because they do not shed them before the inner ones, which are similar, are grown up.

12. And it is probable that the same takes place in other wild animals, since they are said only to shed their canine teeth. Young dogs are known from old ones by their teeth, for young dogs have sharp white teeth, old dogs have them black and blunted. The horse is in this respect different from all other animals; for while the teeth in other animals become darker as they grow older, in the horse they become more white.

13. Those which are called canine teeth are placed between the cutting and the molar teeth, and partake of the nature of both, for they are wide below, but sharp at the top. The male has more teeth than the female in mankind, and sheep, and goats, and swine. This has not been observed in other animals. Those persons which have the greatest number of teeth are the longest lived; those which have them widely separated, smaller, and more scattered, are generally more short lived.

14. The last molar teeth, which are called wisdom teeth, appear, both in the male and female about the age of twenty, and some women cut the molar teeth at eighty years of age, causing great pain in the extremity of the jaw, and some men also: this happens with persons who do not cut their wise teeth at the proper age.

15. The elephant has four teeth on each side, with which he grinds his food, for he reduces his food very small, like meal. Besides these, he has two tusks: in the male these are large, and turned upwards; in the female they are small, and bent in the contrary direction. The elephant has teeth as soon

as it is born; but the tusks are small, and therefore inconspicuous at first. It has so small a tongue within its mouth, that it is difficult to see it.

Chapter IV.

1. ANIMALS have very differently-sized mouths, for some have wide, open mouths, as the dog, the lion, and all animals with pointed teeth; other animals have a small mouth, as man, or a moderately-sized one, as the swine. The Egyptian river-horse has a mane like a horse, and a cloven hoof like the ox; it has a flat face; the talus is like that of other animals with cloven hoofs, and it has large projecting teeth; it has a tail like a hog, and utters a sound like the neighing of a horse; it is about the size of an ass, and its skin is so thick that shields are made of it; its intestines are like those of a horse or ass.

Chapter V.

1. SOME animals unite in their nature the characteristics of man and quadrupeds, as apes, monkeys, and cynocephali. The monkey is an ape with a tail; cynocephali have the same form as apes, but are larger and stronger, and their faces are more like dogs' faces; they are naturally fierce, and their teeth are more like dogs' teeth, and stronger than in other genera.

2. The apes are hairy in their upper parts, so as to bear some resemblance to quadrupeds, and also in the lower, because they are like men, for in this particular, as I said before, there is a difference in men and brutes; their hair is coarse, and apes are rough both above and below. They bear a strong likeness to men in their face, for their nostrils, ears, and teeth, both the fore and back teeth, are like his; and as for eye-lashes, though other animals are entirely without them, the ape has them on the lower eye-lid; they are, however, very thin, and altogether small.

3. Upon the breast are two small mammæ, with two nipples; the arms are like those of man, but hairy; both the arms and legs are bent like those of man, the curves of the limbs being turned towards each other. Besides these, it has hands, fingers, and nails like those of man. but all indicating an approximation to the brute; their feet are peculiar, for they

are like great hands. The fingers upon them are like those on the hands, and the middle one is the longest; the sole of the foot is like a hand, except that it extends the whole length of the hand like a palm, and is hard at the extremity, and is a bad and obscure representation of a heel.

4. The feet are used for both the purposes of hands and feet, and are bent like hands. The humerus and the femur are short compared with the cubitus and the leg. The navel is not prominent, and there is a hard place about the region of the navel. Like quadrupeds, the upper part of the body is much larger than the lower, almost in the proportion of five to three, and the feet are like hands, and as it were made up of hands and feet, a foot as far as the extremity of the heel, and the remainder like a hand, for the fingers are furnished with something like a palm.

5. The ape passes more of its time as a quadruped than a biped, and like a quadruped, it has no nates, nor has it a tail like a biped, but only something in representation of a tail. The pudendum of the female resembles that of a woman; that of the male is more like a dog's. The monkey, as I said before, has a tail, and all the internal parts of the body are like those of man. The external parts of viviparous quadrupeds are of this nature.

Chapter VI.

1. OVIPAROUS and sanguineous quadrupeds (for no sanguineous land animal that is not either a quadruped or apodal is oviparous) have a head, neck, back, upper and lower parts of the body, and fore and hind legs, and something resembling a breast, like oviparous quadrupeds: most of them also have a large tail, some a small one; all of them have many toes and divided feet, and all the organs of sense, and a tongue, except the Egyptian crocodile. And in this respect it resembles some fishes, for the tongue of fishes is thorny, and not free, and in some the place for the tongue is altogether smooth, and without division (so that nothing is visible), unless the lips are drawn aside.

2. They have no ears, only a passage for hearing; neither have they any mammæ, and the penis and testicles are internal, and not external. They have no hair, but are covered with scales, and all are furnished with sharp teeth. The

river-cocodiles have eyes like hogs, and great sharp teeth, strong claws, and an unbroken scaly skin. In the water their sight is imperfect, but very good on land. They pass the greatest part of the day on land, and of the night in the water, for they cannot bear the cold air.

Chapter VII.

1. The chameleon has the whole of its body like that of a lizard, and the ribs, descending downwards, are joined together on the hypogastric region, like those of fish, and the back-bone stands up, like that of a fish; its face is like that of the chœropithecus.[1] It has a very long tail; the extremity is very smooth, and rolled together like a thong. It is raised, upon longer legs than a lizard; the joints of the legs are bent in the same direction as the lizard's.

2. Each of its feet is divided into two parts, having the same relation to each other as our thumbs have to the rest of the hand: and, for a short distance, each of these is divided into toes; in the fore-feet the internal part has three, the external two toes; in the hind feet the internal part has two, and the external three toes; there is a claw upon each of its toes like that of birds of prey; its whole body is rough, like the crocodile.

3. Its eyes are placed in a hollow, and are very large and round; surrounded with skin like the rest of its body, and in the middle is left a small aperture through which it sees; this is never covered with skin. The eye is turned round in a circle, and it can direct its vision to any side, so that it can see where it will. The change in the colour of its skin takes place when it is filled with air. It can acquire either a black colour, like that of the crocodile, or ochreous, like that of the lizard, or spotted with black, like the panther; and this change takes place over the whole body, for the eyes also change like the rest of the body, and so does the tail.

4. Its movements are slow, like those of the tortoise; when dying, it becomes ochreous, and retains this colour after death. The œsophagus and trachea of the chameleon are similar to the same parts in lizards; it has no flesh, except a little on the head and cheeks, and upon the appendage at the end of its tail. It has no blood, except about the heart, and

---

[1] Simia rostrata, or perhaps baboon. (*The identifications of the animals, unless otherwise noted, are taken from the German translation by Strack,* 1816.)

eyes, and the parts above the heart, and the veins that extend from these: and even in these there is very little blood.

5. The brain lies a little above the eyes, and is continuous with them; and when the outside skin of the eye is taken away, a bright object shines through it, like a bright ring of brass. Through the whole of its body many strong membranes are extended, which are much stronger than in other animals. It breathes strongly for some time after it has been dissected, and there are some slight movements of the heart; it also continues to contract its sides, but not the other parts of the body. It has no distinct spleen; and it hides itself in rocks like the lizard.

Chapter VIII.

1. Birds also have many parts like the animals described above. For all these have a head, neck, back, and under parts of the body, and something resembling a breast. They have two legs, and thus resemble men more than other animals, except that the joints bend backwards like those of quadrupeds, as I said before. They have neither hands, nor forefeet, but wings; herein they differ from all other animals. Again, the hip is like a thigh, large and united as far as the middle of the abdomen, so as to look like a thigh, when it is separated from the rest of the body; and the thigh where it is joined to the leg is another part. The class of birds with crooked claws have the largest thigh, and stronger breasts than others.

2. All birds have claws and many divisions of the foot; in most of them the toes are quite separate; but the swimmers have their feet covered with a web, but even these have distinct and jointed toes. All birds that fly high in the air have four toes; and, generally, these are placed three forwards, and one backward, like a heel; a few birds have two toes turned forwards and two backwards, as the bird called jynx.[1] This bird is somewhat larger than the spize,[2] and is variegated in appearance. The formation of its toes is peculiar, and so is that of its tongue, which is like a serpent's. This it can project from its mouth, as much as the width of four fingers, and draw it in again. Like a snake it can turn its neck quite round, whilst the rest of its body is perfectly

[1] Jynx torquilla, wry-neck.   [2] Fringilla, finch.

still. It has large claws, like those of the colius,[1] and it hisses with its voice.

3. Birds have a mouth, but its construction is peculiar, for they have neither lips nor teeth, but a beak, and neither ears nor nostrils, but only passages for these organs, for the nostrils in the beak, and for the ears in the head. They have two eyes like other animals, without eyelashes; when heavy with sleep, they close their eyes with the lower eyelid; and all possess a nictitating membrane, which closes the eye. The owl-like birds also use the upper eyelid. The same is the nature of the scaly animals, as the saurians, and others of this class; all of them close their eyes with the lower eyelid, but they do not all wink like birds. Again, birds have neither scales nor hair, but feathers; all the feathers have a stem.

4. Birds have no tail, but a rump; in birds with long legs, or palmated feet, this is short, in others it is large. These last, when they fly, keep their legs close to the body, but the others stretch them out behind them. All birds have a tongue, but this differs in various kinds: some have it large, others small. Next after man, some birds articulate words better than any other animals; this is particularly the case with those with broad tongues. No oviparous animal has an epiglottis on its trachea: but it can close and open the passage, so as to prevent any heavy thing finding its way into the lungs.

5. Some tribes of birds have spurs; this is never the case with those which have crooked claws. Those with crooked claws are more active in flight; those which have spurs, are heavier in their make.

6. Some birds have a crest, mostly formed of erect feathers; the domestic fowl, alone, is peculiar, for its crest is neither flesh, nor very unlike flesh.

Chapter IX.

1. Among aquatic animals, there is one class of fish, which embraces many forms, and is separated from other animals, for it has a head, and upper and lower parts, in which last are the stomach and bowels, and a continuous and undivided tail. This is not alike in all. They have neither neck nor limb, nor internal and external testicles, nor mammæ, nor

[1] Perhaps Corvus galgulus.

has any other animal mammæ that is not viviparous, nor indeed all viviparous animals, but those only that are internally viviparous, and not first of all oviparous. For the dolphin is a viviparous animal, wherefore it has two mammæ, not indeed above, but near the organs of reproduction. It has not evident nipples, but, as it were, a stream flowing from each side. From these the milk exudes, and the young ones suck as they follow the mother. This has been distinctly observed by some persons.

2. But fish, as we have observed, have neither mammæ nor any external passage for the genital organs. In the branchia they have a distinctive organ, through which they eject the water they have received into their mouths; and they have fins, most fishes have four, but the long fishes, as the eel, have only two placed near the branchia, and in this respect the cestreus,[1] a fish in the lake of Siphæ, is similar to the eel,[2] and so is the fish called tænia.[3] Some of these long fish have no fins, as the muræna, nor have they divided branchia like other fish.

3. Some fish with branchia have coverings over their branchia; in all the cartilaginous fishes they are uncovered. All fishes that have coverings have the branchia placed on their sides; among the cartilaginous fishes some are broad in the lowest part, as the narce[4] and the batos;[5] some very long in the sides, as all the galeodea.[6] In the batracus,[7] although the branchia are on the sides, they are covered with a coriaceous, not a prickly membrane, like those of fishes which are not cartilaginous.

4. In some fishes with branchia they are single, in others double, but the last towards the body is always single. Some have but few branchia, others have many; but their number is always equal on both sides, and those with the smallest number have always one on each side; this is double in the capros;[8] others have two on each side, sometimes these are single, sometimes double, as in the conger[9] and the scarus;[10] others have four simple branchia on each side, as the ellops,[11] synagris, muræna, and eel; others have

---

[1] Mugil, mullet. [2] Muræna anguilla. [3] Perhaps Cepola tænia.
[4] Raia torpedo. [5] Raia batos. [6] The shark tribe.
[7] Lophius piscatorius. [8] Perhaps Cottus cataphractus.
[9] Muræna conger. [10] Scarus cretensis.
[11] Swordfish or sturgeon (L. and S. Lexicon), or Centriscus scolopax.

four, all divided except the last, as the cichle,¹ perca,² glanis,³ and cyprinus;⁴ all the galeodea have five double branchia on each side, the xiphias⁵ has eight, which are double. This is the manner and number of the branchia of fishes.

5. And fish differ in other respects besides their gills, for they have no hair like viviparous quadrupeds, nor scaly plates like oviparous quadrupeds, nor feathers like birds, but the greater number of them are covered with scales; some of them are rough, and a very few are smooth. Some cartilaginous fishes are rough, others smooth. Congers, eels, and tunnies are smooth. All fish except the scarus have pointed teeth, and all have sharp teeth, some several rows of them, and teeth on the tongue; they have also a hard prickly tongue, so united to the mouth as sometimes to appear without a tongue.

6. The mouth of some fishes is wide, like viviparous quadrupeds. They have no external organs of sense, nor even passages for smelling or hearing; but all have eyes without eyelids, though their eyes are not hard. All fishes are sanguineous; some are oviparous, others viviparous; all those that are covered with scales are oviparous. The cartilaginous fishes are all viviparous, except the batrachus.

CHAPTER X.

1. THE remaining class of sanguineous animals is that of serpents; these partake of both characters. The greater portion of them inhabit the land, a few inhabiting water are found in rivers. There are also serpents in the sea very like those on land, except in their head, which is more like that of the conger. There are many genera of sea-serpents, and they are of all kinds of colours; they do not exist in the deepest part of the ocean. Serpents are apodal, like fishes.

2. There are also marine scolopendræ,⁶ very like those on land, but rather less; they live in rocky places; in colour they are redder, and they have more feet, and slighter legs than in the terrestrial species. These also, like the serpents, are not found in deep places.

3. And there is a small fish which lives among the rocks, which some call echineis;⁷ some people use it for trials and philtres; it is not fit for food. Some people say it

---

¹ A variegated fish. ² Perca fluviatilis. ³ Silurus glanis.
⁴ Cyprinus carpis, Carp. ⁵ Xiphias gladius, Swordfish.
⁶ Nereis, or aphrodite. ⁷ Echeneis remora.

has feet, but it has none; the fins, however, are like feet, which gives it this appearance. I have now described the external parts of sanguineous animals, their nature, and their number, and the differences which occur amongst them.

Chapter XI.

1. First of all we will speak of the internal parts of sanguineous animals, for the greatest number of genera differ from other animals, some being sanguineous, others exsanguineous. The sanguineous genera are man, viviparous and oviparous quadrupeds, birds, fishes, and whales, and perhaps others that are anonymous, because they do not form a genus, but simply species amongst each other, as the serpent and the crocodile.

2. All viviparous quadrupeds have an œsophagus and trachea, situated as in man, and so have oviparous quadrupeds and birds, though there is some difference in the formation of these parts; all that breathe by inhaling and exhaling air have lungs, trachea, and œsophagus. The position of the œsophagus and trachea, though similar, is not the same, nor are the lungs alike in all, nor similar in position.

3. All sanguineous animals have a heart, and a division in the middle of the body, called a diaphragm. In small animals its smallness and thinness render it less apparent. The heart of the ox is peculiar; for there is a kind of ox, though not the whole genus, which has a bone in its heart, and there is also a bone in the heart of the horse.

4. Not all animals have lungs, fish and those with gills have no lungs. All sanguineous animals have a liver, generally a spleen also; but in oviparous animals that are not viviparous, the spleen is so small as nearly to escape notice, as in most birds, the pigeon, kite,[1] hawk,[2] and owl. The ægocephalus[3] has none at all. Oviparous quadrupeds are of the same nature, for they have a very small spleen, as the tortoise, emys,[4] phryne,[5] lizard, crocodile, and frog.

5. Some animals have a gall upon the liver, others none. Among viviparous quadrupeds the stag[6] has none, nor the deer,[7] horse, mule, ass, seal, and some swine. The Achaïnian stag appears to have the gall in the tail; that which they call

[1] Falco milvus.   [2] Falco palumbarius.   [3] Stryx otus.
[4] Testudo coriacea.   [5] Cervus elaphus.
[7] Cervus capreolus, or C. Dama.

gall in these animals resembles it in colour, but it is not liquid like gall, but more like the spleen in its internal structure.

6. All, while they are alive, have worms[1] in the head; they are produced in the hollow part under the hypoglottis, and near the vertebræ, where the head is joined on. In size they resemble very large maggots; they are numerous, and continuous, in number not generally more than twenty. Stags, as I have observed, have no gall, but their intestines are so bitter that dogs will not eat them if the deer are fat.

7. The elephant also has a liver without a gall, but when the part where the gall is attached in other animals, is cut open, a quantity of fluid like bile, more or less abundant, runs out. Among those animals which inhale sea-water, and have lungs, the dolphin has no gall. All birds and fishes have galls, and all oviparous quadrupeds, to speak of them at once, have a gall, greater or less; but in some fishes it is placed upon the liver, as the galeodea, glanis, rine,[2] leiobatus,[3] narce, and in some long fish, as the eel, belone,[4] and zygæna;[5] and the callionymus[6] has a gall upon the liver, larger in proportion to its size than any other fish. Others have a gall upon the intestines, extending from the liver by several thin passages; the amia[7] has it stretched out upon the intestines, and equal to them in length, and many times folded upon it. Other fish have the gall upon the intestines, some at a greater, others at a less distance, as the batrachus, elops, synagris, muræna, xiphias.

8. And the same genus often appears to have the gall extended in both directions, as the conger, in some individuals it is turned towards the liver, in others suspended before the liver. The same structure is observed in birds, for some have the gall turned towards the stomach, and others towards the entrails, as the pigeon, crow, quail, swallow, sparrow; in others it is directed both towards the liver and the stomach, as the ægocephalus; in others, as the hawk and kite, it is directed towards the liver and the intestines.

Chapter XII.

1. All viviparous quadrupeds have kidneys and a bladder, but some oviparous animals have neither, as birds and

---

[1] Possibly Œstrus nasalis.   [2] Squalus squatina.
[3] Raia batos.   [4] Syngnathus acus.   [5] Squalus zygæna.
[6] Uranoscopus scaber.   [7] A kind of marked scomber, mackerel?

fishes, and among oviparous quadrupeds the marine turtle is the only one that has them at all proportionate to its size. The marine turtle has the kidneys like those of oxen, and that of the ox is like a great many kidneys joined together. In all its internal parts, the bonassus[1] is like the ox.

2. The position which these parts occupy is the same in all animals, and the heart is in the middle of the body of all creatures, except man. In him it is inclined towards the left side; and, as it was before observed, the apex of the heart is directed forward in all, but in fishes it does not appear to be so, for the apex of the heart is not directed towards the chest, but towards the mouth and head, and the top of the heart is suspended from the place where the right and left branchia are joined to each other, and there are also other passages which extend from the heart to each of the branchia, greater towards the larger branchia, and less towards the smaller; but that to the top of the heart in great fishes is a thick white tube.

3. A few fishes, as the conger and the eel, have an œsophagus, but even in these it is very small; in some of the fish that have a liver, it is placed on the right side, and has no lobes; in others, it is divided from the commencement, and the greater part is on the right side. For in some fish each part of the liver hangs down, and the divisions are not united at their origin, as in the tribe of fish called galeodea, and in a species of hare which is found near the lake of Bolba, in the place called Sycine, and in other places, so that one might suppose that they had two livers, on account of the distances at which the passages unite, as in the lungs of birds.

4. In all animals the spleen is naturally situated on the left side. The case has occurred that an animal having been opened, has been observed to have the spleen on the right side and the liver on the left, but such appearances are considered ominous. In all animals the trachea reaches to the lungs (its nature will be described in another place); and the œsophagus, in all that have this part, reaches to the stomach through the diaphragm. For most fishes (as I observed before) have no œsophagus, but the stomach is united directly with the mouth. So that it often happens that, when great

[1] Bos grunniens.

fishes are pursuing small ones, the stomach falls forward into the mouth.

5. All the animals that have been mentioned have a stomach, and in the same situation, for it is universally placed under the diaphragm, and an intestine follows it, and ends in the exit for the food which is called the anus. But the stomach of different animals is variously formed, for in the first place viviparous horned quadrupeds, which have not teeth in both jaws, have four such passages, and those animals are said to ruminate. For the œsophagus, commencing in the mouth, extends to the parts just below the lungs, and passes through the diaphragm to the great stomach.

6. The internal part of this is rough, and folded together; and it is united, near the junction of the stomach, to the part which, from its appearance, is called the net, for the exterior is like a stomach, but the inside resembles the meshes of a net; in point of size, the net is much less than the stomach. Next to this is the part called echinus, because internally it is rough and channelled; it is nearly the same size as the net. Next to the echinus is the enystrum, which is both larger and longer than the echinus, and internally covered with many large and smooth folds; after this are the entrails.

7. This is the nature of the stomach of animals with horns, and no teeth in the upper jaw. But they differ from each other in the form and size of these parts; and because the œsophagus is sometimes united to the middle, and sometimes to the side of the stomach. Most animals which have teeth in both jaws have but one stomach, as the man, dog, bear, lion, and the wolf. The thos[1] has all its intestines like a wolf. All these have but one stomach, to which the bowel is united. But in some of these the stomach is larger, as the hog and the bear; that of the hog is marked with a few smooth lines. In other animals the stomach is less, not indeed much larger than the intestine, as the dog, lion, and man. In the forms of their bowels other animals are divided into two classes, resembling these types; for in some the stomach resembles a dog's, in others a hog's, both the greater and lesser animals in the same way; and the stomachs of various animals differ in size, form, thickness, thinness, and the position of the junction of the œsophagus.

[1] Felis onza, perhaps also canis aureus.

8. And the nature of the bowels differs in the before-named animals, those, namely, which have not, and those which have teeth in both jaws, in size, thickness, and folding. The intestines of the ruminants are all large, and so are the animals themselves; there are a few small animals of this class, and there is no horned animal which is very small. And some have appendages to the intestines, for none of the animals with teeth in both jaws have straight intestines. There are enlargements in the bowels of the elephant, which give it the appearance of having four stomachs; in these the food is detained, and apart from these there is no receptacle for the food. Its intestines are very like those of the hog, except that the liver is four times greater than that of the ox, and other parts also; the spleen is small in proportion to its size.

9. The stomach and intestines of oviparous quadrupeds bear a similar proportion to each other, as in the land and marine tortoise, the lizard, and both kinds of crocodiles,[1] and similar quadrupeds; for they have one simple stomach, in some it is like that of the hog, in others like that of the dog.

10. The class of serpents in almost every part of their body resemble the saurians, which have feet, and are oviparous, if we add to their length, and take away the feet; for snakes are covered with scales, and have their upper and lower parts like saurians, except that they have no testicles, but, like fish, two passages united in one, and a large and cloven uterus, but in other respects their intestines are so like those of saurians, except that from their elongated figure their intestines are long and narrow, that they might be mistaken for them, from their similarity.

11. For the trachea is very long, and the œsophagus still longer, and the commencement of the trachea is close to the mouth, so that the tongue appears to lie beneath it. The trachea appears to be above the tongue because this last can be retracted, and is not always in one position, as in other animals. Their tongue is long, thin, and black, and can be put forth for some distance. The tongue of serpents and saurians is distinct from that of all other animals, for the extremity of the tongue is cloven; this is most remarkable in serpents, for the extremities of their

---

[1] Crocodilus niloticus and Lacerta stellio.

tongues are like hairs. The seal also has a forked tongue. The serpent has a stomach like a very wide entrail, like that of the dog, afterwards a very long and thin intestine, which is alike to its extremity.

12. Behind the pharynx is a small kidney-shaped heart, so that at times the apex does not appear to be directed towards the chest, next to this is a single lung, divided by a muscular passage, very long, and descending a long distance from the breast. The liver is long and simple, the spleen small and round, like that of the saurians. The gall resembles that of fish, in water serpents it is situated on the liver, in others generally upon the intestines. They all have pointed teeth, and as many ribs as there are days in the month, for they have thirty. Some persons say that in one respect serpents resemble the young of the swallow, for if their eyes are pierced with a pointed instrument, they will grow again, and if the tails of serpents or lizards be cut off, they will be reproduced.

13. The same remarks will apply to the intestines and stomachs of fishes, for they have one simple stomach, but it differs in form, for in some fishes it is like a bowel, as in the one called scarus, and this is the only fish that appears to ruminate, and the size of the intestines is simple and folded together, for it can be resolved into one, by unfolding it. The appendages of the stomach appear to be peculiar to fishes and birds, for birds have them above the stomach, and few in number, but in fish they are above, and around the stomach. Some have many appendages, as the gobius,[1] galeus,[2] perca, scorpios,[3] citharus,[4] trigla,[5] and sparus.[6] But the cestreus has many on one side of the stomach, and only one on the other. Some have only a few, as the hepatus[7] and the glaucus,[8] and the chrysophrys[9] also has only a few, but some individuals differ from others, for one chrysophrys has many, another has only a few. There are some fish which have none of them, as most of the cartilaginous genera; others have a few, and some a great many, and all fish have these appendages very near the stomach itself.

[1] Gobio, gudgeon.
[2] Shark.
[3] Cottus scorpius.
[4] Probably Pleuronectes rhombus.
[5] Mullus surmulentus.
[6] Sparus maina.
[7] Theutis hepatus.
[8] Probably Gobio gozo.
[9] Sparus aurata.

14. Birds have their internal parts different from each other and from other animals; for some have before the stomach a crop, as the domestic fowl, pigeon, dove, and partridge. The crop is a large and hollow skin, into which the food is received before it is digested. Hence from the œsophagus it is narrower, then wider, and where it descends into the stomach it is smaller.

15. In most birds the stomach is fleshy and thick, and on the outside there is a strong skin, which is separated from the fleshy part. Some birds have no crop, but instead of it a wide œsophagus, either wholly so, or in the part extending to the stomach, as in the colœus,[1] raven, and crow. The quail has the lower part of the œsophagus broad, the ægocephalus has it small but wider, and so has the owl. But the duck, goose, gull, diver, and bustard, have a wide and broad œsophagus, and so have many other birds.

16. And some have a part of the stomach itself like a crop, as the cenchreis;[2] and there are some which have neither œsophagus nor a wide crop, but a large stomach; these are small birds like the swallow, and the sparrow. A few have neither a crop, nor a wide œsophagus, but a very long one; these are birds with a long neck, as the porphyrion.[3] Almost all these emit a moister excrement than other birds.

17. The quail has these peculiarities, for it has a crop, and before the stomach a wide and broad œsophagus. And the crop is at a great distance from the part of the œsophagus before the belly, considering the size of the bird. Birds have generally a small intestine, which is single when unfolded, and birds have appendages, a few, as I have said, and not placed above, as in fish, but below, near the end of the intestine. Some birds have not these appendages, though they generally have them, as the domestic fowl, partridge, duck, night-raven,[4] localus,[5] ascalaphus,[6] goose, bustard, owl. Some of the small birds have them, but they are very minute, as the sparrow.

---

[1] Three kinds of birds are called by this name. Corvus graculus, C. monedula, and Pelicanus graculus. [2] Falco tinnunculus.
[3] Fulica porphyrion. [4] Ardea nycticorax. [5] Some kind of heron.
[6] Some kind of owl.

BOOK THE THIRD.

Chapter I.

1. We have treated of the other internal parts of animals, their number, their nature and varieties. It now remains for us to speak of the organs of generation. In females these are always internal; but there is much difference in males, for some sanguineous animals have no testicles at all, in others they are internal; and in some animals with internal testicles, they are placed near the kidneys, in others near the abdomen; in other animals they are external. The penis of these last is sometimes united to the abdomen, in others it is loose as well as the testicles; but in promingent and retromingent animals it is suspended from the abdomen in a different manner. Neither fish nor any other animal with gills, nor the whole class of serpents, have testicles; neither has any apodal animal which is not internally viviparous.

2. Birds have testicles, but they are internal and near the loins, and so have oviparous quadrupeds, as the lizard, tortoise, and crocodile, and among viviparous animals, the hedgehog. In some viviparous animals they are situated internally upon the abdomen, as the dolphin among apodal creatures, and the elephant among quadrupeds. In other animals the testicles are external. It has been previously observed, that the manner and position of their junction with the abdomen is various, for in some they are joined on and do not hang down, as in swine, in others they hang down as in man.

3. It has also been observed that neither fishes nor serpents have testicles, but they have two passages hanging down on each side of the spine from the diaphragm, and these unite in one passage above the anus, by above, we mean nearer the spinal column. At the season of coition these passages are full of semen, which exudes on pressure; the differences

among these may be seen by dissection, and in another place they will each be considered more particularly.

4. All oviparous animals, whether bipeds or quadrupeds, have their testicles placed in the loins below the diaphragm, some of a white colour, others ochreous, but in all surrounded with small veins; from each of these a passage is produced, which afterwards become united in one, and, as in fish, open near the anus. This is the penis, which is inconspicuous in small animals; but in the larger, as the goose and such like, it becomes more conspicuous immediately after coition.

5. And these passages, both in fish and other animals, are joined to the loins below the stomach and between the entrails and the great vein, from which passages proceed to each of the kidneys; and, as in fish, the semen may be seen entering them at the period of coition, when these passages become very conspicuous, but when this season is passed the passages again become invisible. So also the testicles of birds are either small or entirely invisible when not excited, but when urged by desire they become very large; this is so remarkable in pigeons and partridges, that some persons have supposed that they had no testicles during winter.

6. In some of those animals in which the testicles are placed forwards, they are internal and upon the abdomen, as in the dolphin; in others they are externally conspicuous upon the extremity of the abdomen. These animals are similar in other respects, but differ in this, for in some the testicles are uncovered, and others that have external testes they are placed in a scrotum.

7. This is the nature of the testicles of all viviparous animals with feet: from the aortá, passages like veins proceed to the head of each testicle, and two others from the kidneys, these last are full of blood, but those from the aorta contain no blood. From the head of each testicle to the testicle itself, there proceeds a thicker and more muscular passage, which is in each testicle reflected back to the head of the testicle, and from this point they again unite upon the penis towards the fore-part of it.

8. And both these passages which are reflected back upon themselves, and those which are seated upon the testicles, are covered with the same membrane as the testes them-

selves, so that unless this membrane is taken away, they all appear to be one passage. These last passages, which are seated upon the testicle, contain sanguineous fluid, but less than those above from the aorta; but in the reflected passages of the duct which is upon the penis, the fluid is white. A passage also leads from the bladder, and is united to the upper part of this duct, which is enclosed in the part called the penis as in a husk. The accompanying diagram will illustrate the position of these parts.

9. The origin of the passage from the trachea, *a*; the head of the testes and the descending passages, *b b*; the passages which proceed from these, and are seated upon the testicle, *c c*; the reflexed passages which contain the white fluid, *d d*; the penis, *e*; the bladder, *f*; the testicles, *g g*. But when the testicles are cut out or otherwise destroyed, the upper passages are retracted; in young animals castration is performed by bruising the testicles, in older animals by excision. And it has happened that a bull has begotten young if admitted to the female immediately after castration. This is the nature of the testicles of animals.

10. The uterus of the females that possess this organ is not of the same nature, nor alike in all, but they differ from each other both in viviparous and oviparous animals. The uterus is double in all those animals in which it is situated near the external organ of generation, one part lying on the right side, the other on the left, but the origin is one, and there is but one os uteri, which is like a very fleshy tube, and in most animals, especially those of a large size, it is cartilaginous. One part of this organ is called the uterus and delphys (whence the word adelphi, brothers), and the vagina and os uteri are called metra.

11. In all viviparous animals, whether bipeds or quadrupeds, the uterus is placed below the diaphragm, as in the human female, the bitch, sow, mare, and cow, and it is the same in all horned animals. At the extremity of the uterus most animals have a convoluted part called the horns; these are not distinct in all oviparous animals; but in some birds they are placed near the diaphragm, and in some fishes below, as in the viviparous bipeds and quadrupeds. But they are thin, membranaceous, and long, so that in very small fish each part of the roe appears as one ovum, as if the fish

which are said to have a crumbling roe had but two ova, for it is not one ovum but many, and therefore it may be resolved into many.

12. In the uterus of birds the vagina is below, fleshy and tough, but the part near the diaphragm membranaceous and very thin, so that the eggs appear to be outside the uterus. In large birds the membrane is more conspicuous, and if inflated through the vagina, it swells and enlarges at places; in small birds these parts are not conspicuous. The uterus of oviparous quadrupeds, as the tortoise, lizard, frog, and such like, is of the same nature, for the vagina below is one and fleshy, but the division and the ova are higher up and near the diaphragm.

13. In those apodal creatures which are outwardly viviparous and inwardly oviparous, as the sharks and selachea —[The selachea are apodal, furnished with gills, and viviparous]—the uterus is divided, and as in birds, it commences below and extends towards the diaphragm. The ova are situated between the division, and above near the diaphragm; and the animal is produced from the ovum after this has descended into the open space.

14. The difference between the uteri of these fish and others may be studied more accurately in drawings of dissections. Serpents also differ much both among themselves and from other animals, for all serpents except the viper are oviparous; this one is viviparous, though at first internally oviparous, wherefore, in many respects, its uterus resembles that of the cartilaginous fishes. The uterus of the serpent is long, like the body, and descends downwards, beginning from one duct and continuing on either side of the spine as far as the diaphragm, as if each were a passage, in which the ova are placed in order; these ova are not extruded singly, but connected together like a chain.

15. In all animals that are either internally or externally viviparous, the uterus is situated above the abdomen; in all oviparous creatures it is placed below, near the loins. Those that are externally viviparous, but internally oviparous, partake of both characters, for the lower part in which the ova are situated is near the loins, the other part whence the ova are extruded above the intestines. And there is also this difference in the uteri of animals; those which have horns

and not teeth in both jaws have cotyledons in the pregnant uterus, and some of those also with teeth in both jaws, as the hare, the mouse, and the bat. But other viviparous animals with teeth in both jaws, and with feet, have a smooth uterus. The embryo is not united to the cotyledon, but to the womb. This is the manner of the internal and external heterogeneous parts of animals.

Chapter II.

1. Of the homogeneous parts of animals, the blood is common to sanguineous animals; and so is the part in which it is contained, which is called a vein; analogous to these, in exsanguineous animals are the serum and the fibre. That which especially constitutes the body is flesh or its analogue: the bone and its analogue; the spine and the cartilage. Next to this we place the skin, membranes, sinews, hair, nails, and their analogue; after these, adeps, fat, and excrementitious matters; then are fæces, phlegm, and bile, both the yellow and the black.

2. But inasmuch as the blood and the veins seem to occupy the chief place, we will first of all speak of these, both for other reasons, and because former writers do not appear to have described them rightly. The difficulty of understanding them is the reason of their errors, for in dead animals, the nature of the principal veins is obscure, for they collapse as soon as the blood has escaped, and it pours out of them as from a vessel. No part of the body, except the veins, contains any blood, except the heart, which has a little; but it is all in the veins. In living creatures their nature cannot be distinguished, for they are internal, and out of sight; so that those who consider them only in dead and dissected animals, cannot see their principal origins. But some, by the examination of emaciated persons, have distinguished the origin of the veins, from the appearance of those which are external.

3. For Syennesis,[1] a Cyprian physician, speaks thus: "The larger veins are thus constituted. From the navel around the loins, through the back to the lungs, under the breasts; that from the right to the left, and that from the

---

[1] Syennesis, a physician of Cyprus. Very little is known of him; he must have lived in or before the fourth century B.C.

left to the right. That from the left, through the liver to the kidney and the testicle; that from the right to the spleen, the kidney, and the testicle, and from thence to the penis."

4. Diogenes[1] of Apollonia writes thus: "The veins are thus placed in man. There are two very large ones, which extend through the stomach by the spine of the back, one to the right and the other to the left, each to the leg nearest itself, and upwards to the head by the collar-bone, and through the neck. From these great veins others extend through the whole of the body, from the right to the right side, and from the left to the left side. The largest are two from the heart, surrounding the spine of the back; and others, a little higher up, through the breasts under the arm-pits, each to the hand nearest itself; and the one is called the splenetic, the other the hepatic vein.

5. "The extremity of these veins is divided, one branch goes to the thumb, and another to the wrist, and from these many small branches are extended upon each hand, and the fingers; and others, smaller still, branch off from these first veins, from the right side to the liver, from the left to the spleen and kidneys. The veins, which go to the legs, are divided near the junction, and extend through the whole thigh; but the largest of these extends to the back of the thigh, and appears thick; another, less thick, passes through the inside of the thigh, and afterwards veins extend by the knee to the leg and foot. As on the hands, they are distributed upon the tarsus of the foot, and from thence to the toes.

6. "A number of small veins are distributed on the stomach and the lungs. Those that extend to the head, through the jugular region, appear large in the neck. From the extremity of each of these many veins are distributed upon the head, some on the right side to the left, others on the left side to the right, they all end near the ear. And there is a second vein upon the neck on each side, somewhat less than the other, to which the principal veins of the neck are united. These pass inwards, through the neck, and from each of them veins pass beneath the shoulder-blade and to the hands; and near the splenetic and

---

[1] Diogenes of Apollonia was an eminent natural philosopher of Crete, in the fifth century B.C. He wrote a work, περὶ φύσεως, in which he treated of natural philosophy in the widest sense of the words: a few fragments are still extant, of which this quoted by Aristotle is the longest.

hepatic veins there appear others a little less, which they divide when any disease attacks the skin; but the hepatic and splenetic veins are divided for any disease in the neighbourhood of the stomach.

7. Other veins pass from these, beneath the breasts; and there are other small ones, which proceed from each of these through the spinal marrow to the testicles, and others beneath the skin, through the flesh, reach the kidneys; in men they terminate upon the testicles, in women on the uterus. The first veins from the stomach are wider, and afterwards become smaller, until they pass over from the right to the left, and from the left to the right; these are called the spermatic veins. The thickest blood is beneath the flesh, but that which is in excess in these places becomes thin, and warm, and frothy." These are the opinions of Syennesis and Diogenes.

8. Polybus[1] writes thus : "There are four pair of veins, one from the back of the head through the neck, on the outside, near the spine on either side, as far as the thighs and the legs, afterwards through the legs to the ancles, on the outside, and to the feet. Wherefore, in complaints of the back and thigh, they divide the veins upon the poplitic region, or ancles, on the outside. Another pair of veins pass from the head, by the ears, through the neck, these are called the jugular veins; and others within, near the spine, lead by the loins to the testicles and the thighs, and through the poplitic region on the inside, and through the leg to the inner part of the ancle, and the feet; wherefore, in complaints of the loins and testicles, they bleed in the poplitic region and ancles.

9. "The third pair of veins, from the temple through the neck, and beneath the scapula, reach the lungs; those from the right to the left, under the breast, to the spleen and kidneys; and those from the left to the right side, from the lungs, under the breast, and liver, and kidney; and both end beneath the testicles. The fourth pair from the forepart of the head and the eyes, under the neck and collar-bones; from thence they extend through the humerus to the elbow, and through the cubitus to the wrist and the fingers, and through the lower part of the arm to the arm-pits, and the

---

[1] Polybus, a pupil of Hippocrates, a native of the island of Cos; he lived in the fourth century B.C. Many treatises on medical subjects are attributed to him.

upper part of the lungs. The one reaches as far as the spleen, the other to the liver; afterwards they both pass over the abdomen to the pudendum."

Chapter III.

1. The opinions of other persons are nearly these; and there are other physiologists, but they have not treated so accurately of the veins. But all agree in placing their origin in the head and brain, in which they are incorrect. But, as I have remarked before, it is difficult to discern the course of the veins; indeed, it is impossible to understand them unless a person will examine animals which, after emaciation, have been killed by strangulation. The following is the nature of the veins: There are two veins in the interior of the chest, near the spine; the larger of these is placed forward, the smaller is behind; the larger is inclined to the right side, the smaller to the left; and this by some persons is called the aorta, from the sinewy portion which is seen in dead animals.

2. These veins have their origin in the heart, for they pass completely through the other intestines, and always preserve the character of veins. The heart is, as it were, a part of them, and especially of the more forward and larger one, for these veins are above and below, and the heart is in the middle of them. The heart of all animals contains cavities, but in the heart of very small animals the largest cavity is scarcely perceptible, in moderately sized animals the second cavity is scarcely visible, but in large animals they are all three distinct enough. And when the apex of the heart is turned forwards, as I have observed, the principal cavity is on the right side, and above it the least is on the left side, and the middle-sized one is between them; the two smaller are far less than the greater.

3. All these are perforated towards the lungs, but imperceptibly so from the minuteness of the passage, except in one place. The great vein is suspended from the upper portion of the principal cavity; and on the right side; afterwards through the cavity a vein extends again, as if the vein were a part of the cavity in which the blood stagnates. The aorta has its origin from the middle cavity, but in a different manner from the vein, for it communicates with the heart by a much narrower passage, and the vein is continued

through the heart. But the aorta passes from the heart, and the great vein is membranous and like skin, but the aorta is narrow and very sinewy, and as it is continued towards the head and the lower parts of the body, it becomes narrow and quite sinewy.

4. A portion of the great vein is first of all extended upwards from the heart to the lung, and to the junction of the aorta, this vein being undivided and large; from this place it divides into two branches, the one towards the lung, and the other to the spine and the lowest vertebra of the neck. The branch which goes to the lungs is first divided into two branches, and afterwards it is continued upon every tube and passage of the lungs, greater to the greater, and less to the less, so as to leave no part in which there is not a passage and a small vein. These last are invisible from their minute size, so that the whole lung seems to be full of blood.

5. And the passages from the vein are above the tubes which extend from the trachea. And the vein which is continued upon the vertebra of the neck, and upon the spinal column, returns again to the spine, as Homer writes in his poems: "He cut off the whole vein which passes up the back and returns again to the neck;"[1] and from this vein branches extend to each rib and to each vertebra; but that which is upon the vertebra near the kidneys branches in two directions. These branches, then, of the great vein are subdivided in this manner.

6. And above these, from that part which is continued from the heart, the whole is again divided into two directions, for some reach to the sides and the clavicles, and afterwards through the armpits to the arms, in the human subject, but in quadrupeds to the fore-legs, to the wings in birds, and to the pectoral fins in fishes. The commencements of these veins, when they are first of all divided, are called jugular veins; and having branched off in the neck from the great vein, they are continued to the trachea of the lungs. And if these veins are held on the outside, men fall down dead with insensibility, with closed eyes, but without choking.

7. Extending in this manner, and receiving the trachea between them, they reach the place where the jaws unite with the head; and again from this point they are divided into four veins, one of which bends backwards and descends

[1] Iliad. xiii. 546.

through the neck and shoulder, and meets the first division of the vein by the joint of the arm; the other portion terminates in the hand and fingers; and another branch extends from each part near the ear to the brain, where it is divided into many small branches upon the membrane which surrounds the brain.

8. The brain never contains blood in any animal, nor does any vein, small or great, terminate upon it; but some of the other branches that extend from this vein surround the brain in a circle, and others, end upon the organs of sense and the teeth in very small veins. In the same manner, also, the branches of the smaller vein, which is called the aorta, are divided: they are continued beside those of the great vein, but the tubes are smaller and the branches less than those of the great vein.

Chapter IV.

1. The veins, then, are thus distributed in the parts above the heart, but the part of the great vein which is below the heart passes through the middle of the diaphragm, and is united to the aorta and spinal column by membranous flaccid passages. From this a short and wide vein passes through the liver, from which many similar branches extend to the liver, and disappear upon it. There are two branches of the vein, one of which terminates upon the diaphragm, and what is called the præcordia, the other returns through the armpit to the right arm, and unites with the other veins near the interior part of the elbow. For this reason physicians treat certain diseases of the liver by venesection in this vein.

2. From the left of this there is a short and wide vein, which reaches to the spleen, and the branches of this vein are lost upon this organ, and another portion branching off in the same way from the left the great vein passes up to the left arm, except that the last-mentioned pass through the liver, but this one through the spleen. Other branches also separate from the great vein, the one to the omentum, the other to the pancreas; and from this many veins extend through the mesenterium, and all end there in one great vein, which passes through the whole intestine and the stomach, as far as the œsophagus; and many veins branch off from them around these parts.

3. Both the aorta and the great vein continue as far as the kidney each as a single duct; from this point they are more closely united to the spinal column, and are each divided into two parts, like the letter lambda (Λ), and the great vein is placed farther back than the aorta. The aorta is more closely united to the spinal column, near the heart, and the junction is formed by small sinewy veins.

4. The aorta leaves the heart as a large hollow passage, but as it advances it becomes narrower and more sinewy. From the aorta, veins extend also to the mesenterium, like those from the great vein, but far inferior in size, for they are narrow and muscular. They terminate in small hollow muscular veins. No branch of the aorta extends to the liver and the spleen, but the branches of either vein extend to each hip, and both touch upon the bone. Branches reach the kidney both from the great vein and the aorta; they do not, however, enter the cavity, but are taken up in the substance of the kidney.

5. Two other strong and continuous passages reach from the aorta to the bladder, and others from the cavity of the kidney; but these do not communicate with the great vein. From the centre of each kidney a hollow sinewy vein passes through the other veins to the spinal column; first of all they disappear upon each hip, and then appear again in branches towards the hip; their extremities are distributed upon the bladder and penis in the male, and upon the uterus in the female; no branch of the great vein passes to the uterus, but many and thick ones reach it from the aorta.

6. From the aorta and great vein branches are distributed to the nates; at first they are large and hollow, afterwards they pass through the legs, ending upon the feet and toes; and others again pass through the nates and thighs, alternately from right to left, and they join with other veins below the knees.

7. The nature and origin of the veins are evident from this description. In all sanguineous animals, the nature and origin of the principal veins are the same, but the multitude of smaller veins is not alike in all, for neither are the parts of the same nature, nor do all possess the same parts. Nor are the veins equally apparent in all animals; but they are more manifest in

those which have most blood, and in the largest creatures; but in those animals which are small, and have not much blood, either by nature or from excess in fat, they are not so easily investigated, for some of the passages are confused, like rivulets that are lost in beds of mud; and there are some animals which have but few, and these fibres instead of veins. The great vein is very conspicuous in all, even the smallest animals.

Chapter V.

1. The following is the nature of the sinews of animals. The origin of these, also, is in the breast, for there is a sinew in the principal cavity of the heart itself; and that which is called the aorta is a sinewy vein, for its terminations are always sinewy, for they are not hollow, and are extensible, like the sinews which end upon the bending of the bones: for it is not the nature of sinews to be continuous from one origin, like the veins, for the veins have the whole form of the body as in outline sketches, so that in emaciated subjects the whole mass appears full of veins, for the same place is occupied by veins in lean persons that in fat ones is flesh.

2. The sinews are drawn round the joints and flexures of the bones; but, if their nature were continuous, the continuation would be evident in emaciated persons. The principal parts of the sinews are around the part of the body appropriated to leaping, and this is called the poples. Another double sinew is the tendon of the neck, and the epitonus and the sinew of the shoulder, which aid in the support of the body. The sinews around the joints have not received any name, for all the bones where they are contiguous are bound together by the sinews.

3. And there are many sinews round all the bones; there are none in the head; but the sutures of the skull are adapted to each other. It is the nature of sinew to tear readily lengthwise, but across the fibre it is indivisible, and it is very extensible. The sinews are surrounded by a mucous, white, and gelatinous fluid, by which they are nourished, and from which they seem to derive their origin. The vein does not alter its form by combustion, but the sinew is entirely destroyed. Neither does it unite after division.

4. Numbness does not take place in those parts of the body which contain no sinews. The sinews are most abundant on the hands and feet, and on the ribs and shoulderblades, and round the neck and arms. All sanguineous animals have sinews; but in those which have not jointed limbs, and are without feet and hands, the sinews are small and inconspicuous, so that in fishes they are most distinct near the fins.

Chapter VI.

1. The fibres are between the sinews and the veins; but some of them are moistened with serum, and they extend from the sinews to the veins, and from the veins to the sinews. There is also another kind of fibre, which is produced in the blood of most, but not of all animals. When this is extracted from the blood, it does not coagulate, but if it is not taken out of the blood it coagulates. These fibres are present in the blood of most animals, but not in that of the stag, prox,[1] and bubalis,[2] and some others; so that their blood does not coagulate like that of other animals: the blood of stags is very like that of hares; for in both of these coagulation takes place; not firm, as in other animals, but trembling, like that of milk, if no coagulating substance is put into it. The blood of the bubalis coagulates more thickly, only a little less so than that of sheep. This is the nature of veins, sinews, and fibres.

Chapter VII.

1. The bones of animals depend upon one bone, and are connected with each other, like the veins; and there is no such thing as a separate bone. In all animals with bones the spinal column is their origin. The spinal column is made up of vertebræ, and extends from the head to the hips. All the vertebræ are perforated; the upper part of the head is a bone joined to the last vertebra, and is called the skull, the saw-like part is the suture.

2. This is not alike in all animals, for the cranium of some consists of a single bone, as in the dog; in others it is compound, as in the human subject. The female has

---

[1] Cervis Capreolus, or C. dama.   [2] Antilope gnou.

one suture, in a circle; the male has three, meeting at the top of the head, like a triangle; and human skulls have been seen without sutures. The head is not composed of four bones, but of six; two of these are placed above the ears, and are small compared with the rest.

3. From the head the jaw-bones descend. All other animals move the lower jaw, the river-crocodile alone moves the upper jaw. In the jaws are the order of the teeth, which are bony, in some parts they are perforated, in others they are not. These are the only bones too hard to be engraved.

4. From the spinal-column, which is the point of union, originate the clavicles and ribs; the breast also is placed upon the ribs, and some of these are united, others are not, for no animal has a bone round the stomach. There are also the scapulæ upon the shoulders, and these are continued upon the arms, and those again to the hands; and in all animals with fore legs the nature of the bone is the same.

5. At the extremity of the lower part of the spinal column, and next to the hip, is the socket, and the bones of the lower extremity, with those of the thigh and leg, which are called the colenes. The ancles form a portion of these, and the part called the spur in all creatures with ancles. Continuous with these are the bones of the feet. Viviparous animals with blood and feet do not differ much in their bones, but rather by analogy, in hardness, softness, and size. Again, some of the bones contain marrow, whilst others, in the same animal, have none.

6. Some animals do not appear to have any marrow at all in their bones, as the lion, whose bones are very small and slight: or there may be marrow in a few of its bones, as in those of the thigh and fore leg; otherwise, in the lion, the bones are particularly solid, for they are sufficiently hard to emit fire like stones on concussion. The dolphin also has bones, but it has no spine, like fish. Some sanguineous animals differ partially from these, as the class of birds. In others, as fish, the bones are only analogous, for viviparous fish have a cartilaginous spine, like those which are called selachea; the oviparous fish have a spine, which is like the backbone of quadrupeds.

7. It is a peculiarity in fish that some species have small

spines in the flesh separated from each other. Serpents are like fish, for their back-bone is spinous; among oviparous quadrupeds the greater animals have a bony vertebral column; the lesser have a spinous one.

8. For all sanguineous animals have either a bony, or a spinous column. The remainder of the bones exist in some animals, but not in others, for if they have the limbs, they have the bones belonging to them; for those that have not hind and fore legs have not hams, nor are they present in those animals which possess limbs unlike those of quadrupeds, for in these they vary in size and proportion. This is the nature of the bones of animals.

Chapter VIII.

1. Cartilage is of the same nature as bone, but it differs in the greater and less, and neither bone nor cartilage are reproduced if they are cut off. In sanguineous and viviparous animals living on the land the cartilage is imperforate, and does not contain marrow, like the bones; but the flat selachea, which have a cartilaginous spine, have a cartilage analogous to bone containing a liquid marrow. Viviparous animals, with feet, have cartilage about their ears, nostrils, and extremities of their bones.

Chapter IX.

1. There is another class of parts, which, though not the same as these, are not very different, as nails, hoofs, claws, and horns, and besides these, the beak of birds which alone possess this part. For these are both flexible and fissile. But bone is neither flexible nor fissile, but brittle; and the colour of horns, nails, claws, and hoofs follow the colour of the skin and the hair; for in black animals the horns are black, and so are the claws and hoofs in those with claws; in white animals they are white. There are also intermediate colours, the nails also are of the same nature.

2. But the teeth are like bones; wherefore, in black men, Ethiopians, and such like, the teeth and the bones are white, but the nails are black, like the rest of the skin.

The horns of most animals are hollow at their base, and surround a bony process on their heads; but at the extremity the horn is solid and single. The stag's horns are solid throughout, and divided; and these animals alone cast their horns; this is done annually, if they are not cut off. Concerning those that are cut off, we shall speak hereafter.

3. The horns are more nearly allied to skin than to bone, so that in Phrygia and elsewhere there are oxen which have the power of moving their horns, as they do their ears; and of those which have nails (and all that have toes have nails, and those that have feet have toes, except the elephant, which has its toes undivided, and scarcely distinguished, and no nails at all)—and of those with nails, some have straight nails, like men, others crooked, as the lion among beasts, and the eagle amongst birds.

Chapter X.

1. This is the nature of hair and its analogues and skin. All viviparous animals, with feet, have hair; oviparous animals, with feet, have scaly plates; and those fish alone which produce friable ova are covered with scales; for the conger and muræna among long fish have not such ova, and the eel produces no ova. The hair differs in thickness, thinness, and size, according to its situation, both in the parts of the body which it occupies, and the nature of the skin, for upon thick skins the hair is generally harsh and thick, the hair is both thicker and longer in the hollow and moist parts of the body, if they are such as to be covered with hair.

2. And the case is similar in those animals which are covered with plates or scales. If animals covered with soft hair are placed in good pastures their hair will become coarser; and, on the contrary, it becomes finer and less in those that have coarse hair. Warm and cold situations also make a difference, for the hair of natives of warm climates is harsh, but it is soft in those of colder climates. Straight hair is soft, crisped hair is harsh.

3. It is the nature of hair to split; and different kinds of hair are dissimilar in excess and deficiency; some are so changed by harshness as to bear slight resemblance to hair,

and are more like spines, as in the hedgehog, wherein they resemble nails. So again the nails in some animals are not different from bones in point of hardness.

4. Man has the thinnest skin in proportion to his size. There is a mucous, glutinous fluid in the skin of all animals, less in some, more in others, as in the skins of oxen, from which glue is made; and sometimes glue is made from fishes. When the skin alone is cut it is insensible, especially that upon the head, from the absence of flesh between that and the bone. Wherever the skin is without flesh it does not unite again after being cut, as the thin part of the cheek, the prepuce, and the eyelid. In all animals the skin is continuous, and it is only wanting in places where there are natural passages for exudation, and at the mouth and nails. All sanguineous animals have a skin: all, however, have not hair, but those which are described above.

5. The colour of the hair changes in men as they grow old, and the hair becomes grey. This takes place in other animals, but not so remarkably as in the horse. The hair begins to grow white from the extremity. Most white animals are white from their birth, wherefore it is plain that whiteness does not arise from dryness, as some persons suppose, for no animal is born dry. In the exanthematous disease, called whiteness, all the hair becomes hoary; and some patients, who have suffered from illness, after the hair has fallen off on recovery, have regained their dark-coloured hair. Hair which is covered up becomes white more readily than that which is exposed to the air; in man the temples are the first to grow grey, and the fore part of the head before the hind part, and last of all the hair on the pubes.

6. Some of the hair exists on the body at the period of birth, and some appears afterwards. In man alone the hair on the head, eyelashes, and eyebrows exist at birth. The hair on the pubes, in the armpits, and on the chin appear successively after birth, so that the parts on which the hair appears at birth, and those on which it grows afterwards are the same in number. In old age the hair on the head especially is the first to fail, and falls off. This is only in front, for no one ever becomes bald on the back

of the head. The smoothness on the crown of the head is called baldness, that upon the eyebrows depilation; neither of these takes place before the commencement of puberty.

7. Children, women, and eunuchs never become bald. If a person be castrated before puberty, the hair which grows after birth never makes its appearance; if after puberty these alone fall off, except the hair on the pubes. Women have no hair upon the chin, excepting a few of those in whom the catamenia have ceased, and the priestesses in Caria: and this appears ominous of future events. Women also have other hair, but not much. There are some persons, both male and female, who from their birth are without the hair which grows after birth; but those persons are barren who have not hair on the pubes.

8. The rest of the hair grows proportionally, either more or less. That upon the head grows the most, then that on the chin, and thin hair most of all. The eyebrows grow so thick upon some aged persons as to be cut off, for they are placed upon the symphysis of the bone; and this being separated in old persons, a more abundant moisture exudes. Those on the eyelids do not grow, but they fall off, when persons come to puberty, and especially in those of warm sexual desires; they become grey very slowly. If the hair is plucked out during the period of growth, it comes again, but not after it has done growing.

9. Every hair has at its root a glutinous moisture, which will adhere to anything with which it comes in contact, soon after it is drawn out. In spotted animals the spots exist both in the hair and upon the skin, and upon the skin of the tongue. As for the beard, some persons have a thick one, both beneath the chin and upon it; in others, these parts are smooth, and the beard is on the cheeks. Those who have smooth chins are least likely to become bald. The hair grows in some diseases, as in phthisis especially, and in old age, and upon dead bodies, and the hair becomes harder instead of softer. The same is the case with the nails. In persons of strong passions, the hair that is born with them decreases, while that which comes after birth increases.

10. Those who suffer from enlarged veins are less likely

to become bald; and if they have this disease after they are bald, the hair sometimes grows again. The hair, when cut off, does not grow again from the extremity, but increases by growth from the root. The scales of fishes become harder and thicker, and in those that are growing thin and old they become still harder. The hair and wool of old animals becomes thicker, though the quantity decreases; and the hoofs and claws enlarge as they grow old, and the beaks of birds. And the claws grow in the same way as the nails.

11. Feathered animals, like birds, do not change their colour by age, excepting the crane, for this bird is ash-coloured, and becomes black by age. But from the change of season, when it becomes cold, some of those having but one colour, black or grey, become white, as the crow, sparrow, and swallow; but none of those which are white become black. At different seasons of the year many birds change the colour of their plumage, so as to render it difficult for those who are not acquainted with them to recognise them.

12 And many animals change their colour with a change of water; for in one place they are black, and in another white; and the same thing takes place at the season of coition. There are many waters of such a nature that if sheep drink of them before sexual intercourse, they produce black lambs; as at that which is called the cold river in the Thracian Chalcis (in Astyritis). And in Antandria there are two rivers, one of which turns the sheep white, the other black; and the Scamander appears to make the sheep yellow, wherefore some people think that Homer called the Scamander the Xanthus.

13. Other animals have no hair internally, nor upon the bottom of their feet, though it is on the upper part. The hare alone has hair on the inside of its cheeks, and upon its feet, and the mysticetus[1] has no teeth in its mouth, but hairs, like hog's bristles. The hair, if it is cut off, increases below, but not above. Feathers do not grow either above or below, but fall out. The wing of the bee, if it is plucked off, does not grow again, nor that of any other creature which has an undivided wing; nor does the

[1] Balæna Mysticetus.

sting of the bee grow after it is plucked out, but the animal dies.

Chapter XI.

1. There are membranes in all sanguineous animals. Membrane is like a dense thin skin, but it differs in kind, for it is neither divisible nor extensible. There is a membrane round every bone and every intestine, both in the greater and smaller animals; they are inconspicuous in small animals, owing to their thinness and small size. The principal membranes are two, which surround the brain, one round the bones of the head, and this is stronger and thicker than that round the brain itself; and after these, the membrane which surrounds the heart. A thin membrane does not unite after it has been cut asunder, and the bones, when deprived of their membranes, become inflamed.

2. The omentum is a membrane. All sanguineous animals have an omentum; in some it is fat, in others it contains no fat. In viviparous animals, with cutting teeth in both jaws, it has its origin and is suspended from the middle of the stomach, where it appears like a suture of this organ. In those that have not teeth in both jaws, it is suspended in the same way from the principal stomach.

3. The bladder also is membranous, but its character is different, for it is extensible. All animals have not a bladder, but all viviparous animals have this organ, and the tortoise alone of oviparous animals. When the bladder is cut it does not re-unite, except at the very origin of the urethra, or only very rarely, for it has happened sometimes. No moisture passes into the bladder of dead animals; but in living creatures there are dry compounds, from which are formed the stones that are found in persons labouring under this disease; sometimes they are of such a nature in the bladder as to differ in nothing from shells. This, then, is the nature of veins, sinews, and skins, and of muscle and membrane; and of hair, nails, claws, hoofs, horns, teeth and beaks, and of cartilage, bone, and their analogues.

Chapter XII.

1. In all sanguineous animals, flesh, and that which is like flesh, is between the skin and the bone, or what is analogous

to bone: for the same relation which a spine bears to a bone, is also borne by flesh to that which is like flesh, in animals possessing bones and spines. The flesh can be divided in every direction, and so is unlike sinews and veins, which can only be divided in their length. The flesh disappears in emaciated animals, giving place to veins and fibres. Those animals which can obtain abundance of good food have fat instead of flesh.

2. Those that have much flesh have smaller veins and redder blood, and their intestines and stomachs are small; but those which have large veins and dark blood, and large intestines and great stomachs, have also less flesh, for those that have fat flesh have small intestines.

Chapter XIII.

1. Adeps and fat differ from each other, for fat is always brittle, and coagulates upon cooling, but adeps is liquid, and does not coagulate; and broths made from animals with adeps do not thicken, as from the horse and hog, but that made from animals with fat thickens, as from the sheep and goat. These substances also differ in situation, for the adeps is between the skin and the flesh; but the fat only exists upon the extremity of the flesh. In adipose animals the omentum is adipose, in fat animals it is fatty: for the animals with cutting teeth in both jaws are adipose, those that have not cutting teeth in both jaws are fat.

2. Of the viscera in some animals the liver is full of adeps, as in the cartilaginous fishes, for oil is procured from these during the process of decomposition, the cartilaginous fish are particularly free from adeps on their flesh, but the adeps is separated on the stomach. The fat also of fishes is adipose, and does not coagulate; and some animals are furnished with adeps on the flesh, and others apart from the flesh; and those creatures in which the adeps is not separated from the flesh have less of this substance on the stomach and omentum, as the eel: for these creatures have little fat on the omentum. In most animals the adeps collects principally upon the abdomen, especially in those which take little exercise.

3. The brain of adipose animals is unctuous, as in swine; that of fatty animals is dry. Of all the viscera the kidneys

are surrounded by the greatest quantity of adeps in all animals; that on the right side is always the least adipose; and let there be ever so much adeps, there is always a space left between the kidneys. They are also the most fatty of the viscera, and especially in sheep, for this animal sometimes dies from the entire concealment of its kidneys in fat. This excessive fat around the kidneys arises from good pasture, as in the Leontine territory of Sicily; wherefore also in the evening they drive away the sheep which have been feeding during the day, in order that they may take less food.

4. The fat around the pupil of the eye is common to all animals; for all have fat in this part, that possess it, and are not hard-eyed. Fat animals, both male and female, are more inclined to be barren, and all old animals become fat more readily than young ones, especially when they increase in depth, having obtained their proper width and length.

Chapter XIV.

1. The following is the nature of the blood. This is most essential and common to all sanguineous animals, and is not superadded, but exists in all animals that are not in a perishing condition. All the blood is in a vessel called the veins, but in no other part of the body, except the heart. The blood of all animals has no sense of touch, nor has the excrementitious matter in the stomach; neither have the brain, nor the marrow, any sensation of touch; but wherever the flesh is divided, the blood flows in the living subject, unless the flesh is perishing. It is the nature of the blood to have a sweet juice, as long as it is healthy and a red colour, and that is bad which either by nature or disease is black. The best kind of blood is neither very thick nor thin, unless it is vitiated either by nature or disease.

2. In living animals it is always warm and moist, but when taken out of the animal the blood of all creatures coagulates, except that of the stag and deer, and perhaps some others of the same nature. The blood of all other creatures coagulates, unless the fibre is taken out of it. Bullock's blood coagulates faster than that of any other animals. Amongst sanguineous animals, those which are both internally and externally viviparous, have the most blood, and

after them the oviparous sanguineous animals; those which are well disposed, either by nature or by health, have not a great deal of blood, as in those that have just drank; nor a very little, as in those which are very fat. Fat animals have pure blood, though the quantity is small; as they become more fat they lose a portion of their blood, for fat is free from blood. Fat is not corruptible, but blood and the parts that contain blood are very corruptible; of these the parts surrounding the bones are most corruptible.

3. Man has the thinnest and purest blood, that of the ox and ass is the thickest and blackest of all viviparous animals. The blood is thicker and blacker in the lower than in the upper part of animals. The blood palpitates in the veins alike in all animals; this alone of all the fluids exists in every part of the body of living subjects, and as long only as they are alive. The blood first of all exists in the heart of all animals before it is distributed through the body. When deprived of their blood, or if the greater part escapes, they faint away; but when a very great deal is lost, they die. When the blood becomes very much liquefied, illness ensues, for it becomes like serum, and flows through in such a manner, that some have perspired blood; and when taken out of the body, it does not coagulate into a mass, but into separate and divided portions.

4. In sleeping animals, the blood in the extremities is diminished, so that it does not flow freely when they are pricked. Blood is formed from serum, and fat from blood. When the blood becomes diseased, hæmorrhoids are produced, either in the nose or anus, and a disease called ixia.[1] When the blood becomes corrupted in the body, pus is formed, and from pus a scab. The blood in females differs from that of males, for it is more thick and black in females of similar health and age. In the whole of the body the quantity of blood is less in females, but internally they are more full of blood. Of all females, women have the most blood, and the catamenia are more abundant in them than in other females.

5. When this blood is diseased, it is called a flooding. Women have a less share in other diseases; but a few are afflicted with ixia, and with hæmorrhoids and bleeding

[1] Varicose veins.

from the nose; when any of these take place, the catamenia decrease. The blood differs in proportion to the age in quantity and appearance, for when very young, it is more like serum, and very abundant; in the aged it is thick, black, and in less quantity; in those in the prime of life it is between these. In aged persons the blood coagulates quickly in the body, or on the surface; but in young persons this does not take place. Serum is imperfect blood, because it has not ripened, or because it has become more fluid.

Chapter XV.

1. Concerning marrow, for this is one of the fluids which exist in some animals. All the natural fluids of the body are contained in vessels, as the blood in the veins, and the marrow in the bones, and others in membranes, skin, and cavities. The marrow is always full of blood in young animals; but when they grow older, in the adipose it becomes adipose, in fat animals fatty. There is not marrow in all the bones, but only in those that are hollow, and not even in some of these, for some of the bones of the lion have no marrow, others but little; wherefore some persons say the lion has no marrow at all, as was before observed. In the bones of swine there is very little marrow, in some none at all.

Chapter XVI.

1. These fluids are nearly always co-existent with animal life; but milk and the spermatic fluid are produced afterwards. Of these the milk is always secreted in those animals in which it is present. The spermatic fluid is not secreted in all, but in some as in fishes are what are called melts. All animals having milk have it in the mammæ. All animals that are both internally and externally viviparous have mammæ, that is, all that have hair, as man, and the horse, the cetacea, as the dolphin, seal, and whale, for these also have mammæ and milk.

2. Those animals that are only externally viviparous, and oviparous animals, have neither mammæ nor milk, as fish, and birds. All milk has a watery serum, which is called whey, and a substantial part called curds; the thicker kinds of milk have the most curds. The milk of animals without

cutting teeth in both jaws, coagulates, wherefore cheese is made from the milk of domestic animals. The milk of those with cutting teeth in both jaws does not coagulate, but resembles their adeps, and is thin and sweet; the milk of the camel is the thinnest of all, next is that of the horse; in the third place that of the ass. Cow's milk is thicker.

3. Under the influence of cold, milk does not coagulate, but becomes fluid; by heat it is coagulated, and becomes thick. There is no milk in any animal before it has conceived, or but rarely; but, as soon as it has conceived the milk is produced; the first and last milk are useless. Sometimes milk has come in animals not with young, from partaking of particular kinds of food; and even in aged females it has been produced so freely when sucked, as to afford nourishment for an infant. And the shepherds round Æta, when the shegoats will not endure the approach of the males, cut their udders violently against a thorn, so as to cause pain; at first, when milked, they produce bloody, and afterwards putrid milk, but at last their milk is as good as that of those which have young ones.

4. The males, both of man and other animals, rarely produce milk; nevertheless, it is found in some cases: for in Lemnos, a he-goat has given from the two nipples, which are always found on the penis, so much milk, that cakes of cheese were made from it. The same thing happened to another he-goat, which was produced from this one; but such things as these are considered ominous: for, on inquiry being made of the god of Lemnos, he replied that there should be an additional supply of cattle. A small quantity of milk has been forced from some men after puberty; from others a great quantity has been produced by suction.

5. There is a fatness in milk which becomes oily when it is cooked. In Sicily, and other countries, when there is an abundant supply of goat's milk, they mix ewe's milk with it, and it coagulates readily, not only because it contains abundance of curd, but also because it is of a drier nature. Some animals have more milk than enough for the support of their offspring, and this is useful for making cheese, and for putting aside. The best is that of the sheep and goats, and next, that of the cow. Mare's milk and ass's milk are combined with the Phrygian cheese. There is

more cheese in the milk of the cow than of the goat: for the shepherds say, from an amphora of goat's milk they can make nineteen cakes of cheese, each worth an obolus, and thirty from cow's milk. Other creatures have only enough for their young, and no superabundance useful for making cheese, as all those animals which have more than two mammæ, for none of these have a superabundance of milk, nor will their milk make cheese.

6. Milk is coagulated by the juice of figs, and by rennet; the juice is placed upon wool, and the wool is washed in a little milk; this coagulates upon mixture. The rennet is a kind of milk, which is found in the body of sucking animals. This rennet is milk, containing cheese, for the milk becomes cooked by the heat of the body. All ruminating animals contain rennet, and the hare among those with cutting teeth in both jaws. The older coagulum is the better, for such rennet is useful in diarrhœa, and so is that of the hare. The rennet of the fawn is the best.

7. The greater or less quantity of milk drawn from those animals which have milk, differs in the size of the body, and the variety of the food. In Phasis there are very small cows, each of which gives a great deal of milk; and the large cows of Epirus give an amphora and half of milk from each of their two mammæ; and the person who milks them stands up, or only leans a little, because he cannot reach them sitting down. The other animals of Epirus are large except the ass, but the largest are the cows and the dogs. These large cattle require more pasture; but the country has a great deal so excellent, that they can be changed to fit places every hour. The oxen are the largest, and the sheep, called Pyrrhic; they have received this name from king Pyrrhus.

8. Some kinds of food check the milk, as the medic grass, especially in ruminating animals. The cytisus and orobus have a very different effect; but the flower of the cytisus is unwholesome, and causes inflammation; the orobus does not agree with pregnant cattle, for it causes difficulty of parturition. On the whole, those animals which are able to eat the most food, as they are better adapted for parturition, will also give the most milk, if they have enough food. Some of the flatulent kinds of food, when given to

animals, increase the quantity of milk, as beans given freely to the sheep, goat, ox, and chimœra,[1] for they cause the udder to be distended; and it is a sign that there will be plenty of milk when the udder is seen below before parturition.

9. The milk lasts a long time in those that have it, if they remain without sexual intercourse, and have proper food; and in sheep it lasts longer than in any other animals, for the sheep may be milked for eight months. Altogether the ruminating animals produce milk in greater abundance, and more fitted for making cheese. Around Torona the cows fail in their milk a few days before calving, but give milk all the rest of the time. In women dark-coloured milk is better for the children than that which is white; and black women are better nurses than white women. The most nutritious milk is that which contains the most cheese, but that which contains less cheese is better for infants.

Chapter XVII.

1. All sanguineous animals eject the spermatic fluid; the office it performs in generation, and how it is performed, will be treated of in another place. In proportion to his size man ejects more than other animals. This fluid, in animals covered with hair, is glutinous, in others it is not glutinous; in all it is white, so that Herodotus is mistaken when he says that the Ethiopians have black semen.[2] The semen comes out white and thick if it is healthy, but after ejection it becomes thin and black; it does not thicken with cold, but becomes thin and watery, both in colour and density. By heat it coagulates and thickens, and when it has been ejected for any time into the uterus, it comes out more thick, and sometimes dry and twisted together. That which is fruitful sinks in water, but the barren mixes with it. All that Ctesias said about the semen of the elephant is false.

---

[1] Some kind of domestic goat, but not known.
[2] Herodotus, iii. c. 97, 101.

BOOK THE FOURTH.

Chapter I.

1. We have hitherto treated of sanguineous animals, the parts possessed by all as well as those which are peculiar to each class, and of their heterogeneous and homogeneous, their external and internal parts. We are now about to treat of ex-sanguineous animals. There are many classes of these, first of all the mollusca.[1] These are ex-sanguineous animals, which have their fleshy parts external, and their hard parts internal, like sanguineous animals, as the whole tribe of cuttle-fish. Next the malacostraca, these are animals which have their hard parts external, and their interior parts soft and fleshy; their hard parts are rather liable to contusion than brittle, as the class of carabi and cancri.

2. Another class is that of the testacea. These are animals which have their internal parts fleshy, and their external parts hard, brittle, and fragile, but not liable to contusion. Snails and oysters are instances of this class.

3. The fourth class is that of insects, which includes many dissimilar forms. Insects are animals which, as their name signifies, are insected either in their lower or upper part, or in both; they have neither distinct flesh nor bone, but something between both, for their body is equally hard internally and externally. There are apterous insects, as the julus and scolopendra; and winged, as the bee, cockchafer, and wasp; and in some kinds there are both winged and apterous insects; ants, for example, are both winged and apterous, and so is the glowworm.

4. These are the parts of animals of the class mollusca (malacia); first the feet, as they are called, next to these the head, continuous with them; the third part is the abdomen, which contains the viscera. Some persons, speaking incorrectly, call this the head. The fins are placed in a circle round this abdomen. It happens in many of the malacia that the head is placed between the feet and the abdomen.

[1] The Cephalopoda.

5. All the polypi, except one kind, have eight feet, with a double row of suckers. The sepia,[1] teuthis,[2] and teuthos[3] possess as a characteristic part two long proboscidiform members, which have rough suckers at their extremities, with which they seize their food and bring it to their mouth; and when a storm arises they weather it out, fastening these members upon a rock, like an anchor. They swim by means of the fin-like members which are attached to the abdomen. There are suckers upon all their feet.

6. The polypus[4] uses its tentacula both as feet and hands, for it brings its food to its mouth with the two that are above the mouth, and it uses the last of its tentacula, which is the sharpest of all, in the act of coition; this is the only one which is at all white, and it is divided at the extremity, it is placed upon the back; and the smooth part, in front of which are the acetabula, is called the back. In front of the abdomen, and above the tentacula, they have a hollow tube, by which they eject the sea-water which they have received into the abdomen, if any enters through the mouth. This part varies in position, and is sometimes on the right side, sometimes on the left, and by this its ink is ejected.

7. It swims sideways upon the part called the head, stretching out its feet; as it swims it is able to see forwards, for the eyes are upwards, and the mouth is placed behind. As long as it is alive the head is hard, as if it were inflated; it touches and holds with its tentacula bent downwards, a membrane is extended throughout, between the feet, if it falls into the sand, it can no longer hold by it.

8. The polypus and the above-mentioned malacia differ from each other; the abdomen of the polypus is small, and the feet are large; but of the others, the abdomen is large, and the feet small, so that they cannot walk upon them. They have also differences among each other; the teuthis is the smallest, the sepia wider; the teuthos is much larger than the teuthis, for it reaches the length of five cubits. Some sepiæ are two cubits long, and the tentacula of the polypus are as long, and even larger in size.

9. The class of the teuthos is rare, and differs in form from

[1] Sepia officinalis.
[2] Loligo vulgaris (*Owen*).
[3] Loligo media (*Owen*).
[4] Sepia octopodia.

the teuthis, for the extremity of the teuthos is wider; and, again, the fin is placed round the whole abdomen, but it is wanting in the teuthis. It is a marine animal, as well as the teuthis. After the feet, the head of all these animals is placed in the middle of the feet, which are called tentacula; one part of this is the mouth, in which are two teeth; above these are two large eyes; between these is a small cartilage, containing a small brain.

10. In the mouth is a small piece of flesh, for these animals have no tongue, but use this instead of a tongue. After this, on the outside, the abdomen is apparent. The flesh of this can be divided, not in a straight line, but in a circle. All the malacia have a skin around this part. After the mouth, they have a long and narrow œsophagus; and continuous with this is a large round crop, like that of a bird; this contains the stomach, like a net. Its form is spiral, like the helix of a whelk; from this a thin intestine turns back, to the vicinity of the mouth. The intestine is thicker than the stomach.

11. The malacia have no viscus, except that which is called the mytis,[1] and the ink which is upon it. The most abundant and largest of all is that of the sepia; all exclude this ink, when alarmed, but especially the sepia; the mytis lies beneath the mouth; and through this the œsophagus passes; and where the intestine turns back the ink is beneath, and the same membrane surrounds both the ink and the intestine. The same orifice serves for the emission of the ink and the fœces.

12. There are some appearances of hair[2] in their bodies; the sepia, teuthis, and teuthos, have a hard part upon the forward part of the body; the one is called sepium (the bone of the cuttle-fish), the other xiphus (the pen of the loligo). These two are different; for that of the sepia is strong and wide, partaking of the nature of spine and bone, and it contains a spongy, friable substance; but the pen of the teuthis is thin, and cartilaginous. In their form also they correspond with the differences of the animals themselves.

---

[1] Köhler supposes the part called by Aristotle *mytis* to have been the glandular appendages on the vena cava and two visceral veins. (*Owen in Todd's Cyclopedia of Anatomy, Art. Cephalopoda.*)

[2] Probably the branchia.

The polypus has no hard internal part, but a portion of cartilage round the head, which becomes hard as they grow old.

13. The females also differ from the males, for the latter have a passage beneath the œsophagus, extending from the brain to the lowest part of the body. That part to which it reaches is like a teat. In the female there are two such organs, which are placed above. In both sexes, some small red bodies are placed under these. The polypus has one capsule of eggs, which is uneven on the surface; it is large; internally it is all of a white colour, and smooth. The multitude of the ova is so great as to fill a vessel larger than the head of the polypus.

14. The sepia has two capsules, and many eggs are in them, like white hailstones. The position of each of these parts may be seen in anatomical diagrams. In all these creatures the male differs from the female, and especially in the sepia. The fore part of the abdomen of the male is always darker than the back; and more rough than in the female, and variegated with stripes, and the extremity of the body is more acute.

15. There are many kinds of polypus; one, which is the largest of all, is very common. Those near land are larger than those which are caught out at sea. There are smaller kinds, which are variegated; these are not articles of food; and two others, one of which is called eledone,[1] differs in the length of its feet, and is the only one of the malacia with a single row of suckers, for all the rest have two; the other is called bolitæna,[2] and sometimes ozolis.

16. There are two other kinds which dwell in shells, which some persons call nautilus[3] (and nauticus), and others call it the egg of the polypus; its shell is like that of the hollow pecten, and not like that which has its shells close together.[4] This animal generally feeds near the land; when it is thrown upon the shore by the waves, after its shell has fallen off, it cannot escape, and dies upon the land. These animals are small in form, like the bolitæna; and there is another,[5] which

---

[1] Eledone moschata.—*Leach.* (*Owen.*)
[2] Eledone cirrosa.—*Leach.* (*Owen.*)   [3] Argonauta argo. (*Owen.*)
[4] This is probably the meaning of the passage. Two kinds of pectens were distinguished; the one large, hollow, and of a dark colour, the other broad and sweeter, but harsh.
[5] Nautilus Pompilius. (*Owen.*)

inhabits a shell like a snail. This animal never leaves its shell, but remains in it, like the snail, and sometimes stretches out its tentacula. Let thus much be said about the malacia.

Chapter II.

1. Of the malocostraca, there is one genus, of carabi,[1] and another, very like it, of astaci;[2] these differ from the carabi, which have no claws, and in some other respects. There is a third genus, of carides,[3] and a fourth, of carcini.[4] There are more genera of carides, and of carcini; for among the carides are the cyphæ,[5] the crangon,[6] and a small species, for these never grow large.

2. The family of carcini is more various, and not so easily enumerated; the largest genus is that called maia,[7] the next to this the pagurus,[8] and the Heracleot carcini; and, again, those that live in rivers. The other genera are small, and have not received any name. On the Phenician coast there are some that they call horsemen, because they run so fast that it is difficult to catch them, and when opened, they are empty, because they have no pasture. There is another small genus like carcini, but in shape they resemble astaci.

3. All these creatures, as I observed before, have their hard and shelly coats on the outsides of their bodies in the place of skin, the fleshy part is internal. Their under parts resemble plates, upon which the females deposit their ova; the carabi have five feet on each side, including the claws; the carcini, also, have in all ten feet, including the claws, which are last. Of the carides, the cypha have five on each side; those near the head are sharp, and five others on each side of the stomach have flat extremities; they have no plates upon the under part of their body; those on the upper part are like the carabi.

4. The crangon is different, for it has, first of all, four plates on each side, and, afterwards, three slight ones, continuous with those on each side, and the greater part of the remainder of its body is apodal; all the feet are directed outwards to the side, like those of insects; but the claws, in those that have them, all turned inwards. The carabus

---

[1] Palinurus, spiny lobster (Bell's crustacea).   [2] Lobster.
[3] Prawns.   [4] Crabs.   [5] Shrimp.   [6] Perhaps Prawn.
[7] Perhaps Maia squinado.   [8] Cancer pagurus, Great crab.

also has a tail, and five fin-like appendages. The cypha, among the carides, has a tail, with four fin-like appendages. The crangon has fin-like processes on each side of the tail, and the middle of them is spinous on both sides; but this part is wide in the crangon, and sharp in the cypha. The carcini alone are without a tail; the body of the carabi and carides is elongated, that of the carcini is rounded.

5. The male carabus is different from the female, for the female has the first foot divided; in the male it is formed of a single claw, and the fin-like process on the lower part is large in the female, and interchanged with each other in the neck; in the male they are small and not interchanged. In the male, also, the last feet are furnished with large and sharp processes like spurs; in the female these are small and smooth. They all have two large and rough processes, like horns, before their eyes, and two, smaller and smooth, below.

6. The eyes of all these animals are hard, and capable of motion, inwards, outwards, and to the side; the same is the nature of the carcini, in which they are even more moveable. In colour the astacus is all of a dull white, sprinkled with black; it has eight small feet, as far as the large ones; after these the large feet are far greater and wider at the extremity than in the carabus, and they are unequal in size; for on the right side the broad part at the end is long and smooth, on the left side the same part is thick and round; they are both divided from the extremity like a jaw, with teeth above and below, only that in those on the right the teeth are all small and sharp, and they are sharp at the extremity of the left side; in the middle they are like molar teeth; in the lower part are four close together, but in the upper part three, but not close together.

7. In both claws the upper part is moved and pressed down upon the lower; both are placed sideways in position, as if intended by nature for seizure and pressure; above these large feet are two rough ones, a little below the mouth; and still lower, the branchial organs around the mouth, which are rough and numerous, and these are continually in motion; it bends and approximates its two rough feet towards its mouth; the feet near the mouth have smooth appendages.

8. It has two teeth like the carabus, above these the long

horns, much shorter and smoother than in the carabus; four others of the same form as these, but still shorter and smoother; and above these are placed its eyes, which are small and short, and not large like those of the carabus. The part above the eyes is acute and rough, as it were a forehead, and larger than in the carabus: on the whole, the head is sharper and the thorax much wider than in the carabus, and its whole body is more fleshy and soft: of its right feet, four are divided at the extremity, and four not divided.

9. The part called the neck is externally divided into five portions, the sixth and last division is wide and has five plates; in the inside are four rough plates, upon which the females deposit their ova. On the outside of each of these which have been mentioned, there is a short and straight spine, and the whole body, with the part called the thorax, is smooth, and not rough as in the carabus. On the outside of the large feet there are great spines. The female does not in any way differ from the male, for whether the male or female have larger claws, they are never both of them equal.

10. All these animals take in sea-water through their mouths; the carcini also exhale a small portion of that which they have taken in, and the carabi do this through the branchiform appendages, for the carabi have many branchiform appendages. All these animals have two teeth: the carabi have two front teeth, and then a fleshy mouth instead of a tongue, from this an œsophagus continued on to the stomach. And the carabi have a small œsophagus before the stomach, and from this a straight intestine is continued. In the caraboid animals and the carides, this is continued to the tail in a straight passage, by which they eject their excrements, and deposit their ova. In the carcini this is in the middle of the folded part, for the place wherein they deposit their ova is external in these also.

11. All the females also, besides the intestines, have a place for their ova, and the part called mytis[1] or mecon, which is greater or less, and the peculiar differences may be learned by studying the individual cases. The carabi, as I have observed, have two large and hollow teeth, in which there is

[1] Perhaps the liver.

a juice resembling the mytis, and, between the teeth, a piece of flesh resembling a tongue; from the mouth a short œsophagus extends to a membranous stomach; in the part of this nearest the mouth are three teeth, two opposite and one below.

12. And from the side of the stomach there is a simple intestine, which is of equal thickness throughout, reaching to the anus. All these parts belong to the carabi, carides, and carcini; and, besides these, the carabi have a passage suspended from the breast and reaching to the anus; in the female this performs the office of a uterus, in the male it contains the spermatic fluid. This passage is in the cavity of the flesh, so as to appear to be between portions of the flesh, for the intestine is toward the curved part, but the passage towards the cavity in the same way as in quadrupeds. In the male this part differs in nothing from the female, for both are smooth and white, and contain an ochreous fluid, and in both sexes it is appended to the breast.

13. The ova and spirals occupy the same position in the carides. The male is distinguished from the female by having in the flesh upon the breast two distinct white bodies, in colour and position like the tentacula of the sepia; these appendages are spiriform, like the mecon of the whelk; their origin is from the acetabula, which are placed under the last feet. These contain a red sanguineous flesh, which is smooth to the touch, and not like flesh. From the whelk-like appendage there is another spiral fold, about as thick as a thread, below which there are two sand-like bodies appended to the intestine, containing a seminal fluid. These are found in the male, but the female has ova of a red colour; these are joined to the abdomen, and on each side of the intestine to the fleshy part of the body, enclosed in a thin membrane. These are their internal and external parts.

CHAPTER III.

1. It happens that all the internal parts of sanguineous animals have names, for all these have the internal viscera; but the same parts of exsanguineous animals have no names, but both classes have in common the stomach, œsophagus, and intestines. I have before spoken of the carcini, and their

legs and feet, and how many they have, and in what direction, and that, for the most part, they have the right claw larger and stronger than the left; I have also mentioned their eyes, and that most of them are able to see sideways. The mass of their body is undivided, and so is their head, and any other part.

2. In some the eyes are placed immediately below the upper part, and generally far apart; in some they are placed in the middle, and near together, as in the Heracleot carcini and the maia. The mouth is placed below the eyes, and contains two teeth, as in the carabus, but they are long and not round, and over these there are two coverings, between which are the appendages, which the carabus also possesses.

3. They receive water through their mouth, opening the opercula, and emit it again by the upper passage of the mouth, closing the opercula by which it entered; these are immediately beneath the eyes, and when they take in water they close the mouth with both opercula, and thus eject again the sea-water. Next to the teeth is a very short œsophagus, so that the mouth appears joined to the stomach, and from this proceeds a divided stomach, from the middle of which is a single thin intestine; this intestine ends externally beneath the folding of the extremity, as I said before. Between the opercula there is something resembling the appendages to the teeth of the carabi; within the abdomen is an ochreous chyme, and some small elongated white bodies, and other red ones scattered through it. The male differs from the female in length and width, and in the abdominal covering, for this is longer in the female, farther from the body, and more thick-set with appendages, as in the female carabi. The parts of the malacostraca are of this nature.

Chapter IV.

1. The testacea, as cochleæ,[1] and cochli,[2] and all that are called ostrea,[3] and the family of echini, are composed of flesh, and this flesh is like that of the malacostraci, for it is internal; but the shell is external, and they have no hard internal part. But they have many differences amongst themselves, both in regard to their external shells and their

---

[1] Land snails.   [2] Marine.   [3] Bivalves.

internal flesh, for some of them have no flesh at all, as the echinus; in others it is entirely internal and out of sight, except the head, as the land snails and those called coccalia,[1] and in the sea the purpura[2] and the ceryx,[3] the cochlus, and all the turbinated shells.

2. Of the rest some are bivalves, others univalves. I call those bivalves which are enclosed in two shells; the univalves are enclosed in one shell, and the fleshy part is uncovered, as the lepas.[4] Some of the bivalves can open, as the pectens and mya, for all these are joined on one side, and separated on the other, so as to shut and open. There are other bivalves which are joined on both sides, as the solen; others which are entirely enclosed in their shells, and have no external naked flesh, as those which are called tethya.[5]

3. And there is a great difference amongst the shells themselves, for some are smooth, as the solen, mya, and some conchæ, called by some persons galaces;[6] other shells are rough, as the limnostrea,[7] pinnæ, some kinds of conchæ, and the whelk; and of these some are marked with ridges, as the pecten and a kind of concha, others are without ridges, as the pinna and another species of concha. They also differ in thickness and thinness, both in the whole shell and in certain parts of the shell, as about the edges, for in some the edges are thin, as the mya; others are thick-edged, as the limnostrea.

4. Some of them are capable of motion, as the pecten, for some persons say that the pectens can fly, for that they sometimes leap out of the instrument by which they are taken. Others, as the pinna, cannot move from the point of attachment; all the turbinated shells can move and crawl; the lepas (patella) also feeds by going from place to place. It is common to all those with hard shells to have them smooth in the inside.

5. Both in univalves and bivalves the fleshy part is united to the shell, so that it can only be separated by force; it is more easily separated from the turbinated shells; it is a characteristic of all these shells, that the base of the shell has the helix directed from the head. All of them from their birth have an operculum; all the turbinated testacea are

---

[1] Some small land snail with a conical shell.
[2] Purpura.
[3] Whelk.
[4] Patella, limpet.
[5] Ascidians.
[6] Chama, L.
[7] Ostrea edulis.

right-handed, and move, not in the direction of the helix, but the contrary way.

6. The external parts of these creatures are thus distinguished; the nature of their internal structure is similar in all, especially in the turbinated animals, for they differ in size and in the relations of excess, the univalves and bivalves do not exhibit many differences. Most of them have but few distinctive marks from each other, but they differ more from the immovable creatures. This will be more evident from the following considerations. In nature they are all alike, the difference, as before said, is in excess; for in larger species the parts are more conspicuous, and less so in those that are smaller. They differ also in hardness and softness, and such like affections.

7. For all have on the outside of the shell, in the mouth, a hard piece of flesh, some more, some less; from the middle of this are the head and the two horns; these are large in larger species, in the little ones they are very small. The head is protruded in the same manner in all of them, and when the creature is alarmed it is again retracted; some have a mouth and teeth, as the snail, which has small, sharp, and smooth teeth.

8. They have also a proboscis, like that of the fly, and this organ is like a tongue. In the ceryx and the purpura this organ is hard, like that of the myops and œstrus, with which they pierce through the skins of quadrupeds; but this is more powerful in strength, for they can pierce through the shells of the baits. The stomach is joined quite closely to the mouth; the stomach of the cochlus is like the crop of a bird; below this there are two hard white substances like nipples, which also exist in the sepia, but are much harder.

9. From the stomach a long, simple intestine reaches as far as the spiral, which is on the extremity of the body. These are distinct, and in the purpura and the ceryx are in the helix of the shell. The bowel is continuous with the intestine. The intestine and bowels are joined together, and are quite simple, to the anus. The origin of the bowel is around the helix of the mecon,[1] and here it is wider. The mecon is, as it were, a superfluous part in all testacea, afterwards another bend causes it to return to the fleshy part; the end of

[1] The so-called liver (*Strack*). Papaver (*Scaliger*).

the entrail, where the fæces are emitted, is near the head, and is alike in all turbinated shells, whether terrestrial or marine.

10. In the larger cochli a long white passage, contained in a membrane, and in colour resembling the upper mastoid appendages, is joined from the stomach to the œsophagus, and it is divided into segments like the ovum of the carabus, except that it is white, while the other is red. It has neither exit nor passage, but it is contained in a thin membrane, which has a narrow cavity. From the intestine black and rough bodies descend continuously, like those in the tortoise, but they are less black.

11. Both these and white bodies occur in the marine cochli, but they are less in the smaller kinds. The univalves and bivalves are in some respects like these, and in others they are different, for they have a head, horns, and mouth, and something like a tongue, though in smaller species these are inconspicuous from their minute size, and they are not discernible when the animals are dead or at rest. They all contain the mecon, but not in the same position, nor of the same size, nor equally conspicuous. In the lepas it is in the bottom of the shell, in the bivalves near the hinge.

12. They all have hair-like appendages placed in a circle, and so have the pectens, and that which is called the ovarium in those that have it; where it is possessed, it is placed in a circle on the other side of the circumference, like the white portion in the cochli, for this is alike in all. All these parts, as I have said, are conspicuous in the larger kinds, but in smaller not at all, or scarcely so, wherefore they are most conspicuous in the larger pectens, and these have one valve flat like an operculum.

13. The anus is placed in the side in some of these creatures, for this is where the excrement passes out. The mecon, as I have said, is a superfluous part enclosed in a thin membrane in all of them; that which is called the ovarium has no passage in any of them, but it swells out in the flesh. This is not placed upon the intestine, for the ovarium is on the right side and the intestine on the left; the anus is the same as in others; but in the wild patella, as some persons call it, or the sea-ear (haliotis), as it is named by others, the excrement passes out below the shell, for the shell is perforated. The stomach also is distinct behind the mouth, and so is the ova-

rium in this animal. The position of all these parts may be seen in dissections.

14. The creature called carcinium[1] resembles both the malacostraca and the testacea, for this in its nature is similar to the animals that are like carabi, and it is born naked (not covered with a shell). But because it makes its way into a shell, and lives in it, it resembles the testacea, and for these reasons it partakes of the character of both classes. Its shape, to speak plainly, is that of a spider, except that the lower part of the head and thorax is larger.

15. It has two thin red horns, and two large eyes below these, not within nor turned on one side, like those of the crab, but straight forwards. Below these is the mouth, and round it many hair-like appendages; next to these, two divided feet with which it seizes its prey, and two besides these on each side, and a third pair smaller. Below the thorax the whole creature is soft, and when laid open is yellow within.

16. From the mouth is a passage as far as the stomach; but the anus is indistinct; the feet and the thorax are hard, but less so than those of the cancri; it is not united with the shell like the purpura and ceryx, but is easily liberated from it. The individuals which inhabit the shells of the strombus are longer than those in the shells of the nerita.

17. The kind which inhabits the nerita is different, though very like in other respects, for the right divided foot is small, and the left one large, and it walks more upon this than the other; and a similar animal is found in the conchæ, though they are united to their shells very firmly; this animal is called cyllarus.[2] The nerita has a smooth, large, round shell, in form resembling that of the ceryx, but the mecon is not black, but red; it is strongly united in the middle.

18. In fine weather they seek their food at liberty, and if a storm arises, the carcinia hide themselves under a stone, and the neritæ attach themselves to it like the patella, the hæmorrhois, and all that class, for they become attached to the rock, where they close their operculum, for this resembles a lid; for that part which is in both sides in the bivalves is joined to one side in the turbinated shells: the interior is fleshy, and in this the mouth is placed.

[1] Hermit crab.   [2] Cancer Diogenes.

19. The nature of the hæmorrhois, the purpura, and all such animals is the same. But those which have the left foot greater are not found in the shells of the strombus, but in the neritæ. There are some cochli which contain an animal like the small astacus, which is found in rivers; but they differ from them in having the inner part of the shell soft. Their form may be seen by examining dissections.

Chapter V.

1. The echini contain no flesh, but this part is peculiar, for they are all of them void of flesh, and are filled with a black substance. There are many kinds of echinus, one of which is eatable; in this one the ova are large and eatable, both in the greater and the less.

2. And there are two other kinds, the spatangus and that called bryttus; these are inhabitants of the sea, and rare. Those which are called echinometræ[1] are the largest of all. Besides this, there is another small species, which has long and sharp spines; this is procured from the sea, in many fathoms water, and some persons use it for stranguary.

3. Around Torona there are white marine echini, which have shells, and prickles, and ova, and are longer than others; but the prickle is neither large nor strong, but soft, and the black parts from the mouth are more in number, and united to the outward passage, but distinct among themselves, and by these the animal is as it were divided. The eatable kinds are particularly and especially active, and it is a sign of them; for they have always something adhering to their spines.

4. They all contain ova, but in some they are very small, and not eatable: that which is called the head and mouth in the echinus is downwards, and the anus placed upwards. The same thing occurs in the turbinated shells, and the patella; for their food is placed below them, so that the mouth is towards the food, and the anus at or on the upper part of the shell.

5. The echinus has five hollow internal teeth, in the midst of these a portion of flesh like a tongue; next to this is the œsophagus; then the stomach, in five divisions, full of fæculent matter: all its cavities unite in one, near the anus, where the shell is perforated. Beneath the stomach, in an-

---
[1] Echinus esculentus.

other membrane, are the ova, the same number in all, they are five in number, and uneven.

6. The black substance is joined above to the origin of the teeth, this black substance is bitter and not eatable; in many animals there is either this substance or its analogue, for it is found in tortoises, toads, frogs, turbinated shells, and in the malacia; these parts differ in colour, but are entirely or nearly uneatable. The body of the echinus is undivided from beginning to end, but the shell is not so when seen through, for it is like a lantern, with no skin around it. The echinus uses its spines as feet, for it moves along by leaning upon them and moving them.

Chapter VI.

1. The creatures called tethya[1] have a most distinct character, for in these alone is the whole body concealed in a shell. Their shell is intermediate between skin and shell, so that it can be cut like hard leather: this shell-like substance is attached to rocks; in it there are two perforations, quite distant from each other, and not easily seen, by which it excludes and receives water, for it has no visible excrement as other testacea, neither like the echinus, nor the substance called mecon.

2. When laid open, there is first of all a sinewy membrane lining the shell-like substance, within this the fleshy substance of the tethyon. Unlike any other creature, its flesh, however, is alike throughout, and it is united in two places to the membrane and the skin from the side, and at its points of union it is narrower on each side; by these places it reaches to the external perforations which pass through the shell; there it both parts with and receives food and moisture, as if one were the mouth, the other the anus, the one is thick, the other thinner.

3. Internally there is a cavity at each end, and a passage passes through it; there is a fluid in both the cavities. Besides this, it has no sensitive or organic member, nor is there any excrementitious matter, as I said before. The colour of the tethyon is partly ochreous, partly red.

4. The class acalephe[2] is peculiar; it adheres to rocks like some of the testacea, but at times it is washed off. It is not

[1] Ascidian mollusks.   [2] Actiniæ.

covered with a shell, but its whole body is fleshy; it is sensitive, and seizes upon the hand that touches it, and it holds fast, like the polypus does with its tentacula, so as to make the flesh swell up. It has a central mouth, and lives upon the rock, as well as upon shell-fish, and if any small fish falls in its way, it lays hold of it as with a hand, and if any eatable thing falls in its way it devours it.

5. One species is free, and feeds upon anything it meets with, even pectens and echini; it appears to have no visible excrement, and in this respect it resembles plants. There are two kinds of acalephe, some small and more eatable, others large and hard, such as are found near Chalcis. During winter their flesh is compact, wherefore in this season they are caught and eaten; in summer time they perish, for they become soft; if they are touched they soon melt down, and cannot by any means be taken away. When suffering from heat, they prefer getting under stones. I have now treated of malacia, malacostraca, testacea, and of their external and internal parts.

Chapter VII.

1. Insects must now be treated of in the same manner. This is a class which contains many forms, and no common name has been given to unite those that are naturally related, as the bee, anthrene,[1] and wasp, and such like; again, those which have their wings enclosed in a case, as the melolontha,[2] carabus,[3] cantharis, and such like. The common parts of all insects are three—the head, the abdomen, and the third, which is between these, such as in other animals is the breast and back. In many insects this is one, but in the long insects with many legs, the middle parts are equal to the number of segments.

2. All insects survive being divided, except those which are naturally cold, or soon become so from their small size, so that wasps live after they are cut asunder; either the head or the abdomen will live if united to the thorax, but the head will not live alone. Those which are long, and have many feet, will survive division for a considerable time; both the extremities are capable of motion, for they walk both upon the part cut off and upon the tail, as that which is called scolopendra. All of them have eyes, but no other

---

[1] Wild bee.   [2] Chafer.   [3] Beetle.

manifest organs of sense, except that some have a tongue. All the testacea have this organ, which serves the double purpose of tasting and drawing food into the mouth.

3. In some of them this organ is soft; in others very strong, as in the purpura; in the myops and œstrus this member is strong, and in a great many more; for this member is used as a weapon by all those that have no caudal sting.

4. Those with this weapon have no small external teeth, for flies draw blood by touching with this organ, and gnats sting with it. Some insects also have stings, which are either internal, as in bees and wasps, or external, as in the scorpion. This last is the only insect that has a long tail; it has claws, and so has the little scorpion-like creature[1] found in books. The winged insects, in addition to other parts, have wings. Some have two wings, as the flies; others four, as the bees; none of the diptera have a caudal sting. Some of the winged insects have elytra on their wings, as the melolontha; and others no elytra, as the bee. Insects do not direct their flight with their tail, and their wings have neither shaft nor division.

5. Some have a horn before their eyes, as the psychæ[2] and carabi. Of the jumping insects, some have their hind-legs larger; others have the organs of jumping bent backwards, like the legs of quadrupeds. In all, the upper part is different from the lower, like other animals.

6. The flesh of their bodies is neither testaceous nor like the internal parts of testacea, but between the two. Wherefore, also, they have neither spine nor bone, as the sepia; nor are they surrounded with a shell. For the body is its own protection by its hardness, and requires no other support; and they have a very thin skin. This is the nature of their external parts.

7. Internally, immediately after the mouth, there is an intestine which in most insects passes straight and simply to the anus, in a few it is convoluted; these have no bones nor fat, neither has any other exsanguineous animal. Some have a stomach, and from this the remainder of the intestine is either simple or convoluted, as in the acris.[3] The

---

[1] Phalangium Cancroides. *Linn. Schneider.*
[2] Butterfly.   [3] Locust.

tettix (grasshopper) alone of this, or any other class of living creatures, has no mouth; but, like those with a caudal sting, it has the appearance of a tongue, long, continuous, and undivided, and with this it feeds upon the dew alone. There is no excrement in the stomach. There are many kinds of these creatures, they differ in being greater or less; those called achetae are divided beneath the diaphragm, and have a conspicuous membrane, which the tettigonia has not.

8. There are many other creatures in the sea which it is not possible to arrange in any class from their scarcity. For some experienced fishermen say they have seen in the sea creatures like small beams, black and round, and of the same thickness throughout; others like shields, of a red colour, with many fins; others[1] like the human penis in appearance and size, but instead of testicles they had two fins, and that such have been taken on the extremity of grappling irons. This is the nature of the internal and external parts of all animals of every kind, both those which are peculiar to certain species, and those which are common to all.

Chapter VIII.

1. We must now treat of the Senses: for they are not alike in all, but some have all the senses, and some fewer. They are mostly five in number; seeing, hearing, smelling, taste, touch, and besides these there are none peculiar to any creatures. Man, then, and all viviparous animals with feet, besides all sanguineous and viviparous animals, have all these, unless they are undeveloped in any particular kind, as in the mole.

2. For this creature has no sight, it has no apparent eyes, but when the thick skin which surrounds the head is taken away, in the place where the eyes ought to be on the outside, are the undeveloped internal eyes, which have all the parts of true eyes, for they have both the iris of the eye, and within the iris the part called the pupil, and the white; but all these are less than in true eyes. On the outside there is no appearance of these parts, from the thickness of the skin, as if the nature of the eye had been destroyed at birth; for there are two sinewy and strong passages proceeding from the brain, where it unites with

[1] Perhaps Pennatula.

the spinal cord, reaching from the socket of the eye, and ending upon the upper sharp teeth.

3. All other animals are endued with the perception of colours, sounds, smells, and taste. All animals have the fifth sense, which is called touch. In some animals the organs of sense are very distinct, and especially the eyes, for they have a definite place, and so has the hearing. For some animals have ears, and others open perforations: so also of the sense of smelling, some animals have nostrils, others passages, as the whole class of birds. In the same way the tongue is the organ of taste.

4. In aquatic animals and those called fish, the tongue is still the organ of taste, though it is indistinct, for it is bony, and not capable of free motion. In some fish the roof of the mouth is fleshy, as in some cyprini among river fish, so that, without careful examination, it appears like a tongue. That they have the sense of taste is quite clear, for many of them delight in peculiar food, and they will more readily seize upon a bait formed of the amia and other fat fishes, as if they delighted in the taste and eating of such baits.

5. They have no evident organ of hearing and smelling, for the passages which exist about the region of the nostrils in some fish do not appear to pass to the brain, but some of them are blind, and others lead to the gills; it is evident, however, that they both hear and smell, for they escape from loud noises, such as the oars of the triremes, so as to be easily captured in their hiding-places.

6. For if the external noise is not loud, yet to all aquatic animals that are capable of hearing, it appears harsh and very loud; and this takes place in hunting dolphins, for when they have enclosed them with their canoes, they make a noise from them in the sea, and the dolphins, crowded together, are obliged to leap upon the land, and, being stunned with the noise, are easily captured, although even dolphins have no external organs of hearing.

7. And again in fishing, the fishermen are careful to avoid making a noise with their oars or net when they perceive many fish collected in one place; they make a signal, and let down their nets in such a place that no sound of the oar or the motion of the waters should reach the place

where the fish are collected, and the sailors are commanded to row in the greatest silence until they have enclosed them.

8. Sometimes, when they wish to drive them together, they proceed as in dolphin catching, for they make a noise with stones that they may be alarmed and collected together, and thus they are enclosed in a net. Before their inclosure, as it was said, they prevent a noise, but as soon as they have enclosed them, they direct the sailors to shout and make a noise, for they fall down with fear when they hear the noise and tumult.

9. And when the fishers observe large shoals at a distance, collected on the surface in calm, fine weather, and wish to know their size, and of what kind they are, if they can approach them in silence, they avoid their notice, and catch them while they are on the surface. If any noise is made before they reach them, they may be seen in flight. In the rivers, also, there are little fish under the stones, which some persons call cotti:[1] from their dwelling beneath rocks, they catch them by striking the rocks with stones, and the fishes fall down frightened when they hear the noise, being stunned by it. It is evident, from these considerations, that fishes have the sense of hearing.

10. There are persons who say that fish have more acute ears than other animals, and that, from dwelling near the sea, they have often remarked it. Those fish which have the most acute ears are the cestreus[2] (chremps),[3] labrax,[4] salpe,[5] chromis,[6] and all such fishes; in others the sense of hearing less acute, because they live in the deeper parts of the ocean.

11. Their nature of smelling is the same, for the greater number of fishes will not take a bait that is not quite fresh; others are less particular. All fish will not take the same bait, but only particular baits, which they distinguish by the smell; for some are taken with stinking baits, as the salpe with dung. Many fish also live in the holes of rocks, and when the fishermen want to entice them out, they anoint the mouths of these holes with salted scents, to which they readily come.

---

[1] Perhaps Cottus gobio L., miller's thumb. Salmo Fario (*Strack*).
[2] Mullet.   [3] Unknown.   [4] Perca Labrax.
[5] Scomber.   [6] Unknown.

12. The eel also is enticed out in this way, for they place a pitcher of salt food, covering the mouth of the pitcher with another vessel pierced with holes, and the eels are quickly drawn forth by the smell of the bait. Baits made of the roasted flesh of the cuttle fish, on account of its strong smell, attract fish very readily. They say they put the roasted flesh of the polypus upon their hooks for nothing but its strong smell.

13. And the fish called rhyades,[1] when the washings of fish or of fœtid drains are emptied into the water, make their escape as if smelling the fœtid odour. They say that fish soon smell the blood of their own kind; this is plain from their hastening from any place where the blood of fishes may be. On the whole, if any one use a putrid bait, the fish will not come near it; but if a fresh strong-smelling bait is used, they will come to it from a great distance.

14. This is especially observable in what was said of dolphins, for these creatures have not external organs of hearing, but are captured by being stunned with a noise, as was before observed; neither have they any external organs of smell, yet their scent is acute. Therefore, it is evident that all creatures have these senses. Other kinds of animals are divided into four classes; and these contain the multitude of remaining animals, namely, the malacia, malacostraca, testacea, and insects.

15. Of these the malacia, the malacostraca, and insects have all the senses, for they can see, smell, and taste. Insects, whether they have wings or are apterus, can smell from a great distance, as the bee and the cnips[2] scent honey, for they perceive it from a long distance, as if they discovered it by the scent. Many of them perish by the fumes of sulphur: ants leave their hills when origanum and sulphur are sprinkled upon them. Almost all of them escape from the fumes of burnt stags' horns, but most of all do they avoid the smell of burnt styrax.

16. The sepia, also, the polypus, and the carabus are caught with baits; the polypus holds the bait so fast that it holds on even when cut: if a person hold conyza to them, they let go as soon as they smell it. So, also, of the sense of taste, for they follow different kinds of food, and do not

---

[1] A fish living in shoals.   [2] Perhaps some species of ant.

all prefer the same food, as the bee approaches nothing that is putrid, only sweet things; the gnat not what is sweet, but what is acid.

17. As I before observed, the sense of touch belongs to all animals. The testacea have the senses of smelling and tasting. This is plain from the baits used, as those for the purpuræ; for this creature is caught with putrid substances, and will be attracted from a great distance to such baits, as if by the sense of smell. It is evident from what follows that they possess the sense of taste; for whatever they select by smell, they all love to taste.

18. And all animals with mouths receive pain or pleasure from the contact of food. But, concerning the senses of sight and hearing, it is not possible to say anything certain, or very distinct; the solens, if a person touch them, appear to retract themselves, and try to escape when they see an instrument approaching them, for a small portion of them is beyond the shell, the remainder as it were in a retreat; the pectens, also, if a finger is brought near them, open and shut themselves as if they could see.

19. Those who seek for neritæ do not approach them with the wind, when they seek them for baits, nor do they speak, but come silently, as if the creatures could both smell and hear; they say that if they speak, they get away. Of all testacea, the echinus appears to have the best sense of smell amongst those that can move, and the tethya and balanus in those that are fixed. This is the nature of the organs of sense in all animals.

Chapter IX.

1. The following is the nature of the voice of animals, for there is a distinction between voice and sound. Speech, again, is different from these. Voice is due to no other part except the pharynx, the creatures, therefore, without lungs are also without voice. Speech is the direction of the voice by the tongue; the vowels are uttered by the voice and the larynx, the mutes by the tongue and the lips; speech is made up of these: wherefore, no animals can speak that have not a tongue, nor if their tongue is confined.

2. The power of uttering a sound is connected with other parts also; insects have neither voice nor speech, but make

a sound with the air within them, not with that which is external, for some of them breathe not, some of them buzz, as the bee with its wings, and others are said to sing, as the grasshopper. All these make a noise with the membrane which is beneath the division of their body in those which have a division, as some families of grasshoppers by the friction of the air. These insects, bees, and all other insects raise and depress their wings in flight, for the sound is the friction of the air within them. Locusts produce a sound by rubbing themselves with their legs, which are adapted for leaping. None of the malacia utter any sound or natural voice, nor do the malacostraca.

3. Fish also are mute, for they have neither lungs, trachea, nor pharynx. Some of them utter a sound and a squeak; these are said to have a voice, as the lyra[1] and chromi,[2] for these utter, as it were, a grunt; so does the capros, a fish of the Achelous, the chalceus[3] and coccyx,[4] for the one utters a sound like hissing, the other a noise like that of the cuckoo, from whence also its name is derived. Some of these utter their apparent voice by the friction of their gills, for these places are spinous, in others the sound is internal, near the stomach. For each of them has an organ of breathing, which causes a sound when it is pressed and moved about.

4. Some of the selachea also appear to whistle, but they cannot be correctly said to utter a voice, only to make a sound. The pectens also make a whizzing noise when they are borne upon the surface of the water, or flying, as it is called; and so do the sea-swallows,[5] for they also fly through the air in the same way, not touching the sea, for they have wide and long fins. As the sound made by birds flying through the air is not a voice, so neither can either of these be properly so called. The dolphin also utters a whistle and lows when it comes out of the water into the air, in a different way from the animals above-mentioned—for this is a true voice, for it has lungs and a trachea, but its tongue is not free, nor has it any lips so as to make an articulate sound.

5. The oviparous quadrupeds, with a tongue and lungs,

[1] Trigla Lyra. [2] Cottus cataphractus. [3] Zeus faber.
[4] Trigla hirundo. [5] Flying fish.

utter a sound, though it is a weak one. Some of them hiss like serpents; others have a small weak voice, others, as the tortoise, utter a small hiss. The tongue of the frog is peculiar, for the fore-part of it is fixed, like that of a fish; but the part near the pharynx is free and folded up. With this it utters its peculiar sound. The male frogs make a croaking in the water when they invite the females to coition.

6. All animals utter a voice to invite the society and proximity of their kind, as the hog, the goat, and the sheep. The frog croaks by making its lower jaw of equal length, and stretching the upper one above the water. Their eyes appear like lights, their cheeks being swelled out with the vehemence of their croaking; for their copulation is generally performed in the night. The class of birds utter a voice: those which have a moderately wide tongue have the best voice; those also in which the tongue is thin. In some kinds both male and female have the same voice; in others it is different: the smaller kinds have more variety in their voice, and make more use of it, than the larger tribes.

7. All birds become more noisy at the season of coition. Some utter a cry when they are fighting, as the quail; others when they are going to fight, as the partridge; or when they have obtained a victory, as the cock. In some kinds both male and female sing, as the nightingale; but the female nightingale does not sing while she is sitting or feeding her young: in some the males alone, as the quail and the cock; the female has no voice. Viviparous quadrupeds utter different voices; none can speak—for this is the characteristic of man, for all that have a language have a voice, but not all that have a voice have also a language.

8. All that are born dumb, and all children, utter sounds, but have no language; for, as children are not complete in their other parts, so their tongue is not perfect at first; it becomes more free afterwards, so that they stammer and lisp. Both voices and language differ in different places.

9. The voice is most conspicuous in its acuteness or depth, but the form does not differ in the same species of animals; the mode of articulation differs, and this might be called speech, for it differs in different animals, and in the same genera in different places, as among partridges, for in some

places they cackle, in others whistle. Small birds do not utter the same voice as their parents, if they are brought up away from them, and have only heard other singing birds. For the nightingale has been observed instructing her young, so that the voice and speech are not naturally alike, but are capable of formation. And men also have all the same voice, however much they may differ in language. The elephant utters a voice by breathing through its mouth, making no use of its nose, as when a man breathes forth a sigh; but with its nose it makes a noise like the hoarse sound of a trumpet.

Chapter X.

1. Concerning the sleep and wakefulness of animals. It is quite manifest that all viviparous animals with feet both sleep and are awake; for all that have eyelids sleep with the eyes closed; and not only men appear to dream, but horses, oxen, sheep, goats, dogs, and all viviparous quadrupeds. Dogs show this by barking in their sleep. It is not clear whether oviparous animals dream, but it is quite plain that they sleep.

2. And so it is in aquatic animals, as fish, the malacia, the malacostraca, the carabi, and such like creatures. The sleep of all these animals is short: it is plain that they do sleep, though we can form no conclusion from their eyes, for they have no eyelids, but from their not being alarmed; for if fish are not tormented with lice, and what are called psylli, they may be captured without alarming them, so that they can be even taken with the hand. And if fish remain at rest during the night a great multitude of these creatures fall upon and devour them.

3. They are found in such numbers at the bottom of the sea as to devour any bait made of fish that remains any length of time upon the ground; fishermen frequently draw them out hanging like globes around the bait. The following considerations will serve still more to confirm our suppositions that fishes sleep; for it is often possible to fall upon the fish so stealthily as to take by the hand, or even strike them during this time; they are quite quiet, and exhibit no signs of motion except with their tails, which they move gently. It is evident, also, that they sleep, from their starting if

anything moves while they are asleep, for they start as if they were waked out of sleep.

4. They are also taken by torchlight while asleep; those who are seeking for thynni surround them while asleep; it is evident that they can be captured from their stillness, and the half-open white (of their eyes). They sleep more by night than by day, so that they do not move when they are struck; they generally sleep holding by the ground, or the sand, or a stone, at the bottom, concealing themselves beneath a rock, or a portion of the shore. The flat fishes sleep in the sand; they are recognized by their form in the sand, and are taken by striking them with a spear with three points. The labrax, chrysophrys, cestreus, and such-like fish are often taken with the same kind of weapon while asleep in the day time, but if not taken then, none of them can be captured with such a spear.

5. The selache sleep so soundly that they may be taken with the hand; the dolphin, whale, and all that have a blowhole, sleep with this organ above the surface of the sea, so that they can breathe, while gently moving their fins, and some persons have even heard the dolphin snore. The malacia sleep in the same manner as fish, and so do the malacostraca. It is evident from the following considerations that insects sleep; for they evidently remain at rest without motion; this is particularly plain in bees, for they remain quiet, and cease to hum during the night. This is also evident from those insects with which we are most familiar, for they not only remain quiet during the night because they cannot see distinctly, for all creatures with hard eyes have indistinct vision, but they seem no less quiet when the light of a lamp is set before them.

6. Man sleeps the most of all animals. Infants and young children do not dream at all, but dreaming begins in most at about four or five years old. There have been men and women who have never dreamt at all; sometimes such persons, when they have advanced in age, begin to dream; this has preceded a change in their body, either for death or infirmity. This, then, is the manner of sensation, sleep and wakefulness.

Chapter XI.

1. In some animals the sexes are distinct, in others they are not so, these are said to beget and be with young by a likeness to other creatures. There is neither male nor female in fixed animals, nor in testacea. In the malacia and malacostraca there are male and female individuals, and in all animals with feet, whether they have two or four, which produce either an animal, an egg, or a worm from coition.

2. In other kinds the sexes are either single or not single; as in all quadrupeds there is the male and female, in the testacea it is not so, for as some vegetables are fertile and others barren, so it is in these. Among insects and fishes there are some that have no differences of this kind, as the eel is neither male nor female, nor is anything produced from them.

3. But those persons who say that some eels appear to have creatures like worms, of the size of a hair, attached to them, speak without observation, not having seen how they really are; for none of these creatures are viviparous without being first oviparous, none of them have ever been observed to contain ova; those that are viviparous have the embryo attached to the uterus, and not to the abdomen, for there it would be digested like food. The distinction made between the so-called male and female eel that the male has a larger and longer head, and that the head of the female is smaller, and more rounded, is a generic, and not a sexual distinction.

4. There are some fish called epitragiæ, and among fresh-water fish the cyprinus and balagrus are of the same nature, which never have ova or semen; those which are firm and fat, and have a small intestine, appear to be the best. There are creatures, such as the testacea, and plants, which beget, and produce young, but have no organ of coition; and so also in fishes the psetus,[1] erythrhinus,[2] and the channa. All these appear to have ova.

5. In sanguineous animals with feet that are not oviparous, the males are generally larger and longer lived than

---

[1] Pleuronectes Lingua and Rhombus.
[2] Perca marina, or Sparus erithrinus.

the females, except the hemionus, but the females of this animal are both larger and longer lived: in oviparous and viviparous animals, as in fish and insects, the females are larger than the males, as the serpent, phalangium,[1] ascalabotes,[2] and frog; in fish likewise, as in most of the small gregarious selache, and all that inhabit rocks.

6. It is evident that female fishes have longer lives than males, because females are caught of a greater age than the males; the upper and more forward parts of all animals are larger and stronger, and more firmly built in the male; the hinder and lower parts in the female. This is the case in the human subject, and all viviparous animals with feet: the female is less sinewy, the joints are weaker, and the hairs finer, in those with hair; in those without hair, its analogues are of the same nature; the female has softer flesh and weaker knees than the male, the legs are slighter; the feet of females are more graceful, in all that have these members.

7. All females, also, have a smaller and more acute voice than the males, but in oxen the females utter a deeper sound than the males; the parts denoting strength, as the teeth, tusks, horns, and spurs, and such other parts, are possessed by the males, but not by the females, as the roe-deer has none, and the hens of some birds with spurs have none; the sow has no tusks: in some animals they exist in both sexes, only stronger and longer in the males, as the horns of bulls are stronger than those of cows.

[1] Aranea tarantula.   [2] Lacerta Gekko.

BOOK THE FIFTH.

Chapter I.

1. We have hitherto treated of the external and internal parts of all animals, of their senses, voice, and sleep, with the distinctions between the males and females; it remains to treat of their generation, speaking first of those which come first in order, for they are many, and have numerous varieties, partly dissimilar, and partly like each other. And we will pursue the same order in considering them as we did before in their division into classes; we commenced our consideration by treating of the parts in man, but now he must be treated of last, because he is much more intricate.

2. We shall begin with the testacea, and after these treat of the malacostraca, and the others in the order of their succession. These are the malacia and insects, next to these fishes, both viviparous and oviparous; next to them birds, and afterwards we must treat of animals with feet, whether viviparous or oviparous; some viviparous creatures have four feet, man alone has two feet. The nature of animals and vegetables is similar, for some are produced from the seed of other plants, and others are of spontaneous growth, being derived from some origin of a similar nature. Some of them acquire their nourishment from the soil, others from different plants, as it was observed when treating of plants.

3. So also some animals are produced from animals of a similar form, the origin of others is spontaneous, and not from similar forms; from these and from plants are divided those which spring from putrid matter, this is the case with many insects; others originate in the animals themselves, and from the excrementitious matter in their parts; those which originate from similar animals, and have both the sexes are produced from coition, but of the class of fishes there are some neither male nor female, these belong to the same class among fishes, but to different genera, and some are quite peculiar. In some there are females but no males, by these the species is continued as in the hypenemia among birds.

4. All these among birds are barren, (for nature is able to complete them as far as the formation of an egg,) unless persons suppose that there is another method of communicating the male influence, concerning which we shall speak more plainly hereafter. In some fish, after the spontaneous production of the ovum, it happens that living creatures are produced, some by themselves, others by the aid of the male. The manner in which this is done will be made plain in a future place, for nearly the same things take place in the class of birds.

5. Whatever are produced spontaneously in living creatures, in the earth, or in plants, or in any part of them, have a distinction in the sexes, and by the union of the sexes something is produced, not the same in any respect, but an imperfect animal, as nits are produced from lice, and from flies and butterflies are produced egg-like worms, from which neither similar creatures are produced, nor any other creature, but such things only. First of all, then, we will treat of coition, and of the animals that copulate, and then of others, and successively of that which is peculiar to each, and that which is common to them all.

Chapter II.

1. Those animals in which there is a distinction of the sexes use sexual intercourse, but the mode of this intercourse is not the same in all, for all the males of sanguineous animals with feet have an appropriate organ, but they do not all approach the female in the same manner, but those which are retromingent, as the lion, the hare, and the lynx, unite backwards, and the female hare often mounts upon the male; in almost all the rest the mode is the same, for most animals perform the act of intercourse in the same way, the male mounting upon the female; and birds perform it in this way only.

2. There are, however, some variations even among birds; for the male sometimes unites with the female as she sits upon the ground, as the bustard and domestic fowl: in others, the female does not sit upon the ground, as the crane; for in these birds the male unites with the female standing up; and the act is performed very quickly, as in sparrows. Bears lie down during the act of intercourse,

which is performed in the same manner as in those that stand on their feet, the abdomen of the male being placed upon the back of the female: in the hedgehogs, the abdomens of both sexes are in contact.

3. Among the large animals, the roe-deer seldom admits the stag, nor the cow the bull, on account of the hardness of the penis; but the female receives the male by submission. This has been observed to take place in tame deer. The male and female wolf copulate like dogs. Cats do not approach each other backwards, but the male stands erect, and the female places herself beneath him. The females are very lascivious, and invite the male, and make a noise during the intercourse.

4. Camels copulate as the female is lying down, and the male embraces and unites with her, not backwards, but like other animals. They remain in intercourse a whole day. They retire into a desert place, and suffer no one to approach them but their feeder. The penis of the camel is so strong, that bowstrings are made of it. Elephants also retire into desert places for intercourse, especially by the sides of rivers which they usually frequent. The female bends down and divides her legs, and the male mounts upon her. The seal copulates like retromingent animals, and is a long while about it, like dogs. The males have a large penis.

Chapter III.

1. Oviparous quarupeds with feet copulate in the same manner: in some, the male mounts upon the female, like viviparous animals, as in the marine and land turtle, for they have an intromittent organ by which they adhere together, as the trygon and frog, and all such animals.

2. But the apodous long animals, as serpents and murænæ, are folded together, with the abdomens opposite, and serpents roll themselves together so closely, that they seem to be but one serpent with two heads. The manner of the whole race of saurians is the same, for they unite together in the same kind of fold.

Chapter IV.

1. All fish, except the flat selache, perform the act of intercourse by approaching each other with their abdomens

opposite: but the flat fish, with tails, as the batos, trygon, and such like, not only approach each other, but the male applies his abdomen to the back of the female, in all those in which the thickness of the tail offers no impediment. But the rhinæ, and those which have a large tail, perform the act by the friction of their abdomens against each other, and some persons say that they have seen the male selache united to the back of the female, like dogs.

2. In all those that resemble the selache, the female is larger than the male; and in nearly all fish the female is larger than the male. The selache are those which have been mentioned; and the bos, lamia, æetus, narce, batrachus, and all the galeode. All the selache have been frequently observed to conduct themselves in this way. In all viviparous creatures the act occupies a longer time than in the oviparous. The dolphin and the cetacea also perform the act in the same manner, for the male attaches himself to the female for neither a very long, nor a very short time.

3. The males of some of the fish which resemble the selache differ from the females, in having two appendages near the anus, which the females have not, as in the galeodea; for these appendages exist in them all. Neither fish nor any other apodal animal has testicles, but the males, both of serpents and of fish, have two passages, which become full of a seminal fluid at the season of coition; and all of them project a milky fluid. These passages unite in one, as they do in birds; for birds have two internal testes, and so have all oviparous animals with feet. In the act of coition this single passage passes to, and is extended upon the pudendum and receptacle of the female.

4. In viviparous animals with feet, the external passage for the semen and the fluid excrement is the same: internally these passages are distinct, as I said before in describing the distinctive parts of animals. In animals which have no bladder, the anus is externally united with the passage of the semen, internally the passages are close together; and this is the same in both sexes: for none of of them have a bladder, except the tortoise. The female of this animal, though furnished with a bladder, has but one passage; but the tortoise is oviparous.

5. The sexual intercourse of the oviparous fish is less evident,

wherefore many persons suppose that the female is impregnated by swallowing the semen of the male; and they have been frequently observed to do this. This is seen at the season of coition, when the females follow the males, and are observed to strike them on the abdomen with their mouths, this causes the males to eject their semen more rapidly. The males do the same with the ova of the females, for they swallow them as they are extruded, and the fish are born from those ova which remain.

6. In Phœnicia they use each sex for capturing the other; for having taken the male cestreus, they entice the females with it, and so enclose them in a net. They use the females in the same way for catching the males. The frequent observation of these circumstances appears to corroborate this manner of intercourse among them. Quadrupeds also do the same thing, for at the season of coition both sexes emit a fluid, and smell to each other's pudenda.

7. And if the wind blows from the cock partridge to the hen, these last are impregnated; and often, if they hear the voice of the cock when they are inclined for sexual intercourse, or if he flies over them, they become pregnant from the breath of the cock. During the act of intercourse, both sexes open their mouths, and protrude their tongues. The true intercourse of oviparous fish is rarely observed, from the rapidity with which the act is accomplished; for their intercourse has been observed to take place in the manner described.

Chapter V.

1. All the malacia, as the polypus, sepia, and teuthis, approach each other in the same manner, for they are united mouth to mouth; the tentacula of one sex being adapted to those of the other; for when the polypus has fixed the part called the head upon the ground, it extends its tentacula, which the other adapts to the expansion of its tentacula, and they make their acetabula answer together. And some persons say that the male has an organ like a penis in that one of its tentacula which contains the two largest acetabula. This organ is sinewy, as far as the middle of the tentaculum, and they say that it is all inserted into the nostril of the female.

2. The sepia and loligo swim about coiled together in this way, and with their mouths and tentacula united, they swim in contrary directions to each other. They adapt the organ called the nostril of the male to the similar organ in the female; and the one swims forwards, and the other backwards. The ova of the female are produced in the part called the physeter, by means of which some persons say that they copulate.

Chapter VI.

1. The malacostraca, as the carabi, astaci, carides, and such like perform the act of intercourse like the retromingent animals, the one lying upon its back, and the other placing its tail upon it. They copulate on the approach of spring, near the land; for their sexual intercourse has often been observed, and sometimes when the figs begin to ripen.

2. The astaci and the carides perform the act in the same manner; but the carcini approximate the fore part of their bodies to each other, and adapt also the folds of their tails to each other. First of all, the smaller carcinus mounts from behind, and when he has mounted, the greater one turns on its side. In no other respect does the female differ from the male, but that the tail, which is folded on the body, is larger and more distant, and more thick set with appendages: upon this the ova are deposited, and the excrement ejected. Neither sex is furnished with an intromittent organ.

Chapter VII.

1. Insects approach each other from behind, and the smaller one subsequently mounts upon the larger. The male is always the smaller. The female, which is below, inserts a member into the male, which is above, and not the male into the female, as in other animals. In some kinds this organ appears large in proportion to the size of the body, especially in those that are small, in others it is less. The organ may be plainly discerned if two flies are separated while in the act of coition. They are separated from each other with difficulty, for the act of intercourse in such animals occupies a long time. This may be plainly discerned by common observation, as in the fly and cantharis.

2. All adopt the same method, the fly, cantharis, spon-

dyla[1], phalangium, or any other insect that copulates. All the phalangia that spin a web unite in the following manner. The female draws a filament from the middle of the web, and then the male draws it back again, and this they do a great many times till they meet, and are united backwards, for this kind of copulation suits them on account of the size of their abdomen. The copulation of animals is accomplished in this manner.

Chapter VIII.

1. ALL animals have their proper season and age for coition; the nature of most creatures requires them to have intercourse with each other when winter is turning into summer. This is the spring season, in which all animals with wings, feet, or fins, are incited to coition. Some copulate and produce their young in the autumn and winter, as some aquatic and winged creatures. Mankind are ready at all seasons, and so are many other animals which associate with man; this arises from greater warmth, and better food, and is usual among those which are pregnant only for a short time, as the hog, dog, and those birds which have frequent broods. Many animals appear to adapt the season of coition to that which they consider the best for the nurture of their young.

2. Among mankind the male is more disposed for sexual intercourse in the winter, and the female in the summer. Birds, as I have observed, generally pair in the spring and summer, except the halcyon. This bird hatches its young about the time of the winter solstice. Whereupon fine days occurring at this season are called halcyon days, seven before the solstice and seven after it. As Simonides also writes in his poems, "as when in the winter months Jupiter prepares fourteen days, which mortals call the windless season, the sacred nurse of the variegated halcyon."

3. These fine days take place wherever it happens that the solstice turns to the south, when the pleiades set in the north. The bird is said to occupy seven days in building its nest, and the other seven in bringing out and nursing its young. The halcyon days are not always met with in this

[1] A beetle living at the roots of trees, Carabus.

country at the time of the solstice, but they always occur in the Sicilian Sea. The halcyon produces five eggs.

4. The æthuia and the larus hatch their young among the rocks on the sea-side, and produce two or three, the larus during the summer, and the æthuia at the beginning of the spring, immediately after the equinox; it sets upon its eggs like other birds; neither of these kinds conceal themselves. The halcyon is the rarest of all, for it is only seen at the season of the setting of the pleiades, and at the solstice, and it first appears at seaports, flying as much as round a ship, and immediately vanishing away. Stesichorus also speaks of it in the same manner.

5. The nightingale produces her young at the beginning of summer. She produces five or six eggs. She conceals herself from the autumn to the beginning of spring. Insects copulate and produce their young during the winter whenever the days are fine, and the wind in the south, at least such of them as do not conceal themselves, as the fly and ant. Wild animals produce their young once a year, unless, like the hare, they breed while they are nursing their young.

Chapter IX.

1. Fish also generally breed once a year, as the chyti. All those which are caught in a net are called chyti; the thynnus, palamis, cestreus, chalais, colias, chromis, psetta, and such like, the labrax is an exception, for this alone of them all breeds twice a year, and the second fry of these are much weaker. The trichias[1] and rock fish breed twice, the trigla is the only one that breeds three times a year. This is shewn by the fry, which appear three times at certain places.

2. The scorpius breeds twice, and so does the sargus, in spring and autumn, the salpa once only in the spring. The thynnis breeds once, but as some of the fry are produced at first, and others afterwards, it appears to breed twice. The first fry makes its appearance in the month of December, after the solstice, the second in the spring. The male thynnis is different from the female, for the female has a fin under the abdomen, called aphareus, which the male has not.

3. Among the selachea, the rhine alone breeds twice in the year; at the beginning of the autumn, and at the period

[1] Clupea Sprottus.

of the setting of the Pleiades. The young are, however, better in the autumn. At each breeding season it produces seven or eight. Some of the galei, as the asterias, seem to produce their ova twice every month. This arises from all the ova not being perfected at once.

4. Some fish produce ova at all seasons of the year, as the muræna: for this fish produces many ova, and the fry rapidly increase in size, as do those also of the hippurus,[1] for these, from being very small, rapidly increase to a great size; but the muræna produces young at all seasons, the hippurus in the spring. The smyrus differs from the muræna, for the muræna is throughout variegated and weak. The smyrus is of one colour, and strong; its colour is that of the pine tree, and it has teeth both internally and externally. They say that these are the male and the female, as in others. These creatures go upon the land, and are often taken.

5. The growth of all fish is rapid, and not the least so in the coracinus among small fish. It breeds near the land, in thick places full of seaweed. The orphos also grows rapidly. The pelamis and thynnus breed in Pontus, and nowhere else. The cestreus, chrysophrys, and labrax, breed near the mouths of rivers. The orcynes and scorpides, and many other kinds, in the sea.

6. Most fish breed in March, April, and May; a few in the autumn, as the salpe, sargus, and all the others of this kind a little before the autumnal equinox; and the narce and rhine also. Some breed in the winter and summer, as I before observed, as the labrax, cestreus, and belona in the winter; the thynnis in June, about the summer solstice: it produces, as it were, a bag, containing many minute ova. The rhyas also breeds in the summer. The chelones among the cestræi begin to breed in the month of December, and so does the sargus, the myxon, as it is called, and the cephalus. They go with young thirty days. Some of the cestrei do not originate in coition, but are produced from mud and sand.

7. The greater number of them contain ova in the spring, but some, as I observed, in the summer, autumn, and winter. But this does not take place in all alike,

[1] Coryphœna hippurus.

nor singly, nor in every kind, as it does in most fish which produce their young in the spring: nor do they produce as many ova at other seasons. But it must not escape our notice, that as different countries make a great difference in plants and animals, not only in the habit of their body, but also in the frequency of their sexual intercourse and production of young; so different localities make a great difference in fish, not only in their size, and habit of their body, but in their young, and the frequency or rarity of their sexual intercourse, and of their offspring in this place or that.

CHAPTER X.

1. The malacia breed in the spring, and first of all the marine sepia, though this one breeds at all seasons. It produces its ova in fifteen days. When the ova are extruded, the male follows, and ejects his ink upon them, when they become hard. They go about in pairs. The male is more variegated than the female, and blacker on the back. The sexes of the polypus unite in the winter, the young are produced in the spring, when these creatures conceal themselves for two months. It produces an ovum like long hair, similar to the fruit of the white poplar. The fecundity of this animal is very great, for a great number of young are produced from its ova. The male differs from the female in having a longer head, and the part of the tentaculum which the fishermen call the penis is white. It incubates upon the ova it produces, so that it becomes out of condition, and is not sought after at this season.

2. The purpuræ produce their ova in the spring, the ceryx at the end of the winter; and, on the whole, the testacea appear to contain ova in the spring and autumn, except the eatable echini. These principally produce their young at the same seasons, but they always contain some ova, and especially at the full and new moon, and in fine weather, but those which live in the Euripus of the Pyrrhæi are better in winter. They are a small kind but full of ova. All the cochleæ appear to contain ova at the same season.

CHAPTER XI.

1. The undomesticated birds, as it was observed, generally pair and breed once a-year. The swallows and cottyphus

breed twice, but the first brood of the cottyphus is killed by the cold, for it is the earliest breeder of all birds. It is able, however, to bring up the other brood. But the domestic birds, and those capable of domestication, breed frequently, as pigeons during the whole summer, and domestic fowls. For these birds have sexual intercourse, and produce eggs all the year round, except at the winter solstice.

2. There are many kinds of pigeons, for the peleias and peristera are different. The peleias is the smaller, but the peristera is more readily tamed. The peleias is black and small, and has red and rough feet, for which reason it is never domesticated. The phatta is the largest of the tribe, the next is the œnas, which is a little larger than the peristera, the trygon is the least of all. If the peristera is supplied with a warm place and appropriate food, it will breed and bring up its young at any season of the year. If it is not properly supplied, it will only breed in the summer. Its young ones are best during the spring and autumn, those produced in the hot weather in summer are the worst.

Chapter XII.

1. Animals also differ in the age at which sexual intercourse commences. For in the first place the period at which the spermatic fluid begins to be secreted, and the age of puberty is not the same, but different; for the young of all animals are barren, or if they do possess the power of reproduction, their offspring are weak and small. This is very conspicuous in mankind, and in viviparous quadrupeds and birds, for in the one the offspring, in the other the eggs, are small. The age of puberty is nearly the same in the individuals of each kind, unless any alteration takes place, either as ominous, or from an injury done to their nature.

2. In men this period of life is shown by the change of voice, and not only by the size but by the form of the pudendum and of the breasts in women, but especially by the growth of hair on the pubes. The secretion of the spermatic fluid commences about the age of fourteen, the power of reproduction at twenty-one. Other animals have no hair on the pubes, for some have no hair at all, and

others have none upon their under side, or less than on their upper side, but the change of the voice is conspicuous in some of them. And in others different parts of the body signify the period of the formation of the semen, and of the power of reproduction.

3. In almost all animals the voice of the female and of the young is more acute than that of the male and the older animals, for even the stags have a deeper voice than their females. The males utter their cry at the season of copulation, the females when they are alarmed. The voice of the female is short, that of the male longer. And the barking of old dogs is also deeper than of young ones, and the voice of the horse also varies. The females utter a little small cry as soon as they are born, and the males do the same, but their voice is deeper than that of the female, and as they grow older, it still increases. When they are two years old, and reach puberty, the male utters a great deep voice, that of the female is greater and clearer than it was at first; this continues till they are twenty years old at the outside, and after that the voice, both of the male and female, becomes weaker.

4. For the most part, then, as we observed, the voice of the male differs from that of the female in depth, in those animals which utter a lengthened sound. There are, however, some exceptions, as oxen; for in these animals the voice of the female is deeper than that of the male, and the voice of the calf than that of the full-grown animal; wherefore also in the castrated animals, the voice changes the other way, for it becomes more like that of the female.

5. The following are the ages at which animals acquire the power of reproduction. The sheep and goat arrive at puberty within a year after they are born, and especially the goat, and the males as well as the females, but the offspring of these males and of the others is different. For the males are better the second year than when they become older. In hogs, the male and female unite at eight months old, and the female produces her young when she is a year old, for this agrees with the period of gestation. The male reaches puberty at eight months old, but his offspring are useless till he is a year old. But these periods, as we have said, are not always the same, for swine will

sometimes copulate when they are four months old, so as to have young and nurse them at six months old, and boars sometimes reach puberty at ten months old, and continue good to three years old.

6. The bitch reaches puberty within a year after birth, and so does the dog, and sometimes this takes place at the end of eight months, but more frequently in the male than in the female. The period of gestation is sixty days, or one or two, or perhaps three days more, but never less than sixty days, or if they produce young in a less time, it never comes to perfection. The bitch is ready for sexual intercourse again in six months, but never sooner. The horse reaches puberty in both sexes at two years old, and is capable of reproduction, but its offspring at that age are small and weakly. For the most part, sexual intercourse begins at three years of age, and the colts continue to improve from that period till they are twenty years old. The male is useful till he is thirty years old, so that he can beget during almost the whole of his life, for the horse generally lives five-and-thirty years, and the mare more than forty, and a horse has been known to live seventy-five years.

7. The ass reaches puberty in both sexes at the age of thirty months; they rarely, however, produce young till they are three years, or three years and six months old. But it has been known to be pregnant and bring up its young within the year. The cow also has been known to produce young and rear it within the year after birth, which grew to the ordinary size, and no more.[1]

8. These are the periods of puberty in these animals. The seventieth year in man, and the fiftieth in woman, is the latest period of reproduction, and this happens rarely, for only a few have had children at this time of life. Sixty-five is generally the boundary in one sex, and forty-five in the other. The sheep produces young till it is eight years old, and, if well treated, until it is eleven, though the act of copulation is continued in both sexes during the whole period of life.

9. Fat goats are rarely productive, wherefore they compare barren vines with barren goats, but they are pro-

[1] This probably means "to such a size as might be expected from the early age of the parent."

ductive when they are lean. The rams copulate with the old sheep first, but they do not follow after the younger; and the younger, as I before observed, produce a smaller offspring than the older.

10. A wild boar will beget till he is three years old, but the progeny of older animals is inferior; for he has not the same power or strength. He generally goes to the female when full of food, and without having been to another female, or, if not, the act of coition is of shorter duration, and the progeny smaller. The sow produces the smallest number of pigs at her first litter, but at the second they are more flourishing. She also produces young when old, but the act of coition is longer. At fifteen years old, she no longer produces young, but becomes fierce.

11. If well-fed, she will be more ready for sexual intercourse, whether young or old; and, if rapidly fattened when pregnant, she has less milk after parturition. As regards the age of the parent, the young of those in the prime of their age are the best, and those that are born at the beginning of winter. The worst are those born in the summer, for they are small, and thin, and weak. If the male is well fed, he is ready for sexual intercourse at all seasons, by day as well as by night; but if not well fed, he is most ready in the morning, and as he grows old, he becomes less disposed for it, as was said before. And it frequently happens that those which are impotent, through age or weakness, and cannot copulate readily, will approach the female as she lies down tired with long standing. The sow generally becomes pregnant when she hangs down her ears in her heats; if she is not pregnant, she becomes heated again.

12. Bitches do not copulate during the whole of their life, but only to a certain period. Their coition and pregnancy generally takes place till they are twelve years old, but both males and females have been known to perform the act of coition at eighteen and even twenty years of age; but old age takes away from both sexes the power of reproduction, as in other animals.

13. The camel is retroningent, and performs the act of intercourse in the manner already described; the period of its coition in Arabia is in the month of September; the

female goes with young twelve months, and produces one foal, for the animal is one of those which produce but one. Both the male and female arrive at puberty at the age of three years, and the female is ready for the male again at the end of a year after parturition.

14. The elephant arrives at puberty, the earliest at ten years of age, the latest at fifteen, and the male at five or six years old. The season for the intercourse of the sexes is in the spring: and the male is ready again at the end of three years, but he never touches again a female whom he has once impregnated. Her period of gestation is two years, and then she produces one calf, for the elephant belongs to the class of animals which have but one young one at a time. The young one is as large as a calf of two or three months old. This, then, is the nature of the sexual intercourse of those animals which perform this function.

Chapter XIII.

1. We must now treat of the mode of reproduction, both of those animals which use sexual intercourse, and those which do not; and, first of all, we will speak of the testacea, for this is the only entire class which is not reproduced by sexual intercourse. The purpuræ collect together in the spring, and produce what is called their nidamental capsules (melicera), for it is like honey-comb, though not so deeply cut, but, as it were, made up of the white pods of vetches. These capsules have neither opening nor perforation, nor are the purpuræ produced from them; but both these and other testacea are produced from mud and putrefaction. But this substance is an excrementitious matter both in the purpura and the ceryx, for these last also produce similar capsules.

2. The testacea which produce these capsules are generated in the same way as the rest of their class, but more readily when there are homogeneous particles pre-existing among them; for, when they deposit their nidamental capsules, they emit a clammy mucus, from which the scales of the capsules are formed. When all these have been deposited, they emit upon the ground a sort of chyle, and small purpuræ spring up upon the same spot and adhere to the larger purpuræ, though some of these can hardly be dis-

tinguished by their form. But if they are taken before the breeding season, they will sometimes breed in the baskets, not indeed anywhere, but they collect together like they do in the sea, and the narrow limits of their place of captivity make them hang together like bunches of fruit.

3. There are many kinds of purpuræ, some of which are large, as those which are found near Sigeum and Lectum; and others are small, as those in the Euripus and on the Carian coast. Those found in gulfs are large and rough. Most of them contain a black pigment; in others it is red, and the quantity of it small. Some of the largest weigh as much as a mina. Near the shore and on the coast they are small, and the pigment is red. Those which are natives of the north contain a black pigment; in those of the south it is red, generally speaking.

4. They are taken in the spring, about the time that they deposit their capsules, but they are never taken during the dog-days, for then they do not feed, but conceal themselves and get out of the way. The pigment is contained between the mecon and the neck. The union of these parts is thick, and the colour is like a white membrane; this is taken away. When this is bruised, the pigment wets and stains the hand. Something resembling a vein passes through it, and this appears to be the pigment; the nature of the rest resembles alum.[1] The pigment is the worst at the period of depositing their nidamental capsules.

5. The small ones are pounded up, shells and all, for it is not easy to separate them; but they separate the larger kinds from the shells, and then extract the pigment. For this purpose the mecon is divided from the neck, for the pigment lies above the part called the stomach, and when this is taken away, they are divided asunder. They are careful to bruise them while alive, for if they die before they are cut up, they vomit up the pigment; for this reason they keep them in the baskets till a sufficient number is collected, and there is time to procure the pigment.

6. The ancients did not let down or fasten any basket-net to their baits, so that it often happened that the purpura fell off as they were drawn up; but at the present time they

---

[1] Evidently a corrupt reading.

use basket-nets, in order that if the purpura should fall off, it may not be lost. They are most likely to fall off when full, but when empty it is difficult to draw them from the bait. These are the peculiarities of the purpura. The nature of the ceryx is the same as that of the purpura, and so are their seasons.

7. They both have opercula, and so have all turbinated shell-fish, from the period of their birth. They feed by forcing out their tongue, as it is called, beneath the operculum: the purpura has a tongue larger than a finger, with which it feeds upon and pierces the conchylia, and even the shells of its own species. Both the purpura and the ceryx are long-lived; for the purpura lives six years, and its annual increase is seen in the divisions on the helix of its shell.

8. The mya also deposits nidamental capsules; those which are called limnostrea are the first to originate in muddy places, but the conchæ, chemæ, solens, and pectens find their subsistence in sandy shores; the pinnæ grow up from their byssus both in sandy and muddy shores. The pinnæ always contain a pinnophylax, either like a small caris or cancer, and soon die when this is extracted. On the whole, all the testacea are produced spontaneously in mud, different kinds originating in different sorts of mud; the ostrea is found in mud, the conchæ and others that have been mentioned in sand. The tethya, balanus, and others which live on the surface, as the patella and nerita, originate in holes in the rocks. All these reach maturity very soon, especially the purpuræ and pectens, for they are matured in one year.

9. Very small white cancri are produced in some of the testacea, especially in the myæ that inhabit muddy places, and next to this in the pinnæ those which are called pinnoteræ; they occur also in the pectens and limnostrea. These animals apparently never grow; and the fishermen say that they are produced at the same time as the creatures they inhabit. The pectens disappear for some time in the sand, and so do the purpuræ. The ostrea (bivalves) are produced in the manner described, for some of them originate in shallow water, others near the shore, or among rocks, or in rough hard places, or in sand; and some have the power of locomotion, others have not.

10. Among those that are not locomotive, the pinnæ are fixed; the solens and conchæ remain on one spot, though not fixed, and do not survive separation from their home. The nature of the aster[1] is so hot, that if it is captured immediately after swallowing anything, its food is found digested; and they say that it is very troublesome in the Pyrrhæan Euripus. Its form is like the paintings of a star. The creatures called pneumones are spontaneously produced. The shell which painters use is very thick, and the pigment is produced on the outside of the shell; they are principally found in the neighbourhood of Caria.

11. The carcinium also originates in earth and mud, and afterwards makes its way into an empty shell, and when it grows too large for that, it leaves it for a larger one, as the shell of the nerita, strombus, and such like; it frequently occurs in the small ceryx. When it has entered the shell, it carries it about and lives in it, except that as it grows it migrates into a larger shell.

Chapter XIV.

1. The nature of the testacea is the same as that of creatures without shells, as the cnidæ[2] and sponges, which inhabit the holes in rocks. There are two kinds of cnidæ, some which live in holes in the rocks, and cannot be separated from them, and other migrating species which live upon the smooth flat surface of the rocks. (The patella also is free and locomotive.) In the interior of the sponges are found the creatures called pinnophylaces, and the interior is closed with a net like a spider's web, and small fish are captured by opening and closing this web, for it opens as they approach, and closes upon them when they have entered.

2. There are three kinds of sponges; one of them is thin, the other is thick, and the third, which is called the Achillean sponge, is slender, compact, and very strong; it is placed beneath helmets and thigh-pieces, for the sake of deadening the sound of blows; this kind is very rare. Among the compact kinds, those which are very hard and rough are called tragi. They all grow upon the rock or near the shore, and obtain their food from the mud. This is evident, for they are full of mud when they are captured. This is

[1] Star-fish. [2] Actinia.

the case with all other fixed things, that they derive their food from the spot to which they are attached.

3. The compact species are weaker than those which are thin, because their point of attachment is smaller. It is affirmed that the sponge possesses sensation; this is a proof of it, that it contracts if it perceives any purpose of tearing it up, and renders the task more difficult. The sponge does the same thing when the winds and waves are violent, that it may not lose its point of attachment. There are some persons who dispute this, as the natives of Torona. The sponge is inhabited by worms and other living creatures, which the rock-fish eat when the sponge is torn up, as well as the remainder of its roots. But if the sponge is broken off, it grows again, and is completed from the portion that is left.

4. The thin sponges are the largest, and they are most abundant on the Lycian coast; the compact sponges are softer, and the Achillean are more harsh than the others. On the whole, those that inhabit deep places with a mild temperature are the softest, for wind and cold weather harden them, as they do other growing things, and stop their increase. For this reason the sponges of the Hellespont are rough and compact; and, altogether, those beyond Malea, and those on this side, differ in softness and hardness.

5. Neither should the heat be very great, for the sponge becomes rotten, like plants, wherefore those near the shore are the best, especially if the water is deep near the land, for the temperature is moderated by the depth. When alive, before they are washed, they are black. Their point of attachment is neither single nor dispersed over the whole surface, for there are empty passages between the points of attachment. Something like a membrane is extended over their lower part, and the attachment is by several points; on the upper part are other closed passages, and four or five which are apparent. Wherefore some persons say that these are the organs by which they take their food.

6. There is also another species called aplysia, because it cannot be washed. This has very large passages; but the other parts of the substance are quite compact. When cut open it is more compact and smooth than the sponge, and

the whole is like a lung; of all the sponges this one is confessed to have the most sensation, and to be the most enduring. They are plainly seen in the sea near the sponges, for the other sponges are white as the mud settles down upon them, but these are always black. This is the mode of production in sponges and testacea.

Chapter XV.

1. Among the malacostraca the carabi are impregnated by sexual intercourse, and contain their ova during three months, May, June, and July. They afterwards deposit them upon the hollow part of their folded tail, and their ova grow like worms. The same thing takes place in the malacia and oviparous fish, for their ova always grow.

2. The ova of the carabi are sandy, and divided into eight parts; for a cartilaginous appendage, round which the ova are attached, is united to each of the opercula at their junction with the side; and the whole resembles a bunch of grapes, for every one of the cartilaginous appendages is frequently subdivided, and the divisions are apparent to any one who will separate them, but when first seen they appear to be united. Those ova which are in the centre are larger than those which are contiguous to the perforation, and the last are the least.

3. The smallest ova are as large as millet; the ova are not continuous with the perforation, but in the middle. For two divisions extend on each side, from the tail and from the thorax, and this is also the line of junction for the opercula. The ova, which are placed at the side, cannot be enclosed, unless the extremity of the tail is drawn over them; this, however, covers them like a lid.

4. The female, in depositing her ova, appears to collect them on the cartilaginous appendages by means of the broad part of the folded tail. She produces them by pressing with her tail and bending her body. These cartilaginous processes at the season of oviposition increase in size, in order to become appropriate receptacles for the ova. The ova are deposited on these processes, as those of the sepia are deposited upon broken pieces of wood or anything floating in the sea. This is the

manner of depositing them; but after they have been ripened twenty days, they are cast off altogether in a mass, as they appear when separated from the parent; in fifteen days, at the outside, the carabi are produced from these ova, and they are often taken off less than a finger's length. The ova are produced before Arcturus, and after Arcturus they are cast off.

5. The cyphæ among the carides contain their ova about four months. The carabi are found in rough and rocky places, the astaci in those that are smooth; but neither of them inhabit mud. For this cause the astaci are found in the Hellespont and near Thasus; the carabi in the neighbourhood of Sigeum and Athos. Fishermen, when they pursue their calling in the open sea, distinguish the rough and muddy places by the nature of the shore, and other signs. In the spring and winter they come near the shore; in summer time they go into deep water, sometimes for the sake of warmth, and sometimes for the cold.

6. Those called arcti[1] breed nearly at the same time as the carabi, wherefore they are most excellent in winter and in spring before the breeding season, and they are worst after they have deposited their ova. They change their shell in the spring, like the serpent, which puts off its old age, as it is called. Both the carabi and the carcini do this when they are young, as well as afterwards. All the carabi are long-lived.

Chapter XVI.

1. The malacia produce a white ovum after sexual intercourse; in the course of time this becomes sandy, like that of the testacea. The polypus deposits its ova in holes or pots, or any other hollow place; the ovum is like bunches of the wild vine and of the white poplar, as was observed before; when the ova are produced they remain suspended from the hole in which they were deposited: and the ova are so numerous, that when taken out they will fill a vessel much larger than the head of the polypus in which they were contained.

2. About fifty days afterwards the young polypi burst the eggs and escape, like phalangia, in great numbers. The particular shape of each limb is not distinct, though the general

[1] Perhaps, Cancer spinosissimus.

form is plain. Many of them perish from their small size and debility. Some have been observed so small that they could not be distinguished, unless they were touched, when they were seen to move.

3. The sepia also deposits eggs, which resemble large, black, myrtle seeds. They are united together like a bunch of fruit, and are enclosed in a substance which prevents them from separating readily. The male emits his ink upon them, a mucous fluid, which causes their slippery appearance. The ova increase in this way; and when first produced they are white, but when they have touched the ink they become large and black. When the young sepia, which is entirely formed of the internal white of the ovum, is produced, it makes its way out by the rupture of the membrane of the ovum.

4. The ovum which the female first produces is like hail, and to this the young sepia is attached by the head, as birds are attached to the abdomen. The nature of the umbilical attachment has never been observed, except that as the sepia increases the white always becomes less, and at last entirely disappears, like the yolk of the eggs of birds.

5. The eyes are at first very large in these as in other animals, as in the diagram. The ovum is seen at A, the eyes at B and C, and the embryo sepia itself at D. The female contains ova during the spring. The ova are produced in fifteen days; and when the ova are produced they remain for fifteen days longer like the small seeds of grapes, and when these are ruptured the young sepias escape from the inside. If a person divides them before they have reached maturity, the young sepias emit their fœces and vary in colour, and turn from white to red from alarm.

6. The crustaceans incubate upon their ova, which are placed beneath them; but the polypus and sepia and such like incubate upon their ova wherever they may be deposited, and especially the sepia, for the female has often been observed with her abdomen upon the ground, but the female polypus has been observed sometimes placed upon her ova, and sometimes upon her mouth, holding with her tentacula over the hole in which the ova were deposited. The sepia deposits her ova upon the ground among fuci and reeds, or upon any thing thrown in the water, as wood, branches,

or stones; and the fishermen are careful to place branches of trees in the water. Upon these they deposit their long and united ova like branches of fruit.

7. The ova are deposited and produced by repeated exertion, as if the parturition were accompanied with pain. The teuthis oviposits in the sea. The ova, like those of the sepia, are united together. Both the teuthus and sepia are short-lived, for very few of them survive a year. The same is the case with the polypus. Each egg produces one small sepia, and so also in the teuthis. The male teuthus differs from the female; for if the hair (branchia) are drawn aside, the female will be seen to have two red substances like mammæ, which the male does not possess. The sepia also has the same sexual distinction, and is more variegated than the female, as I observed before.

Chapter XVII.

1. It has already been observed that the male insects are less than the female, and that the male mounts upon the female; and the manner of their sexual intercourse has been described, and the difficulty of separating them. Most of them produce their young very soon after sexual intercourse. All the kinds except some psychæ (butterflies and moths) produce worms. These produce a hard substance, like the seed of the cnecus,[1] which is fluid within. From the worm an animal is produced, but not from a portion of it, as if it were an ovum, but the whole grows and becomes an articulated animal.

2. Some of them are produced from similar animals, as phalangia and spiders from phalangia and spiders, and attelabi,[2] locusts, and grasshoppers. Others do not originate in animals of the same species, but their production is spontaneous, for some of them spring from the dew which falls upon plants. The origin of these is naturally in the spring, though they often appear in the winter, if fine weather and south winds occur for any length of time. Some originate in rotten mud and dung; and others in the fresh wood of plants or in dry wood; others among the hair of animals, or in their flesh, or excrements, whether ejected, or still existing in the body, as those which are called helminthes.

[1] Cantharus tinctorius, a plant of the thistle kind. L. and S.
[2] The larva of some species.

3. There are three kinds of these, the flat worms, the round worms, and those which are called ascarides. From these creatures nothing is produced; but the broad worm is attached to the intestine, and produces something like the seed of the colocynth, and this is used by physicians as a proof of the presence of the worm.

4. Butterflies are produced from caterpillars; and these originate in the leaves of green plants, especially the rhaphahus, which some persons call crambe. At first they are smaller than millet, afterwards they grow into little worms, in three days they become small caterpillars, afterwards they grow and become motionless, and change their form. In this state the creature is called chrysalis. It has a hard covering, but moves when it is touched. They are united to something by weblike processes, and have no mouth nor any other visible organ. After a short time the covering is burst, and a winged animal escapes, which is called a butterfly.

5. At first, while in the caterpillar state, they take food and evacuate fœces, but in the chrysalis state they do neither. The same is the case with all other creatures which originate in worms, and those which produce worms after sexual intercourse, or even without this process; for the offspring of bees, anthrenæ, and wasps, while they are young worms, consume food and evacuate excrement, but when from worms they receive their conformation they are called nymphæ, and neither feed nor evacuate, but remain quiet in their covering until they are grown. They then make their escape by cutting through a place where the cell is fastened on.

6. The penia[1] and hypera[2] also are produced from a kind of campe (caterpillar) which make a wave as they walk, and as they advance bend the hinder extremity up to that which has preceded. The creature produced always derives its colour from the campe in which it originates. A certain great worm, which has as it were horns, and differs from others, at its first metamorphosis produces a campe, afterwards a bombylius, and lastly a necydalus. It passes through all these forms in six months From this animal some women unroll and separate the bombycina (cocoons), and afterwards weave them. It is

---

[1] Some species of larva.   [2] Geometra.

said that this was first woven in the island of Cos by Pamphila, the daughter of Plateos.

7. From the worms in dry wood the insects called carabi are produced in the same manner; for at first they are immoveable worms, and afterwards the carabi are produced by the rupture of their case. The crambides originate in the plant called crambe, and these also have wings, and the prasocurides from the plant called prasum (onion). The œstri are produced from the little flat creatures that are found on the surface of rivers. Wherefore also they congregate in the greatest numbers around the waters where such animals are found. The kind of pygolampis which has no wings originates in a small, black, hairy caterpillar. These undergo another change, and turn into the winged creatures called bostrychi.

8. The empides originate in ascarides, and the ascarides originate in the mud of wells and running waters which flow over an earthy bottom. At first the decaying mud acquires a white colour, which afterwards becomes black, and finally red. When this takes place, very small red creatures are seen growing in it like fuci. At first these move about in a mass, afterwards their connection is ruptured, the creatures called ascarides are borne about in the water, after a few days they stand erect in the water without motion and of a hard texture, and subsequently the case is broken and the empis sits upon it until either the sun or the wind enables it to move, then it flies away.

9. The commencement of life in all other worms, and in all creatures produced from worms, originates in the influence of the sun and wind. The ascarides are produced in greater numbers, and more quickly, where the various matters are mixed together, as in the works conducted in the Megarian territory, for putrefaction thus takes place more readily. The autumnal season also is favourable to their increase, for there is less moisture at that time of the year. The crotones[1] originate in the agrostis, the melolonthæ from the worms which originate in the dung of oxen and asses.

10. The canthari which roll up dung, hide themselves in it during the winter, and produce worms, which afterwards

---
[1] Ticks. Acarus ricinus.

become canthari; and from the worms which inhabit the osprea,[1] winged creatures, like those already mentioned, derive their existence. Flies originate in dung which has been set apart, and those who are employed in this work strive to separate the remainder which is mixed together, for they say that the dung is thus brought to putrefaction.

11. The origin of these worms is very small; for first of all a redness is perceived, and motion commences, as if they were united together. The worm then again becomes still, afterwards it moves, and then again is immoveable. From this the worm is completed, and motion recommences under the action of the sun and wind. The myops is produced in wood. The orsodacnæ[2] from the metamorphosis of worms, which originate on the stalks of the crambe. The cantharis from worms which dwell on the fig tree, apium (pear tree), and pitch tree, for there are worms on all these, and on the cynacantha.[3] They assemble round strong smelling things because they originate from them.

12. The conops springs from a worm which originates in the thick part of vinegar; for there seem also to be worms in things which are the farthest from putrefaction, as in snow which has laid for some time: for after having laid, it becomes red, wherefore, also, the worms are such and hairy. Those in the snow in Media are large and white, and furnished with but little power of motion. In Cyprus, when the manufacturers of the stone called chalcitis burn it for many days in the fire, a winged creature, something larger than a great fly, is seen walking and leaping in the fire.

13. The worms perish when they are taken out of the snow, and so do these creatures when taken from the fire. And the salamander shews that it is possible for some animal substances to exist in the fire, for they say that fire is extinguished when this animal walks over it.

14. In the river Hypanis in the Cimmerian Bosphorus, about the summer solstice, capsules larger than grape-seed are floated down the river: when these are ruptured, a four-footed, winged creature makes its escape, which lives and flies about till the evening. As the sun descends, it

---

[1] Vetches, leguminous plants.   [2] Chrysomela oleracea.
[3] Perhaps the dog rose, or sweet briar.

becomes emaciated, and is dead by sunset, having lived but one day; for which cause it is called ephemerum. Most animals which spring from caterpillars or worms, are first of all enclosed in a web, and this is their nature.

15. The wasps which are called ichneumons, which are smaller than the others, kill the phalangia, and carry them to a wall, or some other place with a hole in it; and when they have covered them over with mud, they oviposit there, and the ichneumon wasps are produced from them. Many of the coleoptera, and other small and anonymous creatures make little holes in tombs or walls, and there deposit their worms.

16. The period of reproduction, from its commencement to its conclusion, is generally completed in three or four weeks. In the worms and worm-like creatures, three weeks are usually sufficient, and four weeks are usually enough for those which are oviparous. In one week from their sexual intercourse, the growth of the ovum is completed. In the remaining three weeks, those that produce by generation, hatch and bring forth their ova, as in the spiders, and such like creatures. The metamorphoses generally occupy three or four days, like the crisis of diseases. This is the mode of generation in insects.

17. They die from the shrivelling of their limbs, as large animals do of old age. Those which are furnished with wings have these organs drawn together in autumn. The myopes die from an effusion of water in their eyes.

Chapter XVIII.

1. All persons are not agreed as to the generation of bees, for some say that they neither produce young, nor have sexual intercourse; but that they bring their young from other sources; and some say that they collect them from the flowers of the calyntrus,[1] and others from the flower of the calamus.[2] Others again, say that they are found in the flowers of the olive, and produce this proof, that the swarms are most abundant when the olives are fertile. Other persons affirm that they collect the young of the drones from any of the substances we have named, but that the rulers (queens) produce the young of the bees.

[1] Honeysuckle.   [2] Reed.

2. There are two kinds of rulers, the best of these is red, the other black and variegated: their size is double that of the working bees; the part of the body beneath the cincture is more than half of the whole length: by some they are called the mother bees, as if they were the parents of the rest; and they argue, that unless the ruler is present, drones only are produced, and no bees. Others affirm that they have sexual intercourse, and that the drones are males, and the bees females.

3. The other bees originate in the cells of the comb, but the rulers are produced in the lower part of the comb, six or seven of them separated, opposite to the rest of the progeny. The bees have a sting, which the drones have not: the kings and rulers have a sting which they do not make use of, and some persons suppose that they have none.

Chapter XIX.

1. There are several kinds of bees, the best are small, round, and variegated: another kind is large, like the anthrene: a third kind is called phor; this is black, and has a broad abdomen: the drone is the fourth, and is the largest of all; it has no sting, and is incapable of work, for which reason people often wrap something round their hives, so that the bees can enter, but the drones, being larger, cannot.

2. There are two kinds of rulers among bees, as I observed before. In every hive there are several rulers, and not a single one, for the hive perishes if there are not rulers enough (not that they thus become anarchical, but, as they say, because they are required for breeding the bees); if there are too many rulers they perish, for thus they become distracted.

3. If the spring is late, and drought and rusts are about, the progeny is small. When the weather is dry, they make honey. When it is damp, their progeny multiplies; for which reason, the olives and the swarms of bees multiply at the same time. They begin by making comb, in which they place the progeny, which is deposited with their mouths, as those say who affirm that they collect it from external sources. Afterwards they gather the honey which is to be their food, during the summer and the autumn; that which is gathered in the autumn is the best.

4. Wax is made from flowers. They bring the material of wax from the droppings of trees, but the honey falls from the air, principally about the rising of the stars, and when the rainbow rests upon the earth. Generally no honey is produced before the rising of the Pleiades. We argue that wax is made, as I said, from flowers, but that the bees do not make honey, but simply collect that which falls; for those who keep bees find the cells filled with honey in the course of one or two days. In the autumn there are flowers enough, but the bees make no honey, if that which they have produced is taken away. But if one supply was taken away, and they were in want of food, they would make more if they procured it from flowers.

5. The honey becomes thick by ripening, for at first it is like water, and continues liquid for some days, wherefore it never becomes thick if it is taken away during that time. It requires twenty days to make it consistent; this is very plain from the taste of it, for it differs both in sweetness and solidity. The bee carries honey from every plant which has cup-shaped flowers, and from all those which contain a sweet principle, but does not injure the fruit; it takes up and carries away the sweet taste of plants with its tongue-like organ.

6. The honey-comb is pressed when the wild figs begin to appear; and they produce the best grubs when they can produce honey. The bees carry the wax and bee-bread upon their legs, but the honey is disgorged into the cells. After the progeny is deposited in the cells, they incubate like birds. In the wax cells the little worm is placed at the side; afterwards it rises of itself to be fed. It is united to the comb in such a manner as to be held by it. The progeny both of the bees and drones from which the little worms are produced, is white. As they grow they become bees and drones. The progeny of the king-bees is rather red, and about the consistency of thick honey. In bulk it is as large as the creature which is produced from it. The progeny of the king-bee is not a worm, but comes forth a perfect bee, as they say; and, when the progeny is produced in the comb, honey is found in that which is opposite.

K

7. After the grub is covered up, it has wings and feet; and when it has acquired wings, it bursts through the membrane, and flies away. It evacuates an excrementitious matter while it is a worm, but not afterwards, until it is perfected, as I observed before. If a person cuts off the head of the grub before its wings are acquired, the other bees devour it; if a person having cut off the wings of a drone lets it go, the bees will eat off the wings of the other drones.

8. The bee will live for six years, some have lived for seven, and if a swarm lasts nine or ten years, it is considered to have done well. In Pontus there are very white bees, which make honey twice every month. In Therniscyra, near the river Thermodon, are found bees which make cells in the earth, and in hives with a very small quantity of wax, but their honey is thick. The cells are smooth and homogeneous. They only do this in the winter, and not all the year round; for there is a great deal of ivy in the place, which flowers at this season of the year, and from this they carry away the honey. From the higher regions of Amisus a kind of white honey is procured, which the bees form upon the trees without wax. The same is also found in another place in Pontus. There are also bees which form triple cells in the earth; these form honey, but never have grubs. All such as these, however, are not cells, neither are they formed by every kind of bee.

Chapter XX.

1. The anthrenæ[1] and wasps form cells for their progeny when they have no rulers, but are wandering about in search of them, the anthrenæ upon some high place, the wasps in holes. But when they have the rulers they form their cells underground. All their cells are hexagonal, like those of bees; they are not formed of wax, but of a weblike membrane, made of the bark of trees. The cells of the anthrenæ are far more elegant than those of wasps. Upon the side of their cells they place their progeny, in the manner of the bees, like a drop of liquid united to the wall of the cell. The progeny in all the cells is not alike, but in some they are so large as to be almost ready for flight, in others are nymphæ, in others grubs.

[1] Hornet, Apis terrestris.

2. The only excrementitious matter is found in the cells of the grubs, as in the case of bees. As long as they are nymphæ they remain motionless, and the cell is sealed over, and on the other side of the cell which contains their progeny, there is a drop of honey in the combs of the anthrenæ. The grubs of these creatures are produced in the autumn, not in the spring, but they evidently grow most rapidly at the full moon. The progeny and the grubs are not united to the bottom, but to the side of the cell.

Chapter XXI.

1. Some of the bombycia[1] form an angular cell of mud, which they attach to a stone or something else, and smear with a kind of transparent substance; this is so very thick and hard, that it can scarcely be broken with the blow of a spear. In this they deposit their ova, and the white maggots are contained in a black membrane; and wax is formed in the mud without any membrane, this wax is much more yellow than that of bees.

2. The ants also have sexual intercourse, and produce maggots which they do not attach to anything. As these grow, they change from small round things to long articulated beings. The season for their production is in the spring.

3. The land-scorpions also bring forth many egg-like maggots, upon which they incubate. When the young ones are perfect, they drive out and destroy their parents like spiders, for they are frequently eleven in number.

Chapter XXII.

1. The arachnia copulate in the manner already described, and produce maggots which at first are small. After their metamorphosis they become spiders, not from a part but from the whole of the maggot, for they are round from the first. When the female has produced her ova, she incubates upon them, in three days they acquire limbs. All of them produce their young in a web, which is thin and small in some species, but compact in others. Some are enclosed entirely in a round receptacle, and others are only partially covered by the web. All the young spiders are

[1] Apis cementaria.

not produced at once, but as soon as they are hatched they leap out and shoot forth a web. If they are bruised they are found to contain a thick white fluid like that of maggots.

2. The field-spiders first of all deposit their ova in a web, of which one half is attached to themselves, and the other external, they incubate upon this, and produce their young alive. The phalangia deposit their ova in a thick basket which they weave, upon this they incubate. The smooth kinds produce a small number, the phalangia a great many. When they are grown, they surround their parent in a circle, kill and throw her out. They often seize the male in the same way if they can catch him, for he assists the female in incubation. Sometimes there are as many as three hundred round a single phalangium. The little spiders become full-grown in about four weeks.

CHAPTER XXIII.

1. LOCUSTS copulate in the same manner as all other insects, the smaller mounting upon the larger, for the male is the smaller. They oviposit by fixing the organ which is attached to their tail (the ovipositor) in the ground. The males do not possess this organ. Many of them deposit their ova in one spot, so as to make it appear like a honeycomb. As soon as they have deposited their ova, egg-like maggots are formed, which are covered with a thin coating of earth like a membrane, and in this they are matured.

2. The young are so soft as to collapse if they are only touched. They are not produced on the surface, but a little below the surface of the soil; and as soon as they are matured, they escape from the coat of soil in which they are enclosed as small black locusts. Their skin is subsequently ruptured, and they then attain their full size. They produce their young at the end of summer, and then die.

3. For as soon as they have deposited their ova, small worms make their appearance on their necks, the males also perish at the same time: they come out of the earth in the spring. Locusts never shew themselves in mountainous countries, nor in poor land, but in plains, and broken soil, for they deposit their ova in fissures. The ova remain in

the soil during the winter, and in the summer the locusts are produced from the germs of the preceding year.

4. The young of the attelabi are produced in the same manner, and the parents die after having deposited their ova. Their ova are destroyed by the rains of the autumn, if the weather is wet; but if that season is dry, many attelabi are produced, because they are not equally destroyed; for their destruction appears to be irregular, and to take place by accident.

Chapter XXIV.

1. There are two kinds of grasshoppers: some are small. These are the first to appear, the last to perish. Others, which chirp, are large: these appear last, and disappear first. There is another difference between the small and large kind. Those which chirp have a division in the middle of the body: those which do not chirp have none. The large ones, which chirp, are called achetæ; the small are called tettigonia. Such of these as are divided, sing a little.

2. Grasshoppers do not appear where there are no trees, for which reason they are unknown in the open country of Cyrene, but are abundant near the city, and especially among olive trees, for these do not give much shade, and grasshoppers are not produced in the cold, nor in very shady groves. Both the large and small ones have sexual intercourse with their own kind, copulating with each other on their backs. The male inserts his organ into the female, in the same manner as other insects. The female has a divided pudendum. The female individual is the one which receives the male.

3. They deposit their ova in fields, piercing the soil with the organ at the extremity of their body, like the attelabi; for the attelabi also oviposit in the fields, for which reason they are common in Cyrene. They oviposit also in the reeds which are used to support the vines; these they pierce: and so they do in the stems of the scilla. The young ones are washed into the earth, and are common in rainy weather. The maggot, when it is grown in the earth, becomes a tettigometra: these are sweetest before they have ruptured their covering.

4. And when the season arrives for their appearance,

about the solstice, they come forth by night, and immediately burst their envelope, and the tettigometra becomes a grasshopper. They immediately become black and hard, acquire their full size, and begin to chirp. In both kinds the males chirp; the others, which do not chirp, are females. When first produced the males are the sweetest: after the sexual intercourse, the females are sweetest, for they contain white ova.

5. If a noise is made as they fly along, they emit a fluid like water, which the agriculturists describe as if they emitted both a liquid and solid excrement, and that they feed on dew; and if any one approaches them with a bent finger, which is gradually straightened, they will remain more quiet than if it is put out straight at once, and will climb up upon the finger; for, from the dimness of their sight, they climb upon it as if it were a moving leaf.

Chapter XXV.

1. Those insects which are not carnivorous, but live upon the juices of living flesh, as lice, fleas, and bugs, produce nits from sexual intercourse; from these nits nothing else is formed. Of these insects the fleas originate in very small portions of corrupted matter, for they are always collected together where there is any dry dung. Bugs[1] proceed from the moisture which collects on the bodies of animals: lice from the flesh of other creatures; for before they appear, they exist in little pimples which do not contain matter: and if these are pricked, the lice[2] escape from them. Some persons have been afflicted with a disease arising from excessive moisture in the body, of which people have died, as they say that Alcmon the poet, and Pherecydes of Syria did.

2. And in some diseases lice are very common. There is a kind of lice, which they call wild, and are harder than the common sort, which are difficult to eradicate from the body. The heads of children are most subject to be infested with lice, and men the least so, for women are more liable to them than men. Those that have lice in the head are less subject to headache. Many other animals are infested with lice: for both birds have them, and those which are called phasiani, unless they dust themselves, are destroyed by

[1] Cinex lectularius.   [2] Perhaps Acarus Scabiei, Itch insect.

them. And so are all those creatures which have feathers with a hollow stem, and those which have hair, except the ass, which has neither lice nor ticks. Oxen have both; sheep and goats have ticks, but no lice; hogs are infested with large, hard lice, and dogs with those which are called cynoraïstæ. All lice originate in the animals that are infested with them. All creatures that have lice, and wash themselves, are more liable to them when they change the water in which they bathe.

3. In the sea is a kind of lice[1] growing on fish; but these do not originate in the fish, but in the mud. Their appearance is that of wood-lice with many feet, except that they have a wide tail. There is one species of marine lice which occur everywhere, and especially infest the trigla. All these creatures are furnished with many legs, are exsanguineous, and insects. The œstrus[2] of the thynnus occurs near the fins: in shape it is like a scorpion, and as large as a spider. In the sea between Cyrene and Egypt, there is a fish called the phtheira, which accompanies the dolphin; it is the fattest of all fish, because it enjoys an abundance of the food which the dolphin hunts for.

CHAPTER XXVI.

1 THERE are also other minute animals, as I observed before, some of which occur in wool,[3] and in woollen goods; as the moths, which are produced in the greatest abundance when the wool is dusty, and especially if a spider is enclosed with them, for this creature is thirsty, and dries up any fluid which may be present. This worm also occurs in garments. There is one which occurs in old honeycombs, like the creature which inhabits dry wood: this appears to be the least of all creatures, it is called acari, it is white and small. Others also are found in books,[4] some of which are like those which occur in garments: others are like scorpions;[5] they have no tails, and are very small. And on the whole, they occur in everything, so to say, which from being dry, becomes moist, or being moist, becomes dry, if it has any life in it.

[1] Perhaps Oniscus Ceti, or Isora.
[2] Perhaps Lernœa branchialis.
[3] Tinea pellionella, or T. sarcitella.
[4] Dumestes Pellio, and D. lardarius.
[5] Phalangium cancroides.

2 There is a little worm which is called xylophthorus,[1] which is no less extraordinary than these animals; for its variegated head is projected beyond its case, and its feet are at the extremity, as in other worms. The rest of the body is contained in a case made of a substance like spider's web, and a dry material on the outside of this; so that it appears to walk about with this attached to it. These creatures are attached to their case, and as a snail to its shell, so the whole of the case is joined to the worm, and it does not fall out of it, but is drawn out of it, as if they were joined together. If a person pulls off the case, the creature dies, and becomes as helpless as a snail without its shell. As time advances, this grub becomes a chrysalis, like a caterpillar, and lies without motion: but the nature of the winged creature that is produced has never been ascertained.

3. The wild figs upon the fig-trees contain a creature called psen;[2] this is at first a little worm, and afterwards having ruptured the case, the psen flies out, and leaves it behind. It then pierces the unripe figs, and causes them not to fall off, wherefore gardeners place wild fruit near the cultivated kinds, and plant the wild and cultivated plants near each other.

Chapter XXVII.

1. The sexual intercourse of sanguineous and oviparous quadrupeds takes place in the spring. They do not, however, all copulate at the same season; but some in the spring, others in the summer or autumn, as the season is appropriate for bringing up the young of each species. The tortoise produces hard, two-coloured eggs, like those of birds. Having deposited her eggs, she buries them, and makes a beaten place above them. When this is done, she sits upon them. The eggs are hatched the following year. The emys goes out of the water to deposit her eggs, and digs a hole like a cask, in which she places her eggs and leaves them. Having left them alone for less than thirty days, she digs them up again and hatches them and leads them at once to the water.

---

[1] Tinea graminella, Tinea lichenella, Tinea Xylophorus, or perhaps larva of Phryganea.

[2] Cynips Psenes.

The marine turtles deposit their eggs in the earth like domestic birds, and cover them up with earth and sit upon them during the night. They produce a great many eggs, as many as an hundred.

2. The saurians and both the land and river crocodiles produce their eggs upon the land. Those of the lizards are hatched spontaneously in the earth; for the lizard does not live a whole year, for it is said to live only six months. The river crocodile produces as many as sixty eggs, which are white. She sits upon them for sixty days, for they live a long while. A very large animal is produced from these small eggs; for the egg is not larger than that of a goose, and the young is in proportion, but when full grown the creature measures seventeen cubits. Some persons say that it grows as long as it lives.

Chapter XXVIII.

Among serpents the viper is externally viviparous, but first of all internally oviparous. The ovum, like that of fish, is of one colour and soft skinned. The young are produced in the upper part. They are not enclosed in a shelly covering, neither are the ova of fish. The little vipers are produced in a membrane, which they rupture on the third day, and sometimes they make their escape by eating their way through the mother. They are produced one by one in the course of a day, and their number often exceeds twenty. Other serpents are externally oviparous, but their ova are joined together like women's necklaces. When the female deposits her eggs in the soil, she incubates upon them. These also are hatched in the second year. This is the manner of the production of serpents, insects, and of oviparous quadrupeds.

BOOK THE SIXTH.

Chapter I.

1. The above describes the manner of reproduction in serpents, insects, and oviparous quadrupeds. All birds are oviparous, but the season of sexual intercourse and of bringing out their young is not the same in all; for some copulate and produce eggs at all seasons, as we may say, as the domestic fowl and the pigeon, for the domestic fowl lays eggs all the year round, except two months at the winter solstice. Some of the finest birds will lay sixty eggs before they want to sit, though these are not so fruitful as the more common kinds. The Adrianic fowls are very small, but they lay every day; but they are cruel, and often kill their chickens. Their colour is variegated. Some of the domestic birds lay twice a-day, and some have been known to lay so many eggs that they died very soon.

2. The domestic fowls, as I said, lay continually; but the pigeon, dove, trygon, and œnas lay twice a-year; and the pigeon ten times. The greatest number of birds lay in the spring; and some of them produce many young, and this in two ways; some producing their young often, as the pigeon; others producing many at a time, as the domestic fowl. All birds with crooked claws, except the cenchris,[1] lay but few eggs. This bird lays the most of any of its class; for it has been observed to produce four, and it even produces more. Some birds lay their eggs in nests; but those that do not fly, as partridges and quails, do not make nests, but lay their eggs on the ground and cover them over with rubbish. The lark and tetrix[2] do the same.

3. These birds make their nests in a place sheltered from the wind. That which the Beotians call ærops[3] is the only bird that makes its nests in caverns in the earth. The cichlæ[4] make nests of mud like swallows in the tops of trees; but they place them in order close to each other, so

---

[1] Falco tinnunculus.
[2] Tetrao tetrix or Otis tetrix.
[3] Merops apiaster.
[4] Turdus, thrush.

that from their proximity they look like a chain of nests. Among the birds which make solitary nests, the hoopoe makes no real nest, but lays its eggs in the stumps of hollow trees, without building at all. The coccyx[1] lays its eggs in houses and holes in rocks. The tetrix, which the Athenians call "urax," makes no nest on the ground or in trees, but in herbaceous plants.

Chapter II.

1. The eggs of all birds are alike and have a hard shell, if they are produced by sexual intercourse and are not decayed, for domestic fowls sometimes lay soft eggs. Birds' eggs are two-coloured, externally white, internally yellow. The eggs of birds inhabiting the sides of streams and lakes differ from those living on dry land, for in the eggs of aquatic birds the yolk bears a much larger proportion to the white.

2. The colours of eggs vary in different kinds of birds. Some have white eggs, as pigeons, partridges; some yellow, as those inhabiting streams; others are spotted, as those of the meleagris[2] and phasianus;[3] the eggs of the cenchris are red like vermilion. In the egg itself there is a difference; for one end is pointed, the other round. The round end is produced first. The large, sharp eggs are males; those which are round and circular at the sharp end are females.

3. They are matured by incubation. Some are hatched spontaneously in the earth, as in Egypt, being buried in dung; and they say that in Syracuse a drunkard placed eggs beneath his mat, and drank without ceasing until the eggs were hatched; and eggs placed in warm vessels have been matured and hatched spontaneously.

4. The seminal fluid of all birds is white, like that of other animals; and when they copulate the female receives the male semen near the diaphragm. The egg at first appears small and white, afterwards red and bloody; as it grows it becomes quite ochreous and yellow; when it becomes larger a distinction is made, and the internal part becomes yellow, the external white; and when it is perfected it is set at liberty, and excluded just at the period when it is changing from soft to hard. So that during exclusion it is not har-

---

[1] Cuculus canorus.   [2] Numida Mcleagris.
[3] Phasianus colchicus.

dened; but as soon as it is excluded it thickens and becomes hard, unless it is diseased. And eggs have been known to be excluded in the state in which all eggs are at a certain period of their growth; for they were entirely yellow, as the young bird is afterwards. Such have also been observed in the domestic fowl beneath the diaphragm, where the eggs of the hen are placed, entirely yellow, and as large as eggs usually are. This has been considered ominous.

5. They are mistaken who say that the hypenemia (barren eggs) are the remains of former acts of sexual intercourse; for young birds, as fowls and geese, have been frequently observed to lay such eggs without any sexual intercourse. Barren eggs are smaller, not so sweet, and more fluid than fertile eggs, and they are more numerous. If they are placed under a bird, the fluid part never thickens, but both the yolk and the white remain in their original state. Many birds produce these eggs, as the domestic fowl, partridge, pigeon, peafowl, goose, and chenalopex.[1]

6. Eggs are hatched more readily in summer than in winter; for in the summer the domestic fowl will hatch in eighteen days, but in winter sometimes in not less than twenty-five days. Some birds also are more adapted for incubation than others. A thunder-storm during the season of incubation will destroy the eggs. What are called cynosura and uria (addled eggs) are more frequently produced in the summer. The hypenemia[2] are by some persons called zephyria, because they say that birds receive these winds in the spring. They do the same thing if they are touched with the hand. The hypenemia become fertile; and eggs that are produced by sexual intercourse are changed to another kind, if the hen which contains either hypenemia or fertile eggs has sexual intercourse with another bird before the eggs begin to change from yellow to white, and the hypenemia become fertile, and the fertile eggs produce birds of the nature of the second male.

7. But if the change from yellow to white has already taken place, neither the barren nor the fertile eggs are altered, so as to change to the nature of the second male. And if the sexual intercourse should be discontinued while the eggs are small, those which existed previously undergo no change,

[1] Œnas tadorna.   [2] Eggs formed without sexual intercourse.

but if the act is repeated, a rapid increase in size takes place. The nature of the white and yolk of the egg is different, not only in colour, but in other properties, for the yolk coagulates with cold, while the white remains fluid, but the white coagulates with heat, which the yolk does not, but remains soft, if it is not burnt; and it becomes consistent and dry by boiling rather than roasting.

8. The white and yolk are separated from each other by a membrane. The chalazæ at the extremities of the yolk have nothing to do with generation, as some persons suppose. These spots are two, one below and one above. If many whites and yolks of eggs are taken out, and mixed together in a vessel, and cooked with a slow and moderate heat, the yolks will all collect in the middle, and the whites will surround them. Young domestic fowls begin to lay eggs at the beginning of the spring; they lay more than those which are older, but those of the young birds are smaller, and if birds are not permitted to incubate, they are destroyed and become sick.

9. After copulation birds ruffle and shake themselves, and often cover themselves with chaff, and this also they do when they have laid. Pigeons draw up their tail, geese go and bathe. The pregnancy and conception of barren eggs is quick in most birds, as in the partridge, on account of the violence of their sexual desires; for if the hen stands in the way of the breath of the male, she conceives, and immediately becomes of no use for fowling; for the partridge appears to have a very distinct smell. The production of the egg after copulation, and the production of the young by incubation, do not occupy the same length of time in all birds, but varies according to their size. The egg of the domestic fowl is perfected in ten days after sexual intercourse, and that of the pigeon in a shorter time. Pigeons are able to retain their eggs even in the act of parturition. If they are disturbed by anything occurring in the neighbourhood of their nest, or a feather be plucked out, or if anything else troubles or disturbs them, they retain the egg they were about to lay.

10. This is peculiar to pigeons, and so is the following: for they kiss each other when the male is about to mount, or else they will not endure it. The older bird first gives

a kiss, but afterwards he mounts without kissing, but younger birds always kiss before copulation. This also is peculiar to these birds. The females kiss and mount upon each other like the males, when there is no male present. They do not project anything into each other, but produce more eggs than those which produce fertile ones; from these eggs nothing is hatched, but they are all barren.

Chapter III.

1. The production of the bird from the egg is alike in them all, but the period of completion varies, as I observed before. In domestic fowls the first sign of alteration takes place after three days and nights. This period is longer in larger birds, and shorter in small birds. During this period the upper part of the yolk advances to the small extremity of the egg, which is the beginning of the egg. This is the part from which the chicken is excluded, and the heart is visible like a red spot in the white of the egg.

2. This spot palpitates and moves as though it were endued with life. From this, as it increases, two involved sanguineous passages like veins lead to each of the surrounding tunics; and a membrane which has sanguineous passages encloses the white at this period, and separates it from the venous passages. A short time afterwards the body is distinguished, at first very small and white, but the head is distinct, and in this the eyes are the most enlarged. And this continues for some time, for afterwards the eyes are reduced in size and approach each other, but the lower part of the body has not at first any proportion to the upper part.

3. One of the passages from the heart extends into a circle around the embryo, and the other to the yolk, as if it were an umbilical cord. The origin of the young bird is in the white, its nutriment is derived from the yolk through the umbilical cord. On the tenth day, the whole of the young bird and all its parts are distinct, but its head is still larger than the rest of the body, and the eyes are larger than the rest of the head. They have no sense of sight. If the eyes are taken out at this period, they are larger than beans, and black; when the skin is taken from them, they are seen to contain a white and cold

fluid, very brilliant in appearance, but without any hard substance. This is the manner of the development of the eyes and head.

4. At the same period the viscera are visible, but the stomach, and intestines, and the veins from the heart still appear to extend towards the navel. From the navel a vein appears to extend upon the membrane which encloses the yolk, and the yolk itself is at this period fluid, and more abundant than in its natural state. The other extends to the membrane which encloses the whole membrane containing the embryo, and the membrane of the yolk and the fluid between them, and when the young birds have grown a little more, part of the yolk goes to one end, and part to the other, and between them is the fluid white; but the white is still below the lower part of the yolk, where it was at first, but at the tenth day the white disappears, for it has become small, viscid, thick, and rather yellow.

5. This is the position of all the parts: the first and last part adjoining the shell is the membrane of the egg, not the membrane of the shell, but beneath this. This contains the fluid white; within this is the young bird, and a membrane surrounding it, and separating it from the fluid; beneath the embryo is the yolk, to which one of the veins extends, and the other to the white which encloses it. A membrane containing a fluid resembling sanies encloses the whole, and then another membrane which surrounds the embryo itself, as I observed, and separates it from the fluid. Below this the yolk, enclosed in another membrane, which is reached by the umbilical cord from the heart, and the great vein, so that the embryo does not appear to be in either of the fluids.

6. About the twentieth day, if the hatching has been delayed beyond this period, the young bird is able to chirp when moved externally, and if the shell is taken off, by this time also it is downy. The head is placed over the right leg upon the side, and the wing is over the head. At this period the chorion-like membrane is visible, which is united with the lowest membrane of the shell, to which one of the umbilical cords passes, and the young bird is complete. The other chorion-like membrane is also visible, enclosing the yolk. To this the other umbilical cord extends. Both of these cords are attached to the heart and the great vein. At

the same period the cord which is attached to one chorion falls off, and is separated from the animal, but the one which passes to the yolk remains suspended from the young bird by a thin bowel, and a considerable portion of the yolk is contained in the young bird, and some of it is found in the stomach.

7. At this period also they eject an excrementitious matter into the external chorion, and contain it in the stomach. The external excrement is white, the internal yellow. At last the yolk, which has been continually wasting and advancing, is entirely taken up and enclosed in the young bird. So that portions of it may be observed in the intestines of birds if they are dissected on the tenth day after exclusion from the egg. But it is set at liberty from the navel, nor does any communication remain, but the whole is separated. About the before-mentioned period the young bird sleeps, but it stirs itself, and looks up, and chirps when it is touched, and the heart swells up with the navel, as if the embryo were breathing. This is the manner of the development of the chick in the egg.

8. Birds also produce some barren eggs, as well as those from sexual intercourse, but they produce nothing after incubation. This is particularly observed in pigeons. Double eggs have two yolks; in some a thin division of white prevents the yolks from mixing together; others have not this division, but touch each other. There are some hens which always lay double eggs, and in these the peculiarities of the yolks have been observed; for a certain bird having laid eighteen eggs, hatched two chickens from each of them, except those that were addled; all the rest were productive, except that one of the twin chickens was lrage and the other small in each. The last, however, was monstrous.

Chapter IV.

1. All the pigeon tribe, as the phatta and trygon, generally produce two eggs; the trygon and the phatta are those which generally lay three. The pigeon lays, as I said, at every season; the trygon and the phatta in the spring, and uot more than twice. The second brood are hatched when the first has been destroyed, for many birds destroy them.

It sometimes lays three, as I have said, but it never brings out more than two young ones, and sometimes only one, the remaining egg is always addled. Very few birds begin to lay before they are a year old; but when they have once begun to lay, they all, as we may say, naturally contain eggs to the end of their life, though it is not easy to see them in some birds, from their small size.

2. The pigeon usually produces one male and one female, and of these the male is often hatched first; and having laid an egg one day, she omits many days and then lays another. The male sits during a portion of the day, and the female during the night. The first young one is hatched and able to fly within twenty days, and the egg is billed on the day before it is hatched; both the old birds keep the young ones warm for some time, as they do the eggs. During the time of bringing up their young the female is fiercer than the male: this is also the case in other animals. They produce young ten times in a year, and sometimes eleven times; those in Egypt even twelve times. The cock and hen birds copulate within the year, for they do this at the end of six months.

3. And some say that the phatta and trygon are matured when three months old, and they consider their great numbers as a proof of this. The female contains her eggs fourteen days, and then sits upon them fourteen more; in fourteen days after this the young ones fly so well that it is difficult to catch them. The phatta lives, as they say, forty years; the partridge more than sixteen years. The pigeon, after having brought out her young, lays again in thirty days.

CHAPTER V.

1. THE vulture builds its nest in inaccessible rocks, wherefore its nest and young ones are rarely seen. For this reason Herodorus, the father of Bryson the sophist, says that vultures come from another part of the earth, which is invisible to us, giving as a reason for his opinion, that they are seen in great numbers suddenly following the path of an army. But difficult as it is to observe them, their nests have been seen. The vulture produces two eggs. No other carnivorous bird has been observed to produce young more than once a year; but the swallow more frequently produces young twice a year than the carnivorous birds. If a person

pierces the eyes of young swallows they recover, and are able to see afterwards.

CHAPTER VI.

1. THE eagle produces three eggs, of which two only are hatched. This is also related in the poems of Musæus. The bird which lays three eggs, hatches two, and brings up but one. This frequently happens; but three young have been seen in the nest. When the young begin to grow, one of them is turned out by the parent, because she dislikes the trouble of feeding it. At this period it is said to be without food, so that it does not capture the young of wild creatures, for a few days the talons are turned back, and the feathers become white, so that it then becomes cruel to its young. The phene[1] receives and brings up the ejected young one.

2. The eagle incubates for thirty days; this is the usual period of incubation for large birds, as the goose and the bustard. Moderately sized birds usually sit twenty days, as the ictinus[2] and hierax.[3] The ictinus usually produces two young ones, and sometimes three; the Ætolian kite, as it is called, sometimes produces four. The raven produces not only two, but, as they say, many eggs, which she sits upon for about twenty days. She also turns out some of her young ones. Many other birds do the same thing; and generally those which produce several turn out one.

3. All kinds of eagles do not behave in the same way to their young; but the pygargus is cruel; and the black eagles are careful for the food of their young; but all birds with crooked talons as soon as their young can fly well beat them and drive them from the nest. And most birds of other classes, as I have before observed, do the same thing; and when they have brought them up, they take no more notice of them, except the crow. This bird cares for its young a long while, for as it flies past them it gives them food after they are able to fly.

CHAPTER VII.

1. THE cuckoo is said by some persons to be a changed hawk, because the hawk which it resembles disappears when the

---

[1] Vultur cinereus, ossifragus, osprey.   [2] Kite.   [3] Hawk.

cuckoo comes, and indeed very few hawks of any sort can be seen during the period in which the cuckoo is singing except for a few days. The cuckoo is seen for a short time in the summer, and disappears in winter. But the hawk has crooked talons, which the cuckoo has not, nor does it resemble the hawk in the form of its head, but in both these respects is more like the pigeon than the hawk, which it resembles in nothing but its colour; the markings, however, upon the hawk are like lines, while the cuckoo is spotted.

2. Its size and manner of flight is like that of the smallest kind of hawk, which generally disappears during the season in which the cuckoo is seen. But they have both been seen at the same time, and the cuckoo was being devoured by the hawk, though this is never done by birds of the same kind. They say that no one has ever seen the young of the cuckoo. It does, however, lay eggs, but it makes no nest; but sometimes it lays its eggs in the nests of small birds, and devours their eggs, especially in the nests of the pigeon, when it has eaten their eggs. Sometimes it lays two, but usually only one egg; it lays also in the nest of the hypolais,[1] which hatches and brings it up. At this season it is particularly fat and sweet-fleshed; the flesh also of young hawks is very sweet and fat. There is also a kind of them which builds a nest in precipitous cliffs.

Chapter VIII.

1. In many birds the male alternates with the female in the duty of incubation, as we observed in speaking of pigeons, and takes her place while she is obliged to procure food for herself. In geese the female alone sits upon the eggs, and having once begun, she never leaves them during the whole process of incubation. The nests of all water birds are situated in marshy and grassy places, by which means they can keep quiet and still have food within their reach, so that they do not starve all the while. The females alone, among the crows, sit on the eggs, which they never leave; but the males bring them food and feed them.

2. The females of the pigeons begin to sit at twilight, and remain on the nest the whole night, till dawn; and the male the rest of the time. Partridges make two nests of eggs,

---

[1] Sylvia curucca, hedge sparrow.

upon one of which the male sits, on the other the female; and each of them hatches and brings up its own: and the male has sexual intercourse with its young as soon as they are hatched.

Chapter IX.

1. The peacock lives about twenty-five years, and produces young generally at three years old; by which time also they have obtained their variegated plumage: and it hatches in thirty days, or rather more. It only produces young once a-year, laying twelve eggs, or not quite so many. It lays its eggs at intervals of two or three days, and not regularly. At first they lay only eight. The pea-fowl also lays barren eggs: they copulate in the spring, and lay their eggs immediately afterwards.

2. This bird sheds its feathers when the leaves of the trees begin to fall, and begins to acquire them again with the first budding in the spring. Those who rear these birds place the eggs for incubation beneath domestic fowls; because the peacock flies at, and torments the hen when she is sitting; for which reason some of the wild birds make their escape from the males before they begin to lay and sit. They place only two eggs under domestic fowls, for these are all that they can hatch and bring out; and they take care to put food before them, that they may not get up and desert their incubation.

3. Birds at the season of sexual intercourse have large testicles. In the more lascivious they are always more evident, as the domestic cock and the partridge. In those that are not always lascivious, they are less. This is the manner of the gestation and reproduction of birds.

Chapter X.

1. It has been already observed that fish are not always oviparous, for the selache are always viviparous. All the rest are oviparous. The selache are viviparous, having first of all produced ova internally; and these they bring up in themselves, except the batrachus. Fish have also, as I observed before, very different uteri in different kinds: for in the oviparous genera the uterus is double, and situated low down. In the selache the uterus is more like that of birds. There is this difference, however, that the ova are not placed

near the diaphragm, but in an intermediate position near the spine; and when they have grown they change their place from this part. The ovum in all fish is not of two, but of one colour; and it is more white than yellow, both in its early stages, and after the formation of the embryo.

2. The development of the ovum is different in fish and in birds, in that it has not the umbilical cord which passes to the membrane of the shell; but only the passage which leads to the yolk in the eggs of birds. The rest of the development of the ovum is alike in birds and fish; for it takes place at the extremity, and the veins have their origin in a similar manner in the heart; and the head, and eyes, and upper parts of the body are larger than the rest. As the young fish increases, the ovum continues to diminish, and at last it disappears, and is absorbed, like the yolk in the eggs of birds. The umbilical cord is attached a little below the abdomen. At first the cord is long, but it becomes less as the fish grows, and at last is small, and finally absorbed, like that of birds.

3. The embryo and the ovum are enclosed in a common membrane, and beneath this there is another membrane, in which the embryo alone is enclosed. Between these membranes there is a fluid substance. The nutriment contained in the stomach of the young fish is similar to that in the young birds, partly white, and partly yellow. The form of the uterus must be learned from dissection. This organ is different in different fish, as in the galeode by themselves, and the flat fish by themselves: for in some the ova are attached near the spine to the centre of the uterus, as I observed before, as in scylia.[1] They descend when they begin to increase, when the uterus is double, and are attached to the diaphragm, as in other fish: the ova descend into each division.

4. The uterus of these fish, and of the other galeode, has a small appendage attached to the diaphragm like a white nipple, which is not present unless they are pregnant. The scylia and the batis have a shell-like substance, which contains the fluid of the ovum. In form the shell resembles the tongue of a wind instrument, and hair-like passages are attached to the shells. The young of the scylia, which some persons call nebria galei, are born when the shell falls off and bursts. The young of the batis when they are brought forth

[1] Dog fish. Squalus stellaris.

are excluded by the rupture of the shell. In the acantheas[1] galeos the ova are attached to the diaphragm above the nipples; and when the ovum descends, the young is attached to it after it is set free. The reproduction of the alopex is in the same manner.

5. Most galei which are called smooth have the ova placed between the divisions of the uterus, like those of the scylia; and as they surround it, they descend into each division of the uterus, and they are produced, attached to the uterus by an umbilical cord; so that when the ova are taken out, they appear similar to the embryo of quadrupeds. And the long umbilical cord is attached to the lower part of the uterus, each part, as it were, attached to an acetabulum; and to the middle of the embryo near the liver. And when it is dissected, the food is like an egg, though the ovum be no longer there. There is a chorion, and peculiar membranes surrounding each of the embryos, as in quadrupeds.

6. The head of the embryo when it is just produced, is upwards; but as it grows and reaches maturity, it is placed downwards. The males are placed on the left, and the females on the right, or there are males and females together on the same side. The embryo, when dissected, resembles that of quadrupeds, in having its viscera such as it has, as the liver, large, and full of blood. In all the selache the ova are placed high up, near the diaphragm; many larger, and many smaller: and the embryos are placed below, wherefore it is probable that such fish produce their young, and copulate frequently during the same month, for they do not produce all their young at once, but frequently, and for a long while; but those that are in the lower part of the uterus are matured and brought to perfection.

7. The other galei both emit and receive their young into themselves, and so do the rhine and the narca; and a large narca has been observed to contain eighty young in herself. The acanthias is the only one of the galei which does not admit its young into itself, on account of their thorns. Among the flat fish the trygon and batos do not admit their young, on account of the roughness of the tail. Neither does the batrachus admit its young, on account of the size of their heads, and their thorns; and this is the only one that is not viviparous, as I previously observed. These are

[1] Squalus Acanthias.

their mutual differences, and the manner of the development of their ova.

8. At the season of sexual intercourse, the seminal ducts of the male are full of fluid, so that a white matter escapes when they are pressed. These passages are divided, and originate in the diaphragm and the large vein: at the same season the passages of the male are conspicuous, and may be compared with the uterus of the female. When it is not the season of sexual intercourse, they are less conspicuous, from not being in use. In some fish, and sometimes, they are not visible at all, as it was remarked of the testicles of birds. The seminal and uterine passages are different in other respects also, and because those of the male are attached to the loins, those of the female are easily moved, and enclosed in a thin membrane. The nature of the passages of the male may be seen in works on anatomy.

9. The selachea become pregnant again while with young, and the period of gestation is six months. Among the galei, the asterias produces young the oftenest; for it produces twice in a month: it begins to copulate in the month of September. All the other galei except the scylia produce twice in the year; the scylia but once. Some of them have their young in the spring. The rhine produces its first brood in the spring, and its last in the autumn, near the winter season, and the setting of the Pleiades. The second fry are the most numerous. The narca produces its young in the autumn. The selache descend from the ocean and deep water to the shore, to produce their young, both for the sake of the warmth, and care of their offspring.

10. No other fish but the rhine and the batos have ever been observed to unite with others not of their own kind, but there is a fish called the rhinobatus, which has the head and upper part of the rhine, and the lower part like the batus, as it were made up of both. The galei and the galeoeides, as the alopex, dog-fish, and the flat fish, as the narce batos, leiobatos and trygon, are in this manner ovoviparous.

Chapter XI.

1. The dolphin, whale, and other cetacea which have a blow-hole but no gills, are viviparous, and so are the

pristis and the bos. For none of these have an ovum, but a proper fœtus, from which, when perfected, an animal is developed, as in man and the viviparous quadrupeds. The dolphin usually produces one, and sometimes two young ones. The whale generally and usually produces two and sometimes one. The phocæna is similar to the dolphin, for it is like a small dolphin. It is produced in the Pontus. In some respects the phocæna differs from the dolphin, for its size is smaller, it is wider in the back, and its colour is blue. Many persons say that the phocæna is a kind of dolphin.

2. All these creatures which have a blow-hole, breathe and inhale air; and the dolphin has been observed while asleep with the muzzle above the water, and it snores in its sleep. The dolphin and phocæna give milk and suckle their young. They also receive their young into themselves. The growth of the young dolphins is rapid, for they attain their full size in ten years. The female is pregnant for ten months. The dolphin produces her young in the summer-time, and at no other season. They seem also to disappear for thirty days during the season of the dog-star. The young follow their dam for a long while, and it is an animal much attached to its offspring. It lives many years; for some have been known to live twenty-five or thirty years; for fishermen have marked them by cutting their tails and then giving them their liberty. In this way their age was known.

3. The seal is amphibious, for it does not inhale water, but breathes and sleeps. It produces its young on land, but near the shore, in the manner of animals with feet; but it lives the greater part of its time, and obtains its food in the sea, wherefore it is to be considered among aquatic animals. It is properly viviparous, and produces a living creature, and a chorion, and it brings forth the other membranes like a sheep. It produces one or two, never more than three young ones. It has also mammæ, so that it suckles its young like quadrupeds. It produces its young like the human subject, at all seasons of the year, but especially with the earliest goats.

4. When the young are twelve days old, it leads them to the water several times in the day, in order to habituate

them by degrees. It drags its hinder parts along, and does not walk, for it cannot erect itself upon its feet, but it contracts and draws itself together. It is fleshy and soft, and its bones are cartilaginous. It is difficult to kill the seal by violence, unless it is struck upon the temple, for its body is fleshy. It has a voice like an ox. The pudendum of the female is like that of the batis, in all other animals of the class the pudendum resembles that of the human female. This is the manner of the development and nature of the young of aquatic animals which are either internally or externally viviparous.

Chapter XII.

1. The oviparous fish have a divided uterus placed on the lower part of the body, as I observed before. All that have scales are viviparous, as the labrax, cestreus, cephalus, etelis,[1] and those called white fish, and all smooth fish except the eel. Their ova resemble sand. This appearance is owing to their uterus being quite full of ova, so that small fish appear to have only two ova; for the small size and thinness of the uterus renders it invisible in these creatures. I have before treated of the sexual intercourse of fish. The sexes are distinct in almost all fish, though there is some doubt about the erythrinus[2] and the channa, for all these are found to be pregnant.

2. Ova are found in those fish which have sexual intercourse, though they possess them without intercourse. This is observable in some kinds of river fish; for the phoxini[3] appear to be pregnant as soon as they are born, and when they are quite small. They emit the ova in a stream; and, as I observed before, the males devour great numbers of them, and others perish in the water. Those are preserved which they deposit in their appropriate situations. For, if all were preserved, the numbers that would be found would be immense. Not all those that are preserved are fertile, but only those on which the seminal fluid of the male has been sprinkled. When the female produces her ova, the male follows, and scatters his semen upon them. Young fish are produced from those ova which are thus sprinkled. The remainder turn out as chance may direct.

[1] Perhaps the Sea-bream, Sparus. [2] Perhaps Perca marina.
[3] Cyprinus Phoxinus.

3. The same thing also occurs in the malacia; for the male sepia sprinkles the ova of the female as they are deposited; and it is reasonable to suppose that the other malacia do the same, although it has only been observed in the sepia. They produce their ova near the land, the cobii deposit them upon stones, and that which they produce is flat and sand-like. The rest do the same, for the parts near the land are warmer, and provision is more abundant, and there is better protection for their young against larger fish, for which cause very great numbers deposit their ova near the river Thermodon, in the Pontus, for the place is sheltered and warm, and the water is sweet.

4. The majority of viviparous fish reproduce once in a-year, except the small phycides,[1] which reproduce twice a-year. The male phyces differs from the female, being darker-coloured and having larger scales. All other fish produce from seed, and emit ova; but that which is called the belone, at the season of reproduction bursts asunder, and in this way the ova escape; for this fish has a division beneath the stomach and bowels, like the serpents called typhlinæ.[2] When it has produced its ova, it survives, and the wound heals up again.

5. The development of the ovum is alike, both in those that are internally and those that are externally oviparous. For it takes place at the extremity of the ovum, and it is enclosed in a membrane. The eyes are the first part that is conspicuous; they are large and spherical; so that it is plain that they are mistaken who say that the mode of development resembles that of vermiform creatures, for in them the order is different, and the lower parts are formed first, and afterwards the head and eyes. When the ovum is taken away, they assume a circular form, and for some time continue to grow without taking in any food, by absorbing the moisture of the ovum. They afterwards derive their nutriment, as long as they continue growing, from the water of the river.

6. When the Pontus is cleansed, something is floated out into the Hellespont which is called fucus. It is of a yellow colour. Some say that it is naturally a plant. This takes place at the beginning of summer. The oysters and small fish which live in these places feed upon this fucus;

---

[1] Mugil. Some species of mullet. [2] Lacerta apus.

and some maritime persons say that they obtain their purple from this plant.

Chapter XIII.

1. The pond and river fish begin to reproduce usually when five months old. They all produce their ova at the beginning of summer. Like the marine fish, the females of these kinds never emit all their ova, nor the males all their semen, at once; but both sexes are always found to contain a portion of the reproductive substance; they produce their ova at the proper season. The cyprinus five or six times a-year, and especially under the influence of the stars. The chalcis reproduces three times, all the rest but once a-year.

2. They deposit their ova in the stagnant parts of rivers and ponds among the reeds, as the phoxinus and perca. The glanis and the perca produce their ova in strings, like the frog. That which the perca produces is so involved that, on account of its breadth, the fishermen collect it together from among the reeds in ponds. The larger individuals of the glanis produce their ova in deep water, some where it is a fathom deep; but the smaller ones in shallow water, and especially at the root of the willow or some other tree, and among the reeds and mosses.

3. The fish fold themselves together, sometimes a large one with a small one, and approximate the passages, which some call their navel, from which they eject their respective seminal matter, the females their ova, and the males their spermatic fluid. Those ova with which the semen of the male has been mixed immediately or in the course of a day become whiter and larger, and in a short time the eyes of the fish make their appearance; for in all fish, as in other animals, this part is most conspicuous, and appears the largest. But, if the seminal fluid does not touch any of the ova, as in the case of sea-fish, these become useless and barren.

4. From the fertile ova, as the fish increase in size, something like a shell is separated; this is the membrane which envelopes the ovum and the embryo fish. As soon as the seminal fluid is mixed with the ova a glutinous matter is formed, which fastens them to the roots or other substance on which they are deposited. The male watches over the place where the greatest number of ova are deposited, and

the female departs as soon as she has spawned. The development of the ovum of the glanis proceeds the most slowly, for the male remains by them for forty or fifty days, in order that they may not be devoured by fish chancing to come that way.

5. Next to this is the cyprinus. The ova, however, of these which are preserved escape very quickly. The development in some of the small fish takes place on the third day, and the ova upon which the seminal fluid has fallen begin to increase on the same day, or shortly afterwards. The ova of the glanis become as large as the seed of the orobus. Those of the cyprinus and that class, about the size of millet. The ova of these fish are produced and developed in this manner.

6. The chalcis assembles in great numbers to deposit its ova in deep water. The fish which is called tilon deposits its ova near the shore, in sheltered places; this fish also is gregarious. The cyprinus, balerus, and all others, so to say, hasten into shallow water to deposit their ova, and thirteen or fourteen males often follow a single female, and when the female has deposited her ova and departed, the males that follow her sprinkle their semen upon them. The majority of the ova are lost, for the female scatters them abroad as she is moving forward, unless they fall upon any substance, and are not carried away by the stream. None of them, except the glanis, watch their ova, unless the cyprinus meets with them in great numbers, when, they say, that this fish watches them.

7. All the male fish have semen, except the eel, and this one has neither semen nor ova. The cestreus migrates from the sea into lakes and rivers; the eel, on the contrary, leaves them for the sea. Most fish, therefore, as I observed, proceed from ova.

Chapter XIV.

1. Some originate in mud and sand: even of those kinds which originate in sexual intercourse and ova, some, they say, have appeared both in other marshy places and in those which once surrounded Cnidus, which became dry under the influence of the dog-star, and all the mud was parched up, but with the first rains the waters returned, and small fish appeared with

the return of the waters. This was a kind of cestreus, which originates in coition, about the size of small mænidia,[1] but they had neither ova nor semen. In the Asiatic rivers, which do not flow into the sea, other small fish, of the size of epseti,[2] are produced in the same manner. Some persons say that the cestreus is always produced in this manner, but in this they are mistaken, for both the females are known to have ova and the males semen. But there is some one kind of them which originates in mud and sand.

2. It is evident from the following considerations that some of them are of spontaneous growth, and do not originate either in ova or semen. Those which are neither oviparous nor viviparous are all produced either from mud or sand, or from the putrid matter on the surface, as also the foam in sandy places produces the aphya.[3] This aphya never increases in size, and is barren, and as time advances it perishes, and another fry is formed. Wherefore it may be said to be reproduced at every season, except for a short time; for it continues from the autumn arcturus to the spring. This is a proof that it sometimes originates in the soil, for it is not captured by fishermen in cold weather, but on a fine day it may be taken as it comes up from the ground for the sake of the warmth. When they have dragged the ground and scraped up the surface, the fish are more numerous and better. The other aphyæ are inferior, on account of their rapid growth.

3. They are found in shady and marshy places, when the earth becomes warm in fine weather, as near the temple of Athene in Salamis, and near the tomb of Themistocles, and near Marathon, for foam is formed in all these places. It makes its appearance in such places, and in fine weather: it appears also at times in seasons of much rain, and when foam is formed of rain water, wherefore also it is called aphrus; and sometimes it is found on the surface of the sea, in fine weather, where it is whirled about, and, like the little maggots in dung, so this is found in the foam which floats on the surface; wherefore also this aphya is carried by the sea in many directions, and it abounds and is captured in the greatest abundance when the season is moist and warm.

4. There is another aphya derived from fish, for that which is called cobitis is derived from small and inferior

[1] Sardine. [2] Atherine epsetos. [3] Melanurus juvenculus.

gobii, which bury themselves in the earth. The membrades are produced from the phalerica. The trichides come from these, and the trichiæ from the trichides; from one kind of aphya, which inhabits the port of Athens, the encrasicoli are derived. There is another kind of aphya which originates in the mœnis and cestreus, but the barren aphrus is very soft, and endures only for a short time, as I said before, and at last nothing is left but the head and eyes. The fishermen, however, have now found a mode of conveying it from place to place, for it lasts longer when salted.

Chapter XV.

1. Eels are not produced from sexual intercourse, nor are they oviparous, nor have they ever been detected with semen or ova, nor when dissected do they appear to possess either seminal or uterine viscera; and this is the only kind of sanguineous animal which does not originate either in sexual intercourse or in ova. It is, however, manifest that this is the case, for, after rain, they have been reproduced in some marshy ponds, from which all the water was drawn and the mud cleaned out; but they are never produced in dry places nor in ponds that are always full, for they live upon and are nourished by rain water. It is plain, therefore, that they are not produced either from sexual intercourse or from ova. Some persons have thought that they were productive, because some eels have parasitical worms, and they thought that these became eels.

2. This, however, is not the case, but they originate in what are called the entrails of the earth, which are found spontaneously in mud and moist earth. They have been observed making their escape from them, and others have been found in them when cut up and dissected. These originate both in the sea and in rivers wherein putrid matter is abundant; in those places in the sea which are full of fuci, and near the banks of rivers and ponds, for in these places the heat causes much putridity. This is the mode of generation in eels.

Chapter XVI.

1. The reproductive function is not active in all fish at the same time or the same manner, nor are they pregnant during the same length of time. Before the season of sexual inter-

course the males and females begin to assemble, and at the period of intercourse and the production of their ova they pair together. Some of them do not remain pregnant more than thirty days, and others not so long; but all of them remain so for a number of days, which can be distributed into seven. Those which some persons call marini remain pregnant for the longest period. The sargus becomes pregnant in the month of December, and remains so for thirty days. The kind of cestreus which some persons call the chelon and the myxon are pregnant at the same time as the sargus. All these suffer in their pregnancy, wherefore they are driven to the shore at this season; for in the vehemence of their desire they are carried towards the land, and always continue in motion during this period till they have produced their ova. The cestreus is more remarkable for this than any other fish. As soon as they have deposited their ova, they become quiet.

2. In many fish there is a limit to their reproductive powers, when worms make their appearance in their abdomen. These worms are small living creatures, which expel the reproductive substance. The small fry of the rhyas makes its appearance in the spring, and that of many others about the vernal equinox. Other fish do not produce at this season of the year, but in the summer or near the autumnal equinox.

3. The atherina produces its young first of all, near the land. The cephalus is the last. This is evident from the small fry of the former appearing first, and that of the latter last of all. The cestreus also produces among the first. The salpa in most places deposits its ova during the summer, and sometimes in the autumn. The aulopias, which they call anthias, produces its ova in the summer season. After these the chrysophrys, labrax, mormyrus, and all those which are called dromades; the trigla and cocarinus are the latest of all the gregarious fish. These oviposit in the autumn. The trigla deposits her ova in the mud, which causes her to be late, for the mud continues cold for a long while. The coracimus is next to the trigla, and goes among the sea weed to deposit her ova: consequently they frequent rocky places. It continues pregnant for a long while. The mænides oviposit at the winter solstice. Many other marine fish oviposit in the summer, for they are not captured at this period. The mænis is the most productive of all fish, and

the batrachus the most so among the selache. They are, however, rare, for they perish very readily; they oviposit in shoals and near the land.

4. The selache, as being viviparous, are less productive. These are particularly preserved by their large size. The belone is late in producing its young, and many of them are burst by their ova in the act of parturition; for these ova are not so numerous as they are large. They surround the parent as if they were phalangia; for she produces them attached to herself, and if any one touches them they make their escape. The atherina deposits her ova by rubbing her abdomen against the sand. The thynni burst with fat. They live two years. The fishermen argue thus: when the thynnides fail one year, the thynni fail the year after. They appear to be a year older than the pelamus.

5. The thynni and scombri copulate at the end of February, and produce their young at the beginning of June. They produce their ova, as it were, in a purse. The growth of the thynnides is rapid; for when these fish produce their young in the Pontus, they produce from the ovum creatures which some persons call scordylæ, and the Byzantines call auxidæ, because they grow in a few days. They go out in the autumn with the thynnus, and return in the spring as pelamides. Nearly all other fish grow rapidly, but those in the Pontus more rapidly than in other places; for the amiæ there increase visibly every day. It is necessary to remember that the same fish have not in the same place the identical time of coition and gestation, nor the same period of reproduction and completion of their offspring. For those which are called coracini produce their ova at the time of wheat harvest, though, generally speaking, the order of their reproduction is that which I have mentioned.

6. The conger also becomes pregnant, though this circumstance is not equally distinct everywhere on account of its fat; for the organ of reproduction is long, like that of serpents. It becomes distinct, however, when laid upon the fire; for the fat smokes and consumes away, and the ova, when pressed, jump out with a cracking noise. If any person will feel and rub them with the finger, the fat will appear smooth and the ova rough to the touch. Some congers have fat but no ova; and others, on the contrary, have

no fat but such ova as I have described. We have now treated of nearly all the oviparous animals, whether furnished with fins, or wings, or feet, and of their sexual intercourse, gestation, development, and such like subjects.

Chapter XVII.

1. WE must now treat of the nature of viviparous animals with feet and of man at this period. We have already treated in general and in particular of their mode of coition. It is common to all animals to be elevated with the desire and pleasure of sexual intercourse. The females become savage when their young are produced, the males at the season of coition; for horses bite each other and drive about and pursue their riders. The wild boars are very savage at this season, although coition renders them weak.

2. And they fight wonderfully among themselves, and make themselves as it were breastplates, and render their skin callous beforehand by rubbing themselves against trees and frequently wallowing in the mud and drying themselves. They fight together and drive each other out of the herd so fiercely, that not rarely both of them perish in the fight. The same is the nature of bulls, rams, and goats; for although at other seasons they pasture together, at the period of copulation they quarrel and fight together. The male camel also is violent at this time, whether it is a man or a camel that approaches him, and he will at all times fight with a horse.

3. The nature of wild animals is the same. For bears, wolves, and lions are savage if they are approached at this season; but they do not quarrel much among themselves, for none of them are gregarious. The she bears are savage in defence of their cubs, and bitches for their puppies. Elephants also become wild at this period. Wherefore they say that in India those who have the care of them do not permit them to have sexual intercourse with the females; for they become mad at such season and overturn the houses, which are badly built, and do many other violent acts. They say also that abundance of food will render them more gentle. They also bring others among them which are directed to beat them, and so they punish them and reduce them to a state of discipline.

4. Those creatures which have frequent sexual intercourse,

like domestic animals, as the hog and dog, appear to be less influenced by these circumstances on account of the frequency of their coition. Of all females the mare is the most violent in her sexual desires, and then the cow. Mares are subject to the affection called hippomania, and this name is transferred from this single animal to intemperate and lascivious persons. They are said to be affected by the wind at such seasons: wherefore in Crete they never separate the stallions from the mares. When the mares are thus affected, they separate themselves from the other horses. In swine the same affection is called καπρίζειν, to desire the boar. They never run to the east or the west, but either north or south.

5. When they suffer from this affection, they will allow no one to approach them, till they either are so fatigued that they can go no further, or come to the sea: they then eject some substance, which has received the name of hippomanes, like that on a new-born colt. It resembles the capria of the sow. Poisoners diligently seek for this substance. At the season of sexual intercourse they lean upon each other more than at other times, and move their tails, and utter a different sound from that which is common to them. A fluid like semen also flows from their genital organs, but it is much more thin than that of the male; and some persons call this fluid hippomanes, though it is not that which is produced upon colts. It is difficult to collect this fluid, for it does not appear in large quantities. When they are desirous of sexual intercourse, they often make water, and sport together: this is the nature of horses.

6. Cows desire the bull. They are so taken up by their passion, that the cowherds cannot manage them. Mares and cows shew the vehemence of their desire by the swelling of their genital parts. Cows also, like mares, make water very frequently. The cows also mount upon the bull, and follow, and stand beside him. The younger animals, both among horses and oxen, are the first to desire sexual intercourse; and in fine weather, when their health is good, the vehemence of their desire is still stronger. If the manes of the mares are cut, their desires become weaker, and they are rendered more gentle.

7. The stallions recognise the mares of their own herds by the scent; and if any strangers become mixed with them a few days before the period of coition, they bite them till they go away, and each stallion feeds apart with his own mares. Thirty mares, or rather less, are given to each; and if any male approaches, he turns and goes round the mares in a circle, and then prepares to fight. If any one of the females attempts to move, he bites and prevents her.

8. At the season of sexual intercourse the bull pastures with the cows, and fights with other bulls: at other times the sexes keep themselves separate: this is called ἀτιμαγελεῖν (despising the herd); those in Epirus are often not seen for three months: and generally all, or nearly all, wild animals, do not herd with their females before the season of sexual intercourse: but as soon as they come to puberty the males separate themselves, and cease to feed with the females. Sows, when they are urged by sexual desire, or, as it is called, desire the boar (καπρᾶν), will even attack men. In bitches this affection is called σκυζᾶν, to desire the dog.

9. When females are urged with desire, their genital organs are swollen with heat, and a fluid secretion takes place. Mares scatter about a white fluid at this season. In no creatures are the catamenia so abundant as in women. In sheep and goats at the season of coition, there are certain signs before copulation: there are also signs after copulation, but these again cease till the period of parturition, when they again occur. By this means shepherds understand that they are about to produce their young. After parturition there is a great purification, which at first is not very full of blood, but becomes so afterwards.

10. In the cow, the ass, and mare, this purification is abundant, on account of their great size; but still it is small, considering how large they are. When the cow is urged by desire, she undergoes a brief purification, about half-a-cup full, or a little more. The time of this purification is peculiarly the period for sexual intercouse. Of all quadrupeds the mare suffers the least, and is the most cleanly in parturition: neither is her loss of blood great considering the size of the animal. In cows and mares, the failure of the catamenia in the second, fourth, and sixth month is con-

sidered as a sign of pregnancy; but it is not easy for anyone to understand this, who does not follow and accustom himself to them: and some persons are of opinion that they have no catamenia. The female oreus has no catamenia, but her urine is thicker than that of the male.

11. On the whole, the liquid excrements are thicker in other animals than in man; and those of female sheep and goats thicker than in the males of the same animal. That of the she ass is thinner, of the cow is harsher, than of their respective males. After parturition the urine of all creatures becomes thicker, and especially in those which have no purification. When females begin to feel sexual desires, their milk is like pus; it afterwards becomes useful after parturition. Sheep and goats become fat when they are pregnant, and consume more food; and so do cows, and all other quadrupeds.

CHAPTER XVIII.

1. GENERALLY speaking, the sexual desires of animals are more violent in spring. They do not all, however, copulate at the same seasons, but at the time of year which will cause them to produce their young at the proper season. The period of gestation in domestic swine is four months. They never produce more than twenty pigs; and if they have many, they cannot bring them all up. When aged, they produce in the same manner, but they copulate more slowly. They become pregnant with one act of coition; but they submit themselves to the boar very frequently, on account of their rejection of the capria after they are pregnant. This takes place in all, but some will also eject the semen.

2. If any of the pigs are injured or deteriorated during pregnancy, it is called metachæron. This may take place in any part of the uterus. In parturition the sow gives the first teat to the first pig. It is not necessary that she should go to the boar as soon as the sexual appetite is felt, or before her ears begin to hang down; for otherwise she desires to go again. If she goes to the boar when she is desirous of it, the impregnation is complete in a single act of intercourse. Barley is a proper food for the boar at the period of coition. It should be cooked for the female after parturition. Some

sows produce excellent pigs from the first; others do not produce good offspring and pigs till they are grown up. Some persons say that if one of the eyes of a sow is put out, she generally speaking dies very soon. Most of them live fifteen. Some die in less than twenty years.

Chapter XIX.

1. SHEEP become pregnant after three or four acts of sexual intercourse. If rain falls after the act of intercourse, it must be repeated. The nature of goats is the same. They generally produce two, and sometimes three. Cases have occurred of their producing four. The period of gestation in the sheep and goat is five months; and in some places, where the weather is warm and fine, and food is abundant, they have young twice a-year. The goat will live eight years. The sheep lives ten years, or generally rather less; but the leaders of the flock live fifteen years; for in every flock they select one of the males as a leader, who, when called by the shepherd, places himself at the head of the flock. They are accustomed to this duty even when young. In Ethiopia the sheep live twelve or thirteen years, and the goats ten or eleven.

2. Both the sheep and goat enjoy sexual intercourse as long as they live. Sheep and goats produce twins, if either the pasture is good, or the ram or he-goat, or the ewe belongs to a race producing twins. They produce females or males both from the nature of the water (for there are some waters that cause them to produce males and others females) and from their manner of sexual intercourse; and if the wind is northward during copulation they produce males; and if it is southward, females; and one which naturally produces females will change its nature and produce males; so that it is necessary to see that they stand to the north during the act of sexual intercourse. If any are accustomed to copulate early, and the ram is introduced to them late, they will not endure it.

3. The lambs are white or black according as the veins beneath the tongue of the ram are white or black; for the lambs are white if the veins are white, and black if they are black. If they are both black and white, the lambs also are of two colours; and if red, then the lambs are red. They

are more ready for sexual intercourse if they drink salt water; so that they should be supplied with salted water both before and after parturition, and again in the spring. The herdsmen do not constitute any leader among the flocks of goats, because it is not their nature to be stationary, but they are active and ready to move from place to place. If the older sheep prepare for sexual intercourse at the proper time, the shepherds consider it a sign of a good year for the sheep; if the younger ones are ready first, it will be a bad sheep year.

Chapter XX.

1. THERE are many kinds of dogs. The Lacedemonian dogs, both male and female, begin to have sexual intercourse at eight months old. Some also lift their leg to make water about this period. The bitch becomes pregnant with a single act of coition; this is particularly evident in those which perform the act in secret, for they become pregnant when once united. The period of gestation in the Lacedemonian bitch is the sixth part of a year, that is sixty days, or it may be one, two, or three days more or less. The puppies when they are born are blind for twelve days. The bitch is ready for sexual intercourse six months after she has produced her young, and not sooner. In some the period of gestation is the fifth part of a year, this is seventy-two days. The puppies of such bitches are blind for fourteen days. Others are pregnant the fourth part of a year, that is three whole months; their puppies are blind seventeen days. The female appears to desire the male for the same length of time.

2. The catamenia in bitches last for seven days, and at the same time the genital organs are swollen with heat; during this period they will not endure coition, but during the seven days which follow, for they all appear usually to desire the male for fourteen days. This affection continues in some for sixteen days. The purification from parturition takes place at the birth of the young ones; it is thick and phlegmatic, and the quantity produced in parturition is small in proportion to the size of the body.[1] Bitches generally have milk five days before parturition; in

---

[1] (Or perhaps) after parturition the discharge becomes thinner in consistence.

some cases it appears seven, and in others four days beforehand; the milk is good as soon as the young are born. The Lacedemonian bitch gives milk in thirty days after sexual intercourse; at first it is thick, but becomes thinner afterwards. The milk of the bitch is thicker than that of other animals, except the sow and the hare.

3. There is evidence of their having reached the age of puberty, for as in the human subject the mammæ begin to enlarge and become cartilaginous; it is, however, difficult to detect this without practice, for the enlargement is not very great. This takes place in the female, nothing of the kind occurs in the male. The males generally begin to lift up their leg to make water when they are six months old. Some do not do so till they are eight months old, and others before they are six months old, for, to speak plainly, they do this as soon as they reach puberty; all the females sit down to make water; some, however, even of these lift up their leg for this purpose. The female never produces more than twelve puppies, generally five or six, and sometimes only one; those of Lacedæmon generally have eight; both sexes continue to enjoy sexual intercourse as long as they live.

4. It is a peculiarity of the Lacedemonian dog, that it is more ready for sexual intercourse after hard work than when idle; the male of this kind lives ten years, the female for twelve, most other dogs live fourteen or fifteen years, some even twenty, for which reason some persons think that Homer is right when he makes the dog of Ulysses to have died at the age of twenty. On account of the hard work which the Lacedemonian dogs have to endure the female lives longer than the male; in other races this is not so plainly observed, but the male is usually longer lived than the female. The dog does not shed any teeth except those called the canine teeth, these are shed by both sexes at four months old. Because they shed these only, a question is raised, for some persons altogether deny that they shed only two teeth, for it is difficult to meet with these, and others, when they see that they shed these, think that they must shed all their teeth. People judge of the age of a dog by its teeth, for in young dogs they are white and sharp, in old ones they are black and blunted.

Chapter XXI.

1. The cow is impregnated with a single act of coition, and the bull mounts upon her with such violence that she bends beneath his weight. If he fails to impregnate her after twenty days, she is again admitted to the bull. Old bulls will not mount the same cow several times in the same day unless there is some intermission, but young bulls, incited by the strength of their desires, will force the same cow several times, and will mount upon many in succession. The bull is one of the least lascivious of animals. The conqueror copulates with the female, but if he become impotent from frequent sexual intercourse, the inferior will attack him, and often prevail.

2. Both the male and the female commence sexual intercourse, so as to produce young, at a year old, though not generally till they are a year and eight months old, or two years old according to general agreement. The female is pregnant nine months, and produces her young in the tenth month; some persons affirm that parturition takes place at ten months to a day; if any of them calve before the above mentioned time, the calf is abortive and does not live, and even if born a little before the proper time it cannot live, for the hoofs are imperfect. The female generally produces one at a time, sometimes two. She continues to bear and to have sexual intercourse as long as she lives.

3. The female usually lives fifteen years, and so does the male if he is not castrated; some live for more than twenty years if they have an active body. They usually place castrated oxen as leaders of the herd, as they do in sheep, and these live longer than the others, for they do no work, and feed in a superior pasture. They attain perfection at five years old, wherefore some say that Homer was right when he spoke of the male flourishing at five years old, and the cow at nine years old, for both expressions have the same meaning.

4. Oxen change their teeth at two years old, not all of them, however, but only like the horse; they do not cast their hoofs when they are lame, but only swell very much about the feet. The milk is good immediately after calving, but the cow has no milk beforehand. The milk which is first formed

becomes hard like a stone when it is coagulated; this takes place if it is not mixed with water. They do not produce young before they are a year old, except in some remarkable cases, for some have been known to copulate at four months old. Most of them desire sexual intercourse in the months of April and May. Some, however, are not impregnated before the autumn. When many become pregnant and admit the male, it is a sign of cold and rainy weather. The usual discharges occur in cows as they do in mares, but the quantity is less.

Chapter XXII.

1. Both the horse and mare begin to use sexual intercourse at two years old. Such early cases, however, are rare, and their offspring small and weak; and generally they commence at three years old, and they continue to produce better colts till they are twenty years old. The period of gestation is eleven months; parturition takes place in the twelfth. The male does not impregnate the female in any particular number of days; but at times in one, two, or three, sometimes in more. The ass mounts and impregnates more quickly than the horse; and the act of intercourse is not laborious in horses as it is in oxen. Next to the human subject, the horse in both sexes is the most lascivious of all animals. The sexual intercourse of the younger horses takes place before the usual age according to the goodness and abundance of their food. The horse generally produces but one colt, or sometimes two at the outside. The hemionus has also been known to produce two, but this is considered extraordinary. The horse begins sexual intercourse at thirty months old, so that it can produce proper colts when it has done changing its teeth. Some have been known, they say, to impregnate mares while changing their teeth, unless they were naturally barren.

2. The horse has forty teeth. It sheds its four first teeth at thirty months old, two above and two below. A year afterwards, it sheds four more in the same manner, two above and two below. And again, at the end of the next year, it sheds four more in the same manner. When it is four years and a half old, it sheds no more; and individuals have been known to shed them all at first, and others that

have shed them all in the last year. These circumstances are rare, so that it usually happens that the horse is most fit for sexual intercourse at four years and a half old. The older horses are more full of semen, both the males and the females, than younger ones. Horses will copulate both with their dams and with their offspring; and it is thought to be a sign that the herd is complete, when they copulate with their offspring. The Scythians ride upon their pregnant mares when the embryo begins to turn in the uterus, and say that it renders parturition more easy. All other quadrupeds lie down in the act of parturition; wherefore their young are always produced lying on their side; but when the mare feels that the time for parturition is approaching, she stands upright to part with her colt.

3. Horses generally live eighteen or twenty years; some live twenty-five or thirty years; but if they are carefully treated, their life may be extended to fifty years. Thirty years, however, is a very long life for the male, and twenty-five for the female. Some have been known to live forty years. Males live a shorter time than females, on account of the act of sexual intercourse; and those that are brought up separately longer than those which live in herds. Females attain their proper length and height in five years; the males in six. In six more years the fulness of body is acquired, which continues till they are twenty years old. The females attain perfection more rapidly than the males; but in the uterus the males are the more rapidly developed. This is also the case in the human subject. This also takes place in those animals which produce several at a birth.

4. They say that the mule sucks for six months, but the mare will not permit it to come afterwards, because it drags and hurts her. The horse sucks for a longer time. The horse and the mule attain perfection after casting their teeth; and when they have cast them all, it is not easy to know their age. Wherefore they say that, before casting its teeth, the horse has its mark, which it has not afterwards. After the teeth have been changed, the age is usually ascertained by the canine tooth; for that in riding horses is generally worn down, for the bridle rubs against it. In horses which have not been ridden, it is large and not worn. In young horses it is small and sharp.

5. The male copulates at all seasons, and as long as he lives; the female also as long as she lives; and at all seasons, unless they have on a fastening or some other hindrance, no peculiar time is appropriated for copulation in either sex, for there is no period of coition when they cannot also bring up their young. In Opus there was a horse in a herd which engendered when he was forty years old; but it was necessary to lift up his fore legs for him. Mares begin to desire sexual intercourse in the spring; and when the mare has foaled, she does not become pregnant again immediately, but waits for a time, and produces better foals at the end of four or five years. It is quite necessary that she should wait one year, and should pass through a fallow, as it were.

6. The horse, then, bears young at intervals, as I have observed; but the ass is not subject to intervals. Some mares are quite barren, and others, though they conceive, yet do not produce their young; and they give as a reason for this, that upon dissection the fœtus was found to contain other reniform bodies round the kidneys, so that it appeared to have four kidneys. As soon as the mare has foaled, she eats the chorion, and bites from the head of her foal the substance called hippomanes. In size this substance is somewhat less than a dry fig. Its form is flat and round, and its colour black. If any person is at hand to take it before the mare, and she smells it, the scent renders her wild and mad. For this reason it is sought after and collected by poisoners. If an ass copulates with a pregnant mare, the pre-existing fœtus is destroyed. Those who keep herds of horses do not place a leader over them, as they do over oxen, for they are not naturally stationary, but active and wandering.

Chapter XXIII.

1. The male and female ass begin to copulate at thirty months old, and shed their first teeth at the same period. They lose their second pair of teeth six months afterwards, and their third and fourth in the same way. These fourth teeth are called the marking teeth. Sometimes the ass has become pregnant and brought up its young at a year old. The she ass parts with the semen after coition, if she is not prevented; and therefore, immediately after coition, they

beat her and drive her about. She foals in the twelfth month, and generally produces one foal, for this is their nature, though cases of twin births have occurred. If an ass mounts upon a mare, he destroys her fœtus, as I observed before. But the horse does not destroy the fœtus of the ass, if the mare has been impregnated by a he ass.

2. The pregnant female has milk at the end of ten months. After parturition, she will admit the male on the seventh day, and is very easily impregnated at that period. She will also receive it afterwards. If she does not produce young before losing her marking teeth, she can never be impregnated all the rest of her life. She does not like men to be witnesses of her parturition, nor will she produce her young in the day time; but when it is dark she retires, and so produces her young. She continues to procreate during her whole life, if she has begun before losing her marking teeth. The ass lives more than thirty years, and the female longer than the male. When a horse copulates with an ass, or a he ass with a mare, abortion is more frequent than between congeners, a horse with a mare, or two asses together. When the horse and ass are mixed together, the period of gestation follows from the male parent. I mean to say that it takes the same time as if the parents had been congeners; but in size, form, and strength the produce of their union generally resembles the female parent.

3. If the union takes place frequently, and sufficient time is not allowed to intervene, the female soon becomes barren. For which reason those who attend to this business do not permit them to have continual intercourse, but interpose a proper interval. The mare will not admit the he ass, nor the she ass the horse, unless the he ass has been suckled by a mare. They are careful, therefore, to admit only those asses which they call hippothelæ, *i.e.* asses which have been suckled by a mare. These copulate by force in the pastures, like horses.

Chapter XXIV.

1. The oreus (mule) mounts and copulates after shedding the first teeth, and when seven years old is able to engender; and the ginnus is produced when he mounts upon a mare. After this he no longer continues to copulate. The female

oreus also has been impregnated, but the fœtus has never been known to come to maturity. The hemioni (female mules) of Syria, near Phœnicia, admit the male and procreate. The kind, however, though similar, is not the same. Those which are called ginni are produced from a mare, when the fœtus has received some injury in the uterus, like dwarfs among men and metachœra among swine; and the ginnus, like the dwarf, has a large genital organ.

2. The hemionus has a long life; for they have been known to live for eighty years, as in Athens, when they built the temple, this individual, though failing with age, helped in drawing, and went beside them, and encouraged the yoke mules to their work, so that an edict was made, commanding the corn-dealers not to drive it away from the vessels filled with corn. The female mule (oreus) grows old sooner than the male. Some persons say that she is purified when making water, but the male ages more rapidly from smelling the urine.

3. This is the manner of the reproduction of these animals. Those who are employed in bringing up these animals recognize the young from the old in this way. If the skin, when drawn back from the cheek, soon recovers its shape, the animal is young; if the skin continues wrinkled for a long while, the creature is aged.

Chapter XXV.

1. The camel is pregnant ten months, and always produces a single young one, for this is its nature. They separate the young camel from the herd at a year old. The camel will live more than fifty years. The season of parturition is in the spring, and the female continues to give milk until she conceives again. Their flesh and milk are exceedingly sweet. The milk is drunk mixed with two or three times its quantity of water.

2. Elephants begin to copulate at twenty years old. When the female is impregnated, her period of gestation, some persons say, is a year and a half; other people make it three years. The difficulty of seeing their copulation causes this difference of opinion respecting the period of gestation. The female produces her young bending upon her haunches. Her pain is evident. The calf, when it is born, sucks with

its mouth, and not with its proboscis. It can walk and see as soon as it is born.

3. Wild swine copulate at the beginning of winter. They produce their young in the spring. For this purpose the female gets away into inaccessible and precipitous places, where there are caves and plenty of shade. The males remain with the females for thirty days. The number of pigs and the period of gestation are the same as in the domesticated herd, and their voices are much alike: the female, however, grunts more and the male less. The castration of the male makes them larger and more fierce, as Homer writes. "He brought up a castrated wild boar, which was not like a beast fed upon food, but resembled a woody mountain peak." Castration takes place from a disease like a swelling in the testicles, which they rub against the trees and so destroy them.

Chapter XXVI.

1. The female deer usually copulates, as I observed before, from allurement; for she cannot endure the male on account of the hardness of the penis. Some, however, endure copulation as sheep do. When sexual desire is felt, they lie down beside each other. The male is changeable in his disposition, and does not unite himself to a single female, but in a short time leaves one for another. The season for sexual intercourse is in August and September, after Arcturus. The period of gestation is eight months. The female becomes pregnant in a few days, and frequently in one day.

2. She generally produces one fawn, though some have been known to bear twins. She produces her young by the road side, for fear of wild beasts. The growth of the fawns is rapid. The female has no purification at other times, but after parturition her cleansing is sanguineous. The female usually conducts her fawn to some accustomed place, which serves them for a refuge. It is usually an opening in a rock, with but one entrance, where they can defend themselves against those who would attack them.

3. There are fables about their long life. They do not, however, appear to be worthy of credit; and the period of gestation and growth of the young does not agree with the habits of long-lived animals. In the mountain called Ela-

phoïs, in Arginusa, in Asia, where Alcibiades died, all the deer have their ears divided, so that they can be known if they migrate to another place, and even the fœtus in utero has this distinction. The females have four nipples, like cows.

4. As soon as the females are impregnated, the males go and live apart from them, and, urged by their sexual desires, they each go apart and make a hole, in which they emit a strong smell like he goats, and their faces become black, by being sprinkled like those of goats. This continues till after rain, when they turn again to their pasture. The animal acts in this way on account of its violent sexual desires and its fatness. In summer time this is so great that they cannot run, but are taken by those who pursue them, even on foot, in the second or third race.

5. They frequent the water both on account of the heat and the difficulty of breathing. At the period of sexual intercourse, their flesh is inferior both in taste and smell, like that of he-goats. In winter they are thin and weak, and in the spring are most active for the chase. When chased, they sometimes rest awhile, and remain standing till their pursuers come up with them, when they start afresh. They seem to do this from a pain in their intestines; for their viscera are so thin and weak that if they are only struck gently they are ruptured, though the hide remains sound.

Chapter XXVII.

1. Bears perform the act of sexual intercourse in the manner already described, not mounting upon each other, but lying down upon the ground. The female is pregnant thirty days, when she produces one or two, or at the outside five cubs. The fœtus is smaller, in proportion to the size of the parent, than that of any other animal; for it is less than a weasel, and greater than a mouse. It is without hair and blind, and its legs and almost all its parts are without joints. Its season of sexual intercourse is in March. The cubs are born at the time of concealment. At this season both the female and the male are very fat. When they have brought up their young, they show themselves in the third month of the spring. The porcupine also

conceals itself, and is pregnant for the same number of days, and in other respects resembles the bear. It is very difficult to capture the she bear when pregnant.

Chapter XXVIII.

1. It has already been observed that the lion both copulates and makes water backwards. They do not copulate and produce their young at all seasons of the year, though they produce annually. The young are produced in the spring. The female generally produces two, never more than six, and sometimes only one. The fable which says that the uterus is ejected in parturition is a mistake. It has arisen from the rarity of the animal, those who invented the fable being ignorant of the true state of the case. The race of lions is rare, and not to be found in every place, but only in the country between the Achelous and the Nessus in the whole of Europe. The young of the lion are very small at their birth, so that they can hardly walk at two months old. The Syrian lions produce five times; at first five cubs, and then one less every time. After this they produce no more, but continue barren. The lioness has no mane, though the lion has. The lion only sheds its four canine teeth, two above and two below. They are shed when the animal is six months old.

2. The hyæna is of the colour of the wolf, but it is more hairy, and has a mane along the ridge of its back. It is a mistake to say that each individual has the sexual organs of both sexes. That of the male resembles the same organ in the wolf and the dog. That which has been imagined to be the female organ is placed beneath the tail, and it resembles that of the female, but is imperforate, and the anus is beneath it. The female hyena has an organ similar to that which bears its name in the male. It is placed beneath the tail, and is imperforate. Beneath this is the anus, and below this again the true genital organ. The female hyena has an uterus like that of other animals of the class, but the female is rarely captured. A certain hunter said that he caught eleven hyænas of which only one was a female.

3. Hares copulate backwards, as I formerly observed, for it is a retromingent animal. They copulate and produce

their young at all seasons. They become pregnant a second time while they are pregnant, and produce their young every month. They do not produce their young continually, but as many days as may be intervene. The female has milk before the young are produced. As soon as her young are born, she copulates again and conceives while giving milk. The milk is as thick as that of the sow. The young are born blind, like those of many animals with divided feet.

Chapter XXIX.

1. The fox copulates, mounting on the back of the female. The young are born blind, like those of the bear, and are even more inarticulate. When the season of parturition approaches, the female goes apart, so that it is rare to take a pregnant fox. When the young are born, the dam licks them, in order to warm and mature them. She never produces more than four.

2. The periods of gestation and parturition, both in point of time and the number of the young, are the same in the wolf as in the dog, and the young are blind, like those of the dog. They copulate at one season of the year, and the young are produced in the beginning of summer. A fabulous story is told of their parturition; for they say that all the she wolves produce their young in twelve days in the year; and the reason which is given for this fable is this, that during this number of days Latona was brought from the Hyperborean regions to Delos, in the form of a wolf, for fear of Juno. Whether this is or is not the period of parturition has never yet been ascertained. At present it only rests upon tradition. It does not appear to be true, nor that other tale which says that wolves only produce once in their life.

3. Cats and ichneumons produce their young in the same manner as dogs, and live upon the same things. They live about six years. The young of the panther are born blind. They are never more than four in number. The jackal is impregnated like a bitch, and the young are born blind. They produce two, or three, or four. Its length towards the tail is great. Its height is small. It runs very swiftly, although its legs are short; but on account of the softness of its tissues it can leap a great distance.

4. In Syria there are animals called hemioni which are

different from those derived from a mixture of the horse and ass, though they resemble them in appearance. As the wild ass is named from its resemblance to the domestic kind, the wild asses and the hemioni differ from the domestic race in speed. These hemioni are derived from their own congeners, of which this is a proof. For some came to Phrygia in the time of Pharnaces, the father of Pharnabazus, and remain there still. There are now only three, though they say that at first there were nine.

CHAPTER XXX.

1. THE reproduction of mice is more wonderful than that of any other animal, both in number and rapidity. For a pregnant female was left in a vessel of corn; and after a short time the vessel was opened, and a hundred and twenty mice were counted. There is a doubt respecting the reproduction and destruction of the mice which live on the ground; for such an inexpressible number of field mice have sometimes made their appearance that very little food remained. Their power of destruction also is so great that some small farmers, having on one day observed that their corn was ready for harvest, when they went the following day to cut their corn, found it all eaten.

2. The manner of their disappearance also is unaccountable; for in a few days they all vanish, although beforehand they could not be exterminated by smoking and digging them out, nor by hunting them and turning swine among them to root up their runs. Foxes also hunt them out, and wild weasels[1] are very ready to destroy them; but they cannot prevail over their numbers and the rapidity of their increase, nor indeed can anything prevail over them but rain, and when this comes they disappear very soon.

3. In a certain part of Persia the female fœtus of the mice are found to be pregnant in the uterus of their parent. Some people say and affirm that if they lick salt they become pregnant without copulation. The Egyptian mice have hair nearly resembling that of the hedgehog. There are other kinds which go upon two feet, for their fore feet are small and their hind feet large.[2] They are very numerous. There are also many other kinds of mice.

---

[1] Perhaps ferret, Mustela varo, or weasel.
[2] Serboa, Dipus gerbillus, or D. jaculus.

BOOK THE SEVENTH.

Chapter I.

1. The circumstances attending on the growth of man, from his conception in the womb even to old age, derived from his peculiar nature, are after this manner. We have already treated of the distinctions of the male and female and their parts. The male begins to have semen at about the age of fourteen complete. At the same time hair begins to appear on the pubes. As Alcmæon of Crotona says that flowers blossom before they bear seed, about the same period the voice begins to become more harsh and irregular. It is neither quite harsh, nor deep, nor all alike, but it resembles a discordant and harsh instrument. This is called τραγίξειν, to have a voice like a goat.

2. This is more conspicuous in those who attempt the gratification of sexual desires; for those who are vehement in these desires rapidly pass into a man's voice. In those that refrain themselves the contrary occurs. In those who, like some singers, endeavour to avoid this change, the voice will continue for a long while, and never undergo any great change. The breasts also and pudendum not only increase in size, but their general appearance is changed. At this period of life, if a person is urged to the emission of semen, the discharge is accompanied with pain as well as pleasure.

3. About the same period also the breasts of females enlarge, and the catamenia make their appearance. They resemble the blood of a newly killed animal. In young girls only do they appear white, especially if they make use of fluid food. This complaint stops the growth and weakens the body of girls. The catamenia usually appear when the mammæ are about two fingers high. The voice of girls also becomes deeper at this period, for on the whole the voice of women is more acute than that of men, and the voice of girls than that of old women, as the voice of boys is more

acute than the voice of men. The voice of female children also is more acute than that of males, and the windpipe is more acute in girls than boys.

4. They also want especial care at this period, for their sexual desires are very strong at the commencement, so that if they now take care to avoid every excitement, except such as the change of their body requires, without using venery, they generally remain temperate in after-years. For girls who indulge in venery when young, generally grow up intemperate; and so do males if they are unguarded either one way or both ways; for at this age the ducts open, and afford an easy passage for the fluid through the body, and at the same time the memory of past pleasures causes a desire for present gratification.

5. Some men never have hair on the pubes from their birth, nor seed, on account of the destruction of the parts appropriated to the semen. There are some women also who never have hair on the pubes. The male and female also change their habits of sickness and of health, and the proportions of their body, whether slight or stout, or of a good habit. Some thin boys after they attain puberty become stout and healthy, in others the contrary takes place. This is the case also with females; for whether boys or girls have their bodies loaded with excrementitious matter, this is separated in the one by puberty, in the other by the catamenia. They become more healthy and thriving when that which had prevented health and growth is removed.

6. Those which are of the contrary habit of body become more thin and delicate; for their naturally healthy condition is separated in the puberty of one sex, and the catamenia of the other. There is also considerable variety in the bosoms of young girls, for in some they are very large, in others small. This generally takes place in those girls which have much superfluous humour, for when the catamenia are about to appear, but before they arrive, the more fluid the patient is, the more necessary it is that the breasts should increase until the catamenia make their appearance, and the breasts, which then begin to increase, remain so afterwards. In youths and aged men the breasts are more conspicuous, and more like those of females; and in those who

are of a soft habit of body, and are smooth and not full of veins, and in dark persons also more than fair ones.

7. Until twenty-one years of age the semen is unproductive, afterwards it becomes fertile, though boys and girls produce small and imperfect children: this is also the case with other animals. Young girls conceive more readily, but after conception suffer more in parturition, and their bodies frequently become imperfect. Men of violent passions, and women that have borne many children, grow old more rapidly than others; nor does there appear to be any increase after they have borne three children. Women of violent sexual desires become more temperate after they have borne several children.

8. Women who have attained thrice seven years are well adapted for child-bearing, and men also are capable of becoming parents. Thin seminal fluid is barren. That which is lumpy begets males; what is thin and not clotted, females. The beard also appears on the chin of men at the same period.

Chapter II.

1. The catamenia appear when the moon is on the wane, from which some persons would argue that the moon is a female, for the purification of women and the waning of the moon occur together, and repletion occurs again in both after the purification and waning. In few women the catamenia occur every month, but in most at every third month. Those in whom they continue for only two or three days escape with ease: it is more difficult for those in whom it continues for a longer time, for they suffer during the whole period. In some the purification takes place all at once, in others by degrees; in all, however, the pain is considerable as long as they are present. In many women, when the catamenia are nearly ready to appear, the womb suffers so much from strangulation and disturbance, until they are discharged.

2. Conception naturally takes place immediately after this discharge in women, and those who do not then conceive, are usually barren. Some women, however, who have never menstruated, conceive. Such persons contain in themselves as much of the fluid as is usually left behind

after the purification, but not so much as to make its appearance externally. Some women in whom the uterus has closed immediately after the purification, conceive even while menstruating, but do not conceive afterwards. The catamenia sometimes occur even in pregnant women. Such women usually bear imperfect children, and their offspring either do not grow up, or are weakly.

3. It frequently happens that from the want of sexual intercourse, or from youth and the period of life, or from long abstinence, the uterus descends, and the catamenia occur several times in the month, until they conceive; after which the parts return to their proper place: and sometimes even in women with a good habit of body, if the humours are abundant, an effusion of the semen takes place if it is too moist.

4. It has already been observed that this purification is more abundant in women than in any other creature. In animals that are not viviparous no symptoms of anything of the kind occur, for this superfluous matter is returned into their own body, for in many the females are superior to the males in size, and in many it is turned to the formation of plates, or scales, or abundance of feathers. In viviparous animals with feet, it is turned to the formation of hair and bulk of body (for man is the only animal that is smooth), or of urine; for in almost all animals this secretion is thick and abundant. In women, on the contrary, all the superfluous matter of the body is directed to this purification.

5. The case of the male is the same, for in proportion to his size, man emits more semen than other animals; (wherefore, also, man is the smoothest of all animals,) and among men those which abound in humours, and are not very full fleshed, and fair men more than dark ones. So also among women. For in those that are full fleshed, the greater part of the secretion goes to the supply of the body, and in the act of sexual intercourse, fair women have naturally more seminal fluid than dark ones. Liquid and acid foods also increase this kind of intercourse.

CHAPTER III.

1. It is a sign that women have conceived when the pudendum remains dry after coition. If the labia are smooth they

will not conceive, for it slips out; nor will they if the labia are thick: but if there is a sensation of roughness and resistance when touched with the finger, and the labia are thin, they are then adapted for conception. In order that they may be able to conceive, such women must prepare the uterus, and the contrary that they may not conceive; for if the labia are smooth they do not conceive: so that some women, in order that the semen may fall outside the uterus, anoint themselves with oil of cedar, or with ceruse, or oil mixed with frankincense.

2. If it remain seven days, it is evident that conception has taken place, for in this period what are called the outpourings take place. The purification takes place in many women after conception. Thirty days afterwards in the case of conceiving a female child, and forty in the case of a male. After parturition, also, the purification lasts a similar number of days, though it is not exactly the same in all.

3. In the same number of days after conception the discharge no longer takes its usual course, but is turned towards the mammæ, in which the milk begins to make its appearance. At first the milk appears very small, and like a web in the mammæ. After conception, the first sensation generally takes place in the iliac region, which immediately appears more full in some persons. This is more conspicuous in slight persons. If the child is a male, a movement is usually felt on the right side of the groin, in about forty days; if a female, the movement occurs on the left side, in about ninety days. We must not suppose, however, that an accurate judgment can be formed in this way, for it often happens that the movement is felt on the right side when a female child, and on the left when a male child is conceived. All these, and such like things, vary in a greater or less degree.

4. About this period, also, the fœtus becomes divided; it previously existed as an undivided mass of flesh. If it perishes within seven days, it is called an effluxion; if in forty days, an abortion. The fœtus often perishes within this period. If the male fœtus is excluded within forty days, and is put out into any other fluid, it becomes dissolved, and disappears. If placed in cold water, it becomes, as it were, surrounded with a membrane. When this is taken off, the fœtus appears about as large as a large

ant. Its parts are visible, both those of generation, and all the rest; and the eyes are very large, as in other animals. If the female foetus perishes within the three months, it generally appears without divisions. If it survives to the fourth month, the parts appear formed.

5. The whole completion of the parts is more slow in the female than in the male, and parturition is more frequently delayed to the tenth month. After birth, females attain to youth, and puberty, and old age, more rapidly than males, and those that have borne many children more rapidly than others, as it was observed before.

CHAPTER IV.

1. WHEN conception has taken place, the uterus usually closes immediately for seven months. In the eighth month it opens, and the foetus, if properly developed, begins to descend in the eighth month. If the foetus is not properly developed, but checked in the eighth month in parturition, women who bear in the eighth month do not exclude it, nor does the foetus advance downwards in the eighth month, and the uterus does not open itself. It is a sign that it is not properly developed, when it is born before the circumstances I have described take place.

2. After conception, women suffer throughout their whole body, and their sight becomes dim, and they are afflicted with headache. In some, these symptoms occur very soon, as early as the tenth day; in others they are delayed, in proportion as they have an abundance or deficiency of superfluous matter in their bodies. Nausea and vomiting often seize upon them, and on those especially in whom the purifications become stagnant, and do not yet fly to the mammae. Some women suffer at the commencement of pregnancy, and others in the more advanced stages, when the foetus begins to grow. Retention of urine also frequently attacks them at last.

3. Those that are pregnant with a male foetus, usually pass through the time more easily, and retain a better colour throughout. If a female is conceived, the contrary is the case; for they are generally more discoloured, and suffer more during the period of gestation. In many cases the legs swell, and a swollen condition of the flesh is also com-

mon. In some women, however, the condition is contrary. Pregnant women are apt to have all sorts of fancies, which change very rapidly. Some persons call this longing. These fancies are strongest when a female is conceived, and there is but little pleasure in their gratification. In a few women the condition of the body is better during pregnancy; they suffer most when the hair of the fœtus begins to grow. Pregnant women lose the hair which grows on the parts that are hairy at birth, while it becomes more thick upon the parts on which it appears subsequent to birth.

4. A male fœtus usually moves more freely in the womb than a female, and the parturition is not so long. If a female, the parturition is slower. The pain in the birth of female children is continuous, and dull; in the birth of males it is sharp, and far more severe. Those who, before parturition, have sexual intercourse, suffer less in the process. Sometimes women seem to suffer, not from any pain of their own, but from the turning of the head of the child; and this appears to be the commencement of the pain. Other animals have a single exact period for parturition, for one time is appointed for them all. The human subject alone varies in this particular, for the period of gestation is seven, eight, or nine months, or ten at the outside, though some have even advanced as far as the eleventh month.

5. If any are born before the seventh month, they never live. Those of seven months are the first that are developed, but these are usually weakly, wherefore, also, they wrap them in wool. Many of these infants have the passages, as the ears and nostrils, imperforate. As they grow, however, they assume a proper form, and many of them survive. In Egypt, and some other places, where the women suffer little pain in parturition, and where they bear many children with ease, those even at the end of eight months are capable of living, even although they should be monstrous; but in such places children born in the eighth month may survive and be brought up. In Greece, however, few of them survive, and most of them perish; and people suspect that if any of them survive, the exact period of conception must have been mistaken by the mother.

6. Women suffer most in the fourth and eighth month,

and if the fœtus dies in the fourth or eighth month, they usually die also; so that not only children born in the eighth month often perish, but their mothers also perish with them. In the same way, the period of conception probably is mistaken by those who have been pregnant more than eleven months; for in these cases the beginning of the conception escapes the notice of females, for frequently after the uterus has been distended with flatulence, women have copulated and conceived, and supposed that the former condition in which they observed the usual symptoms, was the commencement of gestation.

Chapter V.

1. The human subject also differs from other animals, as to the number of the perfect offspring produced at a birth. For the human subject differs both from animals which produce but one, and those which produce many; for, generally speaking, and, in most cases, women have but one child at a time, though cases of twins occur frequently, and in many places, as in Egypt, three or four at a birth have been known in some particular places, as I have observed before. Five at a birth are the most that have been produced. This has been observed to take place in many cases, but in one case only have twenty been produced at four births, for five were born each time, and many of them were reared. In other animals, if the twins are male and female, there is no more difficulty in rearing and preserving them, than if they were both of the same sex. In the human subject there are few cases of twins surviving, when one was male and the other female.

2. The human female and the mare copulate after conception more than any other creatures, for all other females, when they have conceived, fly from the males, except those which, like the hare, become pregnant a second time during gestation. But the mare, having once conceived, does not form a second fœtus, but generally produces a single foal. In the human subject it happens sometimes, though rarely. Those which are conceived a long while afterwards never come to perfection, but, from the pain which they cause, destroy the original fœtus; and a case has occurred in which twelve imperfect embryos have been produced at

one time. If the second conception take place soon after the first, they bear and produce the fœtus, as if it were a twin. This, they say, was the case with Iphicles and Hercules.

3. The possibility of the case is manifest, for an adulteress has been known to produce one child like her husband, and another like her paramour; and a case has occurred of a woman having conceived twins, and then conceived a third child upon them; and when the proper time came, the twins were born perfect, the other was only a fœtus of five months old, which died immediately: and in another case, a woman produced, first of all, a fœtus of seven months old, and then twins, perfectly developed; the former perished, but the latter survived. And some women have conceived at the same time as they miscarried, and have ejected one fœtus while they bore the other. In most females, who have cohabited after the eighth month after conception, the child has been born filled with a shining mucous-like substance, and has often appeared full of the food which has been eaten by the mother; and if she has fed upon food more than usually salt, the child has been born without nails.

Chapter VI.

1. The milk that is produced before the seventh month is useless; but as soon as the child is alive the milk becomes good. At first it is salt, like that of sheep. Most women during pregnancy are affected by wine, and if they drink it they become faint and feeble. The beginning and the ending of the reproductive power in both sexes is marked in the male by the emission of the semen, in the female by the catamenia. They are not, however, fertile when these first occur, nor while they are still small and weak. The period of the commencement of these signs has been mentioned. In women the catamenia usually cease at forty; but if they pass over this age, they go on to fifty; and some have even produced children at that period, but none later than this period.

2. The reproductive function in men usually continues active till they are sixty years old; if they pass beyond this period, till they are seventy; and some men have had children at seventy years old. It frequently happens that, when

marriages are unfruitful, both men and women become pregnant, if the marriage is dissolved and they marry again. The same thing takes place respecting the birth of male and female children. For sometimes only children of one sex are produced by a marriage; and if this is dissolved, and the parents marry again, children of the other sex are produced. These things also vary with the age of the parents; for some when young have female children, and when older males, though the contrary sometimes takes place.

3. The same is the case with the whole of the reproductive function. For some persons have no children when they are young, but have them afterwards; others have children at first, but none afterwards; and there are some women who conceive with difficulty, but when they have conceived bear children; others conceive easily, but the fœtus never comes to maturity. There are also both men and women who only produce children of one sex, as the story goes of Hercules, who had but one daughter in seventy-two children. Those who have been barren, and either after great care, or from any other cause, at last conceive, more frequently bear a daughter than a son. It often happens also that men who have engendered become impotent, and subsequently return to their former condition.

4. Maimed parents produce maimed children; and so also lame and blind parents produce lame and blind children; and, on the whole, children are often born with anything contrary to nature, or any mark which their parents may have, such as tumours and wounds. Such marks have often been handed down for three generations; as if a person had a mark on their arm which was not seen in the son, but the grandson exhibited a dark confused spot on the same place. The circumstances, however, are rare; and sound children are generally produced from lame parents; nor is there any complete certainty in these matters; and children resemble their parents or their grandparents, and sometimes they resemble neither. This is handed down for many generations; as in Sicily, a woman cohabited with an Ethiopian, her daughter was not black, but her daughter's child was so.

5. For the most part the girls resemble their mother, and the boys their father; though the contrary is often the case, and the females resemble their father, and the males their

mother, and the different parts of the body resemble either parents. Twins have sometimes no resemblance to each other, but they are generally much alike; and one woman cohabited with a man, and conceived seven days after parturition, when she bore a child as like her former as if they had been twins. Some women, as well as other creatures, produce young resembling themselves, others bear those which resemble the male, as the horse called Dicæa in Pharsalia.

Chapter VII.

1. The seminal fluid in its emission is preceded by wind. The manner of its emission exhibits this; for nothing is expelled to a great distance without pneumatic force. If the seminal fluid is taken up by the uterus and retained there, it becomes inclosed in a membrane. For if it is expelled before it becomes articulated, it appears like an ovum inclosed in a membrane, but without any shell, and the membrane is full of veins. All animals, whether furnished with fins, feet, or wings, whether viviparous or oviparous, are produced in the same manner, except that the umbilicus in viviparous animals is turned towards the uterus, and in others to the ovum; and in some cases both ways, as in a certain kind of fish. Some of them are surrounded by a membrane, others by a chorion. First of all, the fœtus is contained within the last envelope. Then there is another membrane over this, which is in part united to the matrix and is partly separate, and contains water. Between these is a watery or sanguineous fluid, which in women is called prophorus.

2. All animals that have a navel increase by the navel; and in those which have acetabula the navel is united to the acetabulum; and in those which have a smooth uterus the navel is united to the uterus upon a vein. The position of all quadrupeds in the uterus is stretched out; that of fishes is on the side; bipeds, as birds, are folded together. The human fœtus lies folded up with its nose between its knees and its eyes upon them, and its ears turned outwards. All animals are alike in having the head placed upwards at first. As they grow, the head turns round, and the birth of all animals is naturally with the head forwards; for even in those that are folded together the presentation of the feet is unnatural. The embryo of quadrupeds contains excrementitious matter,

as soon as it is matured, both fluid and solid. The latter is contained in the extreme parts of the intestine, the former in the bladder.

3. If animals have acetabula in the uterus, these acetabula always become smaller as the fœtus grows, and at last disappear. The umbilical cord is a covering for veins, of which the origin is in the uterus. In those creatures which have acetabula it originates in them; in those that have not acetabula it originates in the vein. In the larger animals, such as the fœtus of oxen, there are four veins; in smaller animals, two; in very small animals, as in birds, there is but one. Two veins reach the fœtus through the liver, from that part called the gates of the liver, towards the great vein; and two go to the aorta, where it is divided into two parts; and there are membranes round each pair of veins, and the umbilical cord surrounds these membranes like a covering. As the fœtus increases, these veins diminish. The embryo, as it grows, advances into the viscera, where its movements are manifest. Sometimes it remains rolled up near the pudendum.

Chapter VIII.

1. When the pains of parturition come on, they extend to many and various parts of the body, but especially to one or other of the thighs. Those who suffer most in the bowels are delivered most rapidly; those who suffer much in the loins are delivered with difficulty; those whose pain lies in the subumbilical region, more quickly. If the child is a male, a liquid, serum-like discharge, of a pale yellow colour, precedes; if a female, this discharge is sanguineous, but still fluid. Some women have neither during the period of parturition.

2. In other animals parturition is not painful, and it is evident that they suffer but moderately in the pains of labour. In women the pains of parturition are more violent, especially in those that are inactive or that are not well made in their sides, and are unable to hold their breath. They also suffer more in parturition, if they breathe in the meantime, compelled by the necessity of respiration. At first a fluid escapes when the fœtus comes to the birth, and the mem-

branes are ruptured; after this, the embryo is excluded, the uterus being turned, and the uterus being turned inside-out.

Chapter IX.

1. The division of the umbilical cord often requires the careful attention of the midwife; for by skilfulness she may not only assist in difficult labours, but should attend carefully to the circumstances, and apply the ligature to the umbilical cord of the child; for if the secundines fall out with the child, the umbilical cord must be bound with a ligature of worsted, and cut above the ligature, and where it is bound it joins together, and that which is joined with it falls off. If the ligature becomes loose, the child dies from loss of blood. If the secundines do not come out at once, while they remain within, and the child is outside, the umbilical cord must be tied and divided.

2. Frequently the child, if weak, has appeared as if born dead, until the umbilical cord was tied, for the blood flowed from the child to the navel and the surrounding parts; but some skilful midwife being present, by pressure on the navel from within has revived the child, just as if it had been filled with blood from the first. It has been already observed, that all animals are naturally born with the head forwards. Children also have their hands pressed down against their sides. As soon as they are born they begin to cry and bring their hands to their mouth. They emit excrements, some immediately, others very soon, but all in the course of a day. This excrementitious matter is very abundant, considering the size of the child. Women call it the meconium. Its colour is like that of blood, and it is black and pitch-like. Afterwards it becomes milky, for the child immediately draws the breast. The child never cries before it is entirely in the world, not even though its head is protruded in difficult cases, while the body is within the uterus.

3. Those women in whom a flooding has preceded the period of delivery are delivered with more difficulty, and if the purifications are small after parturition, and only as much as they are at first, and do not continue for more than forty days, such women are stronger, and more ready for conception. After children are born, for forty days they neither laugh nor weep when awake, but sometimes do both in their sleep;

nor do they usually feel when they are tickled, but they sleep the greater part of their time. As they grow, the period of wakefulness continually increases; and it is evident that they dream, but it is some time before they remember their imaginations. There is no difference in the bones of other animals, but they are all born perfect. In children the bone called bregma is soft, and does not become strong for some time. Some animals are born with teeth, but children begin to cut their teeth in the seventh month. The front teeth naturally appear first, sometimes the upper teeth and sometimes the under. Children cut their teeth more easily if their nurses have warmer milk.

Chapter X.

After parturition and purification women become full of milk; and in some it not only flows through the nipples but through other parts of the breast, and sometimes from the cheeks; and if this fluid is not matured nor secreted, but remains full, hard knots are formed, which remain for a long time; for every part of the breast is so spongy that, if a hair is swallowed with the drink, pain ensues in the breasts, until it either escapes spontaneously with the milk, or is sucked out, this is called τριχιᾶν. They continue to have milk until they conceive again. It then ceases, and is quenched in other creatures as well as in the human subject. The catamenia seldom take place while milk is secreted, though this sometimes occurs in women while nursing. On the whole, an effusion of fluid seldom takes place from many parts of the body at the same time, and those that have hæmorrhoids have usually less purification. In some it takes place through ixiæ (varices), and is secreted from the loins before it reaches the uterus; and those who vomit blood when the purification is suppressed suffer no harm.

Chapter XI.

Children are very subject to spasms, and especially those that are in a good condition and have abundance of rich milk, or whose nurses are fat. Wine is injurious in this complaint, and dark-coloured wines more so than those that are pale, and food that is not fluid, and windy aliments, and stoppage in the bowels. Children with this complaint generally die before the seventh day: wherefore also this day has received a name, as if it gave some hope of the recovery of the child. Children suffer most at the full moon. Children are in great danger when the spasms originate in the back, especially if they are advancing in age.[1]

[1] The seventh book ends very abruptly, and hence it has been thought that what is now called the tenth book, in which the subject of reproduction is continued, would have its proper place here, as a continuation of the seventh. Whether a portion of the genuine work of Aristotle has been lost which would have completed the subject is another question; but there can be little doubt that the tenth book, in the form in which we have it, is no genuine work of Aristotle ; some of the opinions are contrary to those which he has expressed, and the whole style and language is different from that of Aristotle. Schneider therefore has placed the tenth book at the end of the work, that he may neither entirely exclude that which in former times was considered a portion of Aristotle's treatise on Animals, nor yet allow a fictitious book to interrupt the genuine writings of his Author.

BOOK THE EIGHTH.

Chapter I.

1. The nature of animals and their mode of reproduction has now been described. Their actions and mode of life also differ according to their disposition and their food. For almost all animals present traces of their moral dispositions, though these distinctions are most remarkable in man. For most of them, as we remarked, when speaking of their various parts, appear to exhibit gentleness or ferocity, mildness or cruelty, courage or cowardice, fear or boldness, violence or cunning; and many of them exhibit something like a rational consciousness, as we remarked in speaking of their parts. For they differ from man, and man from the other animals, in a greater or less degree; for some of these traits are exhibited strongly in man, and others in other animals.

2. Others differ in proportion. For as men exhibit art, wisdom, and intelligence, animals possess, by way of compensation, some other physical power. This is most conspicuous in the examination of infants, for in them we see, as it were, the vestiges and seeds of their future disposition; nor does their soul at this period differ in any respect from that of an animal; so that it is not unreasonable for animals to present the same, or similar, or analogous appearances. Nature passes so gradually from inanimate to animate things, that from their continuity their boundary and the mean between them is indistinct. The race of plants succeeds immediately that of inanimate objects; and these differ from each other in the proportion of life in which they participate; for, compared with other bodies, plants appear to possess life, though, when compared with animals, they appear inanimate.

3. The change from plants to animals, however, is gradual, as I before observed. For a person might question to

which of these classes some marine objects belong; for many of them are attached to the rock, and perish as soon as they are separated from it. The pinnæ are attached to the rocks, the solens cannot live after they are taken away from their localities; and, on the whole, all the testacea resemble plants, if we compare them with locomotive animals. Some of them appear to have no sensation; in others it is very dull. The body of some of them is naturally fleshy, as of those which are called tethya; and the acalephe and the sponge entirely resemble plants; the progress is always gradual by which one appears to have more life and motion than another.

4. In the vital actions also we may observe the same manner. For vegetables which are produced from seed appear to have no other work beyond reproduction; nor do some animals appear to have any other object in their existence. This object then is common to them all; but as sensation advances, their manner of life differs in their having pleasure in sexual intercourse, in their mode of parturition and rearing their young. Some of them, like plants, simply accomplish their peculiar mode of reproduction at an appointed season, and others are diligent in rearing their young; but as soon as this is accomplished they separate from them, and have no farther communication; but those that are more intelligent, and possess more memory, use their offspring in a more civilized manner.

5. The work of reproduction is one part of their life, the work of procuring food forms another. These two occupy their labour and their life. Their food differs in the substances of which it consists, and all the natural increase of the body is derived from food. That which is natural is pleasant, and all animals follow that which is pleasant to their nature.

Chapter II.

1. ANIMALS are divided according to the localities which they inhabit; for some animals are terrestrial, others are aquatic. They also admit of a ternary division, those that breathe air and those that breathe water, one of these classes is terrestrial, the other is aquatic; the third class does not breathe either air or water, but they are adapted by nature to receive refreshment from each of these elements; and some of these are called terrestrial, others are aquatic, though they

neither breathe air or water; and there are other animals which procure their food and make their abode in either of these elements. For many that breathe air, and produce their young upon the land, procure their food from the water, where they generally make their abode; and these are the only animals which appear to be doubtful, for they may be arranged either as terrestrial or aquatic animals.

2. Of those that breathe water, none have feet or wings, nor seek their food on land; but many of those that are terrestrial, and breathe air, do so; some of them so much so, that they cannot live when separated from the water, as those which are called marine turtles, and crocodiles, and hippopotami, and seals, and some of the smaller creatures, as the water tortoise and the frog tribe; for all these are suffocated if their respiration is suspended for any length of time. They produce their young and rear them on dry land; others do so near the dry land, while they reside in the water.

3. Of all animals the most remarkable in this particular is the dolphin, and some other aquatic animals and cetacea which are of this habit, as the whale and others which have a blowhole; for it is not easy to arrange them either with aquatic or terrestrial animals, if we consider animals that breathe air as terrestrial, and those that breathe water as aquatics, for they partake of the characters of both classes; for they receive the sea and eject it through their blowhole, and air through their lungs, for they have this part, and breathe through it. And the dolphin, when captured in nets, is often suffocated, from the impossibility of breathing. It will live for a long while out of water, snoring and groaning like other breathing animals. It sleeps with its snout above the water, in order that it may breathe through it.

4. It is thus impossible to arrange it under both of these contrary divisions, but it would appear that the aquatic animals must be further subdivided; for they breathe and eject water for the same reason as others breathe air, for the sake of coolness. Other animals do this for the sake of food; for those animals which obtain their food in the water, must also, at the same time, swallow some of the fluid, and have an organ by which they can eject it. Those creatures which use water instead of air for breathing have gills; those that use it for food have a blowhole. These

creatures are sanguineous. The nature of the malacia and malacostraca is the same; for these swallow water for food.

5. Those animals which breathe air, but live in the water, and those which breathe water, and have gills, but go out upon dry land and take their food there, belong to two divisions of aquatic animals. This last division is represented by a single animal called the cordylus (water newt); for this animal has no lungs, but gills; and it goes on dry land to procure its food. It has four feet, so that it appears natural that it should walk. In all these animals nature appears to be, as it were, turned aside, and some of the males appear to be females, and the females have a male appearance; for animals which have but small diversity in particular parts, exhibit great variations in the whole body.

6. This is evident in castrated animals; for if a small portion only of the body is destroyed, the animal becomes a female; so that it is plain that if a very minute portion in the original composition of an animal becomes changed, if that portion belongs to the origin of the species, it might become either male or female; or, if taken away altogether, the animal might be neuter. And so, either way, it might become a land or aquatic animal, if only a small change took place. . . . . it happens that some become terrestrial and others aquatic animals, and some are not amphibious which others are, because in their original generation they received some kind of substance which they use for food. For that which is natural is agreeable to every animal, as I have said before.

Chapter III.

1. When animals are divided in three ways into aquatic and land animals, because they either breathe air or water, or from the composition of their bodies; or, in the third place, from their food, their manner of life will be found to agree with these divisions. For some follow both the composition of their bodies and the nature of their food, and their respiration of either water or air. Others only agree with their composition and food.

2. The testacea which are immoveable live by a fluid which percolates through the dense parts of the sea, and

being digested because it is lighter than the sea water, thus returns to its original nature. That this fluid exists in the sea, and is capable of infiltration is manifest, and may be proved by experiment; for if anyone will make a thin waxen vessel, and sink it empty in the sea, in a night and a day, it may be taken up full of water, which is drinkable.

3. The acalephe (actinia) feeds upon any small fish which may fall in its way. Its mouth is placed in the centre of its body. This organ is conspicuous in the larger individuals: like the oyster, it has a passage for the exclusion of its food, which is placed above. The acalephe appears to resemble the internal part of the oyster, and it makes use of the rock, as the oyster does of its shell. (The patella also is free, and wanders about in search of food.)

4. Among the locomotive testacea, some are carnivorous, and live on small fish, as the purpura, for this creature is carnivorous, it is therefore caught with a bait of flesh: others live upon marine plants. The marine turtles live upon shell-fish, for which purpose they have a very powerful mouth; for if any of them take a stone or anything else, they break and eat it. This animal leaves the water and eats grass. They often suffer and perish, when they are dried up as they float on the surface, for they are not able to dive readily.

5. The malacostraca are of the same nature, for they eat everything; they feed upon stones and mud, seaweeds and dung, as the rock crabs, and are also carnivorous. The spiny lobsters also overcome large fishes, and a kind of retribution awaits them in turn, for the polypus prevails over the lobster, for they are not inconvenienced by the shell of the lobster, so that if the lobsters perceive them in the same net with them, they die from fear. The spiny lobsters overcome the congers, for their roughness prevents them from falling off. The congers devour the polypi which cannot adhere to them on account of the smoothness of their surface; all the malacia are carnivorous.

6. The spiny lobsters also live on small fish, which they hunt for in their holes, for they are produced in such parts of the sea as are rough and stony, and in those places make their habitations; whatever they capture, they bring to their mouth

with their double claw, as the crabs do. When not frightened they naturally walk forwards, hanging their horns down at their sides. When alarmed they retreat backwards, and extend their horns to a great distance. They fight with each other like rams with their horns, raising them and striking each other. They are often seen in numbers as if they were gregarious.

7. The malacostraca lead this kind of life. Among the malacia the teuthis and sepia prevail over the large fish. The polypus generally collects shells which it empties of their contents and feeds upon them, so that those who seek for them find their holes by the shells that are scattered about. The report that they eat each other is a mistake; but some have the tentacula eaten off by the congers.

Chapter IV.

1. ALL fish at the season of oviposition live upon ova; in the rest of their food they are not all so well agreed, for some of them are only carnivorous, as the selachos, conger, channa, thynnus, labrax, sinodon, amia, orphus, and muræna; the trigla lives upon fuci, shell-fish, and mud; it is also carnivorous. The cephalus lives on mud, the dascillus on mud and dung. The scarus and melanurus on sea-weed, the salpa on dung and fuci, it will also eat the plant called horehound; it is the only fish that can be caught with the gourd.

2. All fish, except the cestreus, eat one another, especially the congers. The cephalus and the cestreus alone are not carnivorous. This is a proof of it. They are never captured with anything of the kind in their stomach, nor are they captured with a bait made of flesh, but with bread; the cestreus is always fed upon sea-weed and sand. One kind of cephalus which some persons call chelone lives near the land, another is called peræas. This last feeds upon nothing but its own mucus, for which reason it is always very poor. The cephalus lives upon mud, wherefore they are heavy and slimy. They certainly never eat fish, on account of their dwelling in mud; they often emerge in order to wash themselves from the slime. Neither will any creature eat their ova, so that they increase rapidly,

and when they increase they are devoured by other fish, and especially by the acharnus.

3. The cestreus (mullet) is the most greedy and insatiable of fish, so that its abdomen is distended, and it is not good for food unless it is poor. When alarmed it hides its head, as if its whole body were thus concealed; the sinodon also is carnivorous, and eats the malacia. This fish and the channa often eject their stomachs as they pursue small fish, for their stomach is near the mouth, and they have no œsophagus. Some are simply carnivorous, as the dolphin, sinodon, chrysophrys, the selache and malacia; others, as the phycis, cobius, and the rock-fish, principally feed upon mud and fuci, and bryum, and what is called caulion, and any matter which may be produced in the sea. The phycis eats no other flesh than that of the shrimps. They also frequently eat each other, as I before remarked, and the greater devour the less. It is a proof that they are carnivorous, that they are captured with bait made of flesh.

4. The amia, tunny, and labrax generally eat flesh, though they also eat sea-weed. The sargus feeds after the trigla when the last has buried itself in the mud and departed, for it has the power of burying itself, then the sargus comes and feeds and prevents all those that are weaker than itself from approaching. The fish called scarus is the only one which appears to ruminate like quadrupeds. Other fish appear to hunt the smaller ones with their mouths towards them, in this way they naturally swim; but the selachea, dolphins and cetacea throw themselves on their back to capture their prey, for their mouth is placed below them, for this reason the smaller ones escape, or if not they would soon be reduced in number; for the swiftness of the dolphin and its capacity for food appear incredible.

5. A few eels in some places are fed upon mud, and any kind of food which may be cast into the water, but generally they live upon fresh water, and those who rear eels take care that the water which flows off and on upon the shallows in which they live may be clear, where they make the eel preserves. For they are soon suffocated if the water is not clean, their gills being very small. For this reason those who seek for them disturb the water. In the Strymon they are taken about the time of the rising of the

Pleiades. For the water is disturbed at this season by the mud which is stirred up by contrary winds, otherwise it is useless to attempt to obtain them. When dead, eels do not rise and float on the surface, like other fishes, for their stomach is small; a few of them are fat, but this is not usually the case.

6. When taken out of the water, they will live five or six days; if the wind is in the north they will live longer than if it is in the south. If they are removed from the ponds to the eel preserves during the summer they perish, but not if removed in the winter; neither will they bear violent changes, for if they are taken and plunged into cold water, they often perish in great numbers. They are suffocated also if kept in a small quantity of water. This takes place also in other fish, which are suffocated if kept in a small quantity of water which is never changed, like animals which breathe air when enclosed in a small quantity of air. Some eels live seven or eight years. Fresh-water fish make use of food, and devour each other, as well as plants and roots, or anything else that they can find in the mud; they generally feed in the night, and during the day dwell in deep holes. This is the nature of the food of fish.

Chapter V.

1. ALL birds with crooked claws are carnivorous, nor are they able to eat corn even when put in their mouths. All the eagles belong to this class and the kites, and both the hawks, the pigeon hawk namely, and the sparrow hawk. These differ in size from each other, and so does the triorches. This bird is as large as the kite, and is visible at all seasons of the year; the osprey and vulture also belong to this class. The osprey is as large as the eagle, and ash-coloured. There are two kinds of vultures, one small and whitish, the other large and cinereous.

2. Some of the night birds also have crooked claws, as the nycticorax, owl, and bryas. The bryas resembles an owl in appearance, but it is as large as an eagle; the eleos, ægolius, and scops also belong to this class. The eleos is larger than a domestic fowl, the ægolius is about the size of that bird, they both hunt the jay. The scops is less than

the owl; all three of these are similar in form, and carnivorous. Some that have not crooked claws are carnivorous, as the swallow.

3. Some birds feed on worms, as the finch, the sparrow, batis, chloris, titmouse. There are three kinds of titmouse; the spizites is the largest, it is as large as the finch. Another is called the orinus, because it dwells in mountains; it has a large tail. The third resembles them in everything except its size, for it is very small. The sycalis also, the megalocoryphus, pyrrhulas, erithacus, hypolaïs, œstrus, tyrannis are of this class. The last of these is the least, it is not much larger than a locust; it has a purple crest, and is altogether a graceful and well-formed bird. The bird called anthus also, which is of the size of the finch; the orospizus is like the finch, and nearly of the same size, it has a blue stripe on its neck, and lives in mountainous places. The wren also lives upon seeds. All these and such like birds either partly or entirely live on worms.

4. These birds, the acanthis, thraupis, and that which is called chrysometris, all live upon thorns, but neither eat worms or any other living creature, and they both roost and feed in the same places. There are others which feed on gnats; these live chiefly by hunting for these insects, as the greater and lesser pipo, both of which are by some persons called woodpeckers. They resemble each other in their cry, though that of the larger bird is the louder, and they both feed by flying against trees. The celeos also, which is as large as a turtle dove, and entirely yellow; its habit is to strike against trees; it generally lives upon trees, and has a loud voice. This bird generally inhabits the Peloponnesus. There is also another called cnipologus, which is small, about the size of the acanthyllis; its colour is cinereous and spotted, and its voice is weak; this bird also pecks trees.

5. There are other birds which live upon fruit and grasses, as the phaps, phatta, peristera, œnas, and trygon.[1] The phatta and peristera are always present, the trygon only in summer time; in the winter it is not seen, for it hides itself in holes. The œnas is generally seen and captured in the autumn. The œnas is as large as the peristera but less than

[1] Different species of pigeons and doves.

the phaps. It is generally captured as it is drinking; it comes to this country when it has young. All the rest come in the summer, and make their nests here, and all, except the pigeon tribe, live upon animal food.

6. All birds, as far as food is concerned, are either terrestrial or live in the neighbourhood of rivers and ponds, or near the sea. Those that have webbed feet pass the greater part of their time on the water; those with divided feet near the water. Some of these dive for their food, such as live upon plants and do not eat flesh; others, as the heron and white heron, live in ponds and rivers. The latter of these is smaller than the former, and has a flat large bill.

7. The pelargus also, and the gull, the latter is ash-coloured, and the schœnilus, cinclos, pygargus, (and tryngas) this last is the largest of these small birds, for it is of the same size as the thrush; all these birds wag their tails. The calidris also, this bird is variegated and ash-coloured. The kingfisher also lives near the water; there appear to be two kinds of this bird, one of which utters its cry as it sits upon the reeds, and the other. which is larger, is silent; they both have a blue back. The trochilus also, and the kingfisher and cerylus also live near the sea. The corona also lives upon animals which are cast on shore, for it is omnivorous. The white gull also, the cepphus, æthyia, and charadrius.

8. The heavier web-footed birds inhabit the neighbourhood of rivers and ponds, as the swan, duck, phalaris, columbis, and the boscas, which is like a duck, but smaller; and the bird called corax, which is as large as the pelargus, but its legs are shorter, it is web-footed and a swimmer, its colour is black; this last bird perches upon trees, and is the only one of this class that builds its nest in such places. The great and small goose also, the latter is gregarious, and chenalopex, the aix, and the penelops. The sea eagle also lives near the sea, and fishes in the waters of lakes. Many birds are omnivorous; those with crooked claws seize upon other animals which they can overcome, and upon birds. They do not, however, devour their own congeners, as fish frequently do; all the tribes of birds drink very little, those with crooked claws do not drink at all, or only a few of them, and these but seldom; of these the cenchris drinks the

most; the kite rarely drinks, though it has been observed to do so.

Chapter VI.

1. Animals covered with scaly plates, as the lizard and other quadrupeds and serpents, are omnivorous, for they eat both flesh and grass, and serpents lick their prey more than any other animal; all these creatures, and indeed all with spongy lungs, drink very little, and all that are oviparous are of this kind, and have but little blood. Serpents are all very fond of wine, so that they hunt the viper by placing vessels of wine in the hedge-rows, and they are captured when intoxicated. Serpents devour any animal that they may have captured, and when they have sucked out the juice, they reject all the remainder; nearly all such animals do this, as also the spiders. But the spiders suck the juice without swallowing the animal. Serpents suck the juice internally.

2. The serpent swallows any food which may be presented to it, for it will devour both birds and beasts, and suck eggs. When it has taken its food it draws itself up, till it stands erect upon its extremity, it then gathers itself up and contracts itself a little, so that when stretched out the animal it has swallowed may descend in its stomach; it does this because its œsophagus is long and thin. Phalangia and serpents can live a long while without food, this may be seen in those that are kept by dealers in medicine.

Chapter VII.

1. Among viviparous quadrupeds, those that are wild and have pointed teeth are all carnivorous, except some wolves, which, when they are hungry, will, as they say, eat a certain kind of earth, but this is the only exception. They will not eat grass unless they are sick, for some dogs eat grass and vomit it up again, and so are purified. The solitary wolves are more eager for human flesh than those which hunt in packs.

2. The animal which some persons call the glanus and others the hyæna, is not less than the wolf, it has a mane like a horse, but the hair all along its spine is more harsh and thick. It also secretly attacks men, and hunts them

down; it hunts dogs also by vomiting like men; it also breaks open graves for the sake of this kind of food.

3. The bear is also omnivorous, for it eats fruit, and on account of the softness of its body it can climb trees; it eats leguminous seeds also; it also overturns hives and eats the honey, and it feeds upon crabs and ants, and is carnivorous, for its strength enables it to attack not only deer, but wild hogs, if it can fall upon them secretly, and oxen. For when it meets the bull face to face, it falls upon its back, and when the bull attempts to throw it, seizes its horns with its fore-legs, and biting upon the shoulder of the bull, throws it down. For a short time it can walk upright on its hind legs. It eats flesh after it has become putrid.

4. The lion, like all other wild animals with pointed teeth, is carnivorous; it devours its food greedily, and swallows large pieces without dividing them; it can afterwards, from its repletion, remain two or three days without food. It drinks very little. Its excrement is small, and is not made more than once in three days or thereabouts, and it is dry and hard like that of a dog. The wind from its bowels has an acrid smell, and its urine is powerfully scented, for which reason dogs smell to trees, for the lion, like the dog, lifts its leg to make water. It produces also a strong smell when it breathes upon its food, and when its bowels are laid open they emit a strong scent.

5. Some quadrupeds and wild animals seek their food in the neighbourhood of ponds and rivers, but none of them except the seal live near the sea; of this class are the creature called beaver, and the satherium, the satyrium, the otter, and that which is called latax. This creature is broader than the enydris, and has strong teeth, for it often goes out in the night and with its teeth gnaws off the osiers. The enydris also will bite men, and they say will not leave its hold till it hears the noise of its teeth against the bone. The latax has rough hair, the nature of which is between that of the seal and that of the deer.

Chapter VIII.

1. Animals with pointed teeth drink by lapping, and some that have not pointed teeth, as mice. Those which have an even surface to their teeth draw in the water as horses and

oxen; the bear neither draws in the water nor laps it, but gulps it down. Some birds draw in the water, but those which have long necks imbibe it at intervals, lifting up their heads; the porphyrion alone gulps it down. All horned animals, both domestic and wild, and those that have not pointed teeth eat fruits and grass, and are incapable of enduring hunger, except the dog, and this animal eats fruit and grass less than any other.

2. The hog eats roots more than other animals, because its snout is well adapted for this operation, it is more adapted to various kinds of food than other animals. In proportion to its size its fat is developed very fast, for it becomes fat in sixty days. Those who occupy themselves in fatting hogs know how fast they fatten by weighing them when lean; they will become fat after starvation for three days. Almost all other animals become fat, after previous starvation. After three days those who fatten hogs feed them well.

3. The Thracians fatten them by giving them drink on the first day, then at first they omit one day, afterwards two, three, or four, till they reach to seven days. These creatures are fattened with barley, millet, figs, acorns, wild pears, and cucumbers. Both this and other animals with a warm stomach are fattened in idleness, and the sow also by wallowing in the mire. They prefer different kinds of food at different ages. The hog and the wolf fight together, a sixth part of its weight when alive, consists of bristles, blood, and fat. Sows and all other animals grow lean while suckling their young. This then, is the nature of these animals.

Chapter IX.

1. Oxen eat both fruits and grass. They become fat on flatulent food, as vetches, broken beans, and stems of beans, and if any person having cut a hole in the skin inflates them and then feeds the older cattle, they fatten more rapidly, and either on whole or broken barley, or on sweet food, as on figs and grapes, wine, and the leaves of the elm, and especially in the sunshine and in warm waters. The horns of the calf, if anointed with wax, may be directed in any way that is desired, and they suffer less in the feet if their horns are rubbed with wax, or pitch, or oil.

2. Herds of cattle suffer less when moved in frost than in snow. They grow if they are deprived for a long time of sexual intercourse; wherefore the herdsmen in Epirus keep the Pyrrhic cattle, as they are called, for nine years without sexual intercourse, in order that they may grow. They call such cows apotauri. The number of these creatures reaches four hundred, and they are the property of the king. They will not live in any other country, though the attempt has been made.

Chapter X.

1. The horse, mule, and ass feed upon fruit and grass, but they fatten especially on drinking, so that beasts of burden enjoy their food in proportion to the quantity of water which they drink, and the less difficulty there is of obtaining drink, the more they profit by abundance of grass. When the mare is in foal, green food causes her hair to be fine, but when it contains hard knots it is not wholesome. The first crop of Medic grass is not good, nor if any stinking water has come near it, for it gives it a bad smell. Oxen require pure water to drink, but horses in this respect resemble camels. The camel prefers water that is dirty and thick; nor will it drink from a stream before it has disturbed the water. It can remain without drinking four days, after which it drinks a great quantity.

Chapter XI.

1. The elephant can eat more than nine Macedonian medimni at one meal, but so much food at once is dangerous; it should not have altogether more than six or seven medimni, or five medimni of bread, and five mares of wine, the maris measures six cotylæ. An elephant has been known to drink as much as fourteen Macedonian measures at once, and eight more again in the evening. Many camels live thirty years, and some much more, for they have been known to live an hundred years. Some say that the elephant lives two hundred, and others three hundred years.

Chapter XII.

1. Sheep and goats live upon grass. Sheep pasture for a long while in one place without leaving it, but goats change

their places very soon, and only crop the top of the grass. The sheep fatten rapidly with drinking, and for this reason during summer they give them salt, a medimnus to each hundred sheep; for in this manner the flock becomes more healthy and fat, and frequently they collect and bring them together for this purpose, that they may mix a great deal of salt with their food; for when thirsty they drink the more. And in the autumn they feed them with gourds which they have sprinkled with salt, for this makes them give more milk. When driven about in the heat of the day they drink more towards evening. If fed with salt after parturition, the udder becomes larger.

2. Sheep fatten on green shoots, vetches, and all kinds of grass, and they fatten more rapidly when their food is salted. They fatten more rapidly if previously starved for three days. During autumn northern water is better for sheep than southern, and pastures towards the west are good for them. Long journeys and weariness make them lean. Shepherds distinguish the strong sheep during winter by the frost adhering to their wool, which is not the case with those that are sick; for those that are not strong move about in their weakness and shake it off.

3. The flesh of all quadrupeds which feed in marshy grounds is inferior to that of those which live on high ground. Sheep with wide tails endure the winter better than those with long tails, and short woolled-sheep better than long-woolled, and those with curly wool are more affected by the cold. Sheep are more healthy than goats, though goats are the stronger. The fleece and the wool of sheep which have been devoured by wolves, and garments made of such wool are more subject to vermin than others.

Chapter XIII.

1. Those insects which have teeth are omnivorous, but those which have a tongue only live upon fluids, which they collect from all sources with this organ. Some of these are omnivorous, for they feed upon all kinds of fluids, as the fly. Others only suck blood, as the myops and œstrus. Others, again, live upon the juices of plants and fruit. The bee is the only insect that never touches anything putrid. It uses

no food that has not a sweet taste. They also take very sweet water, wherever they fall upon any that is pure. The different kinds of animals then use these kinds of food.

Chapter XIV.

1. ALL the actions of animals are employed either in sexual intercourse, or in rearing their young, or in procuring food for themselves, or in providing against excessive heat and cold, and the changes of the seasons. For they all have naturally a sensitiveness respecting heat and cold, and, like mankind, who either change their abodes in cold weather, or those who have large estates, pass their summer in cold countries and their winter in warm ones; so animals, also, if they can, migrate from place to place. Some of them find protection in their accustomed localities, others are migratory; and at the autumnal equinox, escape at the approach of winter, from the Pontus and other cold places; and in spring retreat again before the approach of summer from hot to cold countries, for they are afraid of excessive heat. Some migrate from places close at hand, and others from the very ends of the earth.

2. The cranes do this, for they travel from Scythia to the marshes in the higher parts of Egypt, from which the Nile originates. This is the place where the Pygmies dwell; and this is no fable, for there is really, as it is said, a race of dwarfs, both men and horses, which lead the life of troglodites. The pelicans also are migratory, and leave the river Strymon for the Ister, where they rear their young. They depart in great crowds, and those that are before wait for those behind, for in flying over the mountains those behind cannot see the leaders.

3. The fish also, in the same manner, migrate either from or to the Pontus, and in winter they leave the deep water for the sake of the warmth of the shore, and in summer they escape from the heat by migrating from the shore into deep water. Delicate birds, also, in winter and frosty weather, descend from the mountains to the plains, for the sake of the warmth; and in summer they return again to the mountains for fear of the heat.

4. Those that are the most delicate are the first to make the change at each extreme of heat and cold, such as the

P

mackerel migrate sooner than the tunnies, and the quails than cranes; for some migrate in August, others in September. They are always fatter when they migrate from cold countries, than when they leave warm countries, as the quail is more fat in the autumn than the spring: and so it happens that they migrate alike from cold countries and from warm seasons. Their sexual desires are also more violent in the spring, and when they leave warm countries.

5. Among birds, as it was previously remarked, the crane migrates from one extremity of the earth to the other, and they fly against the wind. As for the story about the stone, it is a fiction, for they say that they carry a stone as ballast, which is useful as a touchstone for gold, after they have vomited it up. The phatta and the peleias leave us, and do not winter with us, nor does the turtle; but the pigeon stays through the winter The same is the nature of the quail, unless a few individuals both of the turtle and quail remain behind in sunny spots. The phatta and turtle assemble in large flocks when they depart, and again at the season of their return. The quails, when they commence their flight, if the weather is fine and the wind in the north, go in pairs, and have a successful voyage. If the wind is south it goes hard with them, for their flight is slow, and this wind is moist and heavy. Those that hunt them, therefore, pursue them when the wind is in the south, but not in fine weather. They fly badly on account of their weight, for their body is large. They therefore make a noise as they fly, for it is a toil to them.

6. When they come hither they have no leader, but when they depart hence, the glottis, ortygometra, otus, and cychramus, which calls them together at night, accompany them; and when the fowlers hear this sound, they know that they will not remain. The ortygometra in form resembles the birds which inhabit marshes. The glottis has a tongue which it projects to a great length. The otus resembles an owl, and has small feathers at its ears. Some persons call it the nycticorax, it is mischievous and imitative, it is taken like the owl, as it dances from side to side, one or other of the fowlers compassing it about. On the whole, birds with crooked claws have short necks, broad tongues, and a capacity for imitation. And so has the Indian bird,

the parrot, which is said to have a tongue like a man. It becomes the most loquacious when intoxicated. The crow, the swan, the pelican, and the small goose, are gregarious birds.

Chapter XV.

1. It has already been observed that fish migrate from the deep water to the coast, and from the coast to the deep water, in order to avoid the excesses of cold and heat. Those that frequent the neighbourhood of the coast are better than those from deep water, for the feeding grounds are better and more abundant. For wherever the sun strikes the plants are more frequent, and superior, and more delicate, as in gardens, and the black shore-weed grows near the land, and the other kinds rather resemble uncultivated plants. The neighbourhood of the coast is also more temperate, both in heat and cold, than the rest of the sea; for which reason the flesh of fish which live near the shore is more compact, while that of fish from deep sea is watery and soft. The sinodon, cantharus, orphos, chrysophrys, cestreus, trigla, cichla, dracon, callionymus, cobius, and all the rock fish live near the shore. The trygon, selache, the white congers, the channa, erythrinus, and glaucus inhabit deep water. The phagrus, scorpius, the black conger, the muræna, and coccyx occupy either situation indifferently.

2. They vary also in different places; as in the neighbourhood of Crete the cobius and all the rock fish are fat. The tunny also becomes good again after Arcturus, for it is not tormented by the œstrus after that period; for which reason also it is inferior during the summer. In lakes near the sea also there are several kinds of fish, as the salpa, chrysophrys, trigla, and nearly all the rest. The amia also is found in such situations as in the vicinity of Alopeconnesus, and in the lake of Bistonis there are many fish. Many of the coliæ do not enter the Pontus; but they pass the summer and rear their young in the Propontis, and winter in the Ægean. The thynnus, pelamis, and amia enter the Pontus in the spring and pass the summer there, and so do nearly all the rhyades and the gregarious fish. Many fish are gregarious, and gregarious fish have a leader of the shoal.

3. They all enter the Pontus for the sake of the food (for the pasture is more abundant and superior, on account

of the fresh water), and for fear of the large creatures, which are smaller there; and except the phocœna and dolphin, there is no other found in the Pontus; and the dolphin is small, but when we leave the Pontus we find a larger dolphin. They enter this sea for the sake of food and rearing their young; for the situation is better for this purpose, and the fresh sweet water nourishes the young fry. When they have reared their young, and the fry begin to grow, they migrate immediately after the Pleiades. If the south wind blow during the winter, they leave the place more slowly; but with a north wind they swim faster, for then the wind helps them along. The small fry is captured in the neighbourhood of Byzantium, for they make no long stay in the Pontus.

4. The other fish are seen both in their egress and ingress. The trichia is only seen as it enters, and is not observed to leave again; and if one is captured at Byzantium, the fishermen purify their nets, for it is unusual for them to return. The reason is this: these are the only fish that swim up into the Ister, and when this river divides they swim down into the Adriatic. The following is a proof; for the converse happens here, and they are never captured entering the Adriatic, but as they leave it.

5. The tunnies, as they enter, swim with their right side to the shore, and leave with their left side to the shore; and some persons say that they do this because they see better with their right eye, and their sight is naturally dim. The rhyades move during the day, and in the night remain quiet and feed, unless the moon is bright, in which case they continue their journey and do not rest themselves. And some persons engaged about the sea say that after the winter solstice they do not move, but remain quiet wherever they may be till the equinox.

6. The coliæ are taken as they enter, but not as they return. The best are taken in the Propontis before the breeding season. The other rhyades are captured more frequently as they leave the Pontus, and are then in perfection. Those that swim near the shore are the fattest when captured; and the farther they are away, the more lean they are; and frequently, when the south wind blows, they swim out in company with the coliæ and mackerel, and are taken

lower down rather than at Byzantium. This is the nature of their migrations.

Chapter XVI.

1. Land animals have also the same disposition for concealment. For in winter they all hasten to conceal themselves, and appear again when the season becomes warmer. Animals conceal themselves to guard against the excesses of temperature. In some the whole race is concealed; in others only a part of them. All the testacea conceal themselves, as those which are marine, the purpura, whelk, and all that class; but the state of concealment is more conspicuous in those which do not adhere to rocks; for these also conceal themselves, as the pectens. Some have an operculum on their exterior, as the land snails; and the alteration of those that are not free is inconspicuous. They do not all conceal themselves at the same period; for the snails are torpid during the winter, the purpura and whelk for thirty days under the dog star, and the pectens at the same period. Most of them conceal themselves in very cold and very hot weather.

2. Almost all insects become torpid, except those which dwell in the habitations of men, and those that perish and do not survive for a year. They are torpid in the winter. Some conceal themselves for a good while, others only in the coldest days, as the bees, for these also conceal themselves. This is shown by their not touching the food which is prepared for them; and if any of them creep out, they appear transparent, and plainly have nothing in their stomach. They remain at rest from the setting of the Pleiades until the spring. Animals pass their torpid state in warm places, and in the spots they are accustomed to inhabit.

Chapter XVII.

1. Many sanguineous animals become torpid, as those which are furnished with scales, the serpent, lizard, gecko, and the river crocodile, during the four winter months in which they eat nothing. Other serpents conceal themselves in the earth, but the viper lies hidden among stones. Many fish also become torpid, especially the hippurus and coracinus during the winter; for these alone are never taken but at

certain seasons, which never vary. Almost all the rest are taken at all seasons. The lamprey, orphus, and conger conceal themselves. The rock fish conceal themselves in pairs as the cichla, cottyphus, and perca, the male with the female in which way also they prepare for their young.

2. The tunny conceals itself during winter in deep places, and they become fattest at this season. The season of capturing them commences with the rising of Pleiades and continues to the end of the setting of Arcturus. All the rest of their time they remain quiet in concealment. A few of these are taken during the period of their concealment. and so are some other hybernating creatures, if they are disturbed by the warmth of their abode or the unusual mildness of the season. For they come out a little from their holes to feed, and also when the moon is full. Most fish are better tasted during the period of concealment. The primades bury themselves in the mud. This is shown by their not being taken, or their seeming to have a great deal of mud on their backs and their fins pressed down.

3. In spring, however, they begin to move and come to the shore to copulate and deposit their ova. At this season they are captured full of ova, and then also they appear to be in season, but are not so good in autumn and winter. At the same season also the males appear to be full of melt. When their ova are small they are taken with difficulty; but as they grow larger many are taken when they are infested by the œstrus. Some fish bury themselves in sand, others in mud, with only their mouths above the surface. Fishes usually conceal themselves only in the winter. The malacostraca, the rock fishes, the batus, and selache only in the most severe weather. This is shown by the difficulty of capturing them in cold weather.

4. Some fish, as the glaucus, conceal themselves in summer time; for this fish hides itself for sixty days in the summer time. The onus and the chrysophrys hide themselves. The reason for supposing that the onus hides itself for a long while appears to be that it is captured at long intervals; and the influence of the stars upon them; and especially of the dog-star, appears to be the cause of their hiding themselves in summer time, for the sea is then disturbed. This is most conspicuous in the Bosphorus; for

the mud is thrown up, and the fish are thus brought to the surface; and they say that, when the bottom is disturbed, more fish are often taken in the same cast the second than the first time; and after much rain animals make their appearance which before were either not seen at all or but seldom.

Chapter XVIII.

1. Many kinds of birds also conceal themselves, and they do not all, as some suppose, migrate to warmer climates; but those which are near the places of which they are permanent inhabitants, as the kite and swallow, migrate thither; but those that are farther off from such places do not migrate, but conceal themselves; and many swallows have been seen in hollow places almost stripped of feathers; and kites, when they first showed themselves, have come from similar situations. Birds with crooked claws, and those also with straight claws, conceal themselves indiscriminately; for the stork, blackbird,[1] turtle dove, and lark hide themselves, and by general agreement the turtle dove most of all, for no one is ever said to have seen one during the winter. At the commencement of hybernation it is very fat, and during that season it loses its feathers, though they remain thick for a long while. Some of the doves conceal themselves; others do not, but migrate along with the swallows. The thrush and the starling also conceal themselves, and among birds with crooked claws the kite and the owl are not seen for a few days.

Chapter XIX.

1. Among viviparous quadrupeds the porcupines and bears hybernate. It is evident that the wild bears conceal themselves; but there is some doubt whether it is on account of the cold or from any other cause, for at this season both the males and females are so fat that they cannot move easily. The female also produces her young at this season, and hides herself until the cubs are of an age to be led forth. This she does in the spring, about three months after the solstice, and she continues invisible for at least forty days. During fourteen days of this period they say that she does not move at all. For more than this period afterwards she remains

Κόττυφος, Turdus merula, *Strack*, blackbird, but probably more than one kind of bird is included under the same name. Compare 9, 36, 2.

invisible, but moves about and is awake. A pregnant bear has either never or very rarely been captured; and it is quite plain that they eat nothing during the whole of this period; for they never come out; and if they are captured, their stomach and entrails appear to be empty; and it is said that, because nothing is presented to it, the intestine sometimes adheres to itself; and, therefore, at their first emergence, they eat the arum, in order to open the entrail and make a passage through it.

2. The dormouse hybernates in trees and is then very fat, and the white Pontic mouse. (Some hybernating animals cast their old age, as it is called. This is the outer skin and the coverings at the period of birth.) It has already been observed, that among viviparous animals with feet there is some doubt as to the cause of the hybernation of bears; but almost all animals with scales hybernate and cast their old age; that is, all that have a soft skin and no shell, as the tortoise; for both the tortoise and the emys belong to the class of animals with scales; but all such as the gecko, lizard, and especially the serpents, cast their skins; for they do this both in the spring, when they first emerge, and again in the autumn.

3. The viper also casts its skin both in the spring and autumn, and is not, as some persons say, the only serpent that does not cast its skin. When serpents begin to cast their skin, it is first of all separated from their eyes; and to those who do not know what is about to happen they appear to be blind. After this it is separated from the head, for first of all it appears entirely white. In a night and day the whole of the old skin is separated from the commencement at the head to the tail; and when cast it is turned inside out, for the serpent emerges as the infant does from the chorion.

4. Insects which cast their skins do it in the same way as the silpha, empis, and the coleoptera, as the beetle. All creatures cast it after birth; for in viviparous animals the chorion is separated, and in the vermiparous, as bees and locusts, they emerge from a case. The grasshoppers, when they cast their skins, sit upon olives and reeds. When the case is ruptured, they emerge, and leave a little fluid behind them, and after a short time they fly away and sing.

5. Among marine creatures the carabi and astaci cast their skins either in spring or autumn, after having deposited their ova; and carabi have been sometimes taken with a soft thorax, because their shell was ruptured, while the lower part, which was not ruptured, was hard. For the process is not the same in them as in serpents. The carabi remain in concealment for about five months. The crabs also cast their old skin, certainly those which have soft shells; and they say that those which have hard shells do the same, as the maia and graus. When they have cast their shells, the new shells are first of all soft, and the crabs are unable to walk. They do not cast their skins once only, but frequently. I have now described when and how animals conceal themselves, and what creatures cast their skin, and when they do so.

Chapter XX.

1. Animals are not all in good health at the same season, nor in the same degrees of heat and cold. Their health and diseases are different at different seasons in various classes, and on the whole are not alike in all. Dry weather agrees with birds, both in respect of their general health and the rearing of their young, and especially with pigeons; and wet weather, with few exceptions, agrees with fish. On the contrary, showery weather generally disagrees with birds, and dry weather with fish; for, on the whole, abundance of drink does not agree with birds.

2. For the birds with crooked claws, generally speaking, as it was before remarked, do not drink. But Hesiod was ignorant of this circumstance; for in relating the siege of Nineveh he represents the presiding eagle of the augury drinking. Other birds drink, but not much; neither do any other oviparous animals with spongy lungs. The sickness of birds is manifest in their plumage; for it is uneven, and has not the same smoothness as when they are well.

3. The generality of fish, as it was observed, thrive the most in rainy years; for not only in such seasons do they obtain a greater supply of food, but the wet weather agrees with them as with the plants that grow on land; for potherbs, even if watered, do not grow so well as in wet weather. The same is the case with the reeds that grow in

ponds; for they never grow, as we may say, except in rainy weather.

4. And this is the reason why so many fish migrate every summer into the Pontus; for the number of rivers which flow into it render the water fresh, and also bring down a supply of food, and many fish also ascend the rivers, and flourish in the rivers and lakes, as the amia and mullet. The cobii also become fat in the rivers; and on the whole, those places which have the largest lakes furnish the most excellent fish.

5. Of all kinds of water, summer showers agree best with fish; and if the spring, summer, and autumn have been wet, a fine winter. And to speak generally, if the season is healthy for mankind, it will be the same for fish. They do not thrive in cold places. Those which have a stone in their head, as the chromis, labrax, sciœna, and phagrus, suffer most in the winter; for the refrigeration of the stone causes them to freeze and be driven on shore.

6. Abundant rain confers health on most fish; but the contrary is the case with the mullet and cephalus, which some call marinus; for if there is a great supply of rain water, they soon become blind. The cephali are particularly liable to this disease in the winter; for their eyes become white. When captured they are lean, and at last perish altogether. They do not, however, appear to suffer so much from the wet as from the cold; for in other places, and especially in the swamps in the neighbourhood of the Argive Nauplia, many are found blind in severe weather, and many also are taken with white eyes.

7. The chrysophrys also suffers from the cold; the arachnas from the heat, which makes it lean. Dry seasons agree better with the coracinus than with any other fish, and for this reason, because it is generally warm in dry weather. Particular localities are favourable to different species, as either the neighbourhood of the land, or the deep waters to those which only frequent one of these localities, or particular places to those which frequent both. There are especial places in which each of them thrive; but, generally speaking, they prefer places full of sea weed; for those which inhabit places with plenty of food are generally found to be fatter; for those that eat fuci obtain plenty of

food, while those that are carnivorous find an abundant supply of fish.

8. They are also affected by northern and southern aspects, for the long fish thrive best in northern situations, and in northern places in the summer time more long fish than flat fish are taken in the same locality. The tunny and xiphia suffer from the œstrus, at the rising of the dog-star, for both these fish at this season have beneath their fins a little worm which is called œstrus, which resembles a scorpion, and is about the size of a spider; they suffer so much from this torment that the xiphias leaps out of the sea as high as the dolphin, and in this manner frequently falls upon ships.

9. The tunny delights in warm weather more than any other fish, and they resort to the sand near the sea-shore for the sake of the warmth, and there they float on the surface; the small fish are safe because they are overlooked, for large fish pursue those of a moderate size. The greater portion of the ova and melt are destroyed . . . . . by the heat, for whatever they touch they entirely destroy.

10. The greatest number of fish are taken before sunrise and after sunset, or just about sunrise and sunset, for the casts made at this period are called seasonable. For this reason the fishermen take up their nets at this time, for the sight of the fish is then most readily deceived. During the night they remain quiet, and at mid-day, when the light is strong, they see very well.

11. Fish do not appear to be subject to any of those pestilential diseases which so often occur among men and quadrupeds, as the horse and ox, and other animals, both domestic and wild. They appear, however, to suffer from ill health, and the fishermen consider that this is proved by the capture of some lean, and apparently weak individuals, and others that have lost their colour, among a number of fat ones of the same kind. This is the nature of sea-fish.

12. No pestilential disease attacks river and pond fish, though some of them are subject to peculiar diseases, as the glanis, from its swimming near the surface, appears to be star-struck by the dog-star, and it is stupefied by loud thunder. The carp suffers in the same way, but not so severely. The glanis, in shallow water, is often destroyed

by the dragon-serpent. In the ballerus and tilon a worm is produced, under the influence of the dog-star, which makes them rise to the surface and become weak, and when they come to the surface they are killed by the heat; a violent disease attacks the chalcis, which is destroyed by a number of lice, which are produced under its gills; no other fish appear to be subject to such a disease.

13. Fishes are poisoned with the plant called mullein, for which reason some persons capture them by poisoning the waters of rivers and ponds; and the Phœnicians poison the sea in the same way. There are two other plans which are adopted for the capture of fish; for since fish avoid the deep parts of rivers in cold weather (for even otherwise the river water is cold), they dig a ditch through the land to the river, which they cover over with grass and stones so as to resemble a cave, with one opening from the river, and when the frost comes on they capture the fish with a basket. The other mode of fishing is practised both in summer and winter. In the middle of the stream they raise a structure with faggots and stones, leaving one part open for a mouth; in this a basket is placed, with which they catch the fish, as they take away the stones.

14. Rainy years agree with all the testacea except the purpura; this is a proof of it, if placed near the mouth of a river, they take the fresh water, and die the same day. The purpura will live about fifty days after it has been taken. They are nourished by each other, for a plant like a fucus or moss grows upon their shells. They say that whatever is cast to them for food is done for the sake of weight, that they may weigh the more.

15. Dry weather is injurious to other testacea, for it renders them fewer in quantity and inferior in quality, and the pectens become more red. In the Pyrrhæan Euripus the pectens perish, not only from the instrument with which the fishermen scrape them together, but also from dry weather. The other testacea thrive in wet weather, because it makes the sea-water fresher. The cold of the Pontus and of the rivers that flow into it renders bivalve shells rare. The univalves, however, are frozen in cold weather. This is the nature of aquatic animals.

Chapter XXI.

1. Among quadrupeds, swine suffer from three diseases, one of these is called sore throat, in which the parts above the jaws and the branchia become inflamed; it may also occur in other parts of the body, and frequently seizes upon the foot, and sometimes the ear. The neighbouring parts then become putrid, until it reaches the lungs, when the animal dies; the disease spreads rapidly, and the animal eats nothing from the period of the commencement of the disease, be it where it will. The swineherds have no other remedy but the excision of the part before the disease has spread far.

2. There are two other diseases which are both called craura. One of them consists in a pain and weight in the head, with which many of them are afflicted; the other is an excessive alvine discharge. This appears to be incurable. They relieve the former by the application of wine to the nostrils, and washing them with wine. Recovery from this disease is difficult, for it generally carries them off on the third or fourth day.

3. They suffer particularly from sore throat, when the summer bears abundantly, and they are fat. The fruit of the mulberry is good for them, and abundant washings with warm water, and scarification beneath the tongue. If the flesh of swine is soft, it is full of small lumps (chalazæ) about the legs, neck, and shoulders; for in these parts the chalazæ are most frequent. If there are but a few, the flesh is sweet; if many, it becomes very fluid and soft.

4. Those which have these chalazæ are easily distinguished; for they exist in the greatest numbers under the tongue, and if the hair is plucked from their mane it appears bloody underneath. Those which have chalazæ cannot keep their hind legs still. They are not thus affected as long as they suck. The grain called tipha, which also forms excellent food, is the remedy for the chalazæ. Vetches and figs are useful both for fattening and rearing pigs; and on the whole their food should not be all of one sort, but varied; for swine, like other animals, derive advantage from a change in their food; and they say that at the same time their food ought to inflate them, and to cover them both with flesh and fat. Acorns are good for their food, but

make their flesh watery; and if they eat too many while pregnant, they produce abortions, as sheep also do; for these animals evidently suffer this from eating acorns. The swine is the only creature that we know of which has chalazæ in its flesh.

Chapter XXII.

1. Dogs suffer from these diseases which have received these names, lytta, cynanche, podagra. The lytta produces madness, and they infect every creature which they bite, except mankind, with the same disease. This disease is fatal to dogs and to any other animal they may bite except man. The cynanche also is fatal to dogs; and there are comparatively few which recover from the podagra. Camels also are seized with lytta. (The elephant does not appear to suffer from any other infirmity except flatulency.)

2. Gregarious oxen suffer from two diseases, one called podagra, the other craurus. The podagra affects their feet; but it is not fatal, nor do they lose their hoofs. They derive benefit from their horns being smeared with warm pitch. When attacked with craurus, their breathing becomes warm and thick. Fever in mankind is the same as craurus in cattle. It is a sign of this disease, when they hang down their ears and will not eat. It soon proves fatal, and when dissected, their lungs appear putrid.

Chapter XXIII.

1. Horses when grazing are free from all diseases except podagra; from this they suffer, and sometimes lose their hoofs, which grow again as soon as they are lost, and the loss of the hoof usually takes place as soon as the first recommences its growth. It is a sign of the disease when the right testicle throbs, or when a wrinkled hollow place appears a little below the middle of the nose. Horses that are brought up in a domestic state suffer from several other diseases; they are attacked with a disorder in their bowels, and it is a sign of the disease when they drag their hind legs up to their fore legs, and keep them under in such a way that they almost strike together: if they go mad after having abstained from food for several days, they are relieved by bleeding and castration.[1]

2. The tetanus is another disease of horses, which is thus

[1] The passage is altogether corrupt.

recognised; all the veins, and the head and neck are extended, and their legs are stiff when they walk; the horses also become full of corrupt matter. They are also attacked by another disease in which they are said to have the crithia;[1] the softness of the roof of the mouth, and heated breath, are the signs of this disease, which is incurable, unless it stays of its own accord. Another disease is called nymphia,[2] which is relieved by the sound of a flute; it causes them to hang down their heads, and when anyone mounts they rush forward until they run against something. The horse is always dejected if afflicted with madness; this is a sign of it, if it lays down its ears upon its mane, and then draws them forward, and pants and breathes hard.

3. These also are incurable if the heart is affected. It is a sign of this disease if the animal suffers from relaxation. And if the bladder alters its position, difficulty in making water is a sign of this disease; it draws up the hoofs and loins. It is also fatal for the horse to swallow the staphilinus, which is of the same size as the spondyla. The bite of the shrew mouse is injurious to other animals also; it causes sores, which are more severe if the creature is pregnant when it bites, for the sores then break. If they are not pregnant, the animal does not perish. The creature called chalkis by some persons and zygnis by others, inflicts either a fatal or very painful bite. It resembles a small lizard, and is of the same colour as the serpent called the blind worm.

4. And, on the whole, those who understand horses say that both these animals and sheep suffer from all the infirmities with which mankind is afflicted. The horse, and every other beast of burden, is destroyed by the poison of sandarach.[3] It is dissolved in water and strained. The pregnant mare casts her young with the smell of a lamp going out. This also happens to some pregnant women. This is the nature of the diseases of horses.

5. The hippomanes, as it is called, is said to be produced upon the foals; the mares when they have bitten it off lick the foal and cleanse it. The fables on this subject have been invented by women and charmers. It is, however, agreed that mares before parturition eject the substance called polion.

6. Horses recognise again the voices of any with which

[1] Indigestion caused by eating barley when heated.
[2] Phrensy. [3] Red sulphuret of arsenic.

they may have fought. They delight in meadows and marshes, and drink dirty water; and if it is clean, they first disturb it with their hoof, and then drink and wash themselves. And on the whole, the horse is an animal fond of water, and still more fond of moisture; wherefore, also, the nature of the river-horse is thus constituted. In this respect the ox is very different from the horse, for it will not drink unless the water is clean, cold, and unmixed.

Chapter XXIV.

1. Asses only suffer from one disease, which is called melis, which first attacks the head of the animal, and causes a thick and bloody phlegm to flow from the nostrils. If the disease extends to the lungs, it is fatal; but that which first attacks the head is not so. This animal cannot bear cold, for which reason there are no asses in the vicinity of the Pontus and in Scythia.

Chapter XXV.

1. Elephants suffer from flatulent diseases, for which reason they can neither evacuate their fluid or solid excrements. If they eat earth they become weak, unless used to such food. If it is accustomed to it, it does no harm. Sometimes the elephant swallows stones. It also suffers from diarrhœa. When attacked with this complaint, they are cured by giving them warm water to drink, and hay dipped in honey to eat; and either of these remedies will stop the disease. When fatigued for want of sleep, they are cured by being rubbed on the shoulders with salt and oil, and warm water. When they suffer from pain in the shoulders, they are relieved by the application of roasted swine's flesh. Some elephants will drink oil, and some will not; and if any iron weapon is struck into their body, the oil which they drink assists in its expulsion; and to those which will not drink it, they give wine of rice cooked with oil. This, then, is the nature of quadrupeds.

Chapter XXVI.

1. Insects generally thrive when the year is of the same kind as the season in which they were born, such as the spring, moist and warm. Certain creatures are produced

in beehives, which destroy the combs, and a little spinning worm, which destroys the wax. It is called clerus, or by some persons pyraustes. This creature produces a spider-like animal like itself, which causes sickness in the hive, and another creature like the moth, which flies round the candle. This produces a creature filled with a woolly substance. It is not killed by the bees, and is only driven out by smoking it. A kind of caterpillar also, which is called teredo, is produced in the hives. The bees do not drive it away. They suffer most from diseases when the woods produce flowers infected with rust, and in dry seasons. All insects die when plunged in oil, and most rapidly if their head is oiled, and they are placed in the sun.

Chapter XXVII.

1. Animals also differ in their localities: for some are entirely absent from some localities which exist in others, though small and shortlived, and not thriving. And frequently there will be a great difference even in adjoining places, as the grasshopper is found in some parts of Milesia, and is absent from those in the immediate vicinity. And in Cephalenia a river divides the country, on one side of which the grasshopper is found, and not on the other.

2. In Poroselene a road divides the country, on one side of which the weasel is found, and not on the other. In Bœotia there are many moles in the neighbourhood of Orchomenus, but in the adjoining Lebadian district there are none, nor if they are imported, are they willing to burrow. If hares are taken into Ithaca they will not live, but are seen dead on the sea coast, turned in the direction in which they were brought. In Sicily the hippomyrmex is not found, and in Cyrene there were formerly no croaking frogs.

3. In all Libya there is neither wild boar, nor stag, nor wild goat. And in India, Ctesias, who is not worthy of credit, says, there are neither domestic nor wild swine; but the exsanguineous and burrowing tribes are all large. In the Pontus there are no malacia, nor all the kinds of testacea, except in a few places; but in the Red Sea all the testacea are of a great size. In Syria there are sheep with tails a cubit in width, and the ears of the goats are a span

and four fingers, and some of them bring their ears down to the ground: and the oxen, like the camels, have a mane upon the point of the shoulder. In Lycia the goats are shorn as the sheep are in other places.

4. In Libya the horned rams are born at once with horns, and not the males only, as Homer says, but all the rest also. In the part of Scythia near the Pontus, the contrary is the case, for they are born without horns. And in Egypt some of the cattle, as the oxen and sheep, are larger than in Greece, and others are smaller, as the dogs, wolves, hares, foxes, ravens, and hawks. Others are nearly of the same size, as the crows and goats. This difference originates in the food which is abundant for some, and scarce for others. For the wolves, hawks, and carnivorous creatures food is scarce, for there are but few small birds. For the dasypus and others which are not carnivorous, neither the hard nor soft fruits are of any long continuance.

5 The temperature is also very influential; for in Illyria, Thrace, and Epirus, the asses are small. In Scythia, and Celtic countries, they do not occur at all, for in these places the winter is severe. In Arabia the lizards are more than a cubit long, and the mice are much larger than those which inhabit our fields, their fore legs being a span long, and their hind legs as long as from the first joint of the finger . . . .

6. In Libya, the serpents, as it has been already remarked, are very large. For some persons say that as they sailed along the coast, they saw the bones of many oxen, and that it was evident to them that they had been devoured by the serpents. And as the ships passed on, the serpents attacked the triremes, and some of them threw themselves upon one of the triremes and overturned it. There are more lions in Europe, and especially in the country between the Achelous and the Nessus. In Asia there are leopards which are not found in Europe.

7. On the whole, the wild animals of Asia are the fiercest, those of Europe the boldest, and those of Libya the most varied in form ; and it has passed into a proverb that Libya is always producing something new. For the want of water brings many heterogeneous animals together at the drinking places, where they copulate and produce young, if

their periods of gestation happen to be the same, and their size not very different. The desire of drinking makes them gentle to each other, for they differ from the animals of other countries, in wanting to drink more in winter than in summer; for on account of the great want of water during the summer they are habituated to do without water; and if the mice drink they die.

8. Other animals are produced by the intercourse of heterogeneous creatures, as in Cyrene the wolves copulate with the dogs, and produce young; and the Laconian dogs are bred between a dog and a fox. They say that the Indian dogs are derived from the tiger and the dog; not directly, but from the third mixture of the breeds; for they say that the first race was very fierce. They take the dogs and tie them up in the desert. Many of them are devoured, if the wild animal does not happen to desire sexual intercourse.

Chapter XXVIII.

1. Different localities produce a variety of dispositions, as mountainous and rough places, or smooth plains. They are more fierce and robust in appearance in mountains, as the swine of Athos; for the males of those which inhabit the plains cannot endure even the females of the other kind: and different situations have great influence on the bite of wild animals. All the scorpions about Pharus and other places are not painful, but in Caria and other localities they are frequent, and large, and fierce, and their sting is fatal to either man or beast, even to sows, which are but little influenced by the bite of other creatures, and black sows are more easily affected than others. The swine die very soon after being stung, if they come near the water.

2. The bite also of serpents varies much; for in Libya the asp is found, from which they form a septic poison, which is incurable. In the plant silphium is found a small serpent, for the bite of which a remedy has been discovered in a small stone, which is taken out of the tomb of one of the ancient kings: this they drink dipped in wine. In some parts of Italy the bite of the gecko is found to be fatal. If one poisonous animal eats another, as, if a

---

[1] Probably assafœtida.

viper eats a scorpion, its bite is the most fatal of all. The saliva of a man is hostile to most of them. There is one small serpent, which some persons call hierus, which is avoided even by large serpents. It is a cubit long, and appears rough. Whatsoever it bites immediately becomes putrid in a circle round the wound. There is also a small serpent in India, the only one for which there is no remedy.

CHAPTER XXIX.

1. ANIMALS also differ in being in good condition or not during gestation. The testacea, as the pectens and the malacostraca, as the carabi and such like, are best when pregnant; for this word is also used of the testacea. For the malacostraca have been observed both in the act of copulation and oviposition; but none of the testacea have ever been seen so occupied. The malacia, such as the teuthis, sepia, and polypus, are most excellent when pregnant; and almost all fish are good during the early part of the period; but as the time advances some are good and some not so.

2. The mænis thrives during gestation. The form of the female is round, that of the male longer and broader. And when the period of gestation commences in the females, the males become black and variegated, and are not fit to eat. Some persons call them tragi at this period. Those which are called cottyphus and cichla also change their colour; and the caris also changes at this season and some birds, which are black in spring and afterwards become white.

3. The phycis also changes its colour; for it is white at all other seasons, and variegated in the spring. This is the only sea fish that, as they say, makes a nest in which it deposits its ova. The mænis, as it was before observed, and the smaris also change their colours, and from being white in summer become black. This is particularly conspicuous about the fins and gills. The coracinus is best when pregnant, and so is the mænis. The cestreus, labrax, and nearly all creatures that swim are inferior at this season.

4. There are a few which are good, whether pregnant or not, as the glaucus. Old fish also are inferior; and old tunnies are not even fit for salting, for much of the flesh is

dissolved. The same thing also happens with other fish. The older fish are distinguished by the size and hardness of their scales; an old tunny has been taken which weighed fifteen talents, and the length of the tail was two cubits and a span.

5. River and pond fish are most excellent, after depositing their ova and semen, and recovering their flesh. Some of them, however, are good while pregnant, as the saperdis; and others bad, as the glanis. In all the male is better than the female; but the female glanis is better than the male. Those which they call female eels are better than the males. They call them females, though they are not so, but only differ in appearance.

BOOK THE NINTH.

CHAPTER I.

1. THE dispositions of obscure and short-lived animals are less easily observed than those of long-lived animals; for they appear to have a certain inclination towards each natural affection of the soul, such as prudence and folly, courage and cowardice, mildness and cruelty, and such other habits. Some also, which have the sense of hearing, appear to be capable of a certain degree of instruction and discipline, both from one another and from mankind, for they not only distinguish the difference of sounds but also of signs.

2. And in all animals in which there is a distinction of the sexes nature has given a similar disposition to the males and to the females. This is most conspicuous in man, and the larger animals, and in viviparous quadrupeds; for the disposition of the female is softer, and more tameable and submissive, and more ingenious; as the females of the Lacedemonian dog are more gentle than the males. In the Molossian race of dogs, those employed in hunting differ in no respect from other dogs; while those employed in following sheep are larger and more fierce in their attack on wild beasts. A mixture of the Molossian and Lacedemonian races is both braver and more capable of enduring fatigue.

3. The females of all animals are less violent in their passions than the males, except the female bear and pardalis, for the female of these appears more courageous than the male. In other animals the females are more soft and insidious, less simple, more petulant, and more active in the care of their young. The disposition of the males is opposed to this; for they are more passionate and fierce, more straightforward, and less invidious. The vestiges of these dispositions exist, as we may say, in all, but are more conspicuous in those which have the strongest moral habits, and most of

all in mankind; for the nature of the human subject is the most complete, so that these habits appear more conspicuous in mankind than in other animals.

4. Wherefore women are more compassionate and more readily made to weep, more jealous and querulous, more fond of railing, and more contentious. The female also is more subject to depression of spirits and despair than the male. She is also more shameless and false, more readily deceived, and more mindful of injury, more watchful, more idle, and on the whole less excitable than the male. On the contrary, the male is more ready to help, and, as it has been said, more brave than the female; and even in the malacia, if the sepia is struck with a trident, the male comes to help the female, but the female makes her escape if the male is struck.

Chapter II.

1. Animals often fight with each other, particularly those which inhabit the same places and eat the same food; for when food becomes scarce, congeners fight together. They say that seals which occupy the same locality will fight, the males with the males and the females with the females, until one party is either killed or ejected by the other, and their cubs also will fight in the same way. All animals also will fight with carnivorous creatures, and these will fight with other animals, for they feed upon living creatures; for which reason augurs observe the disputes and agreements of animals, considering that their disputes betoken war, and their agreements peace with each other.

2. When supplied with plenty of food, animals that are naturally afraid of man and fierce appear to submit themselves to him, and to conduct themselves quietly towards each other. The care which is taken of animals in Egypt demonstrates this circumstance; for even the fiercest creatures live together, when they have food enough, and are not in any want; for they become tame from the supply of their wants which they receive, as the crocodiles are tamed by the priests by the care which is bestowed on their food. The same thing may be observed in other countries and in their different parts.

3. The eagle and the dragon are enemies, for the eagle feeds on serpents. The ichneumon and the spider are also

enemies, for the ichneumon hunts the spider. Among birds the pœcilis and the lark and the wood-pecker and chloreus are enemies, for they eat each others' eggs. The crow and the owl also are enemies; for at mid-day the crow, taking advantage of the dim sight of the owl, secretly seizes and devours its eggs, and the owl eats those of the crow during the night; and one of these is master during the day, the other during the night. The owl and orchilus are enemies; for the latter eats the eggs of the owl. During the day other birds fly round the owl, which is called "astonishing it," and as they fly round it pluck off its feathers. For this reason fowlers use it in hunting for all kinds of birds.

4. The presbys contends with the weasel and crow, for they eat its eggs and young. The turtle and pyrallis are foes, for their food and mode of life are the same. The celeus and libyus, kite and raven are enemies; for the kite, from the superiority of its claws and flight, can take from the raven anything it may have caught, so that their food is the cause of their enmity also. Those that obtain their food from the sea also are foes, as the brenthus, larus, and harpa. The triorches is a foe to the toad and the serpent; for the triorches eats the others. The turtle and chloreus are foes, for the chloreus kills the turtle, and the crow kills the bird called typanus. The little owl and all other birds with crooked claws eat the calaris, from whence their enmity arises.

5. The gecko and the spider are enemies, for the gecko eats spiders. The pipo is a foe to the heron, for it devours the eggs and young of the heron. Enmity also exists between the ægithus and the ass; for the ass frequents thorny places, that it may scratch its sores, and by this means, and when it brays it overturns the eggs and young of the ægithus, for they fall out of the nest from fear of the noise, and the bird, to revenge this injury, flies upon the ass and inflicts wounds. The wolf is the enemy of the ass, bull, and fox; for being a carnivorous animal, it attacks both oxen, asses, and foxes. The fox and circus are enemies for the same reason; for the circus having crooked claws, and being carnivorous, attacks and inflicts wounds with its claws.

6. The raven is an enemy to the bull and ass, for it flies round them and strikes their eyes. The eagle and the heron

are foes, for the eagle has crooked claws and attacks it, and the other dies in defending itself. The æsalon is a foe to the vulture, and the crex to the coleus, blackbird, and chlorion, which some persons fabulously say derives its origin from a funeral pile, for it destroys both themselves and their young. The sitta and trochilus are foes to the eagle, and the eagle, as well for this reason, as because it is carnivorous, is a foe to them all.

7. The anthus is the enemy of the horse, for it drives the horse from its pasture, for the anthus also feeds on grass; it is dim-sighted and not quick; it imitates the voice of the horse, which it frightens by flying at it, and drives it from its pasture; if the horse can seize upon it, he will kill it. The anthus lives near rivers and marshes; it is of a fine colour, and lives well. The ass attacks the colota, a creature which lives in the manger, and prevents it from eating, by making its way into its nostrils.

8. There are three kinds of heron, the black, the white sort, and the one called asterias; of these, the black rests and copulates with difficulty, for it utters a cry, and, as they say, bleeds from the eyes during coition, and the process of parturition is severe and painful; it attacks creatures which injure it, as the eagle, for it seizes upon it, and the fox, for this creature attacks it during the night, and the lark, which steals its eggs.

9. The serpent is an enemy to the weasel and the hog, for if the weasel and serpent live in the same house they both require the same kind of food; and swine eat serpents. The æsalon is a foe to the fox, for it strikes and pecks it, and destroys its young, for it has crooked claws. The raven and the fox are friendly, for the raven also attacks the æsalon, and so they help each other in the attack. The little owl and the æsalon are mutual foes, for both have crooked claws. The little owl and the swan attack the eagle, and the swan often comes off victorious. Of all birds the swans are most disposed to devour[1] each other.

10. Some animals are always ready to attack each other, and others, as mankind, only at particular times. The ass and the acanthis are foes, for the latter feeds entirely on thorns, but the former only when they are tender. The an-

---

[1] To fight with each other.—See Liddell and Scott's Lexicon, s. v. ἀλληλομάχος.

thus, acanthis, and ægithus are foes, and it is said that the blood of the anthus and ægithus will not mix. The crow and heron are friends, and so are the schœnion, lark, laëdus, and celeus, for the celeus lives by the side of rivers and thickets, but the laëdus lives among rocks and mountains, and is fond of the place in which it lives. The piphinx, harpa, and kite are friends; the fox and the serpent also, for both live in holes; and the blackbird and the turtle.

11. The lion and jackal are foes, for both are carnivorous, and live on the same substances. Elephants also fight fiercely with each other, and strike with their tusks; the conquered submits entirely, and cannot endure the voice of the victor: and elephants differ much in the courage they exhibit. The Indians use both male and female elephants in war, though the females are smaller and far less courageous. The elephant can overthrow walls by striking them with its large tusks; it throws down palm trees by striking them with its head, and afterwards putting its feet upon them, stretches them on the ground.

12. Elephant-hunting is conducted in the following way: men mount upon some tame courageous animals; when they have seized upon the wild animals they command the others to beat them till they fail from fatigue. The elephant-driver then leaps upon its back and directs it with a lance; very soon after this they become tame and obedient. When the elephant-drivers mount upon them they all become obedient, but when they have no driver, some are tame and others not so, and they bind the fore legs of those that are wild with chains, in order to keep them quiet. They hunt both full-grown animals and young ones. Such is the friendship and enmity of these wild animals originating in the supply of food, and the mode of life.

CHAPTER III.

1. SOME fish are gregarious and friendly together, others that are less gregarious are hostile. Some are gregarious while they are pregnant, others during the season of parturition. On the whole, the following are gregarious: the tunny, mœnis, cobius, box, saurus, coracinus, sinodon, trigla, muræna, anthia, eleginus, atherinus, sarginus, belona, (mecon,) teuthus

iulus, pelamis, scombrus, and colias. Some of these are both gregarious, and live in pairs, for all the others pair together; and some are gregarious at particular seasons, as it has been said, while they are pregnant, and others in the season of depositing their ova.

2. The labrax and cestreus, though most hostile, will at certain seasons congregate with each other, for not only do congeners congregate together, but all those which feed upon the same kind of food, where it is abundant. The cestreus and the conger often survive after having been deprived of their tail up to the anus, for the cestreus is eaten by the labrax, and the conger by the muræna. The stronger are hostile to the weaker, for the strong fish eat the others. This much concerning marine creatures.

CHAPTER IV.

1. It has been already observed, that the dispositions of animals vary in cowardice, mildness, courage, gentleness, intelligence, and folly. The disposition of sheep, as I have said before, is foolish, and without sense; they are the most cowardly of all animals, and steal away into desert places for no purpose, and in winter often escape from their fold. When overtaken by a snow-storm, they will not get away, unless the shepherd drives them, but will stay behind and perish, unless the shepherds carry off the males, when the rest will follow.

2. If a person takes any of the goats by the beard (which is like hair), all the rest stand by as if infatuated, and look at it. Sheep will sleep in colder places than goats, for sheep are more quiet, and are ready to submit themselves to mankind. Goats do not bear the cold so well as sheep. Shepherds teach sheep to come together when they make a noise, and if any of them is left behind and does not join the flock when it thunders, it will cast its young, if pregnant; wherefore, when a noise is made, they will collect together in their sheds according to their custom. (Bulls are destroyed by wild beasts, if they wander away from their herd.) Sheep and goats lie down to rest separately in their races, and when the sun begins to descend, the shepherds say that the goats do not lie down with their faces to each other, but they turn their backs upon each other.

Chapter V.

1. Cows pasture in herds, and in companies, and if one of them wanders to a distance, all the rest follow, so that the herdsmen, if they do not find her, immediately examine all the herds. Mares in herds, if one of them happens to die, will bring up her foal among them, and the whole race of horses appears to have warm natural affections, of which the following is a proof: the barren mares will take away the foals from their mothers, and treat them with affection, though they soon die for want of milk.

Chapter VI.

1. Of all wild quadrupeds, the deer appears to be one of the most prudent in producing its young by the wayside (where wild beasts do not come, for fear of men); as soon as the young is born, the dam eats the chorion, and runs to the plant called seselis, which she eats, and having so done, returns to her kid. She then leads her kid to the station, to which it may learn to retreat in case of danger; this is usually a chasm in a rock with a single entrance, which they say that it stays and defends. When the male gets fat (which usually happens in the autumn) he does not show himself, but gets out of the way, for his fat makes him an easy prey. He sheds his horns in difficult and scarcely accessible places, from whence arises the proverb, "where the stag sheds its horns," for they are afraid of being seen, as if they had lost their means of defence. It is said that the left horn never has been seen, for he conceals it as if it had some medicinal power.

2. When a year old they have no horns, but only a commencement, as it were a sign of what is to be; this is short, and covered with thick down. When two years old, they have straight horns, like sticks, for which reason they are called pattalia (from πατταλος, a stake). In the third year their horns are divided. In the fourth year they become rough. In this manner they are regularly developed till they are six years old. After this age their horns are always the same, so that their age cannot be distinguished by them. Old stags, however, are recognised by two signs; some of them have no teeth at all, others only a few; and

they never have the defensive part of the horn, that part of the growing horn which bends forwards, with which they defend themselves, this the old stags never possess, but all the increase of their horns is upwards.

3. They cast their horns every year about the month of April. When they cast their horns they hide themselves during the day, as it has been already observed. They conceal themselves in thickets, to protect themselves from the flies. During this period they feed (in the thickets) during the night, until their horns are grown. They are produced at first under the skin, and are covered with down. When they grow they expose them to the sun, that the horn may be matured and hardened. When they cease to give them pain if rubbed against trees, they leave such places, for they are confident in their means of defence. An Achaïnian stag [1] has been taken with a considerable quantity of green ivy growing on its horns as in green wood, for the horns are tender when first produced.

4. When the stags are bitten by the phalangium or any such creature, they collect together a number of crabs and eat them. It appears to be wholesome for mankind to drink the same substance, but it is not pleasant. The females, as soon as their young are born, eat the chorium, and it is not possible to obtain it, for they seize upon it before it can fall to the ground; it appears to have some medicinal properties. The females are captured by the sound of the pipe and by singing, and they are charmed by singing. When two persons go out to capture them, one shows himself, and either plays upon a pipe, or sings, and the other strikes behind, when the first gives him the signal; when the ears of the deer are erect, it hears quickly, and cannot be deceived, as it may be if they hang down.

Chapter VII.

1. When bears are in flight, they drive their cubs before them, or take them up and carry them. When nearly overtaken, they climb up into trees. When they first come from their hiding place they eat the arum, as it has been already observed, and gnaw the trees as if they were cutting teeth. Many other animals also prudently provide themselves with

[1] A bracket, or two year old stag.

remedies, for they say that the wild goats in Crete, when struck with an arrow, seek out the dittany, for this plant assists in working the arrow from their body.

2. And dogs, when they are ill, provide themselves with an emetic from a certain kind of grass. The panther, when it has eaten the poison called pardalianches,[1] seeks for human ordure, for this relieves it. This poison also will kill lions, the hunters, therefore, suspend ordure in a vessel from the trees, in order that the animal may not wander far from them; for the panther jumps at it and attempts to seize it, and dies before it can reach it. They say that the panther is aware that its peculiar scent is grateful to other wild animals, and that it preys upon them in concealment, and when deer approach near, it catches hinds.

3. The Egyptian ichneumons, when they see the serpent called the asp, do not attack it until they have invited others to assist. They roll themselves in mud as a protection against its blows and wounds; they first bathe in water and then roll themselves on the ground. When the crocodile gapes, the trochilus flies into its mouth, to cleanse its teeth; in this process the trochilus procures food, and the other perceives it, and does not injure it; when the crocodile wishes the trochilus to leave, it moves its neck that it may not bite the bird. When the tortoise has eaten a viper, it afterwards eats origanum; this has been observed. A person who had often seen this done, and had observed that when the tortoise had tasted the origanum it went back to the viper, gathered all the origanum, and when this was done, the tortoise died.

4. The weasel eats the herb rue before it attacks a serpent, for the smell of this herb is obnoxious to serpents. When the draco has eaten much fruit, it sucks the juice of the bitter lettuce; it has been seen to do this. When dogs are troubled with worms, they eat the green tops of corn. When the pelargus or any other bird has been wounded in flight, they feed upon marjoram, and many persons have seen the locust[2] settle upon the neck of serpents with which it was contending. The weasel also appears prudent in the way in which it attacks birds, for it kills them in the same manner as wolves kill sheep; it will fight also with serpents, and especially with those that hunt mice; for the weasel pursues the same animals.

[1] Perhaps Aconite.   [2] Spax lacerticida.—*Schneider*.

5. Observations have been frequently made on the instinct of the hedgehog, for when the north and south winds change, those that dwell in the earth alter the position of the entrance of their burrows; those which are kept in houses alter their position from wall to wall, so that they say that in Byzantium there was a person who obtained the character of predicting the change of the weather, from observations made on the hedgehog. The ictis is about the size of a small Maltese dog; in the thickness of its hair, its appearance, its white belly, and the cunning of its disposition, it resembles the weasel; it is easily tamed; it attacks hives of bees, for it is very fond of honey; it eats birds like cats; its penis, as it has been already observed, is bony, and appears to be a remedy for stranguary in the human subject; it is administered in shavings.

Chapter VIII.

1. Many animals in their mode of life appear to imitate mankind, and one may observe greater accuracy of intellect in small than in large animals; as the manufacture of its dwelling by the swallow is remarkable among birds; it has the same method of combining chaff with mud, for it mixes the mud with straw, and if mud is not to be found, it dips in the water and rolls itself in the dust; it uses straw in making its nest as men use it, for it places the largest at the bottom, and makes it commensurate with its own bulk; both the male and female labour in support of the young. They feed each in turn, observing by some agreement the one which was first fed that none may receive food twice; at first they turn the dung out of the nest, but as the young birds increase in size, they teach them to turn themselves, so as to eject their excrement out of the nest.

2. There are some observations which may be made on pigeons, for they will not pair with many mates, nor do they forsake their first companion, unless they become widowed. The care and anxiety of the male at the time of parturition are remarkable, for if the pain causes the hen to feel languid when near the nest, he beats her and drives her in. When the young are hatched, the parent provides salt earth, which is injected into the open mouth of the young birds, as a preparation for the reception of food. When it is time for them to leave the nest, the male copulates with them all.

3. In this manner they have usually a great affection for each other. Some females will copulate with males that are not their own mates. This bird is contentious, they fight together, and attack each other's nests, though not frequently, for although they are beaten when at a distance, they will fight to the last when near their nests; it appears to be characteristic of the pigeon, phaps, and turtle not to lean back when they drink, unless they have had sufficient. The turtle and phatta aways remain faithful to the same male, and will not permit another to approach them, and the male and female share the labour of incubation. The male and female are not easily distinguished, except by their internal structure.

4. The phatta is long-lived, they have been known to live for twenty-five or thirty years, some even forty years; their claws grow when they become aged, and pigeon breeders cut them off, and in no other respect are they inferior when aged. The turtle and the pigeon, if they have been blinded by those who use them as decoy birds, will live eight years. The partridge lives fifteen years, the phaps and the turtle always build in the same places.

5. On the whole, males also live longer than females, but in these birds they say that the males die before the females; this conclusion is derived from the observation of those which are brought up in houses for decoy birds. Some persons say that cock-sparrows only live for one year, considering this as a proof, that early in the spring there are no birds with black beneath the chin; but they have it afterwards, as if none of the former birds had survived. The hen-sparrows have a longer life, for these are taken among the young birds, and are easily known by the hard portion about their bills. The turtle lives during the summer in cold places, and during the winter in warm places. The finch lives during the summer in warm places, and in cold places during winter.

Chapter IX.

1. The heavy birds do not make nests, for it does not agree with their mode of flight, as the quail, partridge, and all such birds; but when they have made a hole in the smooth ground (for they never produce their young in any other

place), they collect together some thorns and sticks for a defence against the hawks and eagles, and there lay their eggs and incubate. As soon as the young are hatched, they lead them out, because their slow flight prevents them from procuring food for them. The quail and partridge shelter their young under their wings, like the domestic fowl.

2. They do not lay and incubate in the same place, lest any one should discover the place while they sat there for a long while; and when any one in hunting falls upon the nest, the partridge halts before him, as if she could be taken, and draws him after her in the hopes of capture, until all the young ones have had time to escape, and after she flies back and recalls them to their nest. The partridge does not lay less than ten eggs, and often sixteen. As it has been already observed, it is a bird of an evil and cunning disposition. In the spring they separate with singing and fighting into pairs with the females which each may happen to take. The partridge being a bird of violent passions, it tries to prevent the female from incubation by rolling and breaking the eggs, if it can find them. The female, opposing this artifice by another, lays her eggs as she runs, and often, from her desire of laying, she drops her eggs wherever she may be, if the male is present; and, that they may all be preserved, she does not return to them. If she is observed by men, she leads them away from her eggs as from her young ones, and shows herself just before them until they are drawn away from the nest.

3. When the hen has escaped for incubation, the cocks crow and fight together. These are called widowers. The vanquished in the combat follows his conqueror who alone has intercourse with him; and if any one is overcome by a second, or by any chance one, the victor has secret intercourse with him. This does not take place always, but only at certain seasons of the year. The quail does the same, and domestic fowls also; for when a new one is offered in the temples, where they are kept without the females, all in turn are united with it. Tame partridges have sexual intercourse with wild ones, and strike and insult them.

4. The leader of the wild partridges attacks the partridge used in fowling, and goes out crowing as if he would fight. When he is taken in the trap, the other goes out and crows

in the same manner. If the partridge used for fowling is a cock, they behave in this way; but if it is a female, and she calls, the leader answers her call; and all the rest rise up and beat him, and drive him away from the female, because he attends to her instead of themselves. For this reason he often comes silently, that the others may not hear his voice and come out to fight him. And some experienced fowlers say that the male approaches the female in silence that the other males may not hear him and compel him to fight them. The partridge not only calls, but also utters a shrill cry and other sounds.

5. And it often happens, when the hen is sitting, that if she sees the male approaching the decoy bird, she will get up from her nest, and remain in his way, that he may have intercourse with her, and not be drawn away by the decoy bird. Partridges and quails have such violent sexual desires that they will fall upon the fowlers and often perch upon their heads.

Chapter X.

1. This is the mode of the sexual intercourse of the partridge, and the way in which they are caught, and the nature of the rest of their crafty disposition. Quails, and partridges, and some other birds make their nest upon the ground, as it has been already observed. Of such birds the lark, woodcock, and quail do not perch upon trees, but upon the ground.

2. The woodpecker does not settle upon the ground, but it strikes trees in order to drive out the worms and flies which they contain, and it picks them up with its tongue as they emerge. Its tongue is wide and large. It walks upon the trees in any position, even beneath the branches, like the gecko. It has claws stronger than those of the coloeus, which provide for its safety in climbing trees; for it fixes them in the bark as it walks up the trees. There is one kind of woodpecker less than the blackbird, covered with small red spots, and another kind larger than the blackbird, and a third kind nearly as large as the domestic hen. It builds its nest upon trees, as it has been already observed, both on olive and other trees; and it feeds upon ants and worms which live in trees. It hunts for worms so diligently that they say it hollows out the trees so much as to throw them

down. A tame bird has been known to place an almond in a crack in wood, to prepare it for the stroke of its bill, and break it with three blows, in order to eat the kernel.

Chapter XI.

Many prudent actions appear to be performed by cranes; for they travel great distances, and fly at a great elevation, in order that they may see farther; and if they see clouds and wintry weather, they descend and rest themselves. They have also a leader in front; and in the rear are those which give a signal by whistling, so that their voice may be heard. When they settle on the ground, the rest sleep with their head under the wing, first on one foot, then on the other; but the leader watches with his neck stretched out, and when he sees anything he gives a signal by his cry. The pelicans, which inhabit the rivers, swallow large smooth shells with their drink, and when they have been digested in the first part of their stomach, they vomit them up, in order that they may pick out and eat their flesh when they open their valves.

Chapter XII.

1. The habitations of wild birds are contrived with relation to their mode of life and the preservation of their young. Some of them are kind to their young and careful of them: others are of a different disposition. Some manage well in their mode of life: others do not. Some dwell in clefts, and holes, and in rocks, as the birds called charadrius. This bird is faulty both in its colours and its voice. It appears during the night, and escapes in the day time.

2. The hawk also builds in precipitous places; and although it is carnivorous, it does not devour the heart of the bird it has killed. Some have observed this with respect to the quail and thrush, and others with other birds. There is also a change in their mode of hunting their prey, for they do not seize them in the same way in summer and in winter. It is said that no one has ever seen the young or the nest of the carrion vulture. Wherefore Herodorus, the father of Brison the sophist, says that they come from some distant elevated land, using this proof, that many of them appear suddenly, but where they come from is not intelligible

to any one. The reason is this, they make their nest in inaccessible rocks, and the bird is not an inhabitant of many countries. It produces one egg or two at the most.

3. Some birds dwell in mountains and in woods, as the hoopoe and brenthus. This bird has a good habit of life and a good voice. The trochilus dwells in thickets and holes. It is taken with difficulty, for it is swift in flight, and its disposition is weak; but its mode of life is good, and it is artful. It is also called presbys and basileus. Wherefore also they say that it fights with the eagle.

Chapter XIII.

1. There are some which live near the sea, as the cinclus. In disposition this bird is cunning and difficult of capture, and when taken easily tamed. It appears to be lame, for its hinder parts are weak. All birds with webbed feet live near the sea, or near rivers and ponds, for their nature teaches them to seek what is advantageous for them. Many of those with divided feet live near waters and marshes, as the anthus in the neighbourhood of rivers. Its colour is beautiful, and its mode of life good. The diver lives near the sea, and when it plunges into the sea it remains as long a time as it would take a man to walk over a plethrum of ground. This bird is less than a hawk.

2. The swan also is web-footed, and lives in ponds and marshes. Its manner of life and disposition is good, and so is its mode of rearing their young and its old age. If an eagle attacks the swan, it defends itself and comes off victorious, but will not commence the fight. Swans have the power of song, especially when near the end of their life; for they then fly out to sea, and some persons, sailing near the coast of Libya, have met many of them in the sea singing a mournful song, and have afterwards seen some of them die.

3. The cymindis is seldom seen, for it inhabits mountains. It is black, and about the size of the hawk called pigeon hawk. Its form is long and slight. (It shines with a metallic lustre, wherefore also it is called chalcis.) The Ionians call it cymindis: wherefore Homer writes in the Iliad, "the bird which the gods call chalcis, and mortals cymindis." (Some persons say that the hybris is the same

bird as the ptynx.) This bird does not show itself in the day-time because its sight is dim; but it hunts its prey during the night like the eagle. It fights so fiercely with the eagle that both are often taken alive by the shepherds. It lays two eggs, and builds in rocks and caverns. Cranes fight so fiercely with each other that these also are taken alive by the shepherds while they are fighting. The crane lays two eggs.

Chapter XIV.

1. The jay changes its voice frequently, for it utters a different one, as we may say, almost every day; it lays about nine eggs; it makes its nest upon trees, of hair and wool; when the acorns fall, it conceals and stores them up. Many persons have reported that the stork is fed by its young, and some people say the merops also, and that they are fed by the young, not only in their old age, but as soon as the young birds are able to do so, and that the parents remain within the nest; in appearance, this bird is green beneath the wings, and blue above, as the kingfisher, and its wings are red at the extremity. It lays six or seven eggs in the autumn, in muddy caverns, and digs as much as four cubits into the ground.

2. The bird called chloris from being yellow beneath, is of the size of the lark, and lays four or five eggs; it makes its nest of symphytum, which it pulls up by the root, and lines it with straw, hair, and wool. The blackbird and jay do the same, and line their nests with the same materials; the nest of the acanthyllis is also artfully constructed, for it is folded together like a ball of flax, and has a small entrance. And the natives of those places say that there is a cinnamon bird, and that they bring the cinnamon from the same places as the bird, and that it makes its nest of it. It builds its nest in lofty trees and among their branches, but the natives of the country tip their arrows with lead, with which they destroy the nests, and then pick out the cinnamon from the other material.

Chapter XV.

1. The halcyon is not much larger than a sparrow; its colour is blue and green, and somewhat purple; its whole

body is composed of these colours as well as the wings and neck, nor is any part without every one of these colours. Its bill is somewhat yellow, long, and slight; this is its external form. Its nest resembles the marine balls which are called halosachnæ,[1] except in colour, for they are red; in form it resembles those sicyæ (cucumbers) which have long necks; its size is that of a very large sponge, for some are greater, others less. They are covered up, and have a thick solid part as well as the cavity; it is not easily cut with a sharp knife, but when struck or broken with the hand, it divides readily like the halosachnæ. The mouth is narrow, as it were a small entrance, so that the sea-water cannot enter, even if the sea is rough; its cavity is like that of the sponge; the material of which the nest is composed is disputed, but it appears to be principally composed of the spines of the belone, for the bird itself lives on fish. It also ascends rivers; it does not produce more than five eggs; it continues to reproduce throughout the whole of its life, from the time of being four months old.

Chapter XVI.

1. The hoopoe generally makes its nest of human ordure. It changes its appearance in summer and winter, like most other wild birds. The titmouse, as they say, lays the greatest number of eggs, some say that the bird called melancoryphus lays the greatest number of eggs after the Libyan sparrow, seventeen have been observed, but it will produce more than twenty, and, as they say, it always lays a great many. This bird also builds in trees, and lives upon worms. It is characteristic of this bird and the nightingale not to have any tip to their tongue. The ægithus has a good mode of life, and is careful of its young, but is lame upon its feet. The chlorion is a clever and diligent bird, but its flight is difficult, and its colours bad.

2. The elea, like some other birds, has an excellent mode of life, and dwells during the summer in groves and in the shade, and during the winter in sunshine, perching upon the reeds on the sides of marshes. It is a small bird, with a good voice.

3. The bird called gnaphalus has a sweet voice, its colours

[1] Probably a Zoophyte, Alcyonia.

are beautiful, its mode of life good, and its form elegant; it appears to be a foreign bird, for it is rarely found in places where there are no houses.

4. The disposition of the crex is pugnacious, but it is ingenious in providing for its own subsistence, though otherwise an unfortunate bird. The sitta is pugnacious, but its disposition is gentle and tractable, and its mode of life good. It is said to be medicinal, for it is skilful in many things. It produces many young, which it treats with kindness, and obtains its food by striking trees.

5. The little owl feeds during the night, and is rarely visible by day. It lives in rocks and caverns, for its food is of two kinds; and in disposition it is diligent and ingenious. There is a small bird called certhius, which is bold in disposition, and lives on trees and eats the thrips (timber worm). In disposition it is diligent in search of food, and its voice is brilliant. The disposition and hue of the acanthis is bad, but it has a shrill voice.

Chapter XVII.

1. Among the herons, as it was before observed, the black heron copulates with difficulty, but it is an ingenious bird. It carries its food about, and is skilful in procuring it. It works during the day. Its colour, however, is bad, and its stomach always fluid. Of the other two (for there are three kinds of them), the white heron is beautifully coloured and copulates without pain, and builds its nest and attends its young carefully in trees. It inhabits marshes and lakes, plains and meadows. The bittern, which is called ocnus (the idle), is said in fables to have been originally a slave. Its name indicates its very idle disposition.

2. The herons live in this manner. The bird called poyx is peculiar, for it is its disposition to eat the eyes of other creatures, and is therefore the enemy of the harpa, which lives upon the same food.

Chapter XVIII.

1. There are two kinds of cottyphus. The one is black, and is found everywhere; the other is white. In size they are alike, and their voice is very similar. The white one is found in Cyllene, in Arcadia, and nowhere else. The læus

is similar to the black cottyphus, but is rather smaller. It makes its house upon rocks and tiles. It has not a dark beak, like the blackbird.

2. Of thrushes there are three forms. The one is called misselthrush, for it lives upon nothing but miseltoe and resin. It is as large as the citta; the other is called fieldfare. The voice of this bird is shrill; its size is that of the blackbird. There is another kind, which some persons call illas, which is smaller than the others and less variegated.

3. There is a certain bird living on rocks, which is called blue thrush. This bird generally inhabits Scyrus. It lives upon the wing. It is less than the blackbird, but larger than the finch. Its feet are black, and it climbs up upon rocks. It is entirely blue. It has a smooth, long beak, but its legs are short, and resemble those of the woodpecker.

Chapter XIX.

1. The oriole is entirely of a yellowish green. This bird is not visible in the winter. It is seen in the greatest numbers at the summer solstice, and takes its departure when Arcturus rises. It is of the same size as the turtle. The malacocraneus always perches upon the same place, and is captured there. This is its appearance: its head is large, and has the form of cartilage; its size is smaller than the thrush; its beak is strong, small, and round; its colour is entirely cinereous; its feet are strong, and its wings weak; it is generally captured by the owl.

2. There is another bird, called the pardalus, which is generally gregarious, and a single bird is never seen. Its colour is entirely cinereous. In size it resembles those already mentioned. Its feet are strong, and its wings are not weak. Its voice is frequent and not deep. The collyrion lives on the same food as the blackbird, and in size much resembles those just named. It is generally taken in the winter. These birds are visible all the year round, and so are those which live in the neighbourhood of towns, the raven and crow; for these are always visible, and neither migrate nor conceal themselves.

3. Of the jackdaw there are three kinds, one called coracias, which is as large as the crow, and has a red beak; another is called lycius; there is also a small one called

bomolochus; there is also another kind of jackdaw in Lydia and Phrygia which is web-footed.

4. Of the lark there are two kinds. One dwells on the ground, and has a crest. The other is gregarious, and not solitary. Its colour is similar, though it is a smaller bird, and has no crest. It is used for food.

5. The ascalopas is generally taken in enclosed gardens. It is of the size of the domestic fowl, it has a long beak, and in colour resembles the attagen. It runs quickly, and is very partial to the neighbourhood of mankind. The starling is variegated, and is of the size of the blackbird.

6. There are two kinds of ibis in Egypt; the white and the black. The white live in all the rest of Egypt, but are not found in Pelusium. The black occur in Pelusium, but not in other parts of Egypt.

7. One kind of scops, called brown owl, is seen throughout the year, but it is not eaten, for it is not fit for food. Others occur sometimes in the autumn, when they appear for one, or not more than two days. They are eatable, and are highly esteemed. They differ in no respect from the brown owl, except in fatness; and they are silent, whereas the other has a voice. No observations have ever been made on their mode of generation, except that they appear when the west wind blows. This is manifest.

Chapter XX.

1. The cuckoo, as it has been already observed, makes no nest, but lays its eggs in the nests of other birds, especially in that of the phaps, and in those of the sparrow and lark on the ground, and in the nest of the chloris in trees. It lays one egg, upon which it does not sit, but the bird in whose nest it lays both hatches the egg and nurses the young bird; and, as they say, when the young cuckoo grows, it ejects the other young birds, which thus perish.

2. Others say that the mother bird kills them, and feeds the young cuckoo with them; for the beauty of the young cuckoo makes her despise her own offspring. People assert that they have been eye-witnesses of most of these circumstances, but all are not equally agreed as to the mode in which the other young birds perish. Some persons say

that the old cuckoo comes and devours the young of the other bird. Others say that the great size of the young cuckoo enables it to seize upon the food which is brought to the nest, so that the rest perish from starvation. Others say that the cuckoo, being the stronger bird, kills those that are brought up with it.

3. The cuckoo appears to act prudently in thus depositing her egg; for it is conscious of its own timidity, and that it cannot defend its young, and therefore places them under the protection of another bird, in order that they may be preserved; for this bird is very cowardly, and when it is pecked by even small birds, it flies away from them.

Chapter XXI.

1. That the swift, which some persons call cypsellus, resembles the swallow, has been already observed, and it is not easy to distinguish them apart, except that the legs of the apos are covered with feathers. These birds rear their young in small nests made of mud, which have a passage sufficient for their admission. The nest is constructed in a narrow place under rocks and caverns, so that it avoids both beasts and men.

2. The goatsucker, as it is called, is a mountain bird, larger than the blackbird, and less than the cuckoo. It lays two, or not more than three eggs, and is slothful in its disposition. It flies against the goats and sucks them, whence its name (ægothelas, the goat-sucker). They say that when the udder has been sucked that it gives no more milk, and that the goat becomes blind. This bird is not quick sighted by day, but sees well at night.

3. The ravens in small districts, and where they have not food enough, are found only in pairs; and as soon as their young birds are able to fly, the old birds first of all turn them out of the nest, and then drive them from the place. The raven lays four or five eggs. When the hired soldiers of Medias perished in Pharsalus, Athens and the Peloponnesus were deserted by the ravens, as if they had some means of communication with each other.

Chapter XXII.

1. There are several kinds of eagles. One which is called pygargus (hen-harrier), which is found in plains and groves,

and in the vicinity of towns. Some persons call it nebrophonus. It is a courageous bird, and flies to mountains, and woods also. The other kinds rarely appear in plains and groves. There is another kind of eagle called plangus, the second in point of size and strength, which lives among thickets, and valleys, and marshes. It is called nettophonus and morphnus. Of this kind Homer speaks at the departure of Priam.

2. There is another kind, which is black. It is smaller, and stronger than the others. It inhabits mountains and woods. It is called melanæetus, and lagophonus. This is the only one that rears and educates its young. It is swift, elegant, liberal, fearless, warlike, and of a good omen, for it neither cries nor screams. There is another kind with spotted wings. It has a white head, and is the largest of all eagles. Its wings are short, and its rump very long, like the vulture; it is called oreipelargus, and hypæetus. It inhabits groves. It has all the faults of the rest, and none of their good qualities; for it is taken and pursued by ravens and other birds. It is a heavy bird, and its mode of life is bad. It carries about dead creatures; it is always hungry, and screams and cries.

3. There is another kind of eagle called sea eagle, which has a long and thick neck, curved wings, and a wide rump. It inhabits the sea and the coast. When they have seized their prey, and cannot carry it away, they are borne down into the sea. There is, again, another kind of eagle, called true eagle. They say that these alone of all other birds are true, for the other kinds are mixed and crossed with each other, both eagles, hawks, and other smaller kinds. This is the largest of all the eagles, greater than the phene; one and a half times as large as other eagles, and of a red colour: it is seldom seen, like that called cymindis.

4. The time for the activity of the eagle, and for its flight, is from dinner till the evening, for it sits aloft till the time when the market-place begins to fill. When eagles grow old, their beaks become more and more curved, so that at last they die of famine. The story goes, that the eagle was once a man, and suffers this as a punishment for inhospitality to a guest. Any superabundant food is put aside for their young in their nests, for it is not easy for them to procure it every day, and sometimes they have no place from whence to bring it.

5. If they find anyone attempting to take their nest, they beat them with their wings, and tear them with their claws. They do not make their nests in plains, but in high places, especially in precipitous rocks, but never on trees. They rear their young till they can fly, and then turn them out of their nests, and drive them to a great distance; for one pair of eagles occupies a wide space of country, so that they will suffer no others to live near them.

6. They do not hunt their prey near their nests, but at a considerable distance; and when they have hunted and taken anything, they lay it down and do not take it away at once, but carry it away when they have tried its weight. They do not capture hares at once, but let them escape to the plain. They do not descend to the plain at once, but with large though gradually decreasing circles. They do this in order that they may not be ensnared. They settle upon eminences, because they cannot rise easily from the ground. They fly aloft, that they may see the greater extent of country. For this cause men say that the eagle is the only divine bird.

7. All birds with crooked claws avoid sitting upon rocks, for its hardness is injurious to their claws. The eagle hunts fawns, hares, and other animals which it is able to conquer. It is a long-lived bird. This is plain from the long continuance of their nests in the same place.

8. In Scythia there is a kind of bird as large as a bustard, which produces two young ones. It does not sit upon its eggs, but hides them in the skin of a hare or fox. It watches them from a neighbouring tree all the while it is not engaged in hunting its prey. And if anyone approaches them, it fights and strikes with its wings, like the eagle.

Chapter XXIII.

1. The owl and nycticorax, and the other birds which see imperfectly by daylight, procure their food by hunting in the night. They do not this all the night, but in twilight and at early dawn. They hunt mice, and lizards, and beetles, and such other small animals.

2. The bird called asprey produces many young, is of a good habit of body, diligent in search of food, and gentle; and feeds both its own young and those of the eagle: for

when the eagle turns out its young, the phene takes them up and feeds them; for the eagle ejects them before the proper time, when they still require feeding, and are unable to fly. The eagle appears to eject its young from the nest from envy; for it is an envious and hungry bird, and not quick in seizing its prey. It captures large creatures when it can. When its young have grown, it envies them, for they are good for food, and tears them with its claws. The young also fight in the nest for particular places, and for the food. The parent then turns them out of the nest and strikes them. When they are turned out they begin to scream, and the phene comes and takes them up. The phene is dim-sighted, and its eyes are imperfect.

3. The sea-eagle is very quick-sighted, and compels its young to gaze on the sun before they are feathered. If any one of them refuse, it is beaten and turned round: and the one of them which first weeps when gazing on the sun is killed, the other is reared. It lives near the sea side, and obtains its food by pursuing marine birds, as it was before remarked. It pursues and takes them one at a time, watching them as they emerge from the sea. And if the bird, as it rises, sees the eagle watching it, it dives again from fear, in order that it may rise again in another place: but the eagle's quick sight enables him to pursue the bird till it is either suffocated, or taken on the wing; but it never attacks them in any numbers, for they drive it away by sprinkling it with their wings.

4. The petrels are taken with foam, for they devour it. They are therefore taken by sprinkling them. All the rest of its flesh is good; the rump alone smells of seaweed, and they are fat.

Chapter XXIV.

1. The buzzard is the strongest of the hawks; next to this the merlin. The circus is less strong; the asterias and phassophonus, and pternis are different. The wide-winged hawks are called hypotriorches, others are called perci and spiziæ; others are the eleii and the phrynolochi; these birds live very easily, and fly near the ground.

2. Some persons say that there are no less than ten kinds of hawks; they differ from each other, for some of them

kill the pigeon as it perches on the ground, and carry it away, but do not touch it in flight; others attack it as it sits upon the trees, or in some such situation, but will not touch it when upon the ground or in flight; other kinds of hawks will not strike the bird when perching upon the ground or anywhere else, but will endeavour to attack it when in flight.

3. They say that the pigeons can distinguish each of these kinds, so that if they see one of those which attack them in the air flying towards them, they remain sitting where they are, but if it is one of those which strike them on the ground, they do not remain still, but fly away.

4. In the city of Thrace, formerly called Cedropolis, men are assisted by hawks in pursuing birds in the marshes. They strike the reeds and wood with sticks in order that the birds may fly up, and the hawks appearing above pursue them, the birds then fall to the earth through fear, when the men strike them with their sticks and take them, and divide the prey with the hawks, for they throw away some of the birds, and the hawks come and take them.

5. On the Palus Mœotis, they say that wolves are accustomed to assist the fishermen in their calling, and if they do not give them their share of the food, they destroy the nets that are laid to dry on the ground. This, then, is the nature of birds.

Chapter XXV.

1. Marine animals also have many artful ways of procuring their food, for the stories that are told of the batrachus, which is called the fisher, are true, and so are those of the narce. For the batrachus has appendages above its eyes, of the length of a hair, with a round extremity to each like a bait; it buries itself in the sand or mud, and raises these appendages above the surface, and when the small fish strike them, it draws them down, till it brings the fish within reach of its mouth.

2. The narce stupefies any fish it may wish to master, with the peculiar force which it has in its body, and then takes and feeds upon them; it lies concealed in sand and

mud, and captures as they swim over it any fish that it can take and stupefy; of this circumstance many persons have been witnesses; the trygon also hides itself, but not in the same manner; the following is a proof of their mode of life, for they are often taken with the cestreus in their stomach, which is the swiftest of fishes, and they are the slowest; and the batrachus, when nothing is left on the hair-like appendages, is taken in an emaciated condition. The narce also has plainly caused stupefaction in men.

3. The onus, batus, psetta, and rhine also bury themselves in the sand, and when they have hidden themselves, the appendage which is in their mouth stands up, this the fishermen call their staff, and the small fish approach it as if it was the sea-weed, on which they usually live. Wherever the anthias is found there are no obnoxious creatures; when this sign is observed, those who collect sponges dive for them there, and call the anthias the sacred fish; this is only a coincidence, just as the pig and partridge are never found where there are snails, for they eat them all.

4. The marine-serpent, in colour and in the form of its body, resembles the conger, but it is darker, and more powerful. If it is captured and allowed to escape, it buries itself in the sand, which it pierces with its snout, for its snout is sharper than that of a serpent. The creature called scolopendra when it has swallowed the hook turns itself inside out, till the hook is ejected, when it turns to its original form. The scolopendra, like that which inhabits the land, is attracted by the smell of cooked meat; it does not bite with the mouth, but stings with the contact of the whole body, like the creatures called sea-nettles.

5. The fish called alopex, when one of them has swallowed the hook, assist each other in this matter, as the scolopendra also does, for they collect together round the line and bite it off; in some places, where the water is swift and deep, they are taken with many hooks in them. The amiæ also collect together when they see any obnoxious creature near them, and the largest swim round them in a circle; when attacked, they defend themselves; they have strong teeth, and the lamia and other creatures when attacking them have been seen to be repulsed with wounds.

6. Among river fish the male glanis is very careful of his young fry, but the female goes away as soon as she has deposited her ova, but the male continues to watch by the greater number of the ova, paying them no more attention than to drive away other fish, that they may not carry away the ova; he is thus employed for forty or fifty days, until the young fry are so far grown that they can escape from other fish; the fishermen know when it is guarding its ova, for it drives away other fish, and as it jumps at them it makes a noise and a murmur. It remains with such affection beside its ova, that if they are deposited in deep water, and the fishermen attempt to bring them into shallow water, the fish will not forsake them; but if young it is easily taken with a hook, from its habit of seizing upon any fish that may come in its way; but if it is experienced, and has swallowed a hook before, it does not leave its ova, but with its hard teeth it will bite and destroy the hook.

7. All creatures with fins, and stationary animals, inhabit either the places in which they were born, or similar localities, for their peculiar food is found in such places. The carnivorous fish are the greatest wanderers; all are carnivorous with a few exceptions, as the cestreus, salpa, trigla, and chalcis. The mucous substance which the pholis emits forms around it, and resembles a chamber. Of the apodal testacea, the pecten is the most locomotive, for it flies by means of its own valves; the purpura and its congeners advance very slowly.

8. All the fish except the cobius leave the Pyrrhic Euripus during the winter on account of the cold, for the Euripus is colder than the sea, and return again in the spring. In the Euripus the scarus, the thrissa, all the thorny fish, the galus, acanthia, carabus, polypus, bolitæna, and some others are wanting, and of those that are produced in the Euripus, the white cobius is not an inhabitant of the sea. Those fish which have ova are in the highest season in the spring, before they produce their ova; those that are viviparous in the autumn, and besides these the cestreus, trigla, and their congeners. In the neighbourhood of Lesbos, both the marine fish and those of the Euripus produce their ova in the Euripus; they copulate in the autumn, and deposit

their ova in the spring. The males and females of the selachea also mix together, in numbers, in the autumn, for the purpose of copulation; but in the spring they separate until they have produced their young; at the period of sexual intercourse, they are often taken united together.

9. The sepia is the most cunning of the malacia, and is the only one which uses its ink for the purpose of concealment, when it is not alarmed. The polypus and teuthis emit their ink only when alarmed. These creatures never emit all their ink, and as soon as it is emitted it is secreted again. But the sepia, as it has already been remarked, makes use of its ink for the purposes of concealment, and when it pretends to advance, it returns into its ink. With its long extended tentacula it not only pursues small fish, but frequently attacks the cestreus. The polypus is a foolish creature, for it will approach a man's hand if brought near it. It is an economical animal, for it collects all its prey in the hole in which it dwells, and when the most useful part has been consumed, it ejects the shells, the coverings of the cancri, and conchylia, and the spines of the fish, it pursues any fish that may come in its way, changing its colour and imitating that of any neighbouring stone. It does the same thing when alarmed.

10. Some persons say that the sepia has power to do the same thing, and that it can imitate the colour of the place it inhabits. The rhine is the only fish endowed with the same power, for it can change its colours like the polypus. The polypus rarely lives for two years, for it is by nature subject to decay. This is a proof of it, that when pressed, this animal always emits something, until at last it consumes away. The females suffer so much from this in the period of parturition, as to become foolish, and not perceive any agitation of the waves, so that they are easily taken by the hand of the diver; they become like mucus, and are not able to pursue their prey.

11. The males become hard and shining. This appears to be a proof that they do not survive a year, that in the summer and autumn, after the production of the young, it is difficult to find a large polypus, though large ones were abundant a short time before; when they have produced their ova, they say that both sexes grow old and be-

come so weak, that they are devoured by small fish, and are easily dragged out of their holes, though before they would have permitted nothing of the kind. They also say that the small and young ones will not endure this, and that they are stronger than the large ones. The sepia also only lives one year; the polypus is the only one of the malacia that ever ventures upon dry land, it advances upon a rough surface, but avoids smooth places. In other respects, it is a strong animal, but its neck, if pressed, becomes very weak.

12. This is the nature of the malacia. They say that .... form their rough shells round themselves like a hard breastplate, which increases as they grow, and that they can leave these, as if they were a hole or a habitation. The nautilus is a polypus peculiar both in its nature and its actions; for it sails upon the surface of the sea, rising up from the depths of the waters. It is brought to the surface with its shell inverted, in order that it may go out more easily and navigate in an empty shell. When it reaches the surface, it turns its shell over. There is a membrane extended between two of its tentacula similar to the web feet of birds, except that theirs is thick and that of the nautilus thin and like a spider's web. This it uses for a sail when the wind blows, and it extends two of its tentacula for rudders. If alarmed, it fills its shell and sinks in the sea. No one has made any accurate observation on the production and growth of the shell. It appears not to originate in sexual intercourse, but to be produced like that of other conchylia, nor is it clear whether it can live when taken out of its shell.

Chapter XXVI.

1. The most laborious of all insects, if compared with the rest, are the tribes of ants and bees, with the hornets, wasps, and their other congeners. Some of the spiders are more neat, graceful, and skilful than others in their mode of life. Every one may see the diligence of the ant; for it is on the surface, and that they always travel in one direction, and make a store and treasure-house of food, for they work even in the night when there is a full moon.

2. There are many kinds of spiders and phalangia. Of the phalangia that bite there are two sorts. The one re-

sembles those called wolves. It is small, variegated, sharp, and active in jumping. It is called psylla. The other is larger. Its colour is black, and its fore-legs are long. Its movements are slow, and it can scarcely walk. It is not strong, nor capable of jumping. The other kinds, which the dealers in medicine offer for sale, either do not bite at all, or very slightly.

3. There is another kind of those called wolves. One is small, and makes no web, and the larger sort makes a coarse inferior web upon the ground or in hedges. It always makes its web over chinks in the soil, and with the origin of the web in the interior it keeps guard until something falls into the web and moves it, when it comes out. The variegated kind makes a small inferior web among trees.

4. There is another third kind, which is very skilful and graceful. It commences the process of weaving by extending its web to the extremities on all sides, and then it draws a thread from the centre, and takes up the centre correctly. Upon these threads it weaves, as it were, the woof, and then weaves them altogether. Its sleeping place and store-room are situated at a distance. In seeking its prey it watches in the middle of its web. When anything falls into the web and the centre is moved, the spider surrounds and encloses it in a web, until it is rendered powerless, and then takes it up and carries it to her store. If hungry, she sucks it, for this is their method of enjoyment; and if not hungry, hastens back for the pursuit of more prey, and in the first place mends her broken web.

5. If anything in the meanwhile has fallen into the web, she first goes to the centre, and from that point, as before, falls upon her victim. If anyone destroys the web, she begins spinning again at the rising or setting of the sun, for it is at this time that her prey usually falls into the web. The female both makes the web and pursues the prey. The male only enjoys it with her.

6. There are two kinds of graceful spiders that spin a thick web, one large and one small. The one with long legs keeps watch suspended above its web, that the creatures which fall into the web may not be frightened when taken, and then it falls upon them from above, for its size prevents

it from being easily concealed. But the smaller kind conceals itself in a small superior chamber of the web.

7. Spiders have the power of emitting their web as soon as they are born, not from within their bodies, as if it were an excrement, as Democritus says, but from the surface of their body, like the bark of a tree, or like the ejected spines of some animals, as the porcupine. They will attack and surround with their web animals larger than themselves; for they will attack small lizards, and beginning at the mouth, will emit the web until their mouth is covered, and then will approach and bite them. This is the nature of these animals.

Chapter XXVII.

1. There is a tribe of insects which has not yet received any name, although in form all the species resemble each other. This tribe includes those that form wax, as the bee and those which resemble it in shape. Of these there are nine sorts, six of which are gregarious, the bee, the king bee, the drone, which dwells among the bees, the annual wasp, the hornet, and tenthredo. These are solitary, the small siren, of a tawny colour, and another siren, which is large, black, and variegated. The third, which is larger than these, is called bombylius. The ants pursue no prey, but only collect that which is already found. The spiders do not make anything, nor lay up a store, but only hunt down their prey.

2. Of the rest of the nine kinds already mentioned we will treat hereafter. The bees do not hunt for prey, but they both produce and lay up stores. The honey is their food. This is plainly shown when the honey dealers attempt to take the combs. When they are fumigated and suffering from the effects of the smoke, they devour the honey greedily, which they are not observed to do at other times; but they spare it and store it up for food. They have also another kind of food, which is called cerinthus (bee bread), which is of an inferior quality, and sweet like figs. They carry this upon their legs as they do the wax.

3. There is great variety in their diligence and mode of life. For when a clean hive is given them, they build their combs, bringing the drops from flowers and trees, such as the willow, the elm, and other glutinous trees. With this also they smear the floor of their hive, for fear of other crea-

tures. The honey dealers calls this substance commosis, and they build up the entrance of their hive if it is too wide. They first build cells for their own habitation, then those for the kings and the drones. They always build cells for themselves, and royal cells when there are many young; but they only build cells for the drones when there is plenty of honey.

4. They make the royal cells near their own. These are small. Those for the drones are placed next. These are of a smaller size than those of the bees. They commence the formation of their combs from the top of the hives, and carry them down until several reach the floor of the hive. The cells, whether for the honey or the grubs, are constructed with two mouths; for there are two cells built on each base, like a double cup, one on the inside, the other on the outside. The cells at the beginning of the comb, near the hives, are joined together for as much as two or three rows in a circle, and are short, and contain no honey. The cells which are formed with the greatest quantity of wax contain the most honey.

5. They spread the substance called mitys at the entrance of their hives, near the opening. This material is black, as if it was the purification of the wax, and of a harsh smell. It is considered a remedy for contusions and suppurations. Next to this the pissocerus is smeared over the floor of the hive. This substance is less useful than the mitys in the healing art. Some persons say that the drones build cells for themselves, dividing both the hive and the wax with the bees; but they make no honey, but both themselves and their young are supported by that of the bees. The drones generally remain in the hives; and if they fly out they rise in the air with a great noise, wheeling about as if they were exercising; and when they have done this they return to the hive and feast themselves on the honey.

6. The king bees never leave the hives, either for food or any other purpose, except with the whole swarm; and they say that, if a swarm wanders to a distance, they will retrace their steps and return until they find the king by his peculiar scent. They say also that, when the king is unable to fly, he is carried by the swarm; and if he perishes, the whole swarm dies with him. And if they continue for a time to form cells, they place no honey in them, and then they also perish.

7. The bees collect the wax by climbing actively on the flowers with their fore feet. They cleanse these upon the middle pair of legs, and their middle legs again on the curved part of their hind legs, and thus loaded they fly away. They are evidently heavily loaded. During each flight the bee does not settle upon flowers of different kinds, but as it were from violet to violet, and touches no other species till it returns to the hive. There they are unloaded, and two or three bees follow every one on its return to the hive. It is not easy to see what is taken, nor has their manner of working it been ever observed. Their manner of collecting wax upon the olive trees has been the subject of observation; for the thickness of the leaves makes them remain a long while in this tree.

8. After having done this they produce their young. There is nothing to prevent there being grubs, and honey, and drones in the same comb. As long as the king bee is alive, they say that the drones are produced in a separate place; but when he is dead they are produced by the bees in their own cells, and such drones are more passionate: for this cause they are called stingers, not that they have any sting, but that they would sting, if they had the power to do so. The drone cells are larger. Sometimes the drone cells are placed by themselves, but are generally combined with those of bees, for which reason they cut them off.

9. There are several kinds of bees, as has been already observed: two kinds of kings, the better sort of which is red, and the other sort is black and variegated, and in size double that of a good bee. The best kind is small, round, and variegated; the other is long, like the wild bee. There is another called phor (the thief); it is black, and has a broad abdomen. The drone is another sort: it is the largest of them all, has no sting, and is stupid. The bees that are produced from those that inhabit cultivated places are different from the natives of mountainous countries, for those produced from wood bees are more hairy, smaller, less, more diligent, and more violent. The best bees elaborate a smooth comb, with a polished surface. The comb also is of one form, as if entirely adapted for honey, or for grubs, or drones; and if it happens that all these are produced in the same comb, each form will be elaborated in order.

10. The long bees make their combs uneven, and the covering swollen, like that of the wild bee. Their offspring, also, and the rest of their productions, are not arranged in any order, but according to chance. Among them there are many bad kings, and many drones, and thieves, as they are called; but little or no honey. The bees sit upon the combs, in order to bring them to maturity. If this is not done, they say that the cells perish and become filled with a web; but if afterwards they are able to continue sitting, something like an abortion is produced: if they cannot sit, the whole perishes. Maggots are formed in those cells that perish, which acquire wings and fly away. If a comb falls down, the bees set it up, and put props beneath it, in order that they may be able to pass underneath; for if they have no path by which to approach the place where they sit, the cells become covered with a web.

11. The thieves and the drones do not work, but only injure the other bees, and when taken they are killed by the useful bees. Many of their rulers are also frequently killed, and especially the bad ones, in order that the swarm may not be dispersed by their numbers. They are the more disposed to kill them when the swarm is not fruitful, and no casts are formed. At such times they destroy the royal cells, if any have been prepared, for they are the leaders of the swarm. They destroy also those of the drones, if honey is scarce, or the swarm is short of honey. They fight boldly for their honey with those that would take it from them, and drive out any drones that may be in the hive, and are often seen sitting upon the hives.

12. The small bees fight eagerly with the long kind, and endeavour to drive them from their hives: and if they prevail, it seems to be a sign of a very strong swarm; but if the others conquer, when left alone, they are idle, and do nothing that comes to good, but perish in the course of the autumn. Whenever the useful bees kill any of them, they endeavour to do so outside of the hive; and if any of them die in the hive, they carry them out. Those which are called thieves injure their own combs, and if they can do it in secret, they will enter those of other bees, but if discovered they are killed. It is, however, difficult to enter unperceived, for there are guards placed at each entrance; and if one con-

trives to enter unnoticed, he is unable to fly from repletion, and is rolled out before the whole swarm; so that it is difficult to escape.

13. The kings themselves are never seen out of the hives, except with a young swarm, and in young swarms all the rest appear to be collected round him. When a swarm is about to separate, a peculiar and singular noise is made for some days, and for two or three days beforehand a few bees are seen flying round the hive; and if the king is among them he is not seen, for it is not easy to see him. And when they are collected, all the rest fly away and separate themselves with their respective kings: and if a few of them happen to be near at hand, they join themselves with one of the numerous swarms. And if the king that they have left follows them, they kill him. This is the manner of their leaving the hive, and of swarming.

14. They all have their proper work to perform. Some bring flowers, others water, and others polish and erect the cells. Water is brought when they are rearing their young. None of them ever settle upon flesh, nor will they eat anything seasoned. They have no particular time for commencing work, but when they are properly supplied, and in good health, they are particularly diligent during the summer. When the day is fine they work without ceasing, and as soon as the young bees are three days old, they set to work, if properly fed. And when the swarm settles some depart for food, and afterwards return. In healthy swarms the progeny of the bees only cease from reproduction[1] for about forty days after the winter solstice. As soon as the young bees are grown, they offer them food, and smear the cells with it, and as soon as they are strong enough, the young bees rupture the covering of the cell, and so escape.

15. The good kinds of bees destroy any creatures that are produced in their hives and destroy the combs; but the other kinds from their inferiority overlook the destruction of their work. When the dealers in honey take the combs, they leave the bees some food for the winter. If sufficient is left, the swarm is preserved; but if not, they either die in the winter, or, if the weather continues fine, desert the hive.

[1] This should probably be read "the bees only cease from their work for forty days during the winter solstice."

They eat honey both in summer and in winter. They also lay up another kind of food, which is as hard as wax, which some persons call sandarache.

16. Wasps are very injurious to them, and so is the bird called titmouse, and the swallow, and merops. The frogs also in marshes destroy them when they come for water, for which reason bee-fanciers destroy the frogs in those marshes where the bees come for water. They also destroy wasps' nests, and the nest of the swallow and merops, if near the swarms of bees. They avoid no animal, except those of their own kind. They fight among themselves, and with the wasps. When at a distance from their hives they will neither injure each other, nor any other creature; but when near at home they will destroy everything that they can conquer.

17. When they have stung anything they perish, for they cannot withdraw their sting from the wound without tearing their own entrails; but they are frequently saved, if the person stung will take care to press the sting from the wound: but when its sting is lost, the bee must perish. They will kill even large animals with their stings, and a horse has been known to perish, if attacked by bees. The rulers are the least cruel and stinging.

18. If any bees die in the hive, they carry them out; and in other respects the bee is a very clean creature. For this reason they also eject their excrement when in flight, for the smell is bad. It has been already observed that they dislike bad smells and the scent of unguents, and that they sting persons who use such things. They also die from other causes, as when the rulers in the hive are in great numbers, and each leads out a portion of the swarm. The toad also destroys bees, for it blows into the entrance of the hive, and watches for and destroys them as they fly out. The bees cannot inflict any injury upon it, but their keepers destroy it.

19. Some bee-keepers say that the kind of bee which makes an inferior and rough comb is the young of the others, and that it is the result of imperfect skill. They are young when a year old; young bees do not sting so severely as old bees; for this reason the swarms are carried to the apiaries, for they are those of young bees. When honey is short

they eject the drones, and put figs and other sweet things near them. The elder bees work in the hives, and become hairy from remaining within. The younger ones go out in the fields, and are smoother: and they kill the drones when they have no longer any room for them, for they are placed in a recess of the hive. When a swarm has been weak, strange bees have been known to come and fight with them, and take away their honey; and when the bee-keeper killed them the others came out, and defended themselves, and would not injure the man.

20. Other diseases, and especially one called clerus, frequently attack strong swarms. In this disease small worms are produced on the floor of the hive, and as these increase, the whole swarm is held, as it were, in a spider's web, and the combs decay. There is another disease, which is like a wildness in the bees, and causes a strong smell in the hives. The bees should be fed on thyme, the white sort is better than the red. In close weather they should have a cool place, and a warm one in the winter. They suffer the most when they work with materials affected with the rust.

21. When the wind is high, they carry a stone with them for a balance. If a river is at hand they never drink anywhere else, first of all laying down their weight. If no river is near, they drink in some other place, and then vomit up their honey, and again set to work. There are two seasons for making honey, the spring and autumn. That formed in the spring is sweeter, whiter, and, on the whole, better than that formed in autumn. The best honey is made from the new wax and young flowers. The red honey is inferior, on account of the wax; for, like wine, it is injured by the vessel which contains it; this honey therefore should be dried up. When the thyme is in flower, and the comb is full of honey, it does not become inspissated. The gold-coloured honey is also good. The white honey is not formed of pure thyme, but is good for the eyes, and for wounds. Weak honey always floats on the surface, and ought to be separated. The pure honey is beneath.

22. When the woods are in flower the bees form wax; at this season, therefore, the wax ought to be taken from the hive, for they immediately make more. These are the plants from which they collect it, atractyllis, melilot, asphodel, myrtle, phleos, agnus, broom. When they can procure

thyme, they mix water with it before they smear the cells. All the bees emit their excrements either on the wing, as it has been said before, or into a single cell. The small bees, it has been already remarked, are more industrious than the large ones, so that their wings become worn at the edges, and their colour black and burnt, but the bright and shiny bees are idle, like women.

23. Bees also appear to have pleasure in noises, so that they say that they collect them into their hives by striking earthen vessels and making noises. But it is very doubtful whether they hear or not, and if they hear, whether they collect together from pleasure or from fear. The bees drive out all that are idle or wasteful. They divide the work, as it has been already said; some work at the honey, others at the grubs, and others at the bee bread; some, again, form the comb, others carry water to the cells, and mix it with the honey, while others go to work. Early in the morning they are silent, until one bee arouses them by humming two or three times, when they all fly to their work; when they return again there is some disturbance at first, which gradually becomes less, until one of them flies round with a humming noise, as if warning them to sleep, when on a sudden they all become silent.

24. It is a sign that the swarm is strong when there is much noise and movement, as they leave and return to the hive, for they are then busy with the grubs. They are most hungry when they begin to work after winter. They are more idle if the person who takes the honey leaves much behind, but it is necessary that a quantity should be left proportionable to the strength of the swarm, for they work less actively if too little is left; they become more idle if the hive is large, for they despair of their labour. The hive is deprived of a measure or a measure and a half of honey; if it is strong, two or two measures and a half. Some few will afford three measures.

25. Sheep and wasps, as it was said above, are hostile to bees. The bee fanciers, therefore, catch the wasps in pans, in which they place pieces of flesh; when many have fallen in, they put on a lid and put them in the fire. It is good for the bees to have a few drones among them, for it makes them more industrious. Bees discern the approach of cold

weather and of rain; this is plain, for they will not leave the hive, but even if the day is fine are occupied in the hive. By this the bee keepers know that they expect severe weather.

26. When they are suspended upon each other in the hive, it is a sign that the swarm is about to leave; and when the bee keepers see this, they sprinkle them with sweet wine. They usually plant about the hive the achras, beans, poa medica, syria, ochrus, myrtle, poppy, herypllus, almond. Some bee keepers recognize their own bees in the fields by sprinkling them with flour. When the spring is late or dry, and when rust is about, the bees are less diligent about their young. This, then, is the nature of bees.

Chapter XXVIII.

1. There are two kinds of wasps, of which the wild sort are rare; they are found in mountains, and do not build their nest in the ground, but on oak trees; in form they are larger, longer, and darker than the other sort; they are variegated, all of them have stings, and are strong, and their sting is more painful than that of the other sorts, for their sting is larger in proportion to their size. These live for two years, and in winter are observed to fly out of trees, when they are cut down; during winter they live in holes. Their place of concealment is in trees; some of them are mother wasps, and some workers, as in those which are more domestic; the nature of the workers and the mother wasps will be explained when we come to speak of the more domestic kind.

2. For there are two kinds of the domestic wasps, the rulers, which they call mother wasps, and the workers; the rulers are larger and more gentle, and the workers do not survive the year, but all of them die, on the arrival of winter. This is plain, for at the beginning of winter the workers become stupid, and about the solstice are seen no more; but the rulers, which are called mother wasps, are seen during the whole of the winter, and bury themselves in the earth; for in ploughing and digging during the winter, the mother wasps have been frequently observed, but no one has ever seen a worker.

3. The following is the manner of their reproduction:

when the rulers have found a place properly situated, at the beginning of summer, they form their combs and build the wasps nests, as they are called; these are small, with four holes, or thereabouts; in these working wasps are produced, and not mother wasps. When these are grown, they afterwards build larger nests, and again larger still, as the swarm increases, so at the end of autumn the nests are very numerous and large, and in these the mother wasps no longer produce workers but mothers. These larger maggots are produced on the top of the upper part of the nest, in four or rather more adjoining cells, very like those of the rulers in their combs. When the working wasps are produced in the combs, the rulers no longer labour, but the workers bring them food; this is evident, from the rulers never flying away from the workers, but remaining quietly within.

4. Whether the rulers of the previous year, when they have produced new rulers, die at the same time as the young wasps, or whether they survive a longer period, no one has ever observed, nor has anyone ever observed the old age of the mother wasps, or of the wild wasps, or any other of their affections. The mother wasp is broad and heavy, and thicker, and larger than the working wasp, and her weight prevents her from being very active in flight, neither can she fly far, but always sits in the wasps' nests, and fashions and arranges the internal parts.

5. There are generally mother wasps in the nests, but there is some doubt whether they have stings or not; they seem, however, like the rulers among the bees, to have stings, though they never put them out nor sting; some wasps, like the drones, are without stings, others have a sting. Those that are without stings are smaller, and not so angry, neither do they defend themselves; those which are furnished with a sting are larger, and strong; some call these the males, and those which have no sting the females. Towards winter many of those that have stings appear to lose them, though we have never met with eye-witnesses of this circumstance.

6. Wasps are more abundant in dry seasons and rough places; they are produced beneath the earth, they make their combs of collected materials and of earth, each springing

from one origin, as if from a root. They procure their food from some flowers and fruits, but generally, they are carnivorous. Some persons have observed them in the act of sexual intercourse, but whether one or both had stings or not, was not seen. Some wild wasps also have been seen in the act of intercourse, one of them had a sting, whether the other had was not observed. Their offspring does not seem to be produced from this intercourse, but is always larger than the offspring of the wasp should be.

7. If a person takes hold of the legs of a wasp, and permits it to buzz with its wings, those that have no stings will fly towards him, which those with stings will not do, and some persons consider this to be a sign that the one are males, the other females. Some are taken in caverns during the winter with stings, and others without them. Some of them make small nests and few in number; others make many large nests. Many of those called mother wasps are taken at the turn of the season in the neighbourhood of elms, for they collect the sticky and glutinous matter. There are a great many mother wasps, when wasps have been abundant during the previous year, and the weather rainy. They are captured in the neighbourhood of precipitous places and straight fissures in the earth, and all appear to have stings. This, then, is the nature of wasps.

Chapter XXIX.

1. The wild bees do not live by gathering honey from flowers like the bees, but are entirely carnivorous, for which reason they frequent the neighbourhood of dung; for they pursue large flies, and when they have taken them they tear off the head and fly away, carrying the rest of the body with them. They will also eat sweet fruit. This, then, is the nature of their food. They have rulers, like the bees and wasps; and in proportion to the size of the wild bee these rulers are larger than those of the bees and wasps. Their rulers also keep in the nest, like those of the wasps.

2. The wild bees make their nest under the soil, which they remove like the ants. They never swarm like bees, neither do wasps; but the young ones always remain with them, and as the nest increases they carry out the heap of earth. The nests become large; and from a flourishing nest three or

four baskets of comb have been taken. They do not lay up any food like bees, but conceal themselves during the winter. The greater number of them die, but it is not known whether all of them perish. There is never more than one ruler in the nest as in the swarm of bees, or they would divide the nest.

3. When some of the wild bees wander from the nest, they turn aside to some material and form another nest, such as are often seen on the surface of the soil, and in this they work themselves out a ruler; and when he is grown he goes out and leads them with him to take possession of a nest, in which they may dwell. No one has ever made any observation on the mode of sexual intercourse in the wild bee, nor on the origin of their offspring. Among bees the drones and kings have no stings, and some of the wasps also are without stings, as it has been remarked already; but all the wild bees appear to have stings, but more accurate inquiry should be instituted as to the rulers, whether they have stings or not.

Chapter XXX.

The humble bees produce their young under stones on the surface of the ground in two or a few more cells. The commencement of a kind of inferior honey is found in them. The tenthredo is like the wild bee, but it is variegated, and as broad as the bee. It is a dainty creature, and the only one which resorts to kitchens, and enjoys fish and such like things. It deposits its young under the earth like the wasps. It is a very productive creature, and its nest is much larger and longer than that of the wasp. This is the nature of the work and economy of bees, wasps, and their congeners.

Chapter XXXI.

1. It has been already observed that we can distinguish a difference in the dispositions of animals, especially in the courage and cowardice, and then in their mildness and fierceness, even in wild animals. The lion in his manner of feeding is very cruel; but when he is not hungry, and is full fed, his disposition is gentle. He is not either jealous or suspicious. He is fond of playing with and affectionate towards those animals which have been brought up with him, and to

which he has become accustomed. When hunted, he has never been seen to retreat or be alarmed; and if compelled to yield to the numbers of his hunters, he retreats slowly and leisurely, and turns himself round at short intervals. If overtaken in a thicket, he flies rapidly till he reaches the open plain, and then again he withdraws slowly. If compelled by numbers to retreat openly on the plain ground, he runs at full stretch, and does not leap. His manner of running is continuous, like that of a dog at full stretch. When pursuing his prey, he throws himself upon it when he comes within reach.

2. It is, however, true, as they say, that the lion is afraid of the fire, as Homer also writes, "The burning faggots which he fears when urged against him;" and that he observes the person who strikes him and attacks him; and if a person aims a blow at him without hitting him, the lion, if he can rush upon and seize him, does not do him any injury, nor tear him with his claws, but shakes and frightens him, and then leaves him. They are more disposed to enter towns and attack mankind when they grow old; for old age renders them unable to hunt, from the disease which attacks their teeth. They live many years; and a lame lion has been captured which had many of its teeth broken, which some persons considered as a sign that it had lived many years. For this could not have happened except by the lapse of time.

3. There are two kinds of lions. One of these has a round body and more curly hair, and is a more cowardly animal. The other is of a longer form, has straight hair, and is more courageous. Sometimes, when retreating, they stretch out their tails like dogs; and a lion has been at times observed, when about to attack a hog, to retreat when that animal erected its bristles. The lion is weak if struck in the belly, but will bear many blows on other parts of the body, and its head is very strong. If they bite or tear anything, a large quantity of yellow serum flows from the wound, which can never be stopped by bandages or sponges. The mode of healing is the same as in the bite of a dog.

4. The jackal is an animal attached to mankind. It does not injure men, nor is it much afraid of them, but it will fight with the dog and the lion. They are not, therefore,

found in the same locality. The small jackal is the best. Some persons say that there are two, others that there are three sorts; but, like some fish, birds, and quadrupeds, the jackal changes at differer t seasons, and has a different colour in summer and in winter. In summer it is smooth; in winter, rough.

Chapter XXXII.

1. The bonassus is found in Pæonia, in Mount Messapius, which forms the boundary between Pæonia and Mædia. The Pæonians call it monapus. It is as large as a bull, and more heavily built; for it is not a long animal, and its skin, when stretched out, will cover a couch for seven persons to recline upon. In form it resembles a bull, but it has a mane as far as the point of the shoulder like the horse, but its hair is softer than that of the horse, and shorter. The colour of its hair is red. The hair is deep and thick as far down as the eyes, and in colour between ash-coloured and red, not like that of roan horses, but darker. Its hair below is like wool. They are never either very black or very red.

2. Their voice is like that of the ox. Their horns are crooked and bent together, of no use for defence, a span long or a little more, so thick that each of them would hold half a measure or a little more. The black part of their horn is good and smooth. The fore lock is so placed between the eyes that the creature can look sideways better than forwards. Like the ox, it has no upper teeth in front, neither have any horned animals. Its legs are rough and its hoofs cloven. Its tail is small in proportion to its size, like that of the ox, and it tears up the ground and digs with its hoof like the bull. The skin upon its sides is strong. Its flesh is excellent food, and for this it is hunted.

3. When wounded it retreats, and stays when it can proceed no farther. It defends itself by kicking and ejecting its dung, which it can do to the distance of four fathoms from itself. It uses this means of defence easily and frequently. Its dung is so caustic as to burn the hair from dogs. The dung is only caustic when the creature is disturbed and alarmed. It is not so when undisturbed. This is the form and nature of this creature. At the season of parturition they collect together in numbers in the moun-

tains, and make a circle of their dung round the place, as it were a fortification, for this animal ejects a large quantity of this excrement.

Chapter XXXIII.

Of all wild animals the elephant is the most tame and gentle; for many of them are capable of instruction and intelligence, and they have been taught to worship the king. It is a very sensitive creature, and abounding in intellect. The male never again touches a female that he has once impregnated. Some persons say that the elephant will live for two hundred years, others an hundred and twenty, and the female lives nearly as long as the male. They arrive at perfection when sixty years old. They bear winter and cold weather very badly. It is an animal that lives in the neighbourhood of rivers, though not in them. It can also walk through rivers, and will advance as long as it can keep its proboscis above the surface; for it blows and breathes through this organ, but it cannot swim on account of the weight of its body.

Chapter XXXIV.

Camels refuse to have sexual intercourse with their dams, even when forced; for once a camel driver, who was in want of a male camel, veiled the dam and introduced her young to her. When the covering fell off in the act of copulation, he finished what he was about, and soon afterwards bit the camel driver to death. It is said also that the king of Scythia had an excellent mare, which always produced good colts. He wished to have a colt out of the mare by the best of these horses, and introduced him for copulation, but he would not do it. When she was covered up, however, he performed the act unwittingly. As soon as the form of the mare was shown after copulation, and the horse saw what was done, he ran away and threw himself down a precipice.

Chapter XXXV.

1. Among marine animals there are many instances reported of the mild, gentle disposition of the dolphin, and of its love of its children, and its affection, in the neighbourhood

of Tarentum, Caria, and other places. It is said that when a dolphin was captured and wounded on the coast of Caria, so great a number came up to the harbour, that the fishermen let him go, when they all went away together. And one large dolphin, it is said, always follows the young ones, to take care of them; and sometimes a herd of large and small dolphins has been seen together, and two of these having left appeared soon after, supporting and carrying on their back a small dead dolphin, that was ready to sink, as if in pity for it, that it might not be devoured by any other wild creature.

2. Some incredible things are also told of their swiftness, for it appears to be the swiftest of all animals, whether marine or terrestrial. They will leap over the sails of large ships. This is especially the case when they pursue a fish for the sake of food; for their hunger will make them pursue their prey into the depths of the sea, if it retreats to the bottom. And when they have to return from a great depth, they hold their breath, as if they were reckoning the distance, and then they gather themselves up, and dart forward like an arrow, desirous of shortening their distance from a breathing-place. And if they meet with a ship they will throw themselves over its sails. Divers also do the same thing when they have sunk themselves into deep water, for they also gather up their strength in order to rise to the surface. The males and females live in pairs with each other. There is some doubt as to the reason why they cast themselves on the land, for they say that sometimes they appear to do this without any cause.

Chapter XXXVI.

1. As the actions of all animals agree with their dispositions, so also their dispositions will change with their actions, and some of their parts also. This takes place among birds; for hens, when they have conquered the cock, desire to copulate with others, and their crest and rump become elevated, so that it is difficult to say whether they are hens or not. In some, also, small spurs are found; and some males, after the death of the female, have been seen to take the same care of the young as the female would have done, leading them

about and feeding them, and neither crowing, nor desiring sexual intercourse. And some male birds have been seen to be so effeminate from their birth, that they neither crowed, nor desired sexual intercourse, and would submit themselves to any males that desired them.

3. Many birds at particular seasons change both their colour and their voice, as the blackbird, which becomes russet instead of black, and assumes another voice, for it sings in the summer time, but in winter it chatters and screams violently. The thrush also alters its colour, for in winter it is grey, and in summer is variegated on the neck; but its voice does not alter. The nightingale sings unceasingly for fifteen days and nights, when the mountains become thick with leaves. As the summer advances it utters another voice, not quick and varied, but simple; its colour also is altered, and in Italy it is called by another name at this season of the year. It only shews itself for a short time, for it lies concealed.

3. The erithacus, and the bird called phœnicurus, are changed one into the other. The erithacus is a winter bird, the phœnicurus a summer bird; they differ in nothing but the colour. The sycalis and melancoryphus are the same, for these also are interchanged. The sycalis is found in the autumn, and the melancoryphus immediately after the end of the autumn. They also differ from each other in nothing but their colour and voice, and to prove that it is the same bird, each kind has been seen immediately after the change took place; and when the change was not quite complete, there was nothing characteristic of either form. Nor is it absurd to suppose that these birds change their voices or their colours, for the dove utters no sound in the winter, unless it may be on a fine day in a severe winter, when it will utter its sound to the astonishment of those that know its habits; and as soon as spring commences, it begins to utter its voice: and, on the whole, birds make the greatest number and variety of voices at the season of coition.

4. The cuckoo also changes its colour, and its voice is not distinct, when it is about to leave us. It goes away about the time when the dog-star rises, it having been with us from the commencement of spring to that time. The œnanthe, as it is called, disappears when Sirius rises, and

comes again when it sets, for sometimes it retreats before the cold, and sometimes before the heat. The hoopoe also changes its colour and its forms, as Æschylus writes. "He had variegated this hoopoe, the witness of its own evils, and has displayed the bold bird that dwells in the rock in all armour. In the early spring it shakes the feathers of the white hawk; for it has two forms, that of the young bird and of itself, from one origin. And when the young corn of the harvest begins to grow, it is clothed in spotted feathers; and it always hates this place of Pallene, and inhabits deserted forests and mountains."

5. Some birds dust themselves, and others bathe. Some neither dust nor bathe. Those that do not fly, but live on the ground, dust themselves, as the domestic fowl, partridge, grouse, lark, and pheasant. Those birds which have straight claws, and live near rivers, marshes, and the sea, bathe themselves. Some, like the pigeon and sparrow, both dust and bathe. Most of those with crooked claws do neither the one nor the other. This is their nature in these matters. The act of breaking wind backwards is peculiar to some birds, as the turtle. Such birds make a strong motion with their rumps when they utter their voice.

CHAPTER XXXVII.

1. ANIMALS not only change their forms and dispositions at particular ages and seasons, but also when castrated. All animals that have testicles may be castrated. Birds and oviparous quadrupeds have internal testicles near their loins. In viviparous animals with feet, they are generally external, though sometimes internal; in all they are situated at the extremity of the abdomen. Birds are castrated near the rump, the part with which they touch the female in copulation, for if they are burnt in that part two or three times with irons after they are full grown, the comb turns yellow, and they cease to crow, and no longer desire sexual intercourse. If they are not full grown, these parts never reach perfection.

2. The same is the case with the human subject, for if a boy is castrated, the hair that is produced after birth never appears, nor does his voice change, but continues sharp; but if a full grown man is castrated, all the hair produced

after birth falls off except that on the pubes, this becomes weaker, but still remains. The hair produced at birth does not fall off, for the eunuch never becomes bald. The voice also of castrated animals changes to that of the female. Other animals, if not castrated when young, are destroyed by the operation; with the boar it makes no difference. All animals, if castrated when young, become larger and more graceful than those not castrated; but if already grown, they never become any larger.

3. If stags are castrated before they are old enough to have horns, these never appear; but if castrated after they have horns, their size never varies, nor are they subject to their annual change. Calves are castrated at a year old, if not they become bad and inferior. The steer is castrated in this manner: they lay down the animal and cut the scrotum, and press out the testicles; they next contract the root of the testicle as much as possible, and fill up the wound with hair in order that the discharge may escape, and if it inflames, they cauterize and sprinkle the scrotum. If adult bulls are castrated, they are still apparently capable of sexual intercourse.

4. The capria of the sow is also cut out, so that they should not desire coition, but fatten rapidly. They are cut after fasting two days. They hang them up by the hind legs and make an incision in the lower part of the belly, where the testicles of the male are generally found; the capria is there formed upon the matrix, from which they cut off a portion, and sew up the wound again.

5. The female camels also are cut when they wish to take them to war, that they may not become pregnant. Some of those in the upper parts of Asia possess as many as three thousand. Such camels, when they run, are far more swift than the Nisæan horses, from the length of their stretch. And on the whole, castrated animals are longer-bodied than those not castrated.

6. All animals that ruminate, derive as much use and pleasure from rumination as from eating. Animals that have not cutting-teeth in both jaws ruminate, as the ox, sheep, and goat. No observations have been made on wild animals except those which occasionally associate with men, as the stag, though this animal ruminates. They all lie down

to ruminate, and do so most in the winter; those which are brought up in shelter ruminate for nearly seven months. Those that live in herds, ruminate for a shorter period, for they live out of doors. Some animals with cutting teeth in both jaws, ruminate, as the Pontic mice and the fish, which, from this process, is called meryx. Animals with long legs have loose bellies, and those with broad chests vomit more easily than others, in quadrupeds, birds, and the generality of mankind.

BOOK THE TENTH.

(ERRONEOUSLY ASCRIBED TO ARISTOTLE.)

Chapter I.

If men and women, after they have reached a certain age, do not have children after cohabition, the fault sometimes rests with both, and sometimes in only one of them. And first, it is requisite to examine the uterus of the female, that if the fault lies there it may be relieved by proper treatment. If the fault is not there, attention must be paid to some other cause of sterility. We may conclude that this organ is in a healthy state, when, like the other parts of the body, it performs its functions without pain, and is free from fatigue after the function is performed. Just as the eye is in a healthy state if it suffers no pain in seeing, and is not disordered with the exercise of its function, or unable to perform it again, so the uterus is healthy which suffers no pain, and is well able to perform its functions, whatever they may be, and after they are performed is not impotent, but is free from fatigue.

2. The uterus is said to be disordered, when, even if it performs its functions properly and without pain, it does not hinder its function by any part of itself.[1] As there is nothing to prevent an eye from seeing accurately, although all its parts are not perfect, or if there happens to be a tumour in it; so the uterus may have received no injury in this respect, if it is properly situated in the right place. In the first place, then, the healthy uterus will not be situated in this place or in that, but will always be in a similar position; but it is not difficult to decide whether it is not placed at too great a distance without suffering and pain, or whether it is devoid of sensation when touched. That these parts ought to be properly placed is evident from the following considerations, for if the uterus is not near, it will not be able to imbibe the semen, for the place from which it

---

[1] A corrupt passage.

ought to receive it will be at too great a distance. If the uterus is near, and not able to retire further, it will be useless, for it will be always touched so as to refuse to open; but it ought to do this, and to be obedient to its function. These things ought to be thus ordered, and if they are not, the case requires attention.

3. The catamenia also should proceed correctly, that is, if the general health is good, they should last for their proper time, and not come irregularly, for when the catamenia are right, the uterus will open properly, and receive the fluids of the body whenever they are secreted; but when they make their appearance too often, or not often enough, or irregularly, while the rest of the body does not sympathise with them, and the general health is good, we must look to the uterus for the cause of their irregularity. The dulness of the uterus prevents its being opened at the proper time, so that it receives but a small portion, or rather the uterus imbibes the fluid from some inflammation of the parts. So that it shows that it requires attention, like the eyes, the bladder, the stomach, and other parts. For all the parts, when inflamed, imbibe the fluid which is secreted into each place, but not such a fluid, or in so great quantities.

4. In like manner, if the uterus secretes more than it ought to do, it exhibits an inflammatory tendency, if the secretion is regular but too abundant; but if the secretion is irregular, or more putrid than it should be in healthy subjects, the disease is then quite manifest, for it is necessary that some pain should show that all is not well. In a healthy subject, at the commencement, and the cessation of menstruation, the secretion appears white and putrid. All those subjects in whom the secretion is more putrid than in healthy persons, or is irregular, or too abundant, or deficient, should receive attention, for this it is that prevents child-bearing. But in those subjects who are only irregular, and unequal in the periods of the secretion, the disease is not the preventive of child-bearing, though it shows that the habit of the uterus is changeable, and does not always remain the same. And this affection is sufficient to prevent those persons from conception who are otherwise well disposed towards it. It is, however, hardly a disease, but an affection which may be restored without medical treatment, unless it is affected by some previous fault.

5. If the regularity and quantity of the discharge is subject to alteration, without any corresponding change in the rest of the body, which is sometimes in a more fluid, at other times in a more dry state, the uterus is not in fault, though it ought to follow the habit of the rest of the body, and receive and secrete in proportion. If the body is in a good state of health, but undergoing a change, when this takes place, and there is no need of medical treatment; but if the secretion is too small from disease, and the secretion is taken through some other source, the body suffers : and if the discharge is too great, from all the secretions of the body being turned in one direction, this does not point to disease of the uterus, but of the whole body. Whenever the catamenia coincide with the general habit of the body, it is evident that the fault does not lie with the uterus, which would perform its functions properly if the general health were correct.

6. Sometimes the uterus is weak, and sometimes strong; sometimes too fluid, and sometimes too dry; and the discharge coincides with the state of the body, it is abundant when that is full, deficient when it is less full. If the body is full of fluid, the discharge is watery; if the body is dry, it is more sanguineous; it begins with being white, like milk, and is without smell. Some are dark-coloured, and when about to cease they become white, at the last secretion. The white discharge has not the smell of putrid matter, but is more harsh and disagreeable, nor has it the smell of pus; and when this is the condition of the symptoms, there is no wearing away, but the body becomes heated. In all that are in this state, the uterus is in a healthy condition for child-bearing.

Chapter II.

WE must, then, first of all inquire whether all these particulars are well ordered; and, next, we must learn the position of the body of the uterus; for it ought to be straight; and if it is not so, the seminal fluid can never reach it. And it is evident that women project their semen forwards, from what happens when they have lascivious dreams; for this part of them then requires attention, being moistened as though they had sexual intercourse, for they also project into the place where the semen of the male is emitted, and not into the uterus; and when projected to this place, the semen is drawn into the uterus by inhalation, as the mucus is drawn into the nose. For this reason they become pregnant in every position; for the seminal fluid both in men and women is always projected forwards; but if it were projected into the female she would not always conceive after copulation.

2. But if the uterus is not straight, but inclined to the hips, the loins, or the hypogastric region, it is impossible to conceive, for the before-mentioned reason, that the uterus cannot take up the seminal fluid. If this deformity is great, either naturally or from disease, the disorder is incurable. If there is a rupture, either by nature or arising from the disease, which contracts the parts with inflammation, the disorder will take a different turn from this. But in order that women may become pregnant, it is necessary, as it was said, that the mouth of the uterus should be straight and, moreover, should be well opened. By this I mean that when the menstrual discharge commences, the os uteri should, on contact, appear softer than before, though not distinctly expanded. But if this is the case, let the first appearance be white.

3. But when the appearances are more the colour of flesh, the uterus will be evidently relaxed without pain when it is touched, and the os uteri is neither dull nor different from itself; and when the discharge ceases, let the aperture be very open and dry, but not hard, for a day and a half or two days; for this shows that the uterus is in a healthy state, and fit to perform its functions. If the os uteri is not immediately relaxed, but appears soft, it shows that both the uterus and the rest of the body are relaxed, and the uterus does not prevent, but first discharges the secretion from the os uteri. And when the rest of the body has discharged a great deal, and the os uteri becomes relaxed, it is a sign of a healthy condition.

4. And when the appearances cease to take place directly, the uterus shows that, if there is any difficulty, it will become empty and dry, and wanting in moisture, and there will be no remains in the passage. When the uterus, therefore, is capable of contraction, it shows that it is in a proper state for receiving whatever is brought to it, when it is in this state without pain, and indeed is insensate; and it is good that the os uteri should not be in any other condition. This shows that there is no reason why it should not close

at the proper time. This is the manner of considering the os uteri, whether it is in a healthy condition or not.

Chapter III.

These ought to be the symptoms of the uterus itself after purification. First of all, that the woman should dream of sexual intercourse, and project her seminal fluid readily, as if a man were lying with her; and if this symptom occur frequently, it is better. And when she has arisen, sometimes she should require the same treatment as if she had been with a man, sometimes she should be dry; but this dryness should not be immediate; but after awaking she should be fluid, sooner or later, about as much as half a short day. The humidity should be of the same kind as if she had been with a man. For all this shows that the uterus is in a fit state to receive what is given it, and that the cotyledons are drawn up and will retain what they have received, and be unwilling to part with it.

2. A flatulent state of the uterus is also a good sign, when it enlarges and discharges the wind as the bowels do without pain, and when it becomes larger and smaller without any symptom of disease; for these symptoms show that the uterus is not in want of what is necessary nor sluggish, either naturally or from disease, but that it will be able to find room by growth for anything that it may receive, for it has the power of dilation. When this is not the case, the uterus is too thick, or some natural defect or disease has rendered it insensible. For this cause it cannot nourish, but it will destroy the embryo, if the symptoms are violent, while the embryo is small; if they are less so, when it is larger; if the uterus is slightly affected, the offspring will be inferior, as if it had been fed in an inferior vessel.

3. Upon contact, the right and left side will be found to be alike, and all the other parts in the same way; and in the act of copulation moisture will be produced, not frequently nor in great abundance. This affection is, as it were, a perspiration of the place, like the saliva, which is frequently produced both in the use of food and in speaking. Tears also are shed from the eyes, when we look upon brilliant objects, and under cold or greater heat, of which these

parts also partake, when they happen to be moist. So the uterus becomes moist when employed, when it is of a more moist disposition. Those that are in the best health suffer from this affection, for which reason women always require more or less attention, as also the mouth requires saliva. In some this moisture is so abundant that they cannot imbibe the seminal fluid of the man in a state of purity, on account of its admixture with this uterine moisture.

4. Besides these affections, the following also is to be considered, whether, when they dream of sexual intercourse, their general health is good or not, as whether they are weak, and whether they are so always, or only sometimes, and whether they are not sometimes strong, and whether they are dry at first and moist afterwards; for this ought to be the condition of a woman capable of child-bearing; for relaxation shows that the body has been profuse of the seminal fluid, and that it can perform its functions; but when the uterus is hard, it is a sign of debility. If a woman has this affection without any disease, it shows that the emission takes place naturally and as it ought to do. For if it were not so, there would be disease and prostration of strength. Sometimes, when the uterus is dry and afterwards becomes moist, it is a sign that the whole body receives and makes away with the seminal fluid, and that both the uterus and the body are strong; for it has been already observed that the uterus absorbs the semen which is placed upon it by the process of inhalation, for it is not emitted into it but upon the same place as that of the man. All that takes by inhalation is accompanied with force, so that it is plain that the body of such a person must have the power of retraction.

5. It sometimes happens that women who have lascivious dreams, or men of strong passions, are robust not from strength but from health. This takes place when a large quantity of seminal fluid has been collected near the place from whence they emit it. If this makes its escape, they are in no ways debilitated; for they are not relaxed by the loss of a portion, if sufficient remains behind, or if that which was emitted was useless, nor if it was emitted easily, as if they parted with superfluous matter. For which reason such persons are not robust from strength but from dullness. But

when any part is emitted which is necessary for the body, they become debilitated.

6. If a person is in good health, and of a proper age, the seminal fluid is rapidly formed This takes place in those that have not done growing and in those that are grown. Women rarely know when they are first pregnant; for they do not think that they have conceived unless they perceive that the semen has been emitted, suspecting that it ought to be emitted at the same time both by the female and the male; and it escapes their notice, more especially when they think that they are unable to conceive, unless they have become dry, and that which they have received has disappeared entirely; but it sometimes happens that both the male and the female emit more than could possibly disappear, and more than enough for conception. When sufficient has been drawn in and much left out, they become pregnant without knowing it.

7. That it is possible that this should take place, and that the affection does not arise from the whole of the seminal fluid, we may learn from those animals which produce many young ones from a single act of intercourse, or from the case of twins produced by a single act. It is evident that they are not produced from the whole semen, but each place receives some portion of it, but the larger portion is left behind; and if many young are produced from a single act of intercourse, which appears to be the case with swine and with twins, it is evident that the semen cannot come from every part of the body, but it is divided out to each form. It is possible, therefore, that it may be separated from every part of the body, and that the whole may be divided among many, so that it is not possible that all should have every part. The female also projects her semen into the os uteri, where the man also emits his, when he approaches her. From thence she imbibes with inhalation as if it were with the mouth or nostrils; for whatever is not joined to the members is either hollow above and united by a symphysis, or is sucked in from this place by the act of inhalation. For which reason they take care that it should be dry, as if this had happened before.

8. The path along which it passes is thus formed in women. There is a tube enclosed in the body like the penis of the male. The inhalation takes place through this by a

small passage above the passage for the urine. When, therefore, they desire sexual intercourse, this part is not in the same condition as it was before. A falling down takes place from this passage, and the fore part of the uterus becomes much larger than the part where it falls into this passage. This resembles the nostrils; for, as the nostrils have a passage into the pharynx and into the external air, so this tube has a very small and narrow passage, like a passage out for the wind. That to the fore part of the uterus is wide and broad, as the nostrils are to the external air between the mouth and the pharynx. So women have a larger passage to the fore part of the uterus, and wider than the external passage.

9. Whatever conjecture is formed concerning these affections, it makes to the same conclusion, that the woman also emits a seminal fluid. The same things arise from the same cause, for to some it seems to be the cause of disease or of death; and these consider the end at the beginning as it ought to be considered; for to some women these are important causes, to some of no importance; and of these causes some are and some are not of consequence. They divide also in proportion the consequences which may result from them. To some it happens to pass through all these affections; to those who have many, through many of them: others through few; and others, again, who have none, through none of them.

10. There are some persons who suffer from the affection called inflation. This ought not to be. The affection is of this kind. In copulation they neither evidently emit semen, nor do they become pregnant. Wherefore they are said to be inflated. The excessive dryness of the uterus is the cause of this complaint; and when it has drawn the fluid into itself, it ejects it again. This becomes dried up, and having become small falls out, without any notice being taken of the circumstance on account of its size. When the uterus is violently affected in this way, and becomes very dry, and ejects it very soon, it is plain that pregnancy cannot take place. If this does not take place very soon, impregnation appears for a time to have taken place until it is ejected. The same thing also takes place at times in those who have conceived properly; if a long time has elapsed, the uterus becomes elevated, so that it plainly appears as if impregnation had

taken place until it falls out. Then all becomes as it was at first. They refer this affliction to a divine origin. It is curable, unless it is natural, or the disease has gone a great way. It is a sign that this disease is not present, when women appear neither to have emitted semen, nor to have conceived after sexual intercourse.

CHAPTER IV.

1. PREGNANCY is prevented also by spasm in the uterus. This complaint attacks the uterus when it is either distended with inflammation, or in the act of parturition. When any large quantity of matter suddenly enters it, and the os uteri is not open, spasm then arises from distension. It is a sign of the absence of spasm, if the uterus does not appear to reach inflammation in its functions: whereas, if spasm were present, there would be some signs of inflammation. Again, a swelling at the mouth of the uterus, if it is much drawn out, will prevent conception. It is a sign that this is not the case, when the uterus appears to open and close properly after the discharge of the catamenia, or the use of the male.

2. In some, also, the os uteri is closed, either from the period of birth, or in consequence of disease. Sometimes this is curable, and sometimes not so. It is not, however, difficult to ascertain the state of the case, for it is not possible either to receive or to emit anything in a proper manner. If it appears to have received and rejected the seminal fluid of the male, it is an evidence of the presence of the disease. But those who have no impediment in the way of conception, but are, as it has been said, as they ought to be, unless the man is impotent, or they are not able to have children together, being unable to emit their semen at the same time, and differ very much, such persons will have no children.

CHAPTER V.

IN order to understand of sterility in the male, we must take other symptoms. These will appear very easy, if he copulates with other women, and impregnates them. When the sexes do not appear to concur with each other, although all the before-mentioned circumstances are present, they do not have children together. For it is evident that this is the only reason of sterility: for if the woman contributes to the semen and generation, it is evident that both the sexes should be concurrent: for if the man is quick, and the woman slow, in the emission of the semen (and many women are comparatively slow), this will prevent conception; for which cause they do not produce children by sexual union with each other. They do so, however, when they happen to be concurrent with each other; for if the woman is desirous, and prepared for the intercourse, and is inclined for it, but the man is suffering previous pain, and of a cold disposition, it is then also necessary that they should be concurrent.

Chapter VI.

It is quite plain when animals desire sexual intercourse; for the female pursues the male, as hens pursue the cock and place themselves beneath him, if the male is not desirous. Other animals also do the same. But if all animals appear to have these affections with respect to sexual intercourse, it is plain that the causes must be the same throughout. This bird, however, has not only the desire of receiving, but also of emitting semen. This is a proof of it. If the male is not present, she will emit the semen into herself, and become pregnant, and produce barren eggs, as if she desired both to emit semen, and when she had done so, soon ceased, just as when the male was present. Others also do the same, for a person has attempted to rear some singing locusts, which he had taken in a young state. When grown, they became pregnant spontaneously.

2. From these considerations it is plain that every female contributes to the semen, if this appears to take place in any one class of animals, for the barren animal differs in no respect from the other, except that it does not produce an animal, and this because it was formed by the union of both sexes. For this reason all the seminal fluid of the male does not appear to be productive, but some parts are barren, when not properly compounded from both sexes. And when women have lascivious dreams, the same affections of weakness and debility often occur, as if they had been lying with a male. It is plain, therefore, that if they appear to have emitted a seminal fluid in their dream, they will then conjecture that after their dream the same place

will become moist, and they will be obliged to bestow the same attention upon themselves as if they had had sexual intercourse. So that it is evident that there must be an emission of semen from both if it is to be productive.

3. But the uterus does not emit its semen into itself, but on the outside, into the place where that of the male also is received, and then draws it into itself. For some females produce spontaneously, as the bird produces barren eggs, and other females do not so, as the horses and sheep; either because the bird projects her semen into the uterus, and the place upon which that of the male is emitted is not external; for which reason, if he does not copulate properly with the female, it is poured out upon the ground. But in quadrupeds there is another place for the reception of the semen, both of the male and female, which in other animals it is combined with other fluids of the body, and is not collected in the uterus, because it does not enter it. But in birds, the uterus receives and matures the seminal fluid, and forms a body similar in other respects though not a living creature. It is necessary, therefore, the living creature should be derived from both sexes.

Chapter VII.

We must enquire whether women speak the truth, when they say that after a lascivious dream they find themselves dry; for it is plain that the uterus draws upwards. And if so, why do not females become pregnant spontaneously, since the male seminal fluid is drawn in, mixed with their own? And why do not she goats draw that part of it which extends outwards? for this affection takes place in some that have been pregnant many years; for they produce what is called myle (an amorphous mass of flesh), a circumstance which has also happened to a certain woman; for having had sexual intercourse, and to all appearance conceived, the size of the uterus increased, and everything at first went on regularly: but when the time of parturition arrived, she produced nothing, nor did the enlargement become any smaller: but after three or four years, a dysentery occurred, which placed her life in danger, when she produced a large mass of flesh, which they call myle. The affection continues in some to old age, even to the day of their death.

2. Does this affection arise from a warm habit of body, when the uterus is warm and dry, and for this reason capable of drawing into itself in such a manner that it is taken up and kept in it? For, in persons so affected, if the seminal fluid of both sexes is not united, but, like the barren egg, is taken up by one sex, then the myle is produced, which is not living creature, for it does not originate in both sexes, nor is it lifeless, for it is taken to have life like the barren egg. It remains, however, a long while, on account of the disposition of the uterus, and because the bird, which has produced many eggs in herself, when the uterus is stimulated by these, goes and lays them: and when the first is produced, the last will also come forth in proper time: for there is nothing to prevent it, but the body being productive as soon as it is full, causes the uterus to be no longer retentive. But in viviparous animals, on account of the change of force, as the fœtus increases, and the diversity of food is required, the uterus causes parturition from a kind of inflammation.

3. But the flesh, because it is not alive, always requires the same kind of food, for it does not cause any weight in the uterus, nor any inflammation. So that the affection would continue, in some cases, throughout life, unless some fortunate debility should take place, as in the woman who was attacked with dysentery. But does this affection arise from warmth, as it was said, or rather from a fluid state, because there is a fulness as it closes, either because the uterus is neither cold enough to reject it, nor warm enough to bring it to maturity? Wherefore, the disease lasts a long while, like those things which remain a long while before they are matured; but those that are about to come to maturity have an end, and that quickly. Such uteri, being very high up, cause a long delay. And, again, not being alive, it does not cause any pain by its movements, for the movement of the ligament which the living fœtus produces, causes pain. And the hardness of the substance is the effect of imperfect production, for it is so hard that it cannot be cut by the stroke of an axe. All ripe and mature things become soft, but imperfectly digested things are immature and hard.

4. Wherefore, many physicians, deceived by the resem-

blance, say that women are suffering from myle, if they only see the abdomen elevated without dropsy, and a cessation of the catamenia, when the disease has lasted for a long while. But this is not the case, for the myle is a rare disease. Sometimes there will be collections of cold and moist excrements and fluids, and sometimes of thick ones in this part of the abdomen, if either the nature or the habit is of this kind. For these things afford neither pain nor heat, on account of their cold nature; but if they increase, more or less, they bring no other disease after them, but remain quiet, like some maimed thing.

5. The cessation of the catamenia takes place on account of the excrementitious matter of the body being directed to this point, as when women are nursing; for they occur either not at all, or only in small quantities. A collection of matter from the flesh sometimes takes place between the uterus and the stomach, which has the character of the myle, but is not it. But it is not difficult to know the difference, by touching the uterus; for if it is correctly placed, and not enlarged, it is evident that the disease is not there; but if it is the same as when with child, it will be warm, and cold, and dry, because all the fluids are turned inwards; and the os uteri will be in the same condition as when they are pregnant; but if the enlargement is of any other kind, it will be cold, and not dry when touched, and the os uteri will always be the same.

APPENDIX.

ESSAY ON THE LITERARY AND PECUNIARY RESOURCES WHICH ARISTOTLE EITHER USED, OR IS SAID TO HAVE USED IN THE EXAMINATION AND COMPOSITION OF HIS HISTORY OF ANIMALS.

Translated from the Latin of Schneider.

ARISTOTLE had very likely more authorities, whom he has followed, or converted to his own purposes, than those whose names he has given. These are, however, a few, whom he has named, as Alcmæon of Crotona; Dionysius of Apollonia; Herodorus of Heracleum in Pontus, the father of Bryson the sophist; Ctesias of Cnidos; Herodotus of Halicarnassus; Syennesis of Cyprus; Polybus; Democritus of Abdera; Anaxagoras of Clazomene; Empedocles of Sicily; and if there are any more which do not just now occur to my memory, they are accurately enumerated in the index, with the names of the places to which they belonged. I have said that it is probable, that Aristotle has derived information from more authorities than he has named; and a reason for this conjecture is found in a passage which he extracts, almost verbatim, from Herodotus, on the Nilotic crocodile (Euterpe, 68). This I have shewn in a note on the passage, book v. ch. 27, 2. And there are many places, both in his natural history and his other works on animals, where our philosopher refers to the ancient fables of men who were transformed into the nature and forms of various animals. The oldest author of such fables is Boeus (or Boeo, in the feminine gender, as some have conjectured). From this book Antoninus Literalis has extracted many chapters in Greek. Nicander of Colophon, and others, followed the example of Bocus. Among Latin writers, the Metamorphoses of Ovid have always commanded attention. All who have read the work of Antoninus, and the Metamorphoses of Ovid, will easily perceive how much information on the nature and habits of animals our philosopher could have derived from the very character of the books which had come down from the remotest antiquity to the time of Aristotle (compare note 9, 17, 1), especially if they bear in mind that the ancient teachers of physics always compared the habits of animals with those of man, and conjectured the causes and reasons of their actions, from similar impulses in man. This may be seen in the fables of Æsop, for they contain the first elements of the doctrines of the ancients on physics and morals. We might also offer a surmise on Eudoxus, and Scylax, and others, who wrote "Travels Round the Earth," in which they described the animals of different countries; for our philosopher appeals to the testimony of both these authors, in his work on Meteorics, and elsewhere. There is more doubt whether Aristotle used, or could have used, the numerous notices of animals, of the interior of Asia and India, which the companions of Alexander, in his Asiatic and Indian expeditions, brought back to Greece; which Theophrastus, the pupil of Aristotle, and his successor in the schools, is found to have used so well in his History of Plants. For this I consider to be proved, that the written notices of the companions of Alexander were published after the death of the king, though we have no proof of the exact year in which they were made public. Indeed I have never found any evidence in the History of Animals which could lead us to suppose that Aristotle was acquainted with the animals of the interior of Asia and India, by information derived from the companions of Alexander; nor have I been able to find the slightest information from which I can form a conjecture as to either the place or time when this history was written: but, in order that others may institute a more rigorous inquiry into the date and place of its authorship, if any such have escaped my notice, I will place before my readers that portion of the Aristotelian chronology which relates to this work, from the disputation of St. Croix, a learned French author (Examen Critique des Historiens d'Alexander le Grand, p. 603, second edition). Aristotle, therefore, at the invitation of Philip, King of Macedon, undertook the education of his son, Alexander, when he was thirteen years of age, in the second year of the 109th Olympiad, when Phythodotus was Archon of Athens. Aristotle returned to Athens in the second year of the 111th Olympiad, in the Archonship of Evænetus. He taught at Athens for thirteen years, from whence he fled to Chalcis, and there he died, in the third year of the 114th Olympiad, during the Archonship of Philocles.

There is, indeed, a passage in Pliny, (book x. ch. 64, sect. 84, on the fecundity of mice,) where he says, that among other things Aristotle has spoken in his History of Animals (vi. 29) of the gravid fœtus of the Persian mice; but the Greek exemplar contains no authority from which Pliny could have derived the words which he has added: " More wonderful than all is the fœtus of the mice, which we cannot unhesitatingly receive, though derived from the authority of Aristotle, and the soldiers of Alexander the Great." In this and in two other places he calls those *soldiers* whom others are in the habit of calling the *companions* of Alexander the Great. But there is also a passage in the Meteorics of Aristotle (iii. 1), where he mentions as a recent event the destruction of the temple of Ephesus, by the incendiary Herostratus, on the day of Alexander's birth, in these words: " As it has just now happened in the burning of the temple of Ephesus." This book, therefore, appears to have been written at the commencement of the 106th Olympiad, and with it the History of Animals is very closely connected, as I have shown in my treatise on the order of the books of Physics; so that we may suppose that they were written in nearly the same Olympiad, if we regard only the series of the works; and no interruption occurred with which we are unacquainted. On the other hand, in the Meteorics (iii. 5), he speaks of a lunar rainbow, and says that it is rarely seen, and then adds, " that it has occurred but twice in more than fifty years." If we reckon these fifty years from the birth of Aristotle, in the first year of the 99th Olympiad, that book will fall in the third or fourth year of the 111th Olympiad; and from this calculation it would follow that this book was also written in Athens, but that the first date is to be taken in a wider sense.

From all this, we may easily perceive that at this day we are entirely ignorant of the sources of information collected either from ancient or contemporary writers, to which our philosopher had access in composing and completing a work of such multiplied and varied information. Even if we assume that they were as large as the mind of Aristotle was great, acute, and transparent, still, for a work so various and extensive, spread over seas, rivers, earth, and heaven, even that mind would require some assistance from other sources to which it might apply in constructing and building up a system of general instruction from the materials collected in different places about various animals, and from the observations used in describing and arranging them together in orders, classes, genera, and species. The following were the sources Aristotle used, according to the narrative of an uncertain author quoted by Pliny (viii. 16, 17)—" King Alexander the Great," he says, " was possessed with the desire of knowing the natures of animals, and therefore delegated the work to Aristotle, a man of very great learning. Some thousands of men in the whole region of Asia and Greece obeyed his commands, all, namely, who obtained their livelihood by hunting, hawking, or fishing, or who had in their care menageries, herds, beehives, fishponds, or aviaries; so that nothing in nature might be unknown to him; and from his examination of these, he compiled those fifty celebrated volumes, which I have collected into one, together with those animals with which he was unacquainted, and I hope that they will be consulted by good scholars." In all this there is nothing contradictory to the mind and liberality of Alexander, or the confidence or strength of his empire. But some may prefer the story published by Ælian, in his various history (iv. 19), who, I know not on what authority, transfers the narrative to Philip, the father of Alexander—" Having supplied abundance of riches to Aristotle, he was the means of many other undertakings, and especially of his knowledge of living creatures; and the son of Nichomachus completed his history by the liberal assistance of Philip; who also honoured Plato and Theophrastus." If this be true, it evidently refers to those seven or eight years in which Aristotle was in Macedonia presiding over the education of Alexander, the son of Philip.

These abundant supplies for the studies of Aristotle are not at all inconsistent, either with the liberality of Philip, or his love for his son and his son's tutor, nor do they surpass credibility. The gold mines of Philippi supplied the munificence and liberality of Philip. But there are difficulties in the narrative which make us question the credibility of the author of this munificence. For instance, the names of Plato and Theophrastus are mentioned; but the name of Theophrastus could not be so great and illustrious, even if it were known to the Greeks at all, as to have attracted the liberality of Philip, before the death of his master Aristotle, whom also he succeeded in the School at Athens. I should, therefore, rather imagine that Ælian, who was more diligent in the accuracy of his Attic diction than his historical fidelity, has committed some error in the name of Philip, or in those of Plato and Theophrastus, whom he has appended to his narrative.

The narrative of Athenæus, (ix. 398,) derived from the report of an unknown author, is very different; he calls the History of Animals a very expensive work, and then adds—" There is a report that Aristotle received 800 talents from Alexander, for writing the History of Animals"— a sum of money which Perigonius, in his Notes on Ælian, estimates at 1,440,000 caroli. To this narrative, or, as it may be more justly termed, rumour, is opposed the opinion of Io. Henr. Schulzius, in his History of Medicine (Leipsic, 1738, p. 358). "When I consider this matter aright, it appears to me that the whole story is very doubtful, and, for the most part, fabulous. And it can easily be proved, that the whole revenue of Macedon, if Alexander had paid it all to Aristotle for several years, would not have amounted to this sum. It is impossible, therefore, that he could have paid so much to Aristotle before the conquest of Asia; and after his expedition had been successfully accomplished, his affection was alienated from Aristotle, and, in order to annoy him, he liberally enriched other philosophers, who had done nothing to deserve his patronage. Their labours, therefore, are in vain, who demand justice of our excellent Aristotle, even in his grave, because he did not use such an immense sum of money in the composition of a more veracious history.

" I am certainly of opinion that a great deal has been made, as usual, of a very little matter, namely, that if Aristotle derived any assistance in that kingdom, all the materials were provided for him while Philip was alive, and before Alexander's expedition was undertaken, or in the first years of the expedition. But afterwards, when Alexander had set out, Aristotle returned to Athens, and was engaged in teaching: nor could he have derived any advantage from the resources which Pliny mentions, and the multitude of persons who were instructed to place themselves under his command, for he was not only occupied with other pursuits, but would have been in danger of being destroyed by the fury of the Athenians, on the plea that he was attempting innovations, if he had even ventured to dissect animals, not to say men."

In a note he adds these observations:—" Aristobulus, no unworthy companion of Alexander in his expedition, bears testimony, according to Plutarch, that the whole military chest did not contain seventy talents of coin. For the preparation of so arduous an undertaking, however, the same person says, that two hundred talents ought to have been taken for mutual exchange. I remember also to have read in Eustathius's commentary on Homer, a very learned disquisition on the scarcity of money amongst the Macedonians, at the time of Alexander's expedition; but I cannot lay my hands upon the passage."

I must confess that I am not influenced by this annotation, nor does the whole of this controversy appear to me to have been properly conducted. For the greatest doubt prevails as to the number of talents which Alexander is said to have paid to Aristotle, to help him in his task; and the report only rests on the authority of a writer who lived centuries after the death of Alexander. To refute this is useless labour, both because its origin is obscure, and also because a sum of money set down in figures might be easily corrupted by transcribers. But the testimony of Aristobulus will give little or no assistance to the opinion of the learned, if we adopt that which is most probable, namely, that Philip, or his son Alexander, gave large sums of money to Aristotle, to enable him to pursue his studies in Natural History, while he lived in Macedon, and was employed in the education of Alexander. The question about the date when Aristotle arranged and published the materials and notes he had collected is quite distinct, and I do not think that it can be precisely ascertained at the present time. The conjecture I have hazarded (light enough, I must confess) does not say much in favour of the story of abundant treasures supplied by Philip, or Alexander, to our philosopher, for the composition of his Natural History. But these persons form a very poor estimate of the study and labour bestowed by Aristotle upon the History of Animals, who imagine that our philosopher had only access to such books as now remain, forgetting those of which time has robbed us.

Most of all we must regret his Ζωϊκὰ, which appears to have given a more accurate description of animals, and his ἀνατομικὰ, which further contained notices of their internal structure, and was illustrated by drawings to which he often refers in his Natural History, as well as in his works on the parts and the generation of animals. It will scarcely be possible to fix with any accuracy on the number of books he employed, after the great carelessness of librarians, and the many facilities for error in copyists, arising from the method of notation by letters. Antigonus Carystius, in his sixty-sixth chapter, increases the number of volumes given by Pliny, for he writes seventy; and if the titles of the books, as they are given by Diogenes Laertius and Athenæus, are compared with those published, the number of books relating to Animal History to which he may have had access are readily estimated, even should every book of every work be reckoned as a separate book, and the list compared with the number given by Pliny.

In the memory of our fathers and grandfathers (for, alas! at the present time few trouble themselves with the works of the ancients) there were many who blamed Aristotle for these works, both for his manner of treating the subjects and his narratives of the lives and habits of animals, and vexed them with questions and disputations.

These objections will be better answered, when we come to those passages of the History. It may, however, be of some general avail to put a stop to these objections, which were urged against his manner of teaching; and I hope to be able to point out some peculiar sources from which Aristotle appears to have derived the more difficult parts of his History, and those which were obnoxious to dispute.

Amongst other foolish and trifling questions with which some Grammarian, in the Deipnosophistæ of Athenæus, (viii. p. 352,) has endeavoured not only to impugn, but even destroy our philosopher's credibility, is the following:—" I do not much admire the diligence of Aristotle, though others praise him so highly. At what time, I should like to know, or from what Proteus or Nereus ascending from the deep, to give him information, did he learn what the fishes were doing there, and in what manner they slept and took their food; for he writes things of this kind, which are only 'the miracles of fools,' as the comic poet says."

I will not follow the rest of his argument, which relates to terrestrial and winged animals; for the aquatic, and especially the marine creatures, seem to offer the greatest opportunity for questioning the fidelity of his narrative. In the first place, then, we may observe, that of all mankind the Greeks were amongst the greatest eaters of fish, at least after the heroic and Homeric ages; for Homer is never found to mention fish at the suppers and festivals of his heroes. So that I should not wonder if the frequent and repeated industry and observation of fishermen, following their labours both in rivers and seas, to adorn the tables of their fellow citizens, supplied ample and varied information to learned men who were engaged in the investigation of natural objects. By the same means they might learn from hunters the haunts and dispositions of wild beasts, and those of domesticated animals from husbandmen. The whole life and labour of such men was devoted to the uses, advantages, and food of man; and their observations would be particularly directed to those animals which could assist in sharing the labours of mankind, or whose flesh or other parts were required for food or medicine. Their parturition and its proper time, the number of their young, the manner of bringing them up, their nutriment, the pastures and food of the parents, and the proper time for hunting them, were observed with the greatest accuracy. And if any diseases arising from the weather, their food, or their drink impended over them, and threatened their production or the life of the wild cattle, or if a peculiar or common enemy laid in wait for the life of one or all, it could not easily escape their observation; and from these circumstances we may manifestly derive the origin of those fables and narratives in which the opinions of animals are compared with the life and manner of human beings, such as the simple minds of hunters, fishers, and rustics could comprehend. In these books of natural history we find traces of many stories of this kind which it is unnecessary here to point out.

In the aquatic and marine orders of animals there is, besides these sources of information, the diligent investigation instituted by certain writers throughout the seas and rivers of Greece, at a time when every useful fish, and marine and river animals of this class, mollusca, shell fish, and worms formed part of their food. The time and manner of their coition, parturition, pregnancy, and life, the nature of their food, places and manner of taking fish, the times in which they were not accessible, the faults and diseases of aquatic animals, were minutely described. The twentieth chapter of the eighth book of our History is on this subject, where the food and diseases of aquatic animals are described, and particular notice is taken of their use as food, besides the observations on the manners of quadrupeds.

It is very evident that the life of one man would hardly suffice for the observation of all these facts even in a single class of animals; but, as I have said, there were writers before the time of Aristotle who provided for the tastes and tables of these fish-eating Greeks a most exquisite apparatus from the rivers and seas of Greece, especially in Sicily, which has been remarkable for its wealth ever since the reigns of Gelo and Hiero, and had surpassed the rest of Greece not only in its knowledge of nature, but in the art of poetry.

There is a passage in Plato's "Gorgias," (sect. 156, p. 246, ed. Heind.) where mention is made of "Mithæcus, the author of a work on Sicilian cookery, and Sarambus, the publican. One furnished the best of food, the other the best of wine." That the art of choosing and preparing food for the table was treated of in this book we may conclude from the use of the word ὀψοποιΐα, which the Greeks especially used to signify the kinds of fish used for food. A passage from this book on the manner of cooking the fish called tenia is quoted by Athenæus, who makes the title of this book ὀψαρτυτικὸν, vii. p. 282, and xii. p. 506.

We cannot accurately ascertain the age of Mithæcus. The most ancient author of such a book that we can call to mind is Epicharmus, a Sicilian poet and physician, from whose fragments, collected by Athenæus, we may certainly conclude he was acquainted with the nature of aquatic animals.

To this class we may, in the first place, refer those passages which are extracted from the drama called the Marriage of Hebe, or the Muses, and not only teach us the nature of fishes, but also the manner of procuring and cooking them. A learned writer in the "Literary Ephemeris" of Jena, 1810, (Nos. 156, 157,) attempted to collect all these and reduce them to order. There remain, however, many more passages which the conjectures of the most learned could hardly amend or explain, from the corruption of the text by librarians and the variety of Sicilian names. And before the time of Epicharmus, Ananius, an Iambic poet, nearly contemporary with Hipponactus, an Ionian poet, composed, among other poems, a similar work on cooking fish, as we learn from a passage extracted by Athenæus, (vii. p. 282.) After Epicharmus there was Terpsion, a Sicilian, who was the first to write a gastrology, in which he taught his disciples from what kind of food they ought to abstain. He is mentioned by Clearchus Solensis, a disciple of Aristotle, in his work de Paræmiis, in "Athenæus," (viii. p. 337.)

Clearchus also mentions Archestratus, the Sicilian, the pupil of Terpsion, who, after having travelled through the whole of Greece, wrote a work in heroic verse on the nature of fishes, those especially which were fit for the table, and on the manner of cooking and preparing them. We learn that his book was called 'Ηδυπάθεια, not only from the testimony of Athenæus, but from an imitation by Ennius. For Ennius, who died A.U.C. 584, one hundred and fifty-two years after the death of Aristotle, translated and in part imitated the poem of Archestratus, and called his work "Carmina Hedypathetica," as Apulegius tells us in his "Apologia." We have good reason for supposing that Archestratus was either contemporary with Aristotle, or a little older. For Archestratus mentions Diodorus Aspendius, the Pythagorean, as his contemporary, to whom Timæus, the historian, tells us that the Epistle of Stratonicus was written (" Athenæus," iv. p. 136). Therefore Archestratus, Diodorus, Aspendius, and Stratonicus, an eminent harpist, were contemporaries, and so they were with Aristotle and Demosthenes; and this conjecture is confirmed by many passages in Athenæus, where Stratonicus is reported to have been alive with those persons whom Demosthenes mentions in his orations. Aristotle, therefore, may have used this work of Archestratus in that part of his Natural History which treats of the nature of fishes.[1]

The writings of physicians who prescribed the food, both of sick and well, have handed down similar and much more extensive observations on the animals and fishes which were brought to the tables of the Greeks. Of this kind Athenæus has given many passages from Dorio, and Diphilus of Siphnus. Oribasius has made a long extract from the work of Xenocrates, on the aquatic animals used in food, which I purpose some day to publish with Xenocrates, if my life should be spared long enough.

[1] To the end of this Essay are appended fragments of Archestratus, on the fishes of Sicily, amounting to 270 lines of heroic verse, together with notes, by the author of the Essay.

INDEX.

A

Ἄγνος, Vitex agnus castus, a tree like a willow, the branches of which the matrons strewed on their beds at the Thesmophoria, 266.

Ἀδριανικαὶ ἀλεκτορίδες, a small kind of domestic fowl, 138.

Ἀείσκωψ, a kind of owl. Stryx aluco, *Strack*, 249. Brown Owl. There is also another migratory kind mentioned, 249, which does not hoot.

Ἀέροψ, the Bœotian name of the Merops, M. apiaster, 138.

Ἀετός, or αἰετός, Eagle, hence the Latin avis, 9, 61; its eggs and young, 146; two species, the Pygargus haliætus, and the black eagle, Aquila anataria or Falco nævius, *ib.*; several species, 201, 250; used in augury, 217; eats serpents, 231; food and manners, 251; true eagles, Falco chrysaetos, *ib.*; the eagle kills the heron, 233; it fights with the vulture and the swan, *ib.*; a kind of eagle in Scythia, 252.

Ἀηδών, nightingale, Sylvia luscinia, its song, 95, 96; reproduction, 108; its tongue, 246; changes its song and colour, 276.

Ἀθερίνη, Atherina presbyter, *Spratt's Lycia*, or A. veru, in modern Greek atherno, 159; its reproduction, 160, 234.

Αἰγίθαλος, Parus, Tit or Titmouse, eats worms, 202; three species, *ib.*; lays many eggs, 246; an enemy to bees, 265; σπιζίτης, parus major, *Strack*. ὀρεινὸς, Parus ater, *Strack*, or P. caudatus. ἐλάχιστος, Parus cœruleus.

Αἴγιθος, Bunting, Emberiza, *Strack*, or hedge sparrow or Parus cœruleus, dislikes the ass, builds in hedges, 232; hostile to the anthus and acanthis, 233; its food and young, 246.

Αἰγοθήλας, goat sucker, Caprimulgus Europæus, 250.

Ἀιγοκέφαλος, Stryx otus, *Strack*, 39.

Αἰγυπιὸς, the Vulture, it is hostile to the Æsalon (small hawk), 9, 23; and fights with the eagle, *ib.*

Αἴγυπτος, Egypt, the Egyptians hatch eggs in manure, 139; two kinds of Egyptian mice, one with stiff hair (Hierax, or Aulacodus Swinderianus), another with long hind legs (Jerboa, or Cavia), 178; the care of animals among the Egyptians, 231; a large kind of oxen in Egypt, 226; asp and ichneumon, 238; white and black ibis, 242.

Αἰγώλιος, a night bird of prey, Stryx passerina, *Strack*. or S. flammea. *Camus*. La chouette, little owl, 201; kills the calaris,

232; its habit and mode of life, 247; in p. 139 this bird is called αἰτώλιος.

Αἰετός, a cartilaginous fish, one of the class selache, Raia aquila, 104.

Αἰθιοπία, Æthiopia, winged serpents in Æthiopia, probably Draco volans, 9; Æthiopian sheep, 165.

Αἰθίοψ, Æthiopian, teeth, 60; semen, 72, 188.

Αἴθυια, a large waterbird, Larus parasiticus, or L. Marinus, Strack, or L. argentatus, 2; its reproduction, 108; food, 203.

Αἴλουρος, cat, Felis cattus, copulation, 103; its young, food, and mode of life, 177; kills birds. 239.

Αἱμορροΐς, or ἀπορραΐς, a kind of shell fish, perhaps Murex, 85, 86.

Αἴξ, goat, male and female, Ibex or wild goat, *Spratt's Lycia*, Caper hircus, Strack, 13, 27, 28, 31, 66; the she goats of Œta, 70; the he goat in Lemnos, *ib.*; it is mentioned with the chimæra or domestic goat in 71; dreams, 97; infested with ticks, 134; discharges of the female, 163, 164; gestation, 165; food, drink, &c., 207; the wild goat, 225; Syrian Caper hircus Mambricus and Lycian goat, C. Angorensis, *ib.*; Egyptian, 226; its mode of life, 235; wild goats in Crete, 238; rumination, 278.

Αἴξ, a water bird, probably Tantalus arquatus, Strack, Scolopax Gallinago, 208.

Αἰσάλων, a small hawk, perhaps sparrow-hawk or merlin, Falco Æsalon, 253.

Αἰτώλιος, see Αἰγώλιος.

Ἀκαλήφη, Medusa, and probably also some species of Actinia, 2, 3; fixed and locomotive kinds, 87, 88; small and edible species, others large and hard, 88; a fleshy kind, 195; a large kind, its food, mouth, and anus, 198.

Ἀκανθίας, a kind of shark, Squalus Acanthias, Strack, 256.

Ἀκανθίς, thistle finch or gold finch, Fringilla carduelis, or Fringilla cannabina, Strack, or F. spinus, brown linnet, 202; hates the ass, lives on worms, 233; a foe to the antbus and ægithus, 234; its food, colour, song, 247.

Ἀκανθυλλίς, Parus pendulinus, or caudatus, Strack, 202; its nest, 245.

Ἄκαρι, mite, Dermestes fatidicus, or perhaps Bostrichus, Strack, 135.

Ἀκρίς, locust, Tetigonia, Strack, Acridium, 89, 95; its birth, 123; reproduction, 132; changes its skin, 216; it is said to contend with serpents, 238: the Spex lacerticida corresponds with this description, Schneider.

Ἄκυλος, the acorn of the evergreen oak, used for fattening pigs, 206.

Ἀλεκτορίς, the domestic hen, Phasianus gallus, different kinds, 111, 138; sometimes produces soft eggs, 139; chickens, 140, 141; barren eggs, and times of laying, *ib.*; growth of the chick in the egg, 142; twin eggs, 144; the hen sometimes takes the form of the cock, 215; rolls in the dust, 277.

Ἀλεκτρυών, domestic fowl, male, also used of the class, 5; his comb, 36; crop, 45; appendages to intestines, *ib.*; crowing, 96; manner of coition, 102; appearances like ova when cut open, 139; testicles, 148; habits in temples, 241; sometimes they assume the form and habits of hens, 275; method of castration, 277.

Ἁλιαίετος, sea-eagle, different from the osprey, perhaps Aquila albicilla or Falco haliœtus, 203, 251, 253.

Ἀλκυών, Alcedo, kingfisher, or perhaps Turdus arundinaceus, reproduction, 107, 108; two species described, 203; materials and form

x

of its nest, 246. It is doubtful whether either of the species is our kingfisher. *Schneider.*

Ἀλοσάχη, probably a species of Zoophyte Alcyonia, 246.

Ἀλώπηξ, fox, Canis vulpes, 6, 29; it breeds with the Laconian dogs, 227; attacks the heron, 233; is friendly with the crow, *ib.*; a troglodyte, *ib.*

Ἀλώπηξ, Vampire, Vespertilio caninus, *Strack*, V. dinops or Sciurus volans, 9; reproduction, 177; it hunts mice, 178.

Ἀλώπηξ, a cartilaginous fish, reproduction, 149; represents a class, 151; Egyptian species, 226; stratagems, 255.

Ἀμία, a kind of tunny, mackerel, Scomber, *Strack*, 4, 40, 91; its rapid growth, 160, 199, 200; lives in bays, 211; and enters rivers, 218; its teeth and mode of defence, 255.

Ἀμυγδαλή, Amygdala communis, almond tree, 268; almonds, 242.

Ἀνθίας, a migratory sea fish, also called αὐλωπίας, Scomber ala longa, 159; gregarious, 234; also called sacred, 255.

Ἄνθος, yellow bunting, Emberiza citrinella, *Strack*, Motacilla barula, 202; feeds in meadows, imitates the neighing of the horse, 233; hostile to the acanthis and ægithus, *ib.*; it lives by the side of rivers, 244.

Ἀνθρήνη, wild bee, Apis terrestris, or Vespa crabro, 88; the larvæ, 124; reproduction, 130; a diligent insect, 258; makes honey, 260; its manners and habits, 270.

Ἄπιος, the pear tree, 126.

Ἀπλυσίας, a dark-coloured sponge, 119.

Ἀπορραΐς, various reading for αἱμορροΐς, Murex, or Natica.

Ἄπους, swift, Hirundo apus, 4; also called κύψελλος, 271.

Ἀράχνης, spider, 5, 85, 135; its web, repro[ ] is driven a[ ] it sucks its[ ] the lizard,[ ] 259. Ψυλ[ ] The smalle[ ] rabilis—th[ ] cola, anoth[ ] tus.

Ἄρκτος, bea[ ] 27, 29, 42[ ] time it bec[ ] of gestati[ ] 175; mod[ ] bernation,[ ] *ib*; the fe[ ] its habits,[ ]

Ἄρκτος, a c[ ] cer spinosis[ ] arctus, rep[ ] and manne[ ]

Ἅρπη, a bir[ ] near the s[ ] and brent[ ] and ictinu[ ] its mode o[ ] of its prey[ ]

Ἀρχάνος, a[ ]

Ἀσκαλαβώτ[ ] Gecko, St[ ] lives in h[ ] skin, 216[ ] some part[ ] spiders, 2[ ] inverted p[ ]

Ἀσκάλαφος, owl, Stryx[ ]

Ἀσκαλώπας, snipe, *Str*[ ] proves of[ ] phæopus,[ ]

Ἀσκαρίδες, [ ] 124.

Ἀσκαρίς, th[ ] (gnat), 12[ ]

Ἀσπάλαξ,[ ] lives in [ ] 90; there[ ] none in L[ ]

Ἀσπίς, Co[ ]

which a poison is made in Lybia, 227; in Egypt it is attacked by the ichneumon, 238.

Ἀστακὸς, lobster, Cancer Gammarus, and Astacus, 138; compared with the spiny lobster, 77, 78, 79; a small fresh-water species, Astacus fluviatilis, crayfish, 86; its reproduction, 106, 121; changes its shell, 217.

Ἀσταφίς, a raisin used for feeding cattle, 206.

Ἀστερίας, a cartilaginous fish, 109, 151. Squalus asterias.

Ἀστερίας, a hawk, 109, 151, 253.

Ἀστερίας, Ardea stellaris, bittern, 233.

Ἀστήρ, star-fish, Uraster rubens, 118.

Ἀσφόδελος, a plant, asphodel, A. ramosus, 260.

Ἀτρακτυλλὶς, a plant of the thistle tribe, Carthamus creticus.

Ἀτταγὴν, grouse, Tetrao bonasia, or T. attagen, 249; it lives on the ground, 276.

Ἀττέλαβος, a kind of locust, Gryllus, 123; reproduction and death, 133.

Αὐλωπίας, the same as ἀνθίας, 159.

Αὐξίς, the young tunny, 160.

Ἀφάκη, plant, a kind of vetch, 208.

Ἀφρὸς, fish spawn, 157.

Ἀφύη, anchovy or sardine, Melanurus juvenculus, 157, its origin, ib.; other kinds, ib.; in modern Greek ἀφρόψαρο.

Ἀχαίνης ἔλαφος, a variety of large stag with a strong mane, Strack; a brocket, or two-year old stag, from his single-pointed horns, Liddell and Scott, 39, 237.

Ἀχάρνας, a sea fish, Anarrhicas rufus, 200; does not bear heat, 218.

Ἀχέτας, the male grasshopper, Cicada Orni, 89.

Ἄχρας, a kind of wild pear, Pyrus communis, 206, 268.

B

Βάλαγρος, a fresh-water fish, Cobitis barbus, 98.

Βάλανος, Balanus, Cirripede, acorn shell, 94, 117.

Βάλανος, acorn, 221.

Βάλλερος, a fresh-water fish, Cyprinus blicca, 156, 219; βάλερος, βαλῖνος, βαρῖνος, are various readings.

Βασιλεὺς, also called trochilus, and presbys, lives in holes, 244; has a bright crest, 202; probably Regulus Cristatus, golden-crested wren; or Sylvia troglodytes.

Βατὶς, a bird that frequents bushes, Sylvia rubicola, eats worms, 202; mentioned with finch and sparrow.

Βατὶς, a fish, the prickly roach, Liddell and Scott, 149, 152.

Βάτος, ray, Raia batos, not the skate, which is perhaps leiobatos, 8, 37; its manner of coition, 104; it does not receive its young into itself, 150, 151; it lives in holes, 214; its manner of taking its prey, 255.

Βάτραχος, frog, Rana esculenta and R. temporaria, 3, 39, 87; croaks, 96; the female larger than the male, 100; coition, 103; tadpole, 154; its united spawn, 155; spoken of as a class, 196; no croaking frogs in Cyrene, 225; marsh frogs are foes to bees, 261.

Βάτραχος, a cartilaginous fish, Lophius piscatorius and L. barbatus, 8, 37, 38, 40; among the selache, 104; oviparous, 148, 150; it produces many young, 159.

Βελόνη, fish, Syngnathus acus, 40; its reproduction, 109, 154, 160; gregarious, 224; the Halcyon builds its nest with the bones of this fish.

Βολίταινα, cephalopod, Eledone moschites, Leach, 76; also called ὀζολις; it does not exist in the Euripus, 256.

Βομβύκια, Apis cementaria, or also Megachile muraria, and Bombus terrestris, forms an angular cell of mud, 131.

Βομβύλιος, larva of silk worm, 124; the humble bee, 260, 271.

Βόμβυξ, silkworm.

Βόνασσος, Antelope bonassus, or Bos Urus, Bison, 26, 28; its country, form, habits, hunting, 273.

Βοσκάς, Anas boscas, or A. Crecca, 203.

Βόστρυχος, insect, Lampyris noctiluca, *Strack*, 125.

Βουβαλίς, Antilope Gnou, 58.

Βοῦς, Bos taurus, Ox, 5, 27, 28, 29, 30, 41, 62; milk, 69; dreams, 97; lowing of the bull, 100, 112; coition, 103; tormented with lice, 135; sexual desires, 161, 162; discharges and urine of the cow, 163; reproductive powers of bull, 168; the castrated animal is taught to lead the herd, *ib.*; teeth, milk, and habits, *ib.*; veins in the embryo, 190; mode of drinking, 205; care of the ox, 206; red cattle of Epirus, 207; diseases, 219, 222; the ox drinks pure water, 224; Egyptian oxen, 226; habits, 236; wild oxen, B. Bubalus, 26; one species of ox has a bone in its heart, 39; oxen in Phrygia which can move their horns, 61; small oxen in Phasis, 71; oxen in Epirus, *ib.*; in Tortona, 72; the cow brings forth at a year old, 113; Syrian oxen, 226; castration of the young, 278; rumination, *ib.*

Βοῦς, a cartilaginous fish, Raia cornuta, 104, 152.

Βρένθος, a sea-bird, Anas tadorna, hostile to the larus and harpa, 232; makes its nest in hills and woody places, 244.

Βρύας, a large owl, Stryx bubo, 201.

Βρύον, algæ, both fresh-water and marine, 155, 200, 220.

Βρύσσος, an echinite, Scutella, 102.

Βωμολόχος, Corvus monedula, 218

Βῶξ, a gregarious fish, Sparus boops, 234; contracted from Βόαξ, from the sound it makes.

Γ

Γάλας, a kind of smooth shell-fish, mya pictorum, 82.

Γαλεός, a cartilaginous fish, Squalus galeus and charachias, *Strack*, or Gadus lota, 8, 44, 49, 108, 149, 151; uterus and ova, 150; receives its young into itself, *ib.*; not found in the Pyrrhœan Euripus, 256.

Γαλεώδη, fish of the shark kind, 37, 40, 41; placed under the selache, 104, 149; the males have appendages, 104; the uterus, 149; galei and galeodes, 151.

Γαλῆ, weasel, martin, polecat, Mustela Faro, M. Erminea, M. vulgaris, 20; the wild kind hunts mice, 178; hostile to the crow 232; it attacks serpents, 233; in Poroselene, 225; it fights with serpents, especially with those called myotheræ, 238; its form compared with the ictis, 239; eat birds' eggs, 232; mode of attacking its prey, 238.

Γέρανος, crane, Ardea grus, 2, 4, 64 coition, 102; migrations of th male bird, 209; they migrat after the quails, *ib.*; the fable o the stone they are said to carry 210; gregarious, *ib.*; migration: leaders, prudence, 243; they figl with each other, the number their eggs, 245.

Γίννος, the offspring of a mule wit a mare or she ass, 11; see ἴννος.

Γλανίς, a fresh-water fish, Siluri glanis, *Strack*, 9, 38, 40, 219 conjoined spawn, 155: two sp cies, the greater and the small the male watches the spawn, *ib* size of the ova, 156; diseases, 21 unfit to eat when in spawn, t female better than the male, 229; the male watches the young, breaks the hook with its teeth, 256.

Γλάνος, Hyæna striata, 204.

Γλαῦκος, a fish of a grey colour, Gobius Gozo, *Strack*, 44; marine, 211; it lives in holes during the summer, 214; when good for food, 228.

Γλαυκώδεις, birds of the owl kind, 36.

Γλαῦξ, owl, 39, 45; has crooked claws, 201; how it may be taken, 210; lives in holes, 215; hostile to the crow and orchilus, 232; is pecked by smaller birds, used in hawking. *ib.*; the time for taking the owl, 252.

Γλωττίς, a bird, Rallus crex, *Strack*, Scolopax glottis, see κύγχραμος and ὀρτυγόμητρα, its tongue and migrations, 210.

Γνάφαλος, probably some Indian bird, its form and food, Ampelis garrulus, 246.

Γνήσιοι ἀετοί, true eagles, Aquila Chrysaetos, 251.

Γόγγρος, conger, Muræna conger, 8, 37, 38, 40, 41, 61, its ova and fat, 160; it is destroyed by the spiny lobster, but destroys the polypus, 198; its food, 199; black and white kinds, 211; lives in holes, 213; it is attacked by the muræna, 235; compared with the sea serpent, 255.

Γραῦς, a crustacean, Dromia lanosa, 217.

Γυπαίετος, or ὑπαίετος, Vultur barbatus, see ὀρειπέλαργος, 251.

Γυρῖνος, tadpole, 154.

Γύψ, vulture, Vultur cinereus, or V. fulvus, eggs and nest, 145, 243; its food, two kinds of vulture, 201.

Δ

Δασκίλλος, a fish, sciæna umbra, 199.

Δασύπους, hare, Lepus timidus, and L. cuniculus, 5, 29, 49, 58, 64, 71; coition, 102; superfetation, 108; reproduction, 176, 186; in Ithaca, 225; smaller in Egypt, 226; another species near Lake Bolba, 41.

Δελφὶς, dolphin, Delphinus delphis. 7, 13, 29, 37, 40, 46, 47, 59, 69, 91, 92, 93, 95; its sleep, 98; the fish called φθείρα follows the dolphin, 135; reproduction, 104, 152; it breathes air, 196: food, 200; throws itself on its back to take its prey, *ib.*; dolphin in the Pontus, 212; gentle habits, 274; its speed, it sometimes throws itself on the shore, 275.

Δίκταμνον, plant, dittany, 238; origanum Dictammum, *Lin.*

Δορκάς, Antelope dorcas, 26.

Δράκων, a sea fish, Trachinus draco, lives near the shore, 211.

Δράκων, a species of serpent in fresh water, attacks the glanis, 219; is hostile to the eagle, 231; sucks the juice of the herb picris, 238.

Δρεπανίς, perhaps the sand martin, Hirundo riparia, 4.

Δρομάδες, migratory fish, perhaps some species of tunny, 4, 155.

Δρυοκολάπτης, woodpecker, 202; three kinds, Picus varius, P. viridis, P. martius, 242; habits, *ib.*

E

Εγκρασίχολος, the parent of the Apua, Clupea encrasicolus, *Strack*, 157.

Ἔγχελυς, eel, Muræna anguilla, 8, 37, 40, 41, 61, 66, 93; is neither male nor female, 99; the so-called male and female are different species, 97; migrates to the sea to spawn, 156; its origin, 158; description and habits, 200, 201; those called female are better for food, 229.

Ἐλαίας ἄνθος, the flower of the olive, 127, 133, 216, 242.

Ἔλαφος, stag, Cervus Elaphus, 5, 26, 27, 28; those called Achaïnæ, 39, 237; blood, 58, 67; horns, 60, 236, 237; the female, 100; coition, 103, 174; voice, 112; habits, 236, 237; the castrated animal, 278; rumination, *ib*.

Ἐλέα, Emberiza arundinacea, or Turdus arundinaceus, *Strack*, or E. schœnilus, 246.

Ἐλεγῖνος, a migratory fish, 234.

Ἐλεδώνη, Eledone cirhosa, *Leach*, (Owen, in Cyclopædia of Anatomy), 76.

Ἐλειός, dormouse, Myoxus Avellanarius; or perhaps squirrel, Sciurus vulgaris, lives in holes in trees, 216.

Ἕλειοι, a kind of hawk, 253; probably an incorrect reading.

Ἐλεός, an owl, Stryx Aluco, *Strack*, see Ἀείσκοψ, 201.

Ἐλέφας, Elephas Indicus, 5, 14, 24, 26, 28, 29, 13, 40, 43, 46, 61, 72; voice, 96; reproduction, 103, 115, 161, 173; food, 207; life and diseases, 222, 224; strength, 234; capture, *ib.*; habits, docility, 274.

Ἔλλοψ, a fish with four simple branchia, sword fish or sturgeon, *Liddell and Scott*, Centriscus scolopax, *Strack*, Accipenser stellatus, 37; ἔλοψ, 40.

Ἕλμινς, worms, especially intestinal worms, tænia and lumbricus, some exist in sponges, 119; origin, 123; three kinds, flat worms, round worms, ascarides, 124; worms in snow, Podura nivalis, 126; some insect larvæ are described as worms, 135; small worms in eels, 158; worms in dogs, Tænia severata, 238.

Ἐμπίς, gnat, larger than κώνωψ, Tabanus, or Phryganea, *Strack*, 3, 9, 206.

Ἐμύς, Testudo coriacea, freshwater tortoise, Emys lutraria, 39; reproduction, 136; habits, 194, 216.

Ἐντελις or ἔτελις, probably sea bream, Sparus, *Strack*, Sparus Rayi, 153.

Ἔντερα γῆς, the decomposing matter in which eels have their origin, 158.

Ἔντομα, insects, as a class, 3, 10, 73, 123.

Ἐνυδρίς, otter, Lutra vulgaris, 2; its food, 205.

Ἐπιλαίς or ὑπολαίς, Sylvia curruca, *Strack*, or perhaps hedge sparrow, 202.

Ἔποψ, hoopoe, Upupa Epops, 1; its nest, 138; lives in woods and mountains, 244; changes its colour, 246, 276.

Ἐρέβινθος, a plant, leguminous seeds, Ervum sativum, 221.

Ἐρίθακη, bee bread, 267.

Ἐρίθρακος, Sylvia erithracus, or S. Phœnicurus, *Strack*, Redstart, 202; in its summer plumage called Phœnicurus, 276.

Ἐρινεός, wild fig tree, 136.

Ἕρπυλλος, Thymus serpyllum, wild thyme, 261.

Ἐρυθρῖνος, a red kind of mullet, Perca marina, Sparus Erythrymus, *Strack*, Perca scriba, all have roes, there are no males, 99, 153, 211.

Ἐρωδιός, heron, Ardea major, 203; a foe to the woodpecker, 212; three kinds, ὁ πέλλος, the black, Ardea cinerea, ὁ λευπος, the white, A. egretta, ὁ ἀστηριας, A. stellaris, 233, 247; a friend of the crow, 323.

Εὐλαι, maggots in flesh.

Ἐφήμερον, ephemera, insect, 10, 126.

Ἐχενηΐς, probably Goby or Blenny, *Forbes in Spratt's Lycia*, not the Remora, which was unknown to the ancients. Echeneis remora, *Strack*, 38.

Ἔχιδνα, viper, Coluber vivipara, C. verus, 10; hides under stones, 213.

Ἐχινομήτρα, Echinus Esculentus, *Forbes in Spratt's Lycia*, 86.

'Εχῖνος, sea urchin, Echinus lividus; another species, with hard spines, is Cidaris hystrix, also a long species, Amphidetus Mediterraneus, *Forbes*, 10, 11; eatable kinds, 86; small species, E. saxatilis; white species at Torone, E. decadactylus, *ib.*, 87, 94; at what season they are full of ova, 110.

'Εχῖνος, hedgehog, Erinaceus Europæus, 10, 46, 61, 81; coition, 102; changes the entrance of its hole when the wind changes, 239.

'Εχις, a serpent, Coluber vivipara, Vipera Reedii, viviparous, 49; reproduction, 137; how captured, 204; changes its skin, 216; becomes more poisonous by eating scorpions, 227.

'Εψητός, a small fish, Atherina Hepsetus, *Strack*, 156.

Z

Ζύγαινα, a shark, Squalus Zygæna, *Strack*, 40.

Ζυγνίς, a lizard, see χαλκίς, 223.

Ζωάρια, several small animals, 135.
1. Tinea pellionella.
2. T. sarcitella.
3. Psorus pulsatorius.
4. T. graminella.

Ζῶον, several unnamed animals.
1. A small crustacean in shell fish, perhaps Pinnotheres, 86.
2. marine creatures like small pieces of wood, Veretillum, 89.
3. marine creatures like shields, Alcyonium, 89.
4. marine creatures like αἰδοῖον ἀνδρος, Pennatula, 89.
5. winged creatures produced from maggots in pulse, Bruchus, 126.

H

Ἡμίονος, mule, offspring of horse and wild ass, the female larger and more long lived, 99, 170; the so-called mules of Syria, Equus hemionus, 11, 172, 177.

Ἧπατος, a fish so called from its colour, Theutis hepatus, *Strack*, Stromatos fiatola, 44.

Ἡπίολος, moth, Tinea mellonella, 225.

Ἡρακλεοτικὸς καρκίνος, Heracleotic crab, has a long tail, 77, 81.

Θ

Θαλλός, a shoot of a plant, especially the olive, 208.

Θηρία, animals larger than flies in fire, 126; animals which destroy honey-combs, 225; an animal like a moth, *ib.*

Θίς, black shore weed, fucus, 211.

Θραυπίς, a small bird like a goldfinch, Fringilla Carduelis, or F. Cannabina, 202.

Θρίσσα, a fish with prickly scales, 256.

Θρίψ, timber worm, 207.

Θύμον, thyme, Thymus vulgaris, 266.

Θυννίς, the female tunny, 108, 109; aged, 160; food, 200; migration, 211; gregarious, 234.

Θύννος, tunny fish, Scomber Thynnus, 4, 38; sleeps, 98; swims in shoals, 108; male and female, *ib.*; reproduction, 109, 135; life, 149; they appear to be a year older than the pelamys, 160; food, 199; migrates after the scombri, 209; when best for food, 211; migrations, 212; how concealed, 214; delights in warmth, 219; old fish unfit for salting, their weight, 228.

Θώς, jackal or ounce, Felis onza, or perhaps Canis aureus, *Strack*, 42; habits, 177; hates the lion, 234; carnivorous, *ib.*; several kinds, 272.

I

Ἶβις, Tantalus Ibis, *Strack*, two species, white, Tantalus sacer, and black, T. falcinellus, 249.

Ἱέραξ, hawk, 9, 39, 40; incubation, 146; like the cuckoo, 146, 147; the young good to eat, 147; a kind which builds in rocks, *ib.*; three species, 201; enumeration of species, 253; the Egyptian hawk, 226; its nest, 243; does not eat the heart of birds, *ib.*

Ἱέρας or ἱερός, a kind of serpent, 228.

Ἰκτῖνος, kite, Falco milvius, 39, 40; incubation, 146; food, 201; drink, 203; migration, 215; a foe to the raven, 232.

Ἴκτις, weasel or ferret, Mustela furo, 29; habits, 239.

Ἰλλάς, a kind of thrush, gregarious, Turdus iliaceus, *Strack*, 248; this identification is very doubtful, *Schneider*.

Ἰξόβορος, a kind of thrush, Turdus viscivorus, *Strack*, 248.

Ἰξός, miseltoe, 248.

Ἴννος, hinnus, the offspring of a horse and she ass, 163.

Ἰουλίς, a red fish, Labrus Iulis, *Strack*, 234.

Ἴουλος, Iulus, scolopendra, centipede, 73.

Ἱππάρδιον, giraffe, Giraffa cameleopardalis, 26.

Ἱππέλαφος, perhaps the Nilghau, Antilope picta, 26.

Ἱππεύς, a crustacean, Ocyopode cursor, 77.

Ἱππομύρμηξ, a large kind of ant, Formica Herculanea, 225.

Ἵππος, horse, Equus Caballus, 13, 26, 27, 29, 39, 62, 66, 69, 70; dreams, 97; neighing, 112; reproduction, age, life, 113, 161, 169; food and drink, 205, 207; small horses in the country of the Pygmies, 209; diseases, 219, 222, 223; story of a Scythian horse, 274.

Ἵππος ὁ ποτάμιος, river horse, Hippopotamus amphibius, 32, 196; in Egypt, 32.

Ἱππουρος, fish, Coryphæna hippurus, 109; hides in holes, 213.

Ἰτέα, willow, 155.

Ἴυγξ, wryneck, Jynx torquilla, 35.

Ἰχνεύμων, Ichneumon, Viverra Ichneumon, 177; attacks the asp in Egypt, 238.

Ἰχνεύμων, Ichneumon (insect) Sphex, hunts spiders, 124, 232.

K

Κάλαμος, reed, Acorus calamus, and perhaps also some of the larger grasses, 122, 155; its flower, 127; used to support vine, 133, 155, 216; flourishes in rainy weather, 217.

Κάλαρις or κόλαρις, a bird preyed on by the little owl. Motacilla alba L., *Schneider*, 232. Fringilla petronia.

Καλίδρις, Tringa, Sandpiper, Scolopax calidris, 203.

Καλλιώνυμος, fish, Uranoscopus, *Strack*, U. Scaber, 40; lives near the shore.

Καλλύντρον, a shrub from the flowers of which the bees are said to procure their young, 127; perhaps Cerinthe, L., *Strack*, honeysuckle.

Κάμηλος, Camel, Camelus Bactrianus and C. Dromedarius, 25, 27, 29, 30, 70; reproduction, 103, 114, 161, 173; endurance of thirst, 207; life, *ib.*; diseases, 222; purity, 274; castration of females, 278.

Κάμπη, caterpillar, 124.

Κανθαρίς, several kinds of beetles, 88; a kind of fly, 106; origin, 126.

Κάνθαρος, beetle, Scarabæus pilularius, *Schneider*, Cantharis lytta, 9; origin, 125; changes its skin, 216.

Κάνθαρος, a sea-fish, lives near the shore, Sparus Cantharus, 211.

Κάπρος, boar, 29; coition, age, 112, 114; castration, 277.

Κάπρος, a fish said to make a grunting noise. Cottus cataphractus, or Squalus centrina, 37; in the Achelous, 95.

Καραβοειδῆ, crustaceans, 79, 85, 228.

ἄραβος, insect, stag-beetle, Cerambyx, *Strack*, 89, 125.

Κάραβος, Palinurus vulgaris, Spiny lobster, 7, 9, 10; as a class, 73, 77; male and female, 78; described, 79, 80, 84, 93; sleep, 97; reproduction, 120; where produced, 121; change their shell, *ib.*; kills other fish, is killed by the polypus, 198; habitation, pursuit, 129; hides itself and changes its shell, 217.

Καρίδιον πιννοφύλαξ, a small crustacean, Pinnotheres veterum, *Bell's Crustaceans*, 117.

Καρίς, shrimp or prawn, Crangon, Palæmon, 77; different kinds, *ib.*; reproduction, 106, 121; changes its colour in winter, 228.

Καρκίνιον, hermit crab, Pagurus Bernhardi, L., *Bell*, and probably other species, 85; in Strombi and Neritæ, *ib.*, 118; also a species in Pinnæ distinguished from καριδίον, 117.

Καρκίνος, crab, of various species. Cancer, Carcinus, &c., 4, 10, 73, 77; several species, 77; fluviatile, Telphura fluviatilis, *ib.*; number of feet, *ib.*; short-tailed *ib.*; description, 80, 81, 85; reproduction, 106; white crabs in various shells, 117; change of shell, 121; rock crabs, 198; black crabs, hard shelled crabs, 217.

Κάστωρ, beaver, Castor Fiber, 205.

Καυλίον, some kind of sea-weed, 200.

Καταρράκτης, diver, Pelecanus bassanus, L., *Schneider*, 45; mode of taking its prey, 244.

Κεγχρίς, Falco tinnunculus, *Schneider*, 45; lays many eggs, 138; red eggs, 139; mode of drinking, 203.

Κελεός, large green woodpecker, Picus viridis, 202, 232, 233.

Κέφρος, petrel, Procellaria pelagica, 203, 253.

Κέρθιος, creeper, Certhia familiaris, 247.

Κερκίς. Populus tremula, osier, 205.

Κεστραῖοι, mullets as a class, 109, 159.

Κεστρεὺς, mullet. Mugil. In the lake Silpha, 37, 44, 92; it sleeps, 98; capture, 87; birth, 108; enumeration of species, 109, 153, 157; enters rivers to spawn, 156, 159; food, 199, 228; habits, 200; near the shore, 211; associates with the labrax, 235; the swiftest of fishes, 256; in season in the autumn, *ib.*

Κέφαλος, grey mullet. *Spratt's Lycia*, Mugil cephalus, 109, 153; reproduction, 159; food, 199; injured by cold, 218.

Κῆβος, monkey, Simia mora or diona, *Strack*, 32. S. Cynologus.

Κηρίς, κυρίς, or κιρρίς, a sea-fish, 228.

Κήρυλος, a sea-bird, mentioned with the Halcyon, 203. Tringa variabilis.

Κήρυξ, whelk, Buccinum, its mecon, 80, 81, 82, 85; appears in the early spring, 110; nidulary capsules, 115, 116; the small whelk, 118; hides itself, 213.

Κῆτος, whale, as a class, 10, 39; whales, 69; other whales, 152.

Κητώδη, Cetacea, 7, 13, 104, 196; turn on their back to seize their prey, 200.

Κηφήν, drone, 260.

Κίγκλος, probably Tringa Cinclus, Linn. Dunlin, 244. Cinclus aquaticus.

Κίθαρος, a kind of turbot, Trigla lyra, 44.

Κιννάμωμον, a spice, cinnamon, 245.

Κιννάμωμον ὄρνεον, cinnamon bird, 245; Herodotus, Book 3, c. 111.

Κίρκος, perhaps Falco nisus, *Liddell and Scott*, 232, 253. Falco pygurgus.

Κισσός, Ivy. Hedera Helix, 130.
Κίττα or Κίσσα, Jay, Corvus glandarius, captured by the Ægolius and Eleus, 201; changes its note, 245; its nest, ib.
Κίχλη, Thrush, Turdus labrus and T. merula, nest, 138; hides, 215; changes its colour in winter, 276; three kinds, 244.
Κίχλη, a sea-fish, 37; near the land, 211; in pairs, 213; changes its colour, 228.
Κλῆρος, also called πυραύστης, an insect injurious to beehives, Galeria cerella and G. mellonella, 226, 266.
Κνίδη, sea-nettle, probably an actinia, 118, 255.
Κνιπολόγος, a species of woodpecker, Picus varius, or minor, 202.
Κνίψ or σκνίψ, an insect, Formica flava, *Strack*, finds honey by the sense of smell, 93; eaten by the woodpecker, 93, 202, 242.
Κόγχη, a bivalve shell, Mya pictorum, 82; several species, *ib.*; a kind of crustacean is found in them, 85; origin, 117, 118; large smooth shell in rivers, 243.
Κογκύλιον, a small bivalve shell, 198, 199.
Κοῖτος or κόττος, a fresh-water fish. Trout, Salmo Fario, *Strack*, 92.
Κοκκάλιον, Helix, land snail, 81.
Κόκκυξ, cuckoo, Cuculus Canorus, 93, 138; habits, form, and eggs, 146; eatable, 147; lays in the nests of other birds, 249; changes its note when about to migrate, 276.
Κολεός, also ἰλεός, and κελεος, woodpecker, 233.
Κολίας, a kind of tunny, Scomber colias, in the Propontis, 211; when taken, 212; gregarious, 234.
Κολιός, Corvus monedula or Picus viridis, 36; in p. 242 colœus should probably be colius.
Κυλλυρίων, Ampelis garrula, L.

Schneider. Lanius garrula or excubitor, 248.
Κολοιός, Pelecanus graculus, four species, 248.
Κολοκύντη, cucumber, Cucumis Sativus, 124, 208.
Κολυμβίς, a sea-bird, diver, Colymbis, 3, 203.
Κόνις, knits, 134.
Κόνηξα, plant, Inula Conyza, or I. pulicaria, flea bane, 93.
Κορακίας, probably the Cornish Chough Pyrrocorax Graculus, 248.
Κορακῖνος, sturgeon, Accipenser huso, *Strack*, Sparus Chromis, 109, 159, 160, 213, 218, 228, 234.
Κορακοειδῶν γένος, the crow tribe, 5.
Κόραξ, raven and rook, Corvus Corax and frugilegus, 40, 45, 64; eggs, incubation, young, 146; Egyptian raven, 226; hostile to the hawk, 232; pecks the ass and bull, *ib.*; friend of the fox, 233; frequent in towns, 248; nest and habits, 250.
Κόραξ, a water-bird, Pelecanus Carbo, *Strack*, 203.
Κορδύλη or σκορδύλη, the young tunny fish, 160.
Κορδύλος, water-newt, Triton aquaticus, 3, 9, 197. Siren Proteus.
Κόρις, cimex, bug, C. lectularius, 134.
Κορυδαλός, lark, Alauda arvensis cristata, 277.
Κορυδός, lark, Alauda cristata, A. arborea, A. arvensis, (though Schneider thinks this identification doubtful), its nest, 146, 249; hybernates, 215; hostile to the pœcilis, 232; is said to eat the eggs of the eagle, 233; friendly to the schœnilus, 234; perches on the ground, 242, 245; two kinds, 249.
Κορώνη, Corvus corone, 45; feeds its young after they are fledged, 146; incubation, 147; lives near the sea, 203; Egyptian, 226; foe to the owl, presbys, and typanus,

232; friend of the heron, 234; always to be seen, 248.

Κότινος, the wild olive tree, Eleagnus angustifolia, used as food for sheep (accidentally omitted in the translation), 208.

Κόττος, see κοῖτος. Cottus Gobio, 92.

Κόττυφος, blackbird, Turdus merula, *Strack*, but apparently not always, Turdus merula, and T. saxatilis, hybernate, 215; changes its colour, 228; nest, 245; two kinds, black and white, 247; changes its plumage and voice in the winter, 276.

Κόττυφος, a sea-bird, 110, 214.

Κόττυφος, a fish, 228. Labrus Merula.

Κοχλίας, snail, Helix, several kinds, 73, 81; land-snails, 83; when full of ova, 110; die when the shell is taken off, 136; form an operculum when they hybernate, 213; eaten by swine and partridges, 255.

Κόχλος, Fresh-water univalve shells, Limnæa, Planorbis, 81, 83, 84, 86.

Κραγγών, prawn, Cancer digitalis (Squilla mantis), *Strack*, Penæus sulcatus, 77.

Κράμβη, cabbage or colewort, Brassica, 124, 126.

Κραμβίς, caterpillars of the cabbage butterfly, Papilio Danais Brassicæ, 125.

Κράστις, green fodder for horses, 207.

Κρέξ, Trigna pugnax, hostile to the celeus, 233; its habits, 247.

Κριθή, barley, 206.

Κριός, Ovis aries, ram, breeding season, 114, 161, 199.

Κροκόδειλος, the Land crocodile, Lacerta stellio, Monitor terrestris, 25, 34; both kinds mentioned, 43, 46; reproduction, 137; brought up in Egypt, 231; Herodotus, Book 4, c. 192.

Κροκόδειλος, the Egyptian crocodile. Crocodilus Niloticus, 3, 14; in Egypt, 33, 59; reproduction, 137; hybernates, 72.

Κρότων, Ricinus, tick, or dog-louse, Hippobosca ovina, 135; Acarus ricinus, 125.

Κτείς, Pecten, 82, 84. A large kind, which has one valve flat, Pecten maximus, 84, 94, 95; origin, 117; small crustaceans in them, *ib.*; hybernate, 213; red pectens, 220; leap, 256.

Κύαμοι, beans, Vicia faba, 72, 206.

Κύανος, Turdus Cyaneus, blue thrush, 248.

Κύγχραμος or κύχραμος, Corncrake, Rallus Crex, *Strack*, probably a species of ortolan, *Liddell and Scott*. Leads the flight of the quails, 210.

Κύκνος, swan, Cycnus olor, 4, 45;[1] food, 203; gregarious, 211; fights with the eagle, 233; habits, 244; when dying they go towards the sea, *ib.*

Κύλλαρος or σκύλλαρος, hermit crab, Pagurus, 85.

Κύμινδις, the Ionic name of the χαλκίς, Stryx Nisoria, 244, 251.

Κυνακάνθη, perhaps the dog-rose, worms in it, 126. Rosa canina.

Κυνοκέφαλος, dog-headed ape, Simia Cynocephalus, 32. S. Porcaria.

Κυνορραϊστής, dog-ticks, Ricinus canis, 135.

Κυπρῖνος, carp, Cyprinus Carpio, 38; inhabits rivers, 91; production and growth of young, 155, 156; star-struck, 219.

Κύτισος, a shrub, Cytisus, Medicago arborea, 71.

Κυφή, a kind of shrimp or prawn, 77. Palæmon Squilla or Crangon vulgaris, also Pagurus.

Κύψελλος, a kind of swallow, martin? Hirundo urbica, makes its nest of mud in rocks and caverns, 250.

Κύων, dog, Canis familiaris, 6,

---

[1] Accidentally omitted in a list of birds in the translation.

26, 27, 29, 30, 31, 32, 42, 58; large dog of Epirus, 71 ; dreams, 97 ; reproduction, barking, &c., 103, 107, 112, 113, 114, 161, 163; Laconian dogs, their habits, 166, 167; when dogs eat grass, 204, 238; diseases, 222; Egyptian dogs, 226 ; Cyrenian dogs, half-bred, with wolves, Laconian with foxes, Indian with tigers, 227; the Molossian shepherd dog, 230 ; intestinal worms in dogs, 238.

Κύων, a cartilaginous fish, Squalus carcharias, *Strack*, S. galeus, 104, 151.

Κωβιός, gudgeon, Gobio, 44; ova, 153, 155; poor ones cast on shore, 157; food, 200; live near the land, 211 ; fatten in rivers, 218; gregarious, 197; in winter does not leave the Pyrrhic Euripus, 256.

Κωλώτης, an animal inhabiting the stables of the ass, a lizard according to some, Scaliger thinks a beetle, 232, Mus minutus.

Κώνωψ, a species of gnat, smaller than the empis, Conops calcitrans, *Strack*, Culex pipiens or C. calcitrans, 89, 94; springs from a worm in vinegar, Mosillus cellarius, 126.

Λ

Λάβραξ, perhaps Perca Labrax, Basse, 8, 92 ; sleeps, 98; reproduction, 108, 109, 153, 159 ; food, 199, 200; has a stone in its head, 218 ; unfit to eat when in spawn, 228; at times associated with cestreus, 244.

Λαγωὸς, hare, Lepus timidus, the Egyptian, 226.

Λαεδὸς, the name of a bird living in rocks and mountains, perhaps it should be λαῖος, 234.

Λαῖος, a species of thrush, Turdus torquatus, 234, 247.

Λαμία, a species of shark, Squalus centrina, or carachias, 104, 255.

Λαμπυρίς or πυγολαμπίς, glowworm, Lampyris notiluca, see Πυγολαμπίς.

Λάρος, gull or 'cormorant, Larus canus and marinus, Sterna, 45 ; colour, 203 ; a white kind, *ib.*; hostile to the brenthus and harpa, 232.

Λάταξ, beaver, Castor fiber, 3, 205.

Λάχανα, potherbs, 217.

Λειόβατος, skate, Raia Batis, 40, 151.

Λεπάς, limpet, Patella, 82, 84, 85, 86, 117.

Λεπιδωτοί, scaly fishes, see πλωτοί.

Λευκερώδιος, white heron, Platalea leucerodia, 203.

Λεύκη, probably the unopened flower-bud of the grape, or Populus alba, 121.

Λεύκος, Ardea argentata, 233.

Λέων, Lion, Felis Leo, 6, 24, 25, 26, 28 ; lioness, 29, 30, 32, 42, 59, 61, 69; reproduction, 102, 161, 176 ; existing in one district of Europe, 226 ; Syrian Lions, 176 ; mane and teeth, *ib.*; food, 205 ; habits, 271, 272 ; two kinds described, 272.

Λιβανωτίς, Rosmarinus officinalis, Rosemary, 183.

Λίβυος, a bird, enemy of the woodpecker, 232.

Λίγυες, Lygians who are said to have seven ribs, 16.

Λιμνόστρεα, oysters, Ostrea edulis, 82, 117; small crustaceans in them, *ib.*

Λόκαλος, a species of heron, Ciconia dubia, 45.

Λόφουρα, animals with hairy tails, horse, ass, &c., 11, 16, 19, 30.

Λύγξ, Lynx, Felis Lynx, 28, 29, 102.

Λύκιος, a kind of Jackdaw or chough, Corvus monedula, C. pyrrocorax, 249.

Λύκος, wolf, Canis lupus, 6, 29;

reproduction, 103, 161, 177; eats grass and earth, 204; Egyptian, 226; attacks the ass, bull, and fox, 232; near the lake Mæotis, 254.

Λύκος, a kind of spider, Aranea tarantula, *Strack*, 259.

Λύρα, a fish, Trigla Lyra, 95.

M

Μαῖα, a crustacean, Maia Squinado, 77, 81, 217.

Μαινίς, sprat or sardine, Sparus mœna, μαινίδια, 157, 158, 159; when the males are called tragi, 228; gregarious, 234.

Μαλάκια, the class of cephalopod mollusks, one species which occupies a shell is probably Camarina mediterranea, *Spratt's Lycia*, 8, 10, 19, 73, 87; reproduction, 105, 110, 121, 154; why they imbibe water, 196; carnivorous, 198, 199; best for food when they have ova, 228.

Μαλακοκρανεὺς, perhaps Loxia pyrrhula, *Schneider*, 248.

Μαλακόστρακα, crustaceans, 10, 73, 77; reproduction, 106, 120; imbibe water, 196; omnivorous, 198; best for food when they have ova, 228.

Μαρῖνος, a sea-fish, 159, 218.

Μαρτιχόρα, a fabulous animal, 30.

Μελαγκόρυφος, probably blackcap, Parus ater, or Muscicarpa atricapilla, 202; food, eggs, nest and tongue, 246; in the autumn called Sycalis, 276.

Μελαναίετος, called also lagophonos, an eagle, Aquila melanaetus, Falco fulvus, 251.

Μελανοῦρος, a sea-fish, Sparus melanurus, 199.

Μελεαγρίς, Guinea fowl, Meleagris Numidica, 139.

Μελίλωτος, plant, Melilotus officinalis, 266.

Μέλιττα, bee, Apis mellifica, 3, 5, 7, 8, 9, 64, 88, 89, 93, 95; they sleep, 98; larva are called nymphæ, 124; reproduction, 127; drones, chiefs, also called mothers and kings, 28; three kinds of bees, *ib.*; life, 130; white bees in plants, and other kinds, *ib.*; food, 208; hybernate, 213; change their skins, 216; diseases, 225; industry, 258; habits, 260.

Μεμβράς, an inferior kind of anchovy, Clupea sardina, 158.

Μέροψ, bee-eater, Merops Apiaster, L. or Congener, L. 138, 245, 265.

Μηδική, a plant, medick grass, Medicago sativa, 71, 207, 268.

Μήκων, a gregarious fish, 234.

Μήκων, plant, poppy, 268.

Μηλολόνθη, cockchafer, Melolonthus aurata, 9, 88, 89, 125.

Μήρυξ, a fish like the Scarus, said to ruminate, Scarus Cretensis, 279.

Μίλτος, vermilion, 139.

Μίτυς, a substance used by bees to cover crevices in their hives, 261.

Μόρμυρος, a sea-fish, Sparus mormyrus, 159.

Μόρφνος, another name of the plangus, Falco nævius, 251.

Μυγαλῆ, shrew mouse, Sorex araneus, 223.

Μυῖα, house fly, Musca domestica, 9, 83, 89; reproduction, 106, 108, 126; omnivorous, 208.

Μύξων, a sea fish, perhaps some kind of mullet, 109, 159.

Μυοθῆραι ὄφεις, serpents that hunt mice, attacked by the weasel, 238.

Μύραινα, sea-lamprey, Muræna helena, *Strack*, 8, 37, 40, 61; reproduction, 103, 109; food, 199; near the shore, 211; hybernates, 213; seizes the conger by the tail, 235.

Μύρινος or Μαρῖνος, a sea-fish, 218.

Μύρμηξ, ant, Formica, 4; winged and wingless, 73, 93, 108; reproduction, 131; industry, 258, 260.

Μυρρίνη, myrtle, Myrtus communis, 266, 268.

Μῦς, mouse, Mus musculus. The Egyptian kind is probably Hierax, those said to walk on two feet are the Jerboa. The Pontic kind said to ruminate. Mus Citillus, *Schneider*, 5, 50; reproduction, 178; Persian, Egyptian, and many other kinds, *ib.*; manner of drinking, 205; white mice in Pontus, 216; Arabian mice, 226; Lybian, *ib.*; the Pontic mouse is said to ruminate, 278.

Μῦς, a bivalve mollusk, perhaps Mitylus, 82.

Μυστίκητος, a whale, Balæna mysticetus, 64. Balænopterus musculus or Boops.

Μύωψ, horse-fly or gad-fly, Tabanus Cæcutiens. T. pluvialis, 9, 83, 89; origin, 126; death, 127; sucks blood, 208.

N

Νάρκη, torpedo, Raia Torpedo, 37, 40, 104; reproduction and young, 109, 150, 151; habits, 275.

Ναυτίλος, cephalopod, the species adhering to its shell is probably the Nautilus Pompilius, another species Argonauta Argo, *Owen in Cyclopædia of Anatomy*, 76, 258.

Νεβρίαι γαλεοί, dog-fish, Squalus catulus, 149.

Νεβρός, fawn, 71.

Νεβροφόνος, a name of the pygargus, 251.

Νεκύδαλος, the larva of the silk-worm, Bombyx, 124.

Νηρίτης, different littoral trochi, Trochus, Nerita, Haliotis, 85, 86, 94, 117, 118.

Νῆττα, duck, Anas Boschas, 45, 203.

Νηττοφόνος or Μόρφνος, 251; a name of the plangus.

Νισσαίοι ἵπποι, Nisæan horses, 278.

Νυκτερὶς, bat, Vespertilio, 4, 9, 50.

Νυκτικόραξ, Ardea Nycticorax, Marabu, 45, 201, 210, 252.

Ξ

Ξιφίας, sword-fish, Xiphias gladius, 38, 40, 219.

Ξυλοφθόρος, insects in wood, Phryganea, Tinea graminella, 136.

O

Ὀξολὶς, a cephalopod mollusk, the same as bolitæna, 76.

Οἰνάνθη, the flower of the vine, 121.

Οἰνάνθη, probably the name of some dark-coloured bird, 276.

Οἰνὰς, a wild pigeon, Columba migratoria, *Struck*, C. œnas, 111, 138, 203.

Ὄις, sheep, Ovis aries, 72; different kinds, 208.

Οἶστρος, gad fly, Tabanus corvinus, 3, 9, 83, 89; origin, 125; a blood sucker, 208; the marine species probably refers to certain parasites on fish, Lernæa brachialis, Phalaugium balænarum, 135, 208, 212, 219.

Οἶστρος, a bird, perhaps Motacilla sibilatrix, or Trochilus, 202.

Ὀλοθούριον, probably an alga Spongodium, *Spratt's Lycia*, Holothuria or Salpa, 4.

Ὄνος, ass, Equus Asinus, 27, 31, 39, 68, 70; not infested with lice or ticks, 135; reproduction, 113, 163, 171; food and drink, 207; diseases, 224; a foe to the Ægithus, 232; eats thorns, 233.

Ὄνος ὁ ἄγριος, the wild ass, 178; in Epirus, 71; the Indian ass, perhaps Rhinoceros, 28.

Ὄνος, fish, perhaps Raia squatina, *Strack*, Gadus mustela, 214, 255.

Ὄνος, woodlouse, Oniscus asellus, 135.

Ὀρεινὸς, a species of titmouse, Parus Ater, 202.

Ὀρσιπέλαργος, Grypaetus Barbatus, *Strack*, 251.

Ὀρεὺς, mule, 5, 11, 27, 31, 39, females and reproduction, 163, 172, 173; food and drink, 207.

Ὀρίγανος, plant, Origanum, 238.
Ὄρκυς, a large kind of tunny, Scomber ala longa, 109.
Ὄρνις, domestic fowl, see ἀλεκτόρις and ἀλεκτρυών.
Ὄροβος, tares, Orobus, Ervum ervilia, 71, 191.
Ὀρόσπιζος, mountain finch, Fringilla montifringilla, *Strack*, 202.
Ὀρσοδάκνη, an insect that eats the buds of plants, Chrysomela oleracea, 126.
Ὀρτυγομήτρα, perhaps Land rail, Rallus Crex, 210.
Ὄρτυξ, quail, Coturnix Vulgaris, 40, 45; nest, 146, 240; migration, 210; does not perch on trees, 242.
Ὄρυξ, Nilghau, Antilope picta, or Antilope Oryx, 27.
Ὀρφὸς, a sea fish, perhaps Scorpæna porcus, *Spratt's Lycia*, 109, 199, 211, 214.
Ὀρχίλος, a bird, Charadrius minor, 232.
Ὀστρακόδερμα, testaceous mollusca, 8, 10, 13, 73, 81; reproduction, 110, 115, 117; compared with plants, 195; hybernate, 213; best for food when they have ova, 228.
Ὄστρειον, oyster, 3, 10, 117; different kinds, 73; origin, 117; have an anus, 198; τὰ ὀστρεώδη, testacea, 228.
Ὄστρειον, the shell used by painters, 118.
Οὔραξ, Otis houbara, 139.
Οὖς θακάττιον, sea ear, perhaps Haliotis, 84.
Ὀφίδιον, a small serpent, found in the plant silphium, 227; a small serpent, Coluber ammodytes, or C. Æsculapii, *Strack*, *ib.*; an Indian serpent, whose bite is fatal, *ib.*
Ὄφις, serpent, 5; winged serpent in Æthiopia, perhaps Draco volans, 9; a horned serpent in Egypt, Coluber cerastes, 28; water-serpents, Coluber natrix, 10, 35, 38, 43, 44, 46, 49, 60; marine serpents, Muræna ophis, or Ammodytes tobianus, *Strack*, 38, 255; there are many kinds. Their hissing, 96; the female larger, 100; reproduction, 103, 137; change their skin, 121, 216; omnivorous, 204; hybernate, 213; a large kind in Lybia, Boa constrictor, 226; the blind serpent, Anguis fragilis, 223.
Ὄφριος, Labrus Anthia, 109.

Π

Πάγουρος, probably the common hermit-crab, Pagurus Bernhardi, 77.
Πανθήρ, panther, Felis Panthera, 177.
Παρδάλια, 34; perhaps the spots on the Leopard's skin: an unknown animal, *L. and S. Lex.*
Παρδαλίαγχες, a plant poisonous to the Leopard, perhaps aconite, Doronicum pardalianches, or aconitum Napellus, 238.
Πάρδαλις, Leopard, Felis Leopardus, 5, 27, 29, 30; Asiatic, 226; the female more bold than the male, 230; hunts by scent, 238.
Πάρδαλος, a bird, perhaps Sturnus Vulgaris, Starling. Tringa Squaratola, *Strack*, 248.
Πάρδιον, see ἱππάρδιον, Giraffe.
Πελαργός, stork, Ardea Ciconia, 203, 215; when wounded applies origanum to its wounds, 238; said to be fed by its young, 245.
Πελειὰς, a kind of dove, distinct from περίστερα, 111; migratory, 210.
Πελεκᾶν, Pelecan, Pelecanus onocrotalus, migrates from the Strymon, 209; gregarious, 210; eats shell-fish, 243.
Πέλλος, black heron, Ardea cinerea, 233, 247.
Πέρδιξ, partridge, Perdix cinerea, and rufa, Tetrao Perdix and Græcus, 5, 45, 47, 96; reproduction, 106, 139, 140, 141, 148;

nest, incubation, habits, 138, 240, 241, 242; life, 145, 240; eats snails, 255; dusts itself, 277.

Περιστερά, House-dove, Columba, 4, 5, 39, 45; differs from πελειάς, 111; reproduction, *ib.*, 138, 139, 140, 141, 144, 145; food, 202; not migratory, 210; habits, 239, 240; those used for lures are blinded, 240; wash and dust themselves, 277.

Περιστοειδῆ the class of pigeon-like birds, 111, 144, 202.

Πέρκη, perch, Perca fluviatilis, 38, 44, 155, 214.

Περκνόπτερος, dusky eagle, Vultur percnopterus or Gypaietos barbatus, or Falco barbatus, 251.

Πέρκος, grey hawk, Falco subbuteo, 253.

Πέρνης or πτερνίς, a kind of hawk.

Πεύκη, pine tree, 126.

Πήγανον, rue, Ruta graveolens, 238.

Πηλαμίς, a tunny fish of a year old, Scomber Thynnus, 4; reproduction, 108; where found, 109; the tunny a year older than the pelamys, 157, 160; migrate to the Pontus, 211; gregarious, 235.

Πηνέλοψ, a kind of duck, Anas Penelope, 203.

Πηνίον, some species of larva, Phalænæ geometræ, 124.

Πιθηκοειδῆ, the ape tribe, 26.

Πίθηκος, ape, Simia Sylvanus, 32.

Πίκρις, a bitter herb, endive, Chicorium intybus, or Helminthia Echionella, 238.

Πίννα, the genus Pinna, 82, 117, 118, 195.

Πιννοθήρης or πιννοτήρης, and πιννοφύλαξ, small crustaceans living in shells and sponges, Pinnotheres veterum, 117.

Πῖπος, πίπρα, πιπώ, woodpecker, Picus viridis, major, minor, 202, 232, 248.

Πισσόκηρος, bees' wax, 261.

Πίφηξ or πίφιγξ, Alauda trivialis, 234.

Πλάγγος, a species of eagle, Aquila albicilla, 251.

Πλόμος or φλόμος, mullein, Verbascum thapsus, fatal to fish, 220.

Πλωτοί, certain fish, as the cestreus and labrax, 153, 256, 228, 273; also of birds, 35.

Πνεύμων, a marine animal of low organization, 118.

Πόα Μηδική and Συρία, Medicago sativa, and lupulina, 268.

Ποικιλίς, perhaps Fringilla Carduelis or Œnanthe, 232.

Πολύπους, Octopus, *Spratt's Lycia*, Sepia octopodia, a small variegated kind, has not been determined, *Owen*, 9, 73, 74, 76; several kinds, 73, 258; reproduction, 105, 110, 121; destroys the lobster, 198; is destroyed by the conger, *ib.*; food, 199; when good for food, 228; ink, 75, 257; changes its colour, *ib.*; grows lean, *ib.*; goes upon shore, 258.

Πορφύρα, Murex trunculus, *Spratt's Lycia*, and probably some other shells, 81, 83, 85, 86, 89, 94; time of appearance, 110, 115, 116, 117; several kinds, 116, 117; said to obtain the purple from Algæ, 155; carnivorous, 200; hybernates, 213, 220, 256.

Πορφυρίων, a bird with a long neck, Fulica porphyrion, *Strack*, 45, 206.

Πράσιον, a species of alga, perhaps Caulerpa prolifera, *Spratt's Lycia*, 199.

Πρασοκουρίς, a grub which destroys leeks, Clerus apiarius, 126.

Πρέσβυς, the same as Trochilus, wren, 232, 244.

Πρημάδες, a kind of tunny, 214.

Πρίστις, perhaps the saw-fish, Squalus pristis, *Strack*, 152.

Πρόβατον, sheep, Ovis aries, 27, 29; black lambs, 64, 66, 67; in Epirus, 71, 72; voice of the ram, 96; dreams, 97; reproduction, 112, 113, 163, 164, 165; sheep-ticks,

134; food, 208; acorns injurious to sheep, 222; diseases, 223; Syrian sheep, 225; Egyptian, 226; habits, 235; hostile to bees, 261; ruminate, 279.

Προξ, roe deer, Cervus Capriolus, 39, 58, 67.

Πτελέα, elm, Ulmus campestris, 206.

Πτερνίς, a species of hawk, 253.

Πτύγξ, or πώϋξ, a water-bird, 244.

Πύγαργος, a kind of eagle, perhaps Circus Cyaneus, hen harrier, 146, 250; also a water-bird, perhaps Tringa Ocrophus, L. *Schneider*, 203, 244.

Πυγολαμπίς, glow-worm, Lampyris noctiluca, 73, 125.

Πυραλίς, a bird, enemy of the turtle dove, 232.

Πυραύστης, a moth, Tinea mellonella, *Strack*, 225.

Πυρρούλας, a red bird, Loxia pyrrula, or enucleator, 202.

Πώϋξ, a bird living in marshes, Ardea purpurea, 247.

P

'Ραφάνος, cabbage or radish, 124.

'Ρητίνη, resin, 248.

'Ρίνη, a species of shark, Squalus Squatina, *Strack*, 49; reproduction, 103, 108, 109, 150, 151; mode of taking its prey, 255; changes its colour, 257.

Ρινόβατης, Raia rhinobatus, a cartilaginous fish, 151.

'Ρυάδες, fish that swim in shoals, 93, 109, 159, 211, 212.

Σ

Σαθέριον, a kind of otter or beaver, Lutra Luteola, *Strack*, 205.

Σαλαμάνδρα, salamander, Lacerta Salamandra, 126.

Σάλπη, the genus Scomber, *Strack*, Sparus Salpa, 92; reproduction, 108, 109, 159; food, 201; lives in bays of the sea, 211; is not carnivorous, 256.

Σανδαράκη, red sulphuret of arsenic, 223; bee bread, 264.

Σαπείριον, σαπήριον, or σατύριον, a plant, probably an orchid, Satyrian, 205.

Σαπερδίς, a fresh-water fish, perhaps Accipenser hugo, 229.

Σαργίνος, the sardine, migratory, Tetragonus niger, 231.

Σάργος, Sparus sargus, *Strack*, a sea-fish, 108, 109, 159, 200.

Σατύριον, Sorex moschatus, 205.

Σαῦρα, Lizard, generic name, 5, 8, 25, 34, 35, 36, 39, 43, 44; reproduction, 103, 137; life, 204; hybernates, 213; change of skin, 216; Arabian lizards, 225, 252.

Σαῦρος, Salmo Saurus, marine, 234.

Σειρῆν, a kind of wild bee or wasp, Megachile muraria, 260.

Σελάχη, the class of cartilaginous fishes, 7, 8, 14, 37, 38, 59, 60, 66; description of the class, 46, 48; sleep, 98; kinds, 99, 104; reproduction, 103, 149, 160; carnivorous, 199; marine, 211; hybernate, 214; male and female, 257.

Σελακοείδεις, cartilaginous fishes, 44, 95, 104, 214.

Σέσελις, an umbelliferous plant, Seseli tortuosum, 236.

Σηπία, Sepia officinalis, *Spratt's Lycia*, cuttle-fish, 7, 9, 10, 73, 74, 75, 80, 83, 93; reproduction, 105, 110, 120, 123, 125, 154; food, 199; the male protects the female when wounded, 231; emission of the ink, 257; said to change its colour, *ib*.

Σής, various kinds of moths in clothes, in beehives, in books, 135.

Σικύη, a kind of long gourd, 246.

Σικυός, gourd or cucumber, Cucurbita lagenaria, 206.

Σίλφη, a stinking insect, Blatta orientalis, or Lepisma, *Strack*, 216.

Σίλφιον, a plant, perhaps Assafœtida, Laserpitium, or Thapsus Silphium, 227.

Υ

Σινόδων, or συνόδων, a carnivorous fish, Tetraodon hispidus, or mola, or Sparus dentex, *Strack*, T. lineatus, 199, 200, 211, 234.

Σίττη, a kind of woodpecker, or perhaps Sitta Europœa, creeper, 233, 247.

Σιττάκη or ψιττάκη, parrot, Psittacus erithacus.

Σκάρος, a sea-fish, supposed by the ancients to ruminate, Scarus oretius, *Spratt's Lycia*, S. cretensis, *Strack*, 37; has not sharp teeth, 38, 44; food, 199; appears to ruminate, 200, 256, 278.

Σκίαινα, a sea-fish, Sciæna nigra, *Strack*, S. cirrhosa, 218.

Σκίλλη, Scilla maritima, 133.

Σκολόπαξ, perhaps the woodcock, Scolopax rusticola, 242.

Σκολόπενδρα, Scolopendra morsitans, Centipede, 8; the marine kinds Nereis or Aphrodite, A. aculeata, 38, 88, 255.

Σκομβρίας, σκόμβρος, fish allied to the tunny, mackerel, Scomber sarda, 109, 160, 210, 212, 235.

Σκορδύλη or κορδύλη, the young tunny, 160.

Σκορπίος, Scorpio Europæus, 89, 131, 135, 227.

Σκορπίος, a sea-fish, Cottus Scorpius, *Strack*, 44, 108, 211.

Σκορπίς, a sea-fish, Scorpæna porcus, 109.

Σκορπιώδες, a small creature in books, Phalangium Cancroides, 89, 135.

Σκυλίον, dog-fish, Squalus Stellaris, S. canicula, 149, 151.

Σκύλλαρος or κύλλαρος, a kind of hermit-crab, 85.

Σκωλήκιον, a worm that eats wood, 136; a small intestinal worm in fish, 159; an insect in honeycombs, 266.

Σκώληξ, worm, especially the earthworm, 8, 123.

Σκώψ, the screech-owl, Strix Scops, Strix Otus, 201, 249.

Σμαρίς, a poor sea-fish, Sparus smaris, 228.

Σμύξον, see μύξων. Σμύραινα, see μύραινα. Σμύρος, see μύρος.

Σπάρος, a sea-fish, Sparus Maina, *Strack*, 44.

Σπάρτον, a shrub, broom, Genista, Stipa tenacissima, 266.

Σπατάγος, Spatangus, sea-egg, 86.

Σπίζα, finch, Fringilla, 35; eats worms, 202; habitation, 240.

Σπιζίας, sparrow-hawk, Falco Nisus, 201, 253.

Σπιζίτης, a kind of titmouse, Parus ater or major, 202.

Σπογγος, sponge, Spongia officinalis, 3; growth, 118; three kinds, *ib.*; very like a plant, 195; pores in sponges, 246.

Σπονδύλη or σφονδύλη, probably a kind of beetle, living in the roots of plants, Carabus, 107, 223, 252.

Σταφυλίνος, an insect like the Sphondyle, Staphylinus murinus, 223.

Στρόμβος, Turbinated shells, Helix, Turbo, &c., 13, 85, 86, 118.

Στρομβώδη, univalve mollusks, 85, 86; on land and marine, 84; have an operculum, 117.

Στρουθός, sparrow, Fringilla domestica, 40, 45, 64, 102; eats worms, 202; the hens are said to live longer, 240; compared with the Halcyon, 245; washes and dusts itself, 277; in Lybia, ostrich, Struthiocamelus, 246.

Στρουθός, a flat fish, Pleuronectes passer, 40.

Στύραξ, the gum storax, Storax officinalis, 93.

Συκαλίς, fig-pecker, Italian beccafico, the melancoryphus in its summer plumage, Motacilla Atricapilla, or Parus ater, *Strack*, Sylvia fidecula, 202, 276.

Συκάμινον, the fruit of the mulberry tree, 221.

Σῦκα, figs, used for feeding swine, 206, 221.

Συκῶν κάμπαι, a caterpillar in figs, 126.
Σύμφυτον, a plant, Symphytun officinale, comfrey, or gypsophila arundinacea, 245.
Συναγρίς, a fish, Sparus dentex, 37, 40.
Συριά πόα, a plant loved by bees, 268.
Σῦς, swine, Sus scropha, no wild swine in Libya, 225; the domestic pig eats snails, 255.
Σφαῖραι θαλάττιαι, a species of zoophyte, perhaps Alcyonia, 246.
Σφήξ, wasp, Vespa vulgaris, V. tectorum, V. crabro, generic name, 3, 4, 88, 89; larva, 124; a kind called ichneumon, Ammophila sabulosa, 127, 130; a diligent insect, 258; the annual wasp, 260; hostile to bees, 265, 267; two species, 268.
Σφύραινα, a gregarious sea-fish, Esox sphyræna, 234.
Σχοινικλος or σχοινίων, a water-bird, Emberiza Schœniclus L. *Schneider*, 203, 234.
Σχοινίων, Sylvia arundinacea, 234.
Σωλήν, Solen, Soleneuntus trigillatus, *Spratt's Lycia*, 82, 94, 117, 118, 195.

T

Ταινία, a long thin fish, probably Cepola tænia, *Strack*, 37.
Ταινίαι πλατεῖαι, flat entozoa, 238.
Ταπύνος, see τύμπανος.
Ταῦρος, bull, Bos taurus, 48, 67, 68, 168; horns, 100; fierce in the breeding season, 161; bulls fight together, 163.
Ταώς, peacock, Pavo cristatus, 6; barren eggs, reproduction, 140, 148.
Τενθρηδών, a kind of bee or wasp, Apis terrestris, *Strack*, makes honey, 260; reproduction, 271.
Τερηδών, a caterpillar in bee-hives, 225.

Τέτριξ, a species of grouse, Tetrao tetrix, or Otis tetrix, *Strack*, 138, 139.
Τεττιγομήτρα, the edible larva of the locust or grasshopper, 134.
Τεττιγόνιον, a small kind of grasshopper, 90, 133.
Τέττιξ, grasshopper, Cicada orni, 90; several kinds, 95; origin, 123, reproduction, 133; Cecropis Spumarius, 134; changes its skin, 216; not found in Milesia and Cephalenia, 225.
Τευθίς, Loligo vulgaris, *Owen*, 9, 10, 74, 75; reproduction, 105, 123; food, 177; its ink, 257.
Τεῦθος, Loligo media, 10, 74, 75, 123; perhaps incorrectly in 234 as the name of a gregarious fish.
Τήθυα, Ascidian mollusks, Ascidia phlusa, *Strack*, 82, 87, 94, 117; fleshy nature of their body, 195.
Τίγρις, Tiger, Felis tigris, the Indian dogs are said to be crossed with the tiger, 227.
Τίλλων, a fresh-water fish, Cyprinus brama, 156, 220.
Τίφαι, grass or straw used as food for swine, Secale, 221.
Τράγος, the he-goat, voice, 96, 161, 175.
Τράγος, the male of the fish mænis, Sparus Maina, *Strack*, 228.
Τρίγλη, Red mullet, *Spratt's Lycia*, Mullus surculentus, *Strack*, 44, 108; suffers from parasites, 135; season of reproduction, 159; gregarious, *ib.*, 234; can bury itself, 200; lives near the land, 211; in estuaries, *ib.*; not carnivorous, 256; in season in the autumn, 257.
Τριόρχης, Buzzard, Buteo vulgaris, 201, eats toads and serpents, 232; the first genus of the hawks, 253.
Τριχάς, Fieldfare or thrush, Turdus trichias, *Strack*, T. pilaris, 248.
Τριχίας or τριχίς, a small kind of fish, or spawn, Clupea Sprattus, 108, 158, 212.

Τροχίλος, Sylvia trochilus, *Strack*, also called Presbys, and Basileus, perhaps the wren, Sylvia troglodytes, S. regulus, 203, 233; also a bird living by the sea, charadrius Egyptiacus, 203; picks the teeth of the crocodile, 238; hates the eagle, 232.

Τρύγγας, perhaps Tringa ochropodes, *Schneider*, T. vanellus, 203, 244.

Τρυγγών, Turtle dove, Columba turtur, the smallest of the dove tribe, 111; young and eggs, 138, 145, 240; food, 202; migrates, 210; hybernates, 215; an enemy to the pyrallis, but killed by the chloreus, 232; friendly with the cottyphus, 234; life, 240; habitation, *ib.*; perhaps Psophila crepitans, or Rallus crex, 277.

Τρυγών, a sea-fish, Raia pastinaca, 8, 104, 149, 211; method of taking its prey, 255.

Τρηγών, some oviparous quadruped, 103.

Τύραννος, golden-crested wren, Motacilla Regulus, 202.

Τυφλίνης, blind worm, Lacerta Apus, *Schneider*, 154, 223.

Υ

Ὕαινα, Hyæna Striata, 176; also called γλάνος, 204.

Ὑβρίς, a night bird of prey, 244.

Ὕδρος, a water-serpent, Coluber natrix, 3, 44.

Ὑπαίετος, a kind of eagle, also written γυπαίετος, 252.

Ὕπερα, a kind of caterpillar, Geometra, 124.

Ὑπολαΐς, hedge sparrow, Sylvia hortensis or curruca, 147, 202, 249.

Ὑποτριόρχης, buzzard, 253, see τριόρχης.

Ὗς, swine, Sus scropha, 26; with single hoof in Pœonia, 27, 29; boar, 31; 32; swine, 35, 42, 46, 66; heats, 69; voice, 96; sow, is without tusks, 100; reproduction, 107, 112, 114, 135, 162, 163; domestic swine, 164; μετάχοιρα, 173; they dig up the runs of mice, 178; eat roots, 206; how fattened, *ib.*; diseases, 221; swine in Mount Athos, 227; killed by scorpions, *ib.*; devour serpents, 233; gelding of sows, 278.

Ὗς ἄγριος, the wild boar, 5, 26, 161, 174.

Ὕστριξ, porcupine, Hystrix cristata, 138; compared with the bear, 175; hybernates, 215; throws out its quills, 260.

Φ

Φαβοτύπος, a kind of hawk, Falco palumbarius, 201.

Φάγρος, a sea-fish, Sparus pagrus, 211, 218.

Φαλάγγιον, a kind of spider, Phalangium, Aranea Tarantula, 100, 107, 121, 123; reproduction, 132; patient of hunger, 204; hostile to the ichneumon, 232; several kinds described, 258, 259.

Φάλαγξ, a spider, 231.

Φάλαινα, whale, Physeter Chacalotus, *Strack*, P. macrocephalus, 8, 69, 152; respiration, 196.

Φαλαρίς, coot, Fulica atra, 203.

Φαληρική ἀφύη, some kind of spawn, 158.

Φασιανός, pheasant, Phasianus Colchicus, 134, 139, 277.

Φασσοφόνος, a hawk, probably the same as φαβοτύλος, 253.

Φάττα, a kind of pigeon, Columba palumbus, 45, 47; the largest of the pigeon kind, 111; reproduction and eggs, 138, 144, 145, 147, 202; migrates, 210; sometimes hybernates, 215; likes drought, 217; mode of drinking, 240; habits, *ib.*; 'does not coo in winter, 276.

Φάψ, a kind of dove, Columba livia,

INDEX. 325

the male and female incubate by turns, 147, 202, 210; nest, 249.

Φήνη, perhaps the osprey, Vultur ossifragus, Buffon, nurses the young of the eagle, 146; its food and shape, 201, 251.

Φθείρ, louse, Pediculus capitis and P. pubis, κόνις, nit, 120, 134; in birds, *ib.*; in fish, Lernea, 97, 135; in the fish chalcis, 220.

Φθείρα, a fish that follows the dolphin, Centronotus, 135.

Φλέως, a water plant, Poterium spinosum, 266.

Φοινοκούρος, redstart, Sylvia Phœnicurus, 276; in winter called ἐρίθακος.

Φοξίνος, a river fish, Cyprinus phoxinus, *Strack*, 153, 155.

Φρύνη, toad, Bufo vulgaris, 39, 87; eaten by the buzzard, 232; injurious to bees, 265.

Φρυνολόχος, a kind of hawk, perhaps the buzzard, 253.

Φυκίον, fucus, sea-weed, 122, 125, 154, 199, 200, 255.

Φυκίς, a fish living on sea-weed, Gobius niger, 154; food, 200; changes its colour, and is the only fish that makes nests, 228.

Φῦκος, fucus, 154, 158, 218, 220.

Φώκαινα, porpoise, Delphinus Phocæna, 152, 212.

Φώκη, seal, Phoca vitulina, P. monachus, 4, 7, 14, 22, 25, 26, 30, 39, 44, 69; reproduction and habits, 103, 152, 153, 196; food, 205; fight together, 231.

Φωλίς, a fish enclosing itself in mucus, 256; Blennius pholis, *Strack*.

Φώρ, a kind of bee, the thief, 259.

X

Χάλαξα, Hydatids in swine, 221.

Χαλκευς, a fish, Dory, Zeus Faber, *Strack*, 95.

Χαλκίς, a lizard, with a bright stripe on its back, Lacerta chalcides, 223.

Χαλκίς, a bird, the same as κύμινδις, Stryx flammea, *Strack*, 244.

Χαλκίς, a fish, perhaps Mugil auratus, *Spratt's Lycia*, Clupea picta, 108, 155, 156, 256.

Χαλκίτις λίθος, lime stone, 126.

Χάννη, or χάνη, a fish with a wide mouth, Perca cabrilla, 99, 153; food, 199; marine, 211.

Χαραδριός, lapwing or curlew, Charadrius œdicnemus, *Schneider*, 203, 243.

Χελιδών, swallow, Hirundo urbica and rustica, 4, 40, 45, 64; reproduction and nests, 111, 139, 145, 239; eat animal food, 202; migration, 215; kill bees, 265.

Χελιδών, flying fish, 95; Exocetus volitans.

Χέδροπες, leguminous plants, 205.

Χέλων, or χάλλων, a fish like the cestreus, 109, 159, 199.

Χελώνη, the river tortoise, Testudo orbicularis and Europæa, 34, 39, 41, 42, 46, 65, 84, 87, 96; reproduction, 103, 104, 123; marine, Chelonia cephalo, 196; lives on shell-fish and sea-weed, 198; does not change its skin, 216, 238.

Χήμη, a large bivalve shell, Chama, 117.

Χήν, goose, Anser domesticus and Anas segetum, 6, 27, 45, 47; gosling, 140, 141; incubation, 146, 147; different kinds, 203, 210.

Χηναλώπηξ, an Egyptian goose, Anas tadorna, *Strack*, 140, 203.

Χίμαιρα, probably the she goat, 72.

Χλωρεύς, perhaps the same as χλωρίων, a foe to the woodpecker, and kills the turtle dove, Falco lanarius, 232.

Χλωρίς, Motacilla fitis, or Loxia chloris, *Strack*, eats worms, 202 shape, eggs, nest, 245, 249.

Χλωρίων, perhaps oriole, Oriolus galbula, *Strack*, attacks the blackbird, 233, 248.

Χοιροπίθηκος, ape, Simia rostrata, S. porcaria, 34.
Χρέμψ, a fish joined with labrax, 92.
Χρόμις, a sea-fish, Sciæna nigra, 92, 94, 108, 218.
Χρυσομήτρις, a bird (thistle finch), Fringilla serinus, 202.
Χρύσοφρυς, Sparus aurata L., 8, 44; sleeps, 98; reproduction, 109, 160; food, 200; near the shore, 211; in estuaries, *ib.*; hybernates, 214; impatient of cold, 218.
Χύμινδις, the same as χαλκίς, 244.
Χυτοί, fish that swim in shoals, 109.

Ψ

Ψάρος, starling, Sturnus vulgaris, 215, 249.
Ψήν, gall insect, Cynips psenes, 136.

Ψήττα, a flat fish, Pleuronectes lingua and Rhombus, and maxima, 99, 109, 255.
Ψιττάκη, Parrot, Psittacus erithacus, 211.
Ψύλλα, flea, Pulex irritans, 134; a kind of spider, Salticus scenicus, 259.
Ψύλλος, parasites on fish, Talitrus locusta, 97.
Ψυχή, butterfly, Papilio, 89, 102, 123.

Ω

Ὠτίς, bustard, Otis tarda, 45, 102; incubation, 147, 252.
Ὠτὸς, horned owl, Strix otus, 210, 252.
Ὤχροι, a kind of pulse, useful to bees, Pisum sativum, 268.

THE END.

www.ingramcontent.com/pod-product-compliance
Lightning Source LLC
Chambersburg PA
CBHW021149230426
43667CB00006B/323